THE BOSTON TEA PARTY

From a facsimile of the original by J. DeCosta in the Map Division of the Yale University Library.

A PLAN OF THE TOWN AND HARBOUR OF BOSTON — 1775

Note King Road and Castle Island. The two vessels near the figures "3" are moored in the Admiral's anchorage. The hill in Boston marked "6" is Fort Hill, immediately south of which is Griffin's Wharf.

THE BOSTON TEA PARTY

Benjamin Woods Labaree

A Classics Edition

NORTHEASTERN UNIVERSITY PRESS

Boston

Northeastern University Press
Copyright 1964 by Oxford University Press
Reprinted in 1979 by Northeastern University Press
by arrangement with Oxford University Press, Inc.

Library of Congress Catalog Card Number 79-5423
ISBN 0-930350-16-2 (cloth)
ISBN 0-930350-05-7 (paper)

Printed and bound by The Courier Corp., Westford,
Massachusetts. The paper is Sebago Antique,
an acid-free sheet.

MANUFACTURED IN THE UNITED STATES OF AMERICA

05 04 03 02 01 00   11 10 9 8 7 6

For Linda

PREFACE TO THE

NORTHEASTERN UNIVERSITY PRESS EDITION

In writing the preface to the second edition of a book an author is tempted to correct a few minor errors as an indication of his fallibility; defend the work against its critics, if any; and assert unswerving loyalty to the book's basic viewpoint. Rather than follow those paths, however, I would prefer to reflect upon the joy that writing such a book as The Boston Tea Party *can bring to its author.*

In the spring of 1962 my dissertation on the merchants of Newburyport was about to be published, and I was looking about for a subject for the critical second book when I came across in some notes from one of Samuel Eliot Morison's lectures his assertion that it was about time somebody wrote a good book on the Boston Tea Party. That stroke of fortune gave me a topic that brought together almost all of my historical interests. First of all, I was fascinated by grass-roots aspects of the coming of the American Revolution, and as a New Englander I felt most at home dealing with a subject focused on that region. Secondly, I had already become interested in political ideas and action, and I had long felt that the British background to the American Revolution had been poorly understood by historians ever since the era of Charles M. Andrews and his students. Finally, the topic had enough to do with the sea to satisfy my interests in maritime history. Altogether, then, this was an ideal topic.

Furthermore, the research required just enough travel to make for an interesting year — a summer in England, an autumn trip to archives in Washington, Pennsylvania, and New York, and a winter at home in the Boston area. To top it off, a delightful spring and sum-

mer of writing all combined to make the actual creation of the book a thoroughly enjoyable process.

I cannot deny the satisfaction that has since come from being the author of an acceptable book on such a well-known topic as the Boston Tea Party. But the real lesson is this: every professional historian should write at least one book for the sheer pleasure of it. With a little luck some of the joy will show through, and the result will inevitably be a better book.

Benjamin Woods Labaree

Mystic Seaport, Connecticut
September 1979

PREFACE

In the autumn of 1773 seven bluff-bowed vessels beat their way across the stormy North Atlantic Ocean toward the American coastline. Stowed away in their holds were cargoes of tea — 600,000 pounds in all — consigned by the famous East India Company of London to small groups of merchants in the ports of Boston, New York, Philadelphia, and Charleston. Although subject to the Townshend duty of threepence per pound, this tea was to be sold at a price low enough to compete with tea smuggled into the colonies from Holland and elsewhere. When the vessels arrived, however, the colonists were determined that none of the tea should be landed and that the Townshend duties should remain unpaid. At Charleston the tea was seized and stored by the customs officials; at Philadelphia and New York the ships were turned back; but on the night of 16 December 1773 the patriots of Boston dumped 340 chests of the dutied tea into the harbor.

The Boston Tea Party is one of the best-known incidents in American history. The boldness of the plan, the swift efficiency of its execution, and the anonymity of its participants help explain why it captured the attention of contemporaries and has continued to fascinate the generations that have followed. In England today the Tea Party is one of the few events of the Revolutionary era familiar to the general populace. In Boston, where the site of the Party has long since disappeared beneath waterfront fill, its memory has been kept alive in various ways — in an annual ceremony sponsored by the Daughters of the American Revolution, in a plaque maintained by the Bostonian Society, in a vial of the original tea preserved by the Massachusetts

Historical Society. One disgruntled Bostonian of today has even helped to immortalize the Tea Party by a graffito inscribed on the wall of the subway: "Why didn't they keep the tea and throw the city in the harbor?"

The place of the Boston Tea Party as a dramatic event in our nation's history is well established. It is the purpose of the present volume to explain its significance in the coming of the American Revolution. For three years before the Tea Party, the thirteen American colonies shared no common cause, and relations between them and the mother country were relatively calm. Within eighteen months after the Tea Party the colonies were united in war against Great Britain. The Boston Tea Party was the catalyst that brought about this revolutionary change. How such an event could take place and why it should have had the effect it did are two of the questions the present volume proposes to answer.

When they learned of the East India Company's plan to send cheap, dutied tea to America, many colonists suspected a conspiracy between the British ministry and Company directors to trick them into recognizing Parliament's claim to the right of taxation in the colonies. Bostonians were willing to go to any length to avoid accepting the tea. Because other Americans shared this suspicion, the dramatic destruction of the tea at Boston reawakened a sense of unity among the colonies. With the Parliament's decision to punish the Bostonians by the Coercive Acts, that town's cause became the cause of all. During the summer of 1774 hundreds of colonists had their first chance to strike a blow for American freedom by sending aid to the beleaguered Bostonians. In the autumn twelve colonies met in congress and supported Boston's refusal to pay for the tea. They adopted a broad program of economic retaliation. As both sides narrowed the possibility of compromise and prepared to defend their positions with force, the War of American Independence became inevitable.

In the preparation of this volume my debts have been many. To Harvard University for a year's leave of absence and for a grant from its Foundation for Advanced Study and Research I am deeply thankful. I wish also to acknowledge my gratitude to the American Philosophical Society for its generous grant-in-aid.

Among my former teachers and colleagues at Harvard University I am especially indebted to: Samuel E. Morison, for suggesting the topic in the first place; Arthur M. Schlesinger for his many personal kindnesses and inspiration; Oscar Handlin, Robert G. Albion, Frank Freidel, and Bernard Bailyn for their helpful suggestions; and particularly David Owen for his friendly assistance. To my present colleagues at Williams College, and particularly to President John E. Sawyer, I am grateful for understanding and encouragement. Fellow devotees of Boston's past, including Stephen T. Riley, Walter M. Whitehill, Malcolm Freiburg, Clifford K. Shipton, and Lyman H. Butterfield, have shared with me their extensive knowledge and wisdom. Hiller B. Zobel and Kinvin Wroth, co-editors of the legal papers of John Adams, have helped me through the puzzling statutes of the period.

No historian could commit a single word to paper without the assistance of archivists to guide him through the manuscripts committed to their care. I am indebted to the staff-members of many libraries, including those of the Massachusetts Historical Society, the Boston Public Library, the New England Historical and Genealogical Society, the Houghton Library of Harvard University, the Harvard Business School, the American Antiquarian Society, the Yale University Library, the Columbia University Library, the New-York Historical Society, the New York Public Library, the American Jewish Historical Society, the American Philosophical Society, the Library Company, and the Historical Society of Pennsylvania. I am similarly grateful for the friendly assistance given me by the staff-members of the following British libraries: the British Museum, the Public Record Office, the Commonwealth Relations Office, the House of Lords Record Office, the University of London Library, the Institute of Historical Research, the William Salt Library in Stafford, the Sheffield City Libraries, the Liverpool Public Libraries, the University of Bristol Library, the Berkshire Record Office, Reading, and the Library of

Manchester College, Oxford. Miss W. D. Coates, Registrar of the National Register of Archives, gave generously of her time and hospitality as she has done for many scholars. Commander P. K. Kemp, Librarian of the Admiralty Library, also made an important contribution to my researches.

I am grateful to the Right Honorable the Earl Fitzwilliam and Earl Fitzwilliam's Settled Estates Co. for use of the papers of the 2nd Marquis of Rockingham and to Lord Dartmouth for permission to publish quotations from the papers of the 2nd Earl of Dartmouth. Unpublished Crown-copyright material in the India Office Records transcribed in this book appears by permission of the Secretary of State for Commonwealth Relations. Unpublished Crown-copyright material in the Public Record Office and the House of Lords Record Office has been reproduced by permission of the Controller of H.M. Stationery Office. I wish also to thank the Trustees of the British Museum for permission to use materials entrusted to their care. Quotations from Matthew Brickdale's Diary have been made with the kind permission of Mr. M. Fortescue-Brickdale.

It is a pleasure to acknowledge particular thanks to my parents for their help, spiritual and otherwise, during the past two years. But it is to my wife for her constant and cheerful support that I am most deeply grateful. To her this book is affectionately dedicated.

B.W.L.

Williamstown, Massachusetts
August 1964

CONTENTS

THE BOSTON TEA PARTY

I

THE COLONIAL TEA TRADE

WHEN Samuel Pepys drank his first cup of tea in 1660, few of his countrymen had ever heard of the beverage. But within a century many Englishmen had become virtually addicted to the exotic Oriental brew. They could sympathize with Samuel Johnson's description of himself in 1757 as "a hardened and shameless Tea-drinker, who has for twenty years diluted his meals with only the infusion of this fascinating plant; whose kettle has scarcely time to cool, who with Tea amuses the evening, with Tea solaces the midnight, and with Tea welcomes the morning."[1]

The rise of tea-drinking had widespread effects on the manners and economy of England. Through its monopoly of importation the East India Company grew rich, and the national treasury reaped an ever increasing revenue from stiff customs duties. Others benefited too — the potters of Staffordshire, the sugar planters of the West Indies, and the thousands of retailers and proprietors of tea and coffeehouses who catered to the public's seemingly unquenchable thirst. Tea-time for the upper classes became a major social occasion, at which the hostess proudly displayed her silver and china while passing a pleasant hour of idle conversation with her guests. The middle class and working folk enjoyed their tea as much, if somewhat less ostentatiously. By the middle of the eighteenth century England had become a nation of tea drinkers.

No one knows when the Chinese first discovered that the leaves of their native tea bush (*Camellia Sinensis*) could be cured and brewed into a tasty and refreshing beverage. In the ninth century of the

3

Christian era Arab travelers reported a drink called "Chah" in wide use throughout China, and it was also known and enjoyed by the Japanese at that time. The first Europeans to try tea were probably the Portuguese, although no regular importations into Europe took place until the Dutch East India Company ventured a shipment in 1610. For half a century the Dutch had the infant trade to themselves. But beginning in 1667 the English East India Company started to import small quantities of tea and twenty years later entered the business in earnest. Once firmly in the trade, the English Company very quickly overtook its rival by procuring tea directly from Canton, while the Dutch obtained theirs at greater cost from Chinese junks sailing to Batavia. In 1729 the Dutch established connections with Canton itself, and when French, Swedish, and Danish merchants formed their own East India companies soon thereafter, a fierce rivalry for the China tea trade began.[2]

All tea came from the same variety of bush, but differences in place of growth and process of curing produced several kinds of tea for the European markets. About one-third of the tea exported from China during the eighteenth century was green tea, grown in the provinces of Chekiang and Anhwei. These leaves, heated after gathering to drive out moisture, were rubbed vigorously between the hands, dried, and then carefully packed for shipment to Canton. The choicest of all was green Hyson tea, made from the first gathering of the tenderest leaves, while leaves for the next grade of green tea, Singlo, were picked two or three times a year. Most teas imported into Europe during the eighteenth century were black, from the region of the Bohea mountains in Fukien province. Here the curing involved a longer drying stage than that for the green teas, during which the leaves were exposed to the air for oxidization, distinctly altering the flavor. The best of the black teas, Souchong, came from the first gatherings of young leaves, while Congo was somewhat less choice. The most common and plentiful sort of tea reaching the European market in the eighteenth century was Bohea. Inclined to be dusty, hastily cured and packed, Bohea nevertheless formed the backbone of the tea trade, for it could be sold so cheaply that almost all Europeans could enjoy it if they wished.[3]

Chinese peasants gathered the tea leaves in mid-summer and after processing, shipped them down to Canton for the autumn sales. There the Hong merchants, organized into their Co-Hong guild, established market regulations and monopolized dealings with the Europeans. To pay for the purchase of tea the English Company relied almost entirely on shipments of bullion until late in the eighteenth century, when woolens, tin, and lead became increasingly important as items of exchange. The Dutch, who managed their Cantonese trade from their East Indian capital at Batavia, were more fortunate in discovering a strong demand in China for pepper. At the end of the year the European ships cleared for home, arriving in mid-spring. In London the English Company then arranged each variety of tea into lots of from three to six chests, putting them up for sale twice a year by inch of candle. Each sort was offered at a minimum, or upset, price. As the auction on each lot began, a candle one inch long was lighted. The lot then went to the last man to make a bid before the candle flickered out.[4]

The tea trade soon became a most profitable line of business for the English East India Company. While at the beginning of the eighteenth century importations amounted to less than 100,000 pounds a year, by the 1730's the figure had increased tenfold. And in the period 1760-67 the Company sold over 4,000,000 pounds annually, paying on the average one shilling per pound in Canton for tea that in London commanded an average price of 4s. 8d. Even after freight, duties, and other costs had been deducted, the Company still enjoyed a handsome net profit. Much of this rise in tea consumption resulted from a concerted effort on the part of the East India Company to increase its sales at the expense of coffee, which had once been equally popular. On the European continent, in fact, coffee remained in much greater demand than tea. Only in Russia, which maintained an overland trade with China, did tea consumption surpass that of coffee. As the consumption of tea increased in

England, the East India Company was able to lower its price, putting the beverage within reach of thousands of new customers each year.[5]

Despite this impressive growth in sales, the Company was by no means satisfied. For the British government had early in the century recognized in the tea trade an excellent source of revenue, adding duty upon duty until by the 1760's tea bore a tax burden averaging about 100 per cent *ad valorem*. In addition to a 25 per cent customs upon importation there was a further excise, the "inland duty," of 25 per cent plus one shilling per pound on all tea sold for domestic consumption. In the case of Bohea tea, for instance, which at the sales in 1767 netted the Company about 2*s*. 1*d*. per pound, the final cost to the wholesale purchasers was in fact just over 4*s*. 5*d*. per pound.[6]

The inevitable result of these high duties was to encourage the smuggling of tea from the Continent. Bohea, for instance, could be bought in Amsterdam for 1*s*. 10*d*. per pound in 1767. This was even three-pence per pound under the English Company's net price, but the real difference lay in the fact that the government in Holland was prohibited from charging a duty on the imports of the Dutch Company. Smugglers therefore had a margin of up to 2*s*. 7*d*. between the two prices within which to find a profit. Hundreds of Englishmen earned a lucrative if dangerous livelihood running tea from France, Holland, and Scandinavia into one of the many isolated beaches from Sussex to Cornwall. One authority calculated that during the 1770's Englishmen actually consumed about 13,000,000 pounds of tea annually, of which he estimated 7,500,000 pounds were smuggled in from the Continent. Englishmen were thus consuming tea at the rate of nearly two pounds per capita, almost 300 cups a year for every man, woman, and child.[7]

Not all the tea imported into England by the East India Company was consumed at home, of course. Exports to Ireland and the American colonies made a small but potentially important market for Company tea, for wherever Englishmen went, the tea-drinking habit was sure to follow. The colonists in America were rather slow in acquiring a taste for tea, however, the first regular importations not taking place until the 1720's. Twenty years later the custom had caught on, and the 1760's Americans were consuming well over 1,000,000 pounds a year. After 1721 the colonists could legally import tea only from the mother country but in all probability less than a quarter of the total came from England; the rest was smuggled in, mostly from Holland.[8]

It is admittedly difficult to estimate the amount of tea smuggled into America and to determine the total consumption there during the years before the Revolution. The best one can do is to work backward from known facts. In the decade 1790-99, the first for which figures are available, Americans consumed tea at the rate of about half a pound per person. But the consumption of coffee had risen more than sevenfold in the years since the Declaration of Independence. Much of coffee's new popularity must have come at the expense of tea, which many Americans stopped drinking by necessity or by preference during the Revolution. It is safe to assume, therefore, that in the 1760's Americans drank at least half again as much tea per capita as the generation that followed, or .75 pounds per year. For the period 1760-66, for instance, that would make an annual consumption of about 1,200,000 pounds, of which 275,000 pounds we know came from England. The balance, 925,000 pounds, was therefore smuggled each year.[9]

This figure is in fact conservative in comparison with most contemporary estimates. One observer calculated that in 1763 the colonies consumed 1,500,000 pounds of tea annually, nine-tenths of it smuggled. Another commentator, writing in 1766, offered the figure 1,800,000 pounds. Still others suggested even greater estimates, one as high as 5,000,000 pounds per year, which would have meant that Americans consumed more tea per capita than their English cousins! It would appear, therefore, that 1,200,000 pounds a year for the period 1760-66 is by no means an exaggerated estimate of colonial tea consumption, three-quarters of which were smuggled. In point

of value by 1767 the tea imported from Britain ranked fourth behind
cotton and woolens, linens, and ironware, among the mother
country's principal exports to her American colonies.[10]

A typical shipment of tea to America consisted of ten or twelve
chests, each with a gross weight of about 450 pounds. The chest
was often lead-lined and contained about 360 pounds of tea, tightly
packed (by barefooted Chinese peasants, American patriots were
later to claim). Allowance for the weight of the chest, or "tare,"
was generally reckoned at 80 or 90 pounds. Half-chests and quarter-
chests, in which finer sorts of tea like Souchong and Hyson were
usually shipped, were of course proportionately smaller.

Certain London merchants came to specialize in the exportation
of tea to the American colonies by the middle of the eighteenth
century, usually in fulfillment of specific orders but sometimes
shipped on consignment at their own risk. These merchants attended
the semi-annual sales of the East India Company to bid on the
various lots of tea put up each season. As Bohea accounted for
nine-tenths of the American trade, very little other tea was purchased, save for occasional small lots of Hyson for the few Americans
able to afford the premium price. The duties for which teas bought
for export were liable in England underwent several successive
changes earlier in the century. In the period 1748-67 tea shipped
to America was exempt from Britain's inland duty but was still
subject to the regular *ad valorem* customs duty (about 25 per cent)
payable upon original importation into England. During the middle
decades of the eighteenth century the prime cost of Bohea teas to
American importers ranged from a high of 4s. 1d. in 1759 to a low
of 2s. 8d. in 1767. Charges for freight, primage, bills of lading, and
commissions to the English exporter, added, on the average, fourpence
per pound to this figure. The wholesale price that this tea could
command in America fluctuated wildly according to the law of
supply and demand.[11]

A comparatively small number of merchants concentrated in Boston, New York, and Philadelphia dominated the American end of
the colonies' tea trade with Great Britain. By 1768 about 90 per cent

of English tea entered at those three ports, and of the twenty-seven other continental customs districts, only Charleston, South Carolina, accounted for more than 5000 pounds that year. Since most tea was imported into the three major ports but was consumed throughout the colonies, it follows that tea was an important commodity in both the coastwise and internal commerce of America. Boston merchants, for instance, dominated the markets of northern New England, while the New Yorkers and Philadelphians vied for control of the middle colonies. Merchants from all three ports pushed their wares in the southern colonies and occasionally invaded the domains of the others, whenever the chance for profit presented itself.[12]

But by far the greatest handicap facing the legitimate importer of tea into colonial America was the fierce competition from smugglers. For tea was one of the illicit traders' favorite commodities. High duties on English tea made importation from Holland particularly lucrative, and few items of common trade were more valuable per pound to begin with. Furthermore, once ashore and out of the original chest, smuggled tea could not be distinguished from its legal counterpart. Both had come, after all, from the same warehouses in Canton. False documents, claiming importation from England, were easily obtained and gave added protection.

The smuggling of tea into colonial America was common knowledge, as contemporary comment indicates. Governor George Clinton of New York reported in 1752 that "although the consumption of tea in the Northern Colonies increases to a great degree yearly, yet it will be found that the exportations from London decrease of late." John Kidd, of Philadelphia, informed his London correspondents in 1757 that the many ships from Holland bringing Palatine immigrants to Pennsylvania carried great quantities of Dutch tea as well. He estimated that about 400 chests of tea had arrived in Philadelphia during the previous two years, only 16 of which had been legally imported from London. In the same year, 1757, Governor Charles Hardy of New York reported illicit trade with Holland to be "in a very flourishing state." Governor Francis Bernard wrote of similar difficulties in Massachusetts during the 1760's. "I receive from divers persons intelligence that there is a great quantity of Dutch Teas stirring about this town," he reported to the Earl of Halifax in 1764; "that carts and other carriages are heard to be continually going about in the dead of the night, which can be for no other purpose than smuggling." In 1767 an observer at New York estimated that from forty to a hundred vessels discharged smuggled goods at various harbors along the northern shore of Long Island Sound, among which must have been many chests of tea.[13]

Most of the tea smuggled into America came from Holland, sometimes via the Dutch-held island of St. Eustatius in the Caribbean. In the fall of 1754 a schooner belonging to the Boston merchant Thomas Hancock made just such a voyage. In January, Hancock had written to Thomas and Adrian Hope, English merchants resident in Amsterdam, with whom Americans did much of their illicit trade. Hancock ordered fifteen chests of Bohea tea to be shipped on his account to the care of a merchant at St. Eustatius. Learning in mid-September that his tea had left Amsterdam, he dispatched one of his loyal captains in the schooner *Lydia* to pick up the goods at Statia. Hancock took care to give *Lydia* an outward cargo of fish, apples, and lumber products in hope of making a profit on both outward and homeward passages. He then instructed his captain to take on a legitimate cargo at the British island of Montserrat before returning home and upon his arrival off Boston to "Stop at the lighthouse where you shall have a letter for your further proceeding." The tea arrived safely, although somewhat damaged from faulty packing. It had cost Hancock 2s. 2d. per pound, including freight from Amsterdam and wages for *Lydia*'s crew. At the time it arrived, the wholesale price of tea at Boston was 3s. 0d., and Hancock realized a net profit over £200.[14]

Other smugglers procured their tea in Holland for themselves. The New York merchant John Ludlow dispatched a vessel in the fall of 1755 first to the West Indies, probably with flour and lumber, and then to the Bay of Honduras to pick up a cargo of logwood for Amsterdam. There the vessel was to take on tea and gunpowder.

Ludlow instructed his captain to be especially careful when returning through Long Island Sound:

> . . . proceed down off of Stamford but don't anchor nearer the Connecticut shore than about the middle of the Sound if moderate weather and if other ways then anchor in Oyster Bay or under Lloyd's Neck on long Island side and go across your self or send [your] Mate in your own boat or otherways directly to Mr. John Lloyd whose direction you are to follow . . .[15]

Sometimes smuggling voyages involved illicit trade both ways. In March 1763 the Plymouth merchant Meletiah Bourne hired Captain Churchill's schooner *Sally*, put aboard 110 tierces of rice, and dispatched him to Amsterdam. This was a patent violation of the Acts of Trade, for rice, as an enumerated commodity, could not be sent to any European port north of Cape Finisterre. Churchill arrived at Amsterdam in early May, sold his rice, and bought twelve chests of tea and a small quantity of dry goods. By mid-August he was safely back home. The papers covering this voyage are unusually complete, and from them an accurate balance sheet of expenses and proceeds can be compiled. The result shows a net profit to Bourne of £258.[16]

American merchants shopping for bargains visited other European ports for illicit tea as well. In November 1759 the New Londoner Nathaniel Shaw joined with two New York firms on a voyage to Hamburg for ten chests of Bohea. The partners subsequently divided net proceeds totaling about £200. Still another popular source was Gottenburg, where tea and hemp could be purchased at rock-bottom prices. Observers at Philadelphia noted shipments from Bordeaux and Lisbon during the 1750's in addition to the many cargoes from Amsterdam. During the latter years of the Seven Years War, when the European coast was carefully watched by British cruisers, American smugglers had to concoct more elaborate schemes to obtain illicit tea. The Philadelphian Tench Francis had seventy-five chests of Bohea delivered to the island of Teneriffe in 1760, where one of his vessels later picked it up. Two years later he ordered thirty-eight chests more, this time to be transferred at Fayal. On these two ventures Francis realized a total profit in excess of £1500.[17]

New York was the center for illicit trade in tea, and much of the commodity brought in there found its way into other ports from Boston to Charleston, as the smugglers sought to take advantage of higher local prices. New York's John Waddell sent a steady supply to Thomas Wharton at Philadelphia in the mid-1750's, sometimes dispatching it overland to Trenton and thence down the Delaware, on other occasions by coaster around Cape May and up-river. The two merchants took elaborate precautions to avoid detection. Generally the tea shipped coastwise was transferred into a shallop downstream at Marcus Hook for the final trip. The river was constantly crawling with small boats, and the overworked customs officers could not possibly inspect them all. Once ashore the tea was divided into several lots and carted off to different stores where it was often transferred from the original chests into old sugar barrels and other innocent-looking containers. Sometimes Wharton was prepared to authenticate his tea with documents left over from a legal shipment. On other occasions Waddell could furnish him with "valid" papers purchased from a corrupt official, and Wharton himself discovered a collector's clerk at Philadelphia not averse to supplementing his meager salary.[18]

Tea-smuggling reached its zenith in proportion to legal imports during the 1750's. Thereafter the legitimate trade gradually increased in volume. Stricter enforcement of the Acts of Trade was one reason for this change. Another was the fact that a gradual drop in the price of tea in London narrowed the smugglers' margin of profit somewhat. Conscience did not seem to be a factor, although two onetime smugglers found it necessary to explain their activities in these terms: "There is nothing to be said in favor of the dutch trade but it was carried on in so publick a manner that all people in trade was obliged to be concerned in it in their defence." [19]

Two aspects of the colonial tea trade deserve special emphasis. The first is its rapid growth during the mid-eighteenth century. By the 1760's the consumption of tea was widespread throughout America.

Both men and women had come to enjoy it as an everyday beverage, although it was most popular among the ladies of the cosmopolitan communities of New England and the middle colonies. Probably few colonists were hopeless addicts like Samuel Johnson, but tea-drinking had nevertheless become with many Americans a habit that they would be loath to give up. Another factor of importance was the remarkable extent of illegal trade carried on by colonial merchants. This smuggling made a significant contribution to the breakdown of law and order throughout the ports of North America, where the Revolution's first seeds were sown. Violent resistance to the hapless customs officers became a common practice, deplored by a few but condoned by the multitude.

The East India Company had of course been well aware of the problem of tea-smuggling both at home and in the colonies. At the suggestion of the Company in 1767 Parliament finally enacted legislation to remedy the situation. As a five-year experiment, the Indemnity Act lowered the inland duty on tea consumed in England. On tea exported to America the Act allowed a full drawback of all customs duties originally charged upon its entry into England (it was already exempt from the inland duty) to encourage the legitimate tea trade with the colonies. The East India Company was put on a more equitable footing with its Continental competitors. English merchants trading with America waited until the Act took effect in July 1767, when the actual price of Bohea was dropped by the drawback from 2s. 9d. to 2s. 1d., and then shipped out enough tea to bring the year's total to about 500,000 pounds. In the year following 869,000 pounds were exported to the colonies, the largest amount yet.[20]

To the American fair trader it must have seemed that justice had finally triumphed. At last he could purchase his tea in London at about the same price as the smuggler paid at Amsterdam without incurring any of the risks attending illicit trade. During the first eighteen months after the new law took effect, legal importations increased by 42 per cent at New York and by 100 per cent at Philadelphia. But optimists who predicted a boom for the importers of English tea overlooked the fact that Parliament had passed another law in late June 1767, one which became far more famous than the Indemnity Act. The Townshend Act, which placed a duty of threepence per pound on all tea imported into the colonies, along with duties on glass, paper, lead, and painter's colors, put a quick end to the fair traders' dream of prosperity.[21]

II

THE TOWNSHEND ACT

THE Townshend Act of 1767 was the last of several attempts by the British Parliament to raise a revenue from the American colonies. That it was exacted at all was due to the political and fiscal complexities following the close of the Seven Years War in 1762. Within a few years after ascending the throne in 1760 George III determined to take an active role in the government of his realm, but to accomplish this end he had to acquire a following of his own. By 1763 political conditions admirably suited his purpose. Throughout the first half of the eighteenth century the Whigs, under the successive leadership of Robert Walpole, Henry Pelham, and the Duke of Newcastle, had completely dominated the government of Great Britain. Long years in power, however, inevitably led to squabbles, and by the early 1760's what had once been a united party split into numerous political factions.[1]

Among the best-known factions of the period were those led by George Grenville, the Duke of Bedford, and William Pitt. The Marquis of Rockingham succeeded the Duke of Newcastle as leader of the remaining Old Whigs, and George III had his own supporters, a small group known as the King's Friends. Each of these factions was held together by an elaborate system of patronage and by the common ambition of its members to gain and hold political office. Family ties were often important bonds, although in the case of the brothers-in-law Grenville and Pitt, for instance, political differences proved still stronger. No faction was large enough to constitute a majority in Parliament, and therefore alliances between them became a commonplace. Less often, the groups left out of the government united in opposition. Government by coalition, however, was predictably unstable, and in the 1760's one ministry after another fell from power whenever political allies withheld support. William Pitt, for instance, was forced to resign in 1762 because many of the independent members of Parliament who had backed his ministry throughout the Seven Years War joined the ranks of the King's Friends.

In the spring of 1763 the King chose George Grenville as successor to William Pitt. Supported by the Bedford faction, Grenville soon turned his attention to solving a serious financial crisis facing the Empire. On top of the enormous debt resulting from the war with France, Great Britain was saddled with the expense of maintaining an army in America (the colonial militia did not find frontier garrison duty to its liking) and of supporting numerous government officials there. Grenville and his ministry not surprisingly looked to the colonies for revenue to help defray these costs. One scheme, incorporated in the Sugar Act of 1764, reduced the duties on foreign sugar and molasses imported into the colonies, gave the customs officials there increased powers of collection, and established vice-admiralty courts in America for better enforcement of the Acts of Trade, all with the avowed purpose of producing an American revenue. Adding another plan in the following year, Grenville secured passage of the Stamp Act, which extended to America a program of internal taxation long practiced in England. But the colonists immediately objected to the new policy on the grounds that Parliament had no authority to tax them. Resolutions of protest, a boycott of English goods, and numerous riots brought the crisis to a head by the autumn of 1765, but by that time Grenville was no longer in office. George III, angered by a slight to his mother the minister had made in the Regency Act of 1765, accepted Grenville's resignation and turned instead to the Old Whigs in July 1765.

Led by the ineffectual but well-intentioned Marquis of Rockingham, the new Ministry was immediately faced with the crisis in America when Parliament convened in December 1765. From the start Rockingham's political position was tenuous. United against him were the Bedford and Grenville forces. Pitt remained aloof. Aside from a few King's Friends, his only reliable support came from some fifty members of Parliament who represented the interests of the nation's merchants and manufacturers. Alarmed by the American boycott of English goods, this group clamored for a settlement of the crisis. In the spring of 1766 the Old Whigs managed to secure the repeal of Grenville's Stamp Act, but not until Pitt and his followers had stepped in with decisive help.

Although Americans immediately proclaimed him a hero, Rockingham did not share the colonists' view that the mother country had no right to tax them. He believed with most Britons that Parliament enjoyed legislative supremacy over the colonies in all cases whatsoever. He saw to it that this principle was adopted in the Declaratory Act before Parliament voted to rescind the stamp taxes. Repeal was successful solely because enough members of Parliament considered it the only way to restore Anglo-American trade. But the decision was regarded by many Britons and Americans alike as a concession to the colonists. As such it would have important political consequences. In the mother country those opposed to the apparent policy of leniency toward America became the nucleus for a new conservative coalition; in America patriots mistakenly concluded that many Englishmen supported their claims to exemption from Parliamentary taxation.[2]

Weak to begin with, Rockingham's coalition fell apart altogether in the late spring of 1766. The King turned immediately to William Pitt, who took office in July and accepted the title Earl of Chatham at the same time. The new minister brought with him several of his staunchest supporters, including the Earl of Shelburne, who as Secretary of State for the Southern Department assumed responsibility for colonial policy. But Chatham needed help from the King's Friends to maintain a majority, and several places in the new administration went to members of that faction. In order to make room Chatham drove all but one of the Old Whigs from office.[3]

In February 1767 the Old Whigs retaliated. Their leader in the House of Commons, the veteran William Dowdeswell, sought to embarrass the new administration by moving that the land tax be reduced to its pre-war level of three shillings. Dowdeswell had served as Chancellor of the Exchequer under Rockingham and knew that such a step would deprive the government of about £500,000 revenue per year, but enough members from the counties found the proposal irresistible to assure its passage by a narrow margin. Ironically, this irresponsible action on the part of the Old Whigs led to a reopening with the American colonies of the dispute ostensibly settled by repeal of the Stamp Act.[4]

Defeat on a money bill such as that suffered by the Chatham administration had not occurred for twenty-five years. Ordinarily the Ministry was expected to resign unless funds could be found elsewhere to make up the deficit. Chatham had long hoped that the East India Company would prove to be a promising source of revenue. But in the early weeks of the new year Chatham was suffering from one of the attacks of gout that would grow more serious in the coming months. In his absence the rest of the Ministry was hopelessly divided. Shelburne was the most logical man to take over, but the others distrusted him. Instead, the young, dynamic Chancellor of the Exchequer, Charles Townshend, saw his opportunity and stepped into the breach.[5]

Townshend had his own ideas about budgetary matters. In direct contrast to Chatham he believed Parliament had a right to tax the colonies, and in January 1767 he had hinted to the House of Commons that he would soon introduce legislation to this effect. At a Cabinet meeting held in early March, when Chatham was absent, Townshend presented a series of proposals concerning America. Because New York had refused to support British troops quartered there, that colony was to be punished by a suspension of its assembly. To provide a revenue for the support of civil officers in America duties were to be levied upon the importation of glass, paper, lead, colors, and tea. And to tighten the enforcement of the Acts of Trade against smugglers, Townshend proposed that commissioners be stationed in an American port to oversee the collection of customs throughout the colonies. Both Shelburne and the Duke of Grafton meekly accepted Townshend's American program. Since no other Cabinet members were opposed and Chatham was too ill to intervene, the Chancellor of the Exchequer carried the day. Introducing his legislation to the House of Commons in mid-May, he guided all the bills through to adoption by late June 1767.[6]

The origins of the Townshend Revenue Act are somewhat mysterious. As far back as March 1763 its author, as president of the Board of Trade, had devised a scheme of colonial taxation, but the plan was laid aside. Townshend was a staunch supporter of Grenville's Stamp Act in 1765, and when that measure was repealed in the following year, he remained convinced that colonial taxation was both proper and expedient. It is safe to assume, therefore, that when Townshend accepted the post of Chancellor of the Exchequer under Chatham, the idea of an American revenue was firmly implanted in his mind.[7]

There was understandably some confusion in Great Britain concerning the Americans' opposition to British taxation. Benjamin Franklin, in his testimony before Parliament in 1766 favoring repeal of the Stamp Act, suggested that the colonists had only denied Parliament's right to lay internal taxes. They were not opposed to external taxation, he implied. Always the astute tactician, Franklin took this position to disguise the contention of most Americans—that there was no difference between internal and external taxation and that Parliament had no right to raise a revenue in the colonies by any means whatever.[8]

For opposite reasons few English officials distinguished between external and internal taxation in America either, for they believed with the Declaratory Act that Parliament had the right to legislate for the colonies in all matters whatsoever, including means of taxation. While denouncing the distinction, Townshend saw at the same time an opportunity to justify a new revenue bill by using

Franklin's testimony. If the Americans objected to internal taxation, he reasoned, let us instead raise a revenue by placing duties on certain commodities imported by them from Great Britain.[9]

It is not clear why Townshend selected most of the articles he did to be taxed upon importation into America. Glass, painter's colors, lead, and paper were not among Britain's major exports to the colonies. Perhaps he planned to expand the list later, when the colonists became accustomed to the idea of revenue duties. Or possibly Townshend realized that the manufacturers of British woolens and linens, articles far more profitable for taxation, would object if their products were subjected to an additional cost when imported into America.

The inclusion of tea among the dutied commodities is easier to explain, however. In the first place, several officials had had the idea before. When Grenville undertook the revision of the colonial revenue system that resulted in the Sugar Act of 1764, one of his undersecretaries, Charles Jenkinson, considered including a duty on all English tea entering colonial ports. Although the idea was dropped at that time, two years later, at the height of the Stamp Act crisis, George Spencer recommended replacing the stamp duties with a levy of one shilling per pound on tea shipped to America. Pointing out how inexpensive Bohea was in the colonies, Spencer concluded that Americans could hardly complain of "so small a duty." Perhaps Townshend's decision to include tea in his Revenue bill was prompted by one of these suggestions.[10]

There is a still more likely reason why Townshend included tea among the articles to be taxed. In the spring of 1767 Parliament had before it an elaborate series of proposals dealing with the East India Company. Among them, as we have seen, was the Indemnity bill, with its provisions that on tea shipped to America the Company be granted a full drawback of all customs duties originally charged upon its entry into England. At current prices, this meant that the Treasury would lose about ninepence on each pound, and Americans could buy their tea that much more cheaply than before. Why not recover some of this loss, Townshend reasoned to the House of

Commons, by including tea among those articles to be taxed in America? The Indemnity bill and the Townshend Revenue bill were under Parliament's consideration at the same time, and it was natural that the legislators should consider them related at least in respect to tea. As South Carolina's agent, Charles Garth, reported in mid-May 1767, "I understand the Plan is to allow a Drawback of this [the English customs duty] also upon Tea exported to America, and *in lieu thereof* to impose a Duty of Six pence per pound on all Tea imported lawfully into the Colonies." In a sense, then, what Parliament did in respect to tea was to remove a duty collectable in England and partially replace it with one collectable in America.[11]

As passed by Parliament in June 1767, Townshend's Revenue Act contained several principles that would surely stir up strong opposition in America. First and most important was the clear statement of purpose to raise a revenue in the colonies, no pretence being made that this was an act to regulate colonial commerce. Second, the Act provided that proceeds from the duties would go for the support of a colonial civil list. These officials would thus be made independent of the colonial legislatures for their salaries. Finally, the provision to collect the duties in America underscored the fact that colonists were paying them directly.[12]

Opposition in America to the Townshend Act developed rather slowly. To be sure, John Hancock predicted in early September 1767 that the Americans would soon enter into non-importation agreements in protest to the new taxation, and he resolved to stop importing goods from England and to persuade others to take the same action. By November, however, he had broken down and had ordered the usual assortment of spring goods from London.[13] When the Boston merchants met late that month to consider the situation, no less a patriot than James Otis asserted, according to Governor Bernard, that opposition to the new duties would be "imprudent" at that time, "when every other town in the province in America seemed to acquiesce in them." [14]

Otis, however, was soon proved wrong. One report to Benjamin Franklin in London claimed that the Townshend Act had set off a clamor in every town save New York, and the conservative Philadelphia merchant Thomas Wharton was convinced that a fearful crisis impended. Indeed it was Philadelphia's John Dickinson who galvanized the colonists into action with his *Farmer's Letters*, appearing first in December, although oddly enough his own town would be last to respond to the call. By the end of January Massachusetts Bay had drawn up protests to be sent to England.[15]

In some areas the protest movement against the Townshend Act grew out of an earlier drive to promote colonial frugality. In late October 1767 Boston town meeting had adopted resolutions against the consumption of a large number of luxuries in reaction to the generally depressed times and a shortage of specie. As winter progressed, the movement swept through other provinces until colonists in all parts of America pledged themselves not to purchase such items as ribbon, lace, and expensive foreign clothing. Coupled with this drive was an elaborate promotion of home manufactures, as ladies took to their wheels and looms to vie with neighboring towns and parishes in the production of homespun. By spring the American public had seemingly caught the spirit of thrift, and the ground was laid for a protest movement specifically organized against the Townshend Act.[16]

Although at first opposition to the new taxes was made on the basis of frugality, the merchants obviously had another object in mind — to put economic pressure on Parliament to rescind the duties by an organized boycott of British goods. Patriots believed that a similar scheme had been instrumental in forcing repeal of the Stamp Act two years before; perhaps it would succeed again. In early March 1768 a small group of Boston merchants tentatively agreed not to import British manufactures for one year and sent copies of their resolutions to other trading towns to enlist support. Signatures were hard to come by even in Boston, however, despite the arguments and threats of the patriots. Many of the most prominent importers, including the Hutchinsons and the Clarkes, refused to join. When only a trickle of favorable responses from other provinces came in during the spring, the Boston movement ground to a halt.[17]

Meanwhile New Yorkers had drawn up their own agreement in April, contingent upon support from merchants in Boston and Philadelphia. But the Pennsylvanians withheld their approval at a meeting later that month, and the New York venture collapsed. No group of merchants dared make a move alone during the spring of 1768. So great was the degree of mutual suspicion that many Philadelphians, for instance, regarded the whole idea as simply another trick of the New Yorkers to corner the market on British importations. Nor did they trust the Bostonians. While the merchants bickered, town meetings and colonial legislatures continued to adopt resolutions against the consumption of all British products. Obviously the merchants would have to find some way to catch up with public opinion, for criticism of their dilatory behavior poured into the public prints from all quarters.[18]

In August 1768 the Boston merchants tried again, this time agreeing not to import any British manufactures after 1 January 1769, and particularly to boycott all goods taxed by the Townshend Act. Again the Bostonians sought the support of New York and Philadelphia, although this time they made it clear that they planned to go it alone if necessary, and, indeed, they threatened to suspend their trade with any colony whose merchants continued to import duued goods. The response from New York was immediate and favorable, the merchants there agreeing in late August not to accept any goods shipped from Great Britain after 1 November. In both cases the merchants appended a list of excepted articles, the Bostonians allowing the importation of materials needed for the fisheries, and the New Yorkers permitting a miscellany of articles such as coal, tin, german steel, and grindstones. Curiously enough, the New York merchants agreed as well not to import any merchandise from Hamburg or Holland, except tiles and bricks. Apparently the smuggling of Dutch tea was about to end.[19]

Among the major ports only Philadelphia now hung back. Supported by conservative Quakers in London, the Philadelphians held fast throughout the winter of 1768-69, seemingly impervious to denunciations by colonists elsewhere. Twice they had written directly to the merchants and manufacturers of Great Britain urging them to demand repeal of the Townshend Act. Only when this tactic had once again failed in March 1769 did the merchants of Philadelphia reluctantly come into the non-importation movement in protest to the Townshend Act. Most of the smaller ports along the North Atlantic seaboard had long since fallen into line. By the spring of 1769 only the merchants in Portsmouth, Providence, and Newport continued to hold out, although of course in each major port individual merchants managed to buck the tide of popular resentment by refusing to sign the agreements.[20]

The non-importation agreement had no sooner been concluded among the major ports in the spring of 1769 than the patriots of Boston found it necessary to reaffirm their decision and to launch an all-out drive against those few merchants who continued to remain outside the pact. A house-to-house subscription against purchasing from the hold-outs was circulated in the summer, and in mid-August their names were struck off on handbills for distribution throughout the province as enemies of the people. Rumors that Parliament was about to repeal the Townshend Act made the task of enforcement more difficult, for apparently some weak-hearted merchants considered the battle against Parliamentary taxation won.[21]

But in mid-October 1769 the Boston patriots overplayed their hand. The original non-importation agreement was due to expire on 1 January 1770; plans had to be made for its continuation. Spurred on by the movement's apparent success, they decided to extend their goal beyond simply repeal of the Townshend Act. On 17 October the merchants of Boston agreed not to import goods from Great Britain until *all* the revenue acts were repealed. This meant in particular the acts of 1764 and 1766 putting duties on foreign wines, molasses, and sugar. As the Boston committee explained it to their counterparts in other ports, these acts were also designed to raise a revenue in the colonies, and were therefore just as reprehensible as the Townshend Act of 1767. The Boston merchants, however, all but twelve of whom signed the new agreement, were not willing to bind themselves to the plan without the concurrence of their counterparts in the other major centers. To their disappointment the merchants at both New York and Philadelphia refused to go along with the change, the latter arguing that they had too long accepted the other acts as commercial regulations to alter their position now. The Bostonians then backed down themselves, but at least they had successfully extended their boycott beyond the original date of 1 January 1770.[22]

Despite their best efforts the patriot merchants at Boston found it necessary constantly to reinforce the non-importation agreements. One of the most persistent violators, John Mein, was doubly annoying because he was the printer of the *Boston Chronicle*. When proscribed by the committee in August 1769 as an importer, he became so angered that he determined to expose all other violators in his journal. With the probable co-operation of the customs officials, Mein published lists of the cargoes and their importers that had entered Boston since the beginning of 1769. It did not matter that most of the violators, like the Clarkes and Hutchinsons, were his political allies. Merchants and shopkeepers of inland towns and other ports were shocked to see the ease with which some Bostonians ignored the agreement while they themselves made great sacrifices to honor their word. The effect of Mein's vengeance on the reputation of the Boston patriots was devastating.[23]

Stephen Salisbury of Worcester, for instance, became so disgusted by the end of the year that he told his brother and partner in Boston that he would start selling his stored English goods immediately. "It is impossible to conceive the damage I have sustained by coming into the first agreement," he complained, "and now to behold a large an assortment of goods brought up her[e] & sold. . . . I will not sacrifice my interest to serve the publick any longer," he angrily concluded.[24] When his brother Samuel tried to persuade him that only a few Boston merchants had actually violated the agreement, Stephen refused to believe it. "I am afraid that blind credulity and enthusiastick Zeal in the Cause of Liberty has got the better of your reason. That Instide of Serving the Publick we have been the making of Individuals, and when it is too Late we shall begin to consider & look into our Familys where to our Un-speakable sorrow, we shall find destruction & poverty come upon us without recompense or hope of reward. . . ." [25] Not until spring, when Stephen temporarily changed places with Samuel at Boston, did he become fully convinced that the situation there was not hopelessly out of the patriots' control.[26]

Not that the Bostonians were having an easier time enforcing their boycott. In the spring of 1770 shipments of prohibited goods began arriving from England, some ordered by colonial merchants, others sent on consignment by English houses. Earlier cargoes like these had been stored away either by the merchants' committee or by the recipients themselves, honor-bound not to put the goods up for sale. The former procedure was expensive, however, and the latter difficult to enforce. In October 1769 the Philadelphia patriots had tried a new approach—sending the prohibited goods back to England, often by the same vessels on which they had come. In December the Boston committee adopted the same tactic. When the spring shipments arrived in April 1770, the Bostonians were ready. John Hancock offered his ship *Lydia* to carry back the forbidden cargoes, and in mid-May she sailed for London with about £15,000 worth of English goods. Tea could not be returned, however, for, as a Boston merchant explained to a critical New Yorker, an Act of Parliament passed in 1724 expressly prohibited the reimportation of that article into England upon pain of forfeiture.[27]

Long before the non-importation movement had gained wide acceptance, the campaign for frugality made significant headway in colonial America. Among the imports singled out for condemnation, tea received a large share of attention. One could argue in the first place that tea was expensive and of foreign growth, whether imported from England or Holland. Secondly, it was a needless luxury, especially when compared with other imports like woolens, paper, and glass. In the third place, patriots even argued that perfectly good substitutes for China tea could be brewed from numerous American shrubs.

The first proposal of an anti-tea campaign seems to have come from Connecticut's London agent, William S. Johnson. Writing to Governor William Pitkin in June 1767, even before passage of the Townshend Act, he suggested that Americans substitute for English tea "some of the more salutary herbs of their own country." Beginning in the autumn of 1767 and continuing through the remainder of the pre-Revolutionary period, newspaper articles, resolutions in town meetings, and private petitions railed against the use of foreign tea. By the spring of 1768, when the frugality movements became absorbed into the non-importation protest against the Townshend duties, English tea become a double target, for it was by far the most commonly used article taxed by the new law. In all parts of colonial America the inhabitants were familiar with the beverage, and for confirmed addicts, giving up tea was a major sacrifice.[28]

The patriots' principal line of attack was to urge the ladies of America to drink Labradore instead of English tea. This concoction, known also as Hyperion tea, was made from the red-root bush, found in abundance in swampy regions along the banks of most New England rivers. Its quality, however, was subject to dispute. According to an Englishman to whom a sample was sent, Labradore tea possessed "a very physical taste." The beverage allegedly was first used by Indians, then by Canadians. Its American promoters employed every trick of modern advertising, claiming, for instance, that it had become so popular in France that the East India Company there had to seek a governmental ban on its further importation. It was even suggested in 1768 that the Townshend duty would be reduced because of the competition from Labradore tea. The campaign included newspaper doggerel to win converts to the patriotic drink. One Boston newspaper featured the following verse:

> Throw aside your Bohea and your Green Hyson Tea,
> And all things with a new fashioned duty;
> Procure a good store of the choice Labradore
> For there'll soon be enough here to suit ye;

These do without fear, and to all you'll appear
Fair, charming, true, lovely; and clever;
Though the times remain darkish, young men may be sparkish,
And love you much stronger than ever.[29]

In Boston, Edes and Gill had Labradore tea for sale at their printing shop in January 1768, and patriots everywhere had learned of its existence by spring. Procedures for curing its leaves and brewing from them an acceptable drink gained wide circulation through the journals of the day. As another alternative to English tea some Americans attempted the cultivation of the Chinese tea bush. In Boston a Captain Harrison gained wide fame for his early success in this undertaking, but other efforts to transplant the bush met with disappointment.[30]

Persuading colonial housewives to change their tea-drinking habits or to abandon them altogether proved to be as difficult as growing the Chinese tea plant in America. Part of the campaign consisted of a vigorous if not convincing attack on English Bohea as a deadly poison. To this "enervating" plant were ascribed the causes of an impressive range of human ailments from stomach complaints to the most tormenting nervous disorders. Naturally Labradore tea produced none of these deplorable effects, nor, oddly enough, were such results apparently expected from Dutch tea, although of course it came from the same sources in China. Clearly, whatever the disease spread by English tea, it infected the political rather than the physical constitution of its American victim.[31]

Almost from the beginning of the non-importation movement political writers concentrated their attack on tea. One observer pointed out that however firmly Americans might resolve in favor of frugality, as long as they went on drinking dutied tea, the cause was doomed.

> The produce from all the duties upon glass, paper, print, etc. would be but a trifle and quite insufficient for the purpose of supporting civil government and the administration of justice. . . . But TEA was known to be imported into America in such immense quantities, and the taste, I might properly say, the

passion for it, to be grown so universal and so strong, that the politicians who planned our ruin, I mean the placemen and pensioners, who expect to be supported by it, selected this article as a bait to allure us to their snare. . . .

Although the duty was now only threepence per pound, he admitted, once Americans acknowledged Parliament's right to impose that tax, there was nothing to prevent an increase to three shillings or more. "Can the spirit of man submit to the insolence of a crew of little dirty tyrants?" he concluded. "Let us abjure the poisonous baneful plant and its odious infusion — poisonous and odious, I mean, not on account of its physical qualities but on account of the political diseases and death that are connected with every particle of it." [32]

A COUNTRYMAN had several reasons for supporting the anti-tea campaign. He told first of a friend's family who consumed so much butter with its tea biscuits that there was no longer enough to take to market. "There is my daughters Jemma and Keziah," the friend noted, "two hearty trollups as any in town, forenoon and afternoon eat almost a peck of toast with their tea, and they have learned me and their mother to join them," he ruefully admitted; "and as for Jeremiah, he can hardly live without it, a booby." A COUNTRYMAN insisted that the Commissioners of Customs, currently residing at Castle William for protection against the Boston mob, were laughing at the Americans because the continued high consumption of tea meant a larger salary for themselves. "As for glass, paper, and paint," COUNTRYMAN concluded, "it is not to be mention'd the same day with . . . TEA. Leave Tea and you will find the C[ommissione]rs will soon leave you; for they are a kind of eagle that will be in no place longer than there is a carcase to eat. . . ." [33]

The primary campaign against English tea took the form of voluntary agreements to abstain among the ladies of the various parishes or towns, well publicized to serve as an incentive for others. Newport, Rhode Island, was one of the earliest towns to organize an anti-tea program, while Boston could report in December 1767 that "a considerable number" of the ladies had agreed not to use foreign teas. Sometimes the pledges involved ladies gathered at their parsonage to spin yarn for the minister's wife. On these occasions Labradore tea was served instead of the formerly popular Bohea, and the company invariably recorded their delight at discovering such a satisfactory substitute. The spirit of competition more often than not prompted the ladies of other congregations in town to similar manifestations of patriotism.[34]

From town to town the movement spread on into the spring and summer of 1768. Tiny Windham, Connecticut, joined Boston and New York to proscribe the poisonous herb. From New Bern, North Carolina, came the report that "Yeopann tea" was a delicious substitute for Bohea, and its plant had the advantage of being found in sandy soil all over the province. In Huntington, Long Island, Ever-Green tea reputedly vied with imported Green tea for popularity. Even the students at Harvard joined in the ban against English tea.[35]

It is difficult to tell just how effective the campaign against English tea was during the first year of protest. To be sure, assertions were made that merchants at Boston had to send their tea to other provinces for want of a local market. A common report going the rounds in December 1768 claimed that merchants there did not sell one-fifth the amount they had before the non-consumption movement began. In November 1768 Newburyport merchants Jonathan Jackson and John Bromfield wrote their London correspondents that "Tea is growing daily out of use in this country." Eighteen months earlier, in the spring of 1767, they had described the commodity as having been "as necessary in our business as any one thing." A similar change was apparently taking place in other parts of the country, one Boston shipmaster testifying that he had been able to sell only eight pounds of tea to prospects in North Carolina on a voyage in the autumn of 1768. In New York, Pennsylvania, and many southern colonies English tea virtually disappeared as the list of towns enacting resolutions against dutied tea grew steadily longer.[36]

Evidence beneath the surface, however, indicates that by the middle of 1769 the anti-tea campaign was running into difficulties. Sometime during that year a cynical colonist reported to his English correspondent as follows:

> . . . As to our people's quitting the use of tea, it is really a Joke. It would be full as reasonable to imagine they will cease to drink New England Rum or Cyder. The flourishes in newspapers are designed only as deceptives and therefore ought to be treated as such. The Inhabitants are very strongly possessed in favor of it, & not capable of being actuated by principles of modern Patriotism. . . . I don't believe there are ten chests of tea less consumed in this province in a year than there were before the Act took place. . . .[37]

A better indication that many New Englanders had resumed their old tea-drinking ways lies in the fact that in the early months of 1770 the patriots found it necessary to institute a new round of anti-tea pledges and to stir up the town meetings to adopt another series of resolutions proscribing the baneful herb. The dimensions of this new drive were so large as to suggest that, although the 1768 campaign might have made temporary gains, the enthusiasm of the day soon gave way to the deep-rooted American love for a good cup of tea.

In January 1770 a meeting of the Boston merchants agreed to abstain totally from the use of tea until repeal of the Townshend Act. The movement quickly spread into the community at large, and by early March hundreds of householders had once again pledged themselves not to drink tea. The ladies of the South End vied with their counterparts in the North part of town, while younger girls signed resolutions of their own. The campaign gained support from the tea sellers of both Boston and Charlestown, who agreed to suspend that line of business for the duration. In Newburyport only fifty out of some 1400 adults refused to sign against the use of tea, and for their obstinacy these fifty were listed at the Town House as enemies to their country. Other towns in New England followed suit, and by late spring of 1770 the ban against tea appeared to be once more in force.[38] An English skeptic maintained, however, that the drive would have an effect opposite to that intended. "Tea," he wrote, "becoming a forbidden fruit, will only give ["your fair American Eves"] more ardent longings to taste it." [39]

Figures for the importation of tea into the colonies during 1769 and 1770 indicate the effectiveness of the movement. According to the agreements entered into by the merchants of Boston in the summer of 1768 the importation of dutied tea was specifically prohibited after 1 January 1769. The New Yorkers resolved not to accept any tea (or other proscribed goods) shipped from London after 1 November 1768. Both 1767 and 1768 had been boom years for the legitimate tea trade to the colonies, for during that twenty-four-month period nearly 1,400,000 pounds of tea had been shipped from England, a total no previous two-year period had come close to equaling. With the protest movement against the Townshend Act taking effect by the end of 1768, however, the importation of tea from England was bound to drop off. In fact the 1769-70 total fell to 446,000 pounds, less than a third of the previous two-year figure. Perhaps most surprising is that during this period so much dutied tea did come into America, despite the concerted efforts of patriots in all parts of the country. [40]

By far the most egregious offender against the anti-tea agreements was the town of Boston, where duties were paid on nearly 150,000 pounds of tea during the years 1769-70. There were a number of reasons for this, not the least of which was the fact that New York, Philadelphia, and other communities supplied by them had long since established permanent smuggling routes to Holland and its West Indian possessions. Colonists in those provinces could patriotically swear off dutied tea without the agony of abandoning their favorite beverage. For the Bostonians the situation was quite different. Although Dutch tea had reached their town through Connecticut and Rhode Island, they had always relied heavily on imports from England. A complete cessation of those shipments would mean that many Bostonians would have to do without tea altogether, an unbearable prospect. A more direct reason for the continued flow of dutied tea into Boston after January 1769 was simply the obstinacy of two mercantile firms there, Richard Clarke & Sons and Thomas & Elisha Hutchinson.[41]

Richard Clarke had become one of the major importers of tea into Boston by the mid-1760's, and with passage of the Indemnity Act of 1767, the firm looked forward to greatly increased business. When the Townshend Act finally provoked the Boston merchants into a definite non-importation agreement in August 1768, the Clarkes refused to co-operate. By the end of that year they had a large stock of English tea on hand, and they continued to order more well into the summer of 1769.[42]

At first the Clarkes anticipated a rise in the price of tea, for as they pointed out, the non-importation agreement would eventually result in a shortage of that article. But they failed to take into consideration the initial effectiveness of the non-consumption campaign. "A great number of Inhabitants of this & other towns have agreed to disuse the drinking of India teas from a resentment of the Act," they reported in October. "From this circumstance teas are become a very slow Sale." By February 1769, however, they had reason to believe that many of the signers against tea had begun to lose their early enthusiasm and that the market for dutied tea would show improvement. In May they joined with the Hutchinson brothers in an attempt to fix their prices at a profitable level. But they did not take into account the fact that smuggling, despite the letter of the regulations against all European tea, would continue to offer stiff competition. A large quantity run into Boston in the summer upset their expectations of making a good profit from the English tea they had patiently stored through the previous winter and spring.[43]

Some of the Clarkes' old wholesale customers continued to buy tea from the Boston firm after January 1769 as though no agreements had ever been made. Buckeley Emerson of Newburyport and Thomas Robie of Marblehead apparently had no difficulty getting rid of their usual quantities, despite the fact that both those towns had been enthusiastic endorsers of non-consumption agreements in 1768.[44]

But not even the Clarkes could hold out forever against the

pressure of public opinion. Acknowledging the embarrassing arrival of fifteen chests of tea, in August 1769, they wrote Peter Contincen to explain that the cargo came at an "unlucky time." The opposition against importations from Great Britain

> . . . is so firmly fixed and extensively prevalent that although we were determined to maintain the struggle as long as prudence would admit we were obliged at length to give way to the torrent and consent that these goods [the 15 chests of tea] should lay unexposed to sale for some time, we apprehended that if we did not submit to these and some other mortifying terms some bad consequences might perhaps follow.[45]

Although the Clarkes were forced to suspend the sale of tea, other merchants in Boston continued to risk the consequences. By far the most daring was the firm of Thomas & Elisha Hutchinson. It was of course popularly believed among the patriots that the young men's father, Lieutenant-Governor Thomas Hutchinson, was actively associated with his boys in the importation of tea, but in the absence of concrete evidence it is probably safer to assume that he was busy enough running the government (he had been acting Governor since the departure of Francis Bernard in 1769). The Hutchinsons imported altogether about 50,000 pounds of English tea during 1769, over half of Boston's total shipments for that year. Oddly enough, much of this tea came over on vessels owned by such notable patriots as John Hancock.[46]

The Hutchinsons proved to be a more stubborn firm than even the Clarkes. They resisted the threats and insults of the Boston patriots until nearly the end of 1769. Several times that autumn they apparently agreed to lock up their latest shipment of tea, only to renege on their promise and face the abuse of press and mob once more. By January 1770, however, they seemed finally to have given in, but on the last day of that month they were accused of another broken promise. Not until May 1770 did they finally turn over their remaining stock of tea to the customhouse, where it apparently remained until the end of non-importation, in November.[47]

Boston merchants bent on circumventing the non-importation agreement had a number of alternatives to choose from. John Powell somehow managed openly to defy the regulation without being apprehended. As late as October 1769 he boasted to a friend in Rhode Island that his was the only tea in town not locked up by the merchants' committee of inspection. He eagerly awaited the price rise that would inevitably come "if no Dutch should be smugled." [48] Another dodge was to "smuggle" duties tea into Boston from Rhode Island, where many merchants had refused to boycott British goods. In fact shipments of legal tea into that colony jumped from a normal 3500 pounds annually to a 17,000 pound average for the three years 1769-71. Obviously much of this tea was destined for Boston. [49]

Another way employed by violators of the agreement in Boston was to enter tea at Halifax, paying duty there, and then to ship it down by coaster to Boston, again "smuggling" it into town sometimes through Salem, Plymouth, or some other outport. In 1770 Halifax tea imports rose to over 13,000 pounds, in contrast to the previous two-year average of only 500 pounds. Portsmouth, New Hampshire, proved to be still another easy entry for duties articles. Thomas Hutchinson pointed out the irony of legal tea being "smuggled" in a letter to the Earl of Hillsborough. "Tea from Holland may lawfully be sold," he wrote in April 1770; "it's a High crime to sell any from England." [50]

Despite the best efforts of the patriots New Englanders still found it possible to obtain tea throughout most of the non-importation period. In the summer of 1769, for instance, several Boston importers combined to open a store in Salem, where they sold tea and other duties articles to their own customers as well as to the local inhabitants. The goods were shipped overland from Boston and Newport or were imported by sea from Halifax. Other stocks of Boston tea went to Worcester and Hartford. [51] From Marblehead the impertinent Thomas Robie wrote of tea in January 1770 with unknowing irony:

> I fancy that some how or other supplies of this article have found a way into the Town, notwithstanding the Vigilance of

our worthy Patriots, who are assiduous in detecting and removing any trifling package, as if all the Evils of Pandora's Box
were inclosed or the Fate of Empires depending—[52]

These were the loopholes that prompted the new round of non-
consumption pledges in the early months of 1770. Despite their
boasts to other towns, however, Boston patriots soon discovered that
the ban against tea was again to be only temporary.

The non-importation agreements at New York and Philadelphia
resulted in the virtual disappearance of duned tea from both markets
by 1770. In 1768 New York had imported over 350,000 pounds from
England, under encouragement from the Indemnity Act. In the following year the figure dropped to 17,000 pounds, and in 1770 only
147 pounds of legal tea entered there. At Philadelphia one large
shipment of legal tea came in just three days before the non-importation agreement was to take effect on 1 April 1769. But the total for
that year, 112,000 pounds, fell to a skimpy 65 pounds of duned tea
for 1770. Neither New York nor Philadelphia would see as much as
3000 pounds of legal tea again. Further to the south the pattern was
similar, with the exception of Virginia, where the customarily small
imports remained unchanged. At Charleston, however, entries fell
from about 25,000 pounds in both 1768 and 1769 to less than 1000
pounds in 1770.[53]

Tea addicts in the middle and southern colonies continued to be
supplied by the New York and Philadelphia smugglers throughout
the period of non-importation despite the theoretical ban on all tea.
From Holland came reports of large shipments for American continental and West Indian ports, the British consul at Amsterdam
recording the departure of about forty vessels engaged in this trade
during 1768 alone. In April following he wrote of the arrival of
two ships with Carolina rice, illegal of course, which were taking
aboard a great quantity of liquor, brandy, and tea, undoubtedly
destined for the American colonies. The *New York Journal* reprinted
from the *London Evening Post* in the spring of 1770 that over
200,000 pounds of tea had been shipped on board a Dutch vessel
bound for St. Eustatius in March of that year. In June a Rhode

Island merchant dispatched a small vessel to Gottenburg with rice and sugar in exchange for a cargo of Swedish Company tea. The fact that tea continued to be available with only temporary shortages throughout the middle and southern colonies clearly shows that the smugglers remained active during the period of non-importation.[54]

Despite leaks in the boycott English tea had become a marked commodity in the months after passage of the Townshend Act. Unlike glass and paper, which the colonists manufactured in modest quantities, there was no satisfactory substitute for dutied tea in those areas not regularly supplied from Holland. Besides, tea-drinking was a peculiarly English custom. And as an article commonly used in America, tea constantly reminded the colonists that Parliament claimed the right to tax them at its pleasure. Resentment against this claim had become focused on the tea duty during the years 1768-70. On the local level opposition to the Townshend Act itself was almost exclusively concentrated on the tea duty.

III

THE TEA TAX CONTINUES

IN the months following passage of the Revenue Act of 1767
several major changes took place within the British ministry.
Charles Townshend died suddenly in September 1767 and was succeeded as Chancellor of the Exchequer by King's Friend Lord North.
Chatham's illness grew steadily worse. In his absence the young
Duke of Grafton was left with the responsibility of heading the
government. Grafton desperately needed support from other factions and finally succeeded in forming an alliance with the Bedfordites. His new allies insisted, however, that Chatham's old friend
the Earl of Shelburne be removed. This was accomplished by
dividing his post as Secretary of State for the Southern Department and creating from it a new office — The Secretary of State
for the Colonies. Into this position went another of the King's
Friends, Lord Hillsborough. By mid-autumn 1768 both Shelburne
and Chatham himself had resigned in protest. When the new
Parliament convened in November the conservative King's Friends
and Bedfordites had greatly increased their influence within the
government.[1]

Americans in England and in the New World watched these
developments with grave concern. Colonial affairs, although not a
cause of the recent political upheavals, would surely be affected by
them. In the spring of 1768, for instance, North and Hillsborough
had appeared ready to move the repeal of the Townshend Act at
the next session of Parliament, on the grounds that taxation of
British manufactures imported into the colonies was economically

unsound. But the news of American opposition to the Act and to the Customs Commissioners sent over to enforce it changed their minds. The pompous Hillsborough went so far as to demand that the General Court of Massachusetts Bay rescind the circular letter it had sent around to the other colonies in February 1768 protesting the Townshend Act. Even though Hillsborough himself heartily wished it had never been enacted, the Secretary told a meeting of colonial agents in December that as long as Americans insisted that Parliament had no right to tax them, repeal of the Townshend Act would be unlikely. Put the argument in terms of expediency instead, suggested Dennys DeBerdt, agent for Massachusetts Bay, and then repeal might soon be forthcoming.[2]

When Parliament opened in November 1768, however, there was little evidence of the Ministry's kindly disposition toward the colonists noted by DeBerdt. Several speakers, exasperated by riots in Boston during the previous summer, accused the Americans of striving for no less than complete independence and spoke in threatening terms of military rule. Lord North, reported several observers, declared in an opening address that he would not consider a repeal of the Townshend duties "until he saw America prostrate at his feet."[3] And Hillsborough had proposals ready to alter the charters of Massachusetts Bay and several other colonies, but the King disapproved of strong measures at that time.[4]

As the discussion of American affairs continued, members of the Opposition argued against a policy of coercion. One of the colonies' staunchest defenders was Colonel Isaac Barré, whose cheek bore a jagged scar, a reminder of his part in the Quebec campaign of 1759 when he had fought alongside American militia. Barré spoke in the House of Commons in late January 1769 in rebuttal to Lord North's rash statement of the opening session. William Dowdeswell, Edmund Burke, and others joined the defense of American interests. In the House of Lords, the Duke of Richmond, the Earl of Dartmouth, and of course Rockingham, supported the colonies. "We still abide by that Opinion that the Idea of making America — a *Revenue Mine*, is absurd," wrote the latter in May.[5]

But one observer warned that not even Rockingham's followers were to be depended upon as true friends to America. As soon as they obtained power, they too would support the supremacy of Parliament over the colonies, as they had done in the Declaratory Act, he might have added. In February 1769 the London merchants appointed a committee to petition for repeal of the Townshend duties, but the political atmosphere remained so unfavorable that its members decided to await a more opportune moment. Rockingham himself advised against such a petition at that time, for he feared that the ensuing debate would only produce more recriminations against America.[6]

While more cautious members of the Opposition held back, a staunch friend of America and former colonial governor, Thomas Pownall, moved in mid-April 1769 that Parliament repeal the Townshend Act. His speech was moderate in tone, an attempt to find a compromise between Parliament's asserted right to tax the colonies and the Americans' most recent denials of that claim. Pownall also pointed out that the duties had during their first year produced little net revenue, partly because of American opposition but mainly because of the high cost of collection. Although the Ministry succeeded in persuading the House to postpone the issue until the next session, its hand was now forced.[7]

Grafton called a Cabinet meeting on 1 May to discuss the question of American taxation. He himself proposed that at the next session of Parliament all of the Townshend duties be repealed, but a majority of those present promptly overruled him. King's Friends North and Hillsborough joined forces with the Bedfordites Weymouth and Gower, and the independent Lord Rochford. Relative newcomers to the Cabinet, they insisted on the retention of one duty — that on tea — as a symbol of Parliament's right to tax the Americans. Grafton found himself in a minority along with Granby, Camden, and Conway, all members of Chatham's original Cabinet formed nearly three years before. By the narrow margin of 5 to 4 the new conservatives within the Cabinet had made a policy decision of far-reaching consequences. Perhaps North and Hillsborough had changed their minds to oppose total repeal because of the recent disturbances in America. More likely, it was due indirectly to the influence of George III, who in February had recommended that if repeal were to be considered, the duty on tea should be retained.[8]

On 13 May 1769, two weeks after the Cabinet meeting, Lord Hillsborough sent a circular letter to the governors in America. In rather terse language he explained that the King and his ministers had decided not to levy further taxes in America and in the next session of Parliament would move for repeal of the duties on glass, paper, and colors, on the grounds that they were "contrary to the true principles of commerce." Hillsborough enclosed his version of the cabinet minutes, in which he falsely claimed that the resolution had passed unanimously. Nor did he include numerous phrases suggested by his more moderate colleagues to placate the colonies. Shortly after dispatching his letter, Hillsborough informed several colonial agents in London of the Cabinet's decision. Meanwhile, he had also explained it to several British merchants and urged them to pass the news along to their American correspondents. Within a few short weeks colonists learned of the intended repeal.[9]

William Johnson, agent for Connecticut, immediately suspected that the Ministry had leaked its decision concerning eventual repeal to entice American merchants into giving up their non-importation agreements. Johnson was quick to point out that the Cabinet had decided to retain the tea duty and that the principle of Parliamentary taxation would not be altered one bit by partial repeal. Through the remaining months of 1769 he and other Americans in England urged the colonists not to abandon their boycott of British manufactures, although they could not agree as to that measure's effectiveness. A number of writers insisted that non-importation had made no impression whatever in England, save possibly to increase the general prejudice against America and thus hinder the chance of repeal. It was reported that in Yorkshire the boycott was merely regarded as an idle menace. Richard Henry Lee wrote in November 1769 that he had not heard any complaints concerning the loss in trade. Johnson himself admitted in December that due to commercial opportunities elsewhere the American boycott had had no noticeable effect on English commerce and manufacturing. The Bristol merchant Richard Champion claimed that non-importation had lost the colonists many friends from among his colleagues, who saw themselves, rather than the Ministry, made the objects of American retaliation.[10]

The boycott must have had some effect, for in February 1770 the London merchants trading with America finally presented to Parliament their long-delayed petition for repeal of the Townshend Act. Pointing out that their business was in "an alarming state of suspension" because of the American duties, they prayed for relief.[11] Francis Bernard, now residing in London after his removal from the governorship of Massachusetts Bay, threw his influence behind partial repeal of the Act, which he had never approved of anyway. Bernard wrote to North late in the month enclosing evidence he had received from Boston that a number of merchants there were successfully ignoring the boycott. "It will not probably be in the Power of the Party at Boston to keep up the non-importation much longer," he suggested, and partial repeal would give a good excuse for many others to back out of the agreement. According to Dennys DeBerdt, colonial agent for Massachusetts, there was little demand among Britons that the tea duty be repealed along with the others.[12]

Meanwhile, in late January 1770, still another political upheaval had led to the dismissal of the Duke of Grafton as Prime Minister. To the surprise of no one he was replaced by Lord North. Now at last the King's own Friends were in firm control. For the next twelve years George III would exercise a degree of influence in the government of his realm not enjoyed by any British sovereign for over half a century.

On 5 March, in one of his first acts after taking office, Lord North opened debate on the merchants' petition requesting a repeal of the Townshend duties. North was still unsure enough of himself and his support to proceed with great caution. He agreed that many members might think that the abuse that England had lately received from the colonists made concession inappropriate at that time. But, he argued, the proposed measure was designed to alleviate a hardship placed on Englishmen at home. Repeal of those duties on English products sent to America would bring relief to both merchant and manufacturer.[13]

North, however, refused to consider the possibility of repealing the duty on tea. He claimed that at one time he had favored such a move, but when the colonists had greeted the Earl of Hillsborough's circular letter in the summer of 1769 with even stiffer enforcement of non-importation, he had become disenchanted about how reasonable the Americans were. To give in entirely to their demands would have the same dismal effect as that produced by repeal of the Stamp Act, he now argued. This was no time to grant the Americans concessions, when they continued to defy Parliamentary authority by riots and illegal boycotts. "The properest time to exert our right of taxation," North concluded, "is when the right is refused. The properest time for making resistance is when we are attacked." Besides, the duty on tea was a small one, and by the Indemnity Act passed at the same time as the Townshend Act, Parliament had actually lowered the cost of tea in America. He therefore moved that the duties on paper, glass, painter's colors, and lead alone be repealed.[14] It was misleading for North to contend that only the uncharitable reception given Hillsborough's letter in America had persuaded him to retain the tea duty. For, as we have seen, he had already determined his position on the tea duty at least two weeks before Hillsborough's letter was sent out.

After North had finished, Thomas Pownall rose to give the longest speech of the day. Pownall had tried to bring in a motion for total repeal the previous spring without success, and in January he had told North that repeal would be useless unless all the duties were taken off. Now he proposed amending North's motion to include repeal of the duty on tea as well. Pownall maintained that its retention would only serve to perpetuate American opposition to Parliament's authority and to hinder the settlement of issues between the mother country and her colonies. In fact, he pointed out, some Americans hoped the ill-feeling would continue, as it encouraged colonial manufacturing and the development of a general spirit of independence. Repeal of the tea duty would not be a surrender to American demands, he argued. It was the politic thing to do on several counts: first, because it would help restore British trade with her North American colonies, now in an alarming state; second, because the colonists would continue to boycott English tea as long as it bore any duty, a policy ultimately resulting in the total loss of the tea trade to the Dutch; finally, because there was no need to continue this duty as a symbol of British authority to tax the colonies, for that principle was already stated in the Declaratory Act and maintained by the Sugar Act. The tax on tea was therefore superfluous.[15]

Pownall was followed by three strong Opposition members, General Henry Conway, Sir William Meredith, and Colonel Isaac Barré. Conway advanced the argument that Parliament had no right to tax the colonies as long as they were not represented in that body. Meredith pointed out that retention of the tax on tea meant maintaining the whole structure of the customs service in America at a cost greater than the expected revenue. How unnecessary all this expense was, he concluded, when, as Pownall pointed out, the authority to tax was already declared and in practice. To Colonel Barré, the interest of the East India Company merited consideration. The Company contributed heavily to the support of government, and in return Barré felt that Parliament had a responsibility to preserve its tea trade against the encroachments of the Dutch.[16]

Two members spoke against even partial repeal. Mr. Welbore Ellis, a rather lackluster M.P. who generally supported the Ministry, thought it would be a mistake to repeal any of the duties until the Americans had first rescinded their non-importation agreements. Lord Barrington suggested that the way to bring this about was to repeal the duties only at those ports that had not supported the boycott movement. When the vote was taken, Governor Pownall's motion to include repeal of the tea duty failed 142 to 204. The Commons then adopted partial repeal without a division.[17] What little chance the Opposition had in the House of Lords was lost by the absence of

Lord Chatham, who personally favored total repeal, and who might have succeeded in rallying some support for that position.[18]

But the question of the tea duty was not quite dead. Alderman Trecothick, agent for New Hampshire and staunchly pro-American, tried to bring up the matter again on 9 April. The Ministry took the position, however, that the topic was out of order, since a motion to repeal the tea duty had already been rejected in that session of Parliament. The Opposition seemed unprepared for this argument, and after a brief debate on the parliamentary issue, the House voted to move on to other business. The tea duty remained in force.[19]

The East India Company's position on the tea tax remains unclear. In January 1770 agent Johnson wrote that the Company would probably petition Parliament for a repeal of the tea duty, but a few weeks later he reported that the Company directors were badly divided on the question. Under the terms of the Indemnity Act of 1767 the Company was obliged to compensate the government for any loss in revenue resulting from the drawback on duties allowed by that Act on tea exported to America. The accumulated deficit was considerable, and the directors sought relief from this requirement. But they reportedly claimed that the Company had so completely captured the Continental market for Bohea tea (the only kind Americans bought) that they no longer depended upon the colonies and therefore did not care whether the Townshend duty continued or not.[20]

But these reports were clearly erroneous. In the first place, the East India Company was not allowed to export tea to the Continent and would have had difficulty underselling Dutch tea there anyway. Secondly, the Company did care very much about the American market. Although it did not in fact petition for a repeal of the tea duty when the issue came up in March, the directors apparently did try to make a bargain with Lord North. They suggested that at some later date the tea duty be repealed but that at the same time the drawback on tea exported to America be rescinded also. At 1770 prices the drawback amounted to about 7½d. per pound. If both the Townshend duty of 3d. and the drawback were removed

simultaneously, the net gain in governmental revenues would have
been about 4½d. per pound of tea exported to America. Of course
the price of English tea in the colonies would have risen by the
same margin, but the Company probably expected that removal of
the objectionable Townshend duty would be enough to win back
a large share of the colonial market. Furthermore, there would no
longer be a revenue deficit to make up. In his speech on 5 March
asking for partial repeal, North in fact alluded to the possibility
of such an arrangement at some future date. But nothing ever
came of it, probably because the Ministry was loath to give up
Great Britain's only remaining tax on the colonists.[21]

In the end total repeal of the Townshend Act failed of adoption for
two basic reasons. In the first place, American opposition, and particularly the demand that Parliament had no right to tax the colonies,
convinced the King and his Friends that a full concession would be
unwise. The fact that the Opposition had urged repeal ever since
enactment of the law and had encouraged Americans in their
non-importation movement did not make concession any more acceptable to the majority. Secondly, a number of factors convinced the
Ministry that total repeal was unnecessary as well. Bernard had reported to Lord North in February 1770 that the non-importation
movement was already weakening and that partial repeal would
quickly bring it to an end. The London merchants and the East
India Company itself failed to make a strong campaign for total
repeal. Parliament therefore readily supported the Ministry in its
demand that the tea duty be retained both as a symbol of the right
of taxation and as a promising source of colonial revenue.[22]

News of partial repeal of the Townshend Act reached the colonies
in early May. The patriots immediately faced a difficult quandary,
for in most ports merchants had originally agreed not to import
British goods until all of the Townshend duties had been repealed.
The question now was whether four-fifths of a loaf was better than
none. With the backlog of English goods imported before the agreement steadily dwindling, the less enthusiastic merchants had begun
to grow restless. Partial repeal seemed to them a considerable

victory, and pressure mounted to rescind the non-importation agreements. As usual, contradictory advice poured in from English merchants during the late spring. Some offered the hope that if the colonists ended their boycott Parliament would repeal the tea duty at its next session. Others maintained that only by holding fast would such favorable action take place. American patriots of course took the latter position, and throughout the summer of 1770 the great debate raged in Boston, New York, and Philadelphia.[23]

The merchants at New York were the first to weaken. Governor Colden reported on 16 May that a majority was ready to resume importing now that partial repeal was confirmed. On the 18th a meeting of merchants discussed the question, then decided to hold off a few weeks longer in hopes of learning that the tea duty had also been rescinded. The patriot forces strove to stem the tide, and a popular meeting at the end of May denounced a recent shipment of English goods and expressed its continued support of the boycott. But in mid-June those favoring importation gained control of the merchants' committee which had been appointed to enforce the agreement. As a result two of its staunchly patriotic members, Isaac Sears and Peter Van devoort, resigned in disgust. The end was now in sight.[24]

The New York committee proposed that a congress of merchants from all the major ports meet to discuss the whole problem. The patriots at Boston, Philadelphia, and elsewhere still controlled their local committees, however, and they all refused to admit that there was anything to talk about. New York thereafter was on its own. Taking a leaf from the patriots' book of operations, those favoring reopening of trade drew up a subscription paper to be circulated throughout the town. The proposal was to permit thenceforth the importation of all English goods save those subject to a duty, at that time only tea. The patriots countered with a subscription of their own to sustain the boycott, but the result was an overwhelming victory for importation.[25]

Outsiders expected that the merchants at other ports would immediately follow suit, but the news from New York was met only with indignation. "You have certainly weakened that union of the colonies on which their safety depends," wrote the committee of Philadelphia merchants. "We cannot forbear telling you, that however you may colour your proceedings, we think you have in the day of trial deserted the cause of liberty and your country." The students at Princeton staged a protest, the merchants of New Haven agreed to boycott New York importers, and the Boston committee tried desperately to get the decision reversed. But the patriot forces were on the defensive. They could not stem the tide for long.[26]

Philadelphia was next to succumb to the temptation of reopening trade with Great Britain. In May 1770 Governor Penn had predicted that the merchants there would hold out until repeal of the tea duty, and the merchants confirmed their agreement at a meeting on 5 June. But discontent particularly among the dry-goods merchants mounted steadily. When news reached Philadelphia of the defection at New York, a mass rally was called in mid-July to drum up support for the boycott. For a time public opinion backed the patriots in their efforts, but the task was made more difficult by the arrival of pamphlets from Boston printed by John Mein, revealing the violations of non-importation there. Anger at some of the tactics used by Charles Thomson, the patriot leader, and the steady flow of importations by Maryland merchants won many more converts to the cause of importation. In mid-September a number of the city's most respectable merchants suggested to the committee of enforcement that "an alteration" in the non-importation agreement now seemed appropriate. On 20 September, the merchants of Philadelphia met at Davenport's tavern and voted to allow importation of all goods from England save those subject to a duty. Now only Boston among the major ports remained in the fold.[27]

Despite the well-publicized violations in the agreement at Boston, patriots there remained in control throughout the summer of 1770. The decision to return goods by Hancock's ship *Lydia* had boosted local morale enormously. Not all Bostonians wanted to stand by the boycott, however, and a meeting of conservative merchants in mid-

May voted to resume importation, but the patriots quickly re-enforced the ban.[28] In late July, one observer contended that a large majority of importers wanted to reopen trade but that "they are kept in continual dread by the noise and threats of a set of Villains who are for reducing every one to the same necessitous desperate condition with themselves." [29]

During the summer Boston patriots even extended their jurisdiction by sending committees to investigate suspected importations at Portsmouth, Newburyport, Salem, and Newport, to the great resentment of the local inhabitants. Boston greeted the defection of New York with bitterness and defiance, despite Governor Hutchinson's prediction that the movement would soon collapse in Massachusetts. But with Philadelphia's decision to resume importation in late September, the Bostonians followed suit less than two weeks later. Sam Adams hid his disappointment well, expressing surprise that the boycott had lasted as long as it had, but other patriots, including John Dickinson and Arthur Lee, were bitterly disillusioned. Some English merchants believed that had the boycott continued but three months longer, the Ministry would have been forced to repeal the tea duty. By mid-October 1770 the great protest movement against the Townshend Act was at an end.[30]

The non-importation movement ultimately failed of its purpose to bring about repeal of all the Townshend duties. Some commentators suggested that only the duties articles ought to have been boycotted, but in that case perhaps the British merchants would never have petitioned for repeal. The boycott did of course focus attention on the Act both in America and in England as a major colonial grievance. But by recommending the repeal of the duties on English products on the grounds of commercial expediency, the British ministry easily ducked the Americans' challenge to Parliament's right of taxation. And this was a decision reached by government officials long before the economic effect of the boycott could be felt in Great Britain. As North pointed out to Parliament in March 1770, most of the loss in Anglo-American trade during 1769 had been due to overstocking the year before by American merchants in anticipation of non-importation. The retention of the duty on tea served its purpose well — a symbol of Parliamentary authority.[31]

The unity brought about by the non-importation agreements among the merchants of the major ports was of course significant. But of equal importance was the mutual distrust caused by suspected violations at Boston and ultimately by New York's precipitate decision to resume importation after partial repeal was announced. The years 1771-73 could as accurately be called "the period of disunity" as the more familiar "period of calm."

Within a few shorts weeks after the break-up of the non-importation agreement in October 1770, it was business as usual for the Boston shopkeepers fortunate enough to have tea in storage. "The article of Tea is so generally and openly sold in this Town," wrote Samuel Salisbury to his brother in Worcester in mid-November, "that was it in my way as it is in some other People, I should sell it myself." The Boston merchant rationalized: "I see no advantage in your being the only person that excludes themselves from the sale of it. . . ."[32] Solemn pledges not to sell or consume dutied tea, nominally reaffirmed as the general boycott against English goods was abandoned, were quietly forgotten all over New England, and mention of Labradore tea all but disappeared. Shopkeepers openly advertised their English tea at prices nearly competitive with the Dutch imports, for until the Indemnity Act expired in mid-1772 the full drawback on English duties continued in force. Only the Townshend duty remained, but as far as Boston was concerned, it was but a slight economic handicap. Although the boycott of 1768-70 had managed to reduce legal importations there to 48,000 pounds by 1770, 265,000 pounds arrived in 1771, and an almost equal amount over the next two years.[33]

As might be expected, Richard Clarke & Sons were back in the thick of the tea trade within a few months, a shipment of twenty-six chests arriving in April 1771. Altogether that year the Clarkes imported more than 15,000 pounds, either on consignment or on their own account. The firm quickly re-established its markets in outlying towns, Buckeley Emerson in Newburyport and Thomas Robie in Marblehead receiving steady supplies. With the drawback, Bohea cost about 2s. 4d. in London, subject of course to freight costs and the threepenny duty upon landing in Boston. Throughout most of 1771 and into 1772 the Clarkes sold Bohea wholesale for about 3s. 0d. As long as the Indemnity Act continued and Dutch tea remained scarce in the Boston area, the Clarkes carried on. They even succeeded in developing a modest export trade, as they sent potash, pearlash, and whale oil to London in partial payment for their purchases. By early 1773, however, their importations of tea fell off somewhat, partly due to the expiration of the Indemnity Act in July 1772. Thereafter only three-fifths of the English duty on tea exported to America was drawn back.[34]

By no means could all those who imported duties tea into Boston during the period 1771-73 be dismissed as Tories eager to defy the restrictive edicts of the patriots. For among their ranks were some of those merchants who had firmly supported the non-importation agreements of a few years back. Samuel Salisbury maintained a stock at the Boston store and steadily supplied his brother's shop in Worcester. Newburyport's arch-patriot, Jonathan Jackson, did not hesitate to order Hyson and Bohea from his equally patriotic brother-in-law, Oliver Wendell, while Caleb Davis busily fulfilled orders from his wholesale house at Boston. Even John Hancock profited from the trade, his vessels freighting 45,000 pounds of duties tea into Boston during 1771 and 1772. The only evidence that any of this tea belonged to Hancock, however, is the fact that in November 1772 he returned to his London correspondents, Hayley & Hopkins, a certificate for the landing of one chest. Not until the autumn of 1773 did the Bostonians come in for any major criticism on account of their importations of duties tea. And by that time the American patriots had other things to think about.[35]

Boston merchants were not alone in violating the ban against importing duties tea from England after 1770. Customhouses throughout the Chesapeake Bay area reported entries equaling those in the years before non-importation, and the situation at Charleston, South

Carolina, was the same. But imports at these places altogether amounted to less than half those entered at Boston alone during the years 1771-73. Of greatest significance was the fact that only 1000 pounds of English tea paid duty at New York and Philadelphia in the period after collapse of non-importation. The over-all figures clearly show what had happened to England's tea trade with her American colonies. In the last three years before non-importation took effect, 1766-68, the colonies had imported 1,800,000 pounds from the mother country: in the three years following the boycott's end, the total fell off by more than half to only 787,000 pounds. The revenue Lord North hoped to gain by continuation of the tea duty simply failed to materialize. In all the colonies together, the Townshend duty on tea produced a total return of £9790 after 1770. This was enough to pay the salaries of Governors Hutchinson and Dunmore, but little remained for the support of other colonial officials.[36]

The failure of the East India Company to regain its earlier share of the colonial tea market was due mainly to the continuation of smuggling from Holland and elsewhere. New Yorkers and Pennsylvanians had little difficulty plying the now-familiar routes of clandestine trade, and with continuation of the Townshend duty on tea they had little incentive to change their ways. Clearest evidence for this fact was that, although a mere 1000 pounds of tea were legally imported from England into New York and Philadelphia during the years 1771-73, only once was there a scarcity at either place, and tea continued to sell at prices consistently below the cost of English tea on the Boston market. The only alternative explanation, that the people of the middle colonies ceased to drink tea after 1770, is unsupported by historical evidence. A sudden scarcity at Philadelphia in November 1773 sent the wholesale price up 33 per cent in a few weeks, indicating that tea was still very much in demand.

From Massachusetts, Governor Hutchinson explained the situation at New York as soon as he heard about the end of non-importation there. He announced to Hillsborough that New Yorkers would soon be ordering fall goods, "except Teas, which they have no occasion for from England, their Dutch Trade being under no restraint. . . ."[37]

The Customs Commissioners at Boston ordered the collectors at all American ports in early 1771 to be especially vigilant and warned that illicit tea was often packed in containers resembling rice and wine casks. John Swift, at Philadelphia, replied that "smuggling was never carried to such a height as it has been lately. I do believe there has been more goods smuggled into this Port within the last six months, than ever there was before in as many years." [38] Swift was referring to all illicit trade, of course, and what otherwise might be regarded as a gross exaggeration is explained by the fact that the Philadelphians had taken to smuggling other articles besides tea, particularly woolen goods from Ireland.

In January 1772 the Customs Commissioners issued another general warning that "large quantities of teas and other East India Goods were bought up at the Annual Sales of the Danish and Swedish East India Company . . . on Commission for America and the West Indies." The Commissioners went on to point out that "it is notorious that large quantities of teas and other prohibited goods were introduced in the course of last year 1771" by negligence or connivance of customhouse employees. [39]

Charles Wharton carried on the family business at Philadelphia of importing Dutch tea from New York, either overland to the Delaware or by coaster around Cape May. During the period after non-importation he was supplied principally by the New York firms of Ten Eyck & Seaman, John & Cornelius Sebring, and John Vanderbilt. Although wholesale prices of Bohea fell steadily throughout the period from a high of 3s. 9d. to a low of 2s. 3d., Wharton made a steady profit on a large volume of business. As in the case of dutied tea at Boston, the Philadelphia shopkeepers did not hesitate to advertise their stocks despite the obvious fact that the tea had been smuggled. Such was the demand that Wharton often sold out a shipment within a week of its arrival. While the Whartons brought their tea in from New York, Richard Waln, among others, engaged in the more conventional contraband trade with St. Eustatius. [40]

Conditions in America continued to make strict enforcement of the laws of trade virtually impossible. Except for occasionally effective crackdowns, such as that in Long Island Sound during the late 1750's, smugglers could still with impunity run their contraband goods into any one of the hundreds of coves along the coast. Even if apprehended, the illegal trader had a good chance of winning acquittal in court. At Boston only one of six trials during a thirty-month period resulted in a conviction. But getting caught was a rare event, even if one landed his cargo at a port which had a custom-house. For one thing, the underpaid officers could often be bribed. At various times the ports of New London, Stamford, and Perth Amboy were reportedly wide-open because of corruption.

Even the most conscientious officer had an almost hopeless task. New York, for instance, had but one ship-of-war on station, and during the four winter months it remained at its wharf because of bad weather. The collector's office employed only three men as "outdoor" officers to search incoming vessels. The situation at Philadelphia and elsewhere was not much better.[41]

In an attempt to tighten enforcement, Parliament had provided in 1763 that the captains of men-of-war making a seizure share in the proceeds. But this plan quickly backfired, as Governor Bernard pointed out in 1766, for the collectors no longer called on the man-of-war officers for assistance. Likewise, the governors' zeal in enforcement was reduced, for "if a governor receives an information of contraband goods, and engages a Captain of a Man of War to seize them," Bernard complained, "he forfeits all his share. . . . It must frequently happen," he realistically concluded, "that Contraband Goods will escape by the Contrariety of Interests of the Governor and Customhouse Offices on the one hand, and the Captains of Men of War on the other, which must always prevent their acting in Concert, as the King's Service requires they should do." [42]

Intimidation and violence also hindered enforcement of the law. Bernard reported in the spring of 1766 that although he knew a vessel had just arrived at Barnstable from St. Eustatius with a cargo of tea, yet the customs officer made no effort to intercept it. "He durst not make any use of his Intelligence," wrote Bernard, "as in his attempting to make a Seizure, he would be sure to hazard his Life in a great degree. . . ." [43]

John Swift at Philadelphia had good reason to know what Bernard was talking about. In late November 1771 he sent his customhouse schooner down-river to inspect a pilot boat coming up from Chester. When the officers boarded her, they found a cargo of suspicious-looking chests and cases, which, they were afterwards informed by some of the crew, contained smuggled tea. The officers took command, but before they could maneuver their prize up to Philadelphia, the tide had turned and they were forced to lay to, alongside the cutter. In the dark of the night, the two vessels were boarded by a force of men from another pilot boat, and the officers were attacked with clubs, cutlasses, and guns. After locking the customs men below in their own cutter, the ruffians slashed its rigging, cut it adrift so that it grounded on a mudbank, and made off with the prize. Neither the governor nor the chief justice of the vice-admiralty court showed much interest in assisting Swift to apprehend the criminals. As he sadly reported to the Commissioners in Boston, "we have no reason to believe that any discovery will ever be made. . . ." [44]

The officials at London did what they could to help, but their contribution was of little significance. Whenever they learned of shipments of tea departing from Amsterdam or other European ports, they informed the American customs officers of the fact, but usually the news came too late to be of use. Sometimes the captain of a suspected vessel managed to outwit the officers even though they were forewarned. In November 1770, for instance, the Philadelphia office received notice that the ship *Speedwell*, loaded with tea, was about to sail from Gottenberg for either New York or Philadelphia. The letter arrived the day after the vessel did, and Swift immediately went aboard to investigate. *Speedwell*'s papers indicated that she had come from Liverpool, and on board was a cargo of coal and white salt. Suspecting that the tea was concealed underneath the coal, Swift ordered the hold emptied, at customhouse expense, but with no luck. He remained suspicious, however, when the captain wanted to clear immediately for Carolina, and

Swift seized the vessel in order to interrogate the crew, but those whom he could find refused to testify on the grounds of self-incrimination! With great reluctance Swift let *Speedwell* depart, convinced that its captain had followed the usual practice of landing his tea at the mouth of the Delaware before bringing the vessel upstream.[45]

Swift had burned his fingers badly on this case. He ruefully reported to the Treasury in London:

> In this country an officer of the Customs ought to see his way very clear before he ventures to make a seizure, because he is sure of having every possible difficulty thrown in his way; he is looked upon as an enemy to the community and treated accordingly, and whether he succeeds or not he is sure never to be forgiven, and thinks himself fortunate if his punishment is defer'd to a future day. . . .[46]

By the eve of the Revolution smuggling had become a habit with a significant minority of colonial merchants, particularly those importing sugar, molasses, and tea. These merchants had no quarrel with the theory underlying the Acts of Trade — they never denied that Parliament had the right to regulate the commerce of the Empire. In the beginning they had smuggled not as patriots struggling for freedom against tyrannical oppression; they smuggled because of their greed for profit. And they continued to import Dutch tea after passage of the Townshend duty for the same reason — it was cheaper than English tea, and so the margin of profit was greater. In 1769 one observer even doubted that repeal of the tea duty would have had much effect on illicit importations. Smugglers traded with Holland not only because of the low price of Dutch tea, he said, but also because they could often get better prices for their American exports in Holland than in England.[47]

Not until Parliament finally provided for stricter enforcement of the laws did the smugglers claim their activities to be patriotic. Then they succeeded in convincing the American public that their search for illegal profit was somehow a part of the common fight for freedom. To a large extent abuses on the part of customhouse officers made this argument plausible. Mobbing the King's officials and burning his vessels became justifiable blows against "tyranny," and by 1773 law and order had completely broken down along waterfront America. Into the resulting anarchy stepped Sam Adams, Isaac Sears, Charles Thomson, and other skilled leaders to organize a massive opposition to British authority. In America the stage was set for a showdown.[48]

IV

THE EAST INDIA COMPANY

IN 1773 the East India Company inadvertently precipitated the final crisis between Parliament and the American colonies. The Company, known officially as The United Company of Merchants trading to the East Indies, was formed in 1709 by the merger of two predecessors. The "Old" London East India Company, founded in 1603, had enjoyed a virtual monopoly of English trade to the Far East until 1690, when Parliament authorized the incorporation of a "New" English East India Company. Competition between the two organizations threatened to ruin them both and leave the trade open to serious inroads by the commercial enterprises of other nations. Union was the obvious answer, and in 1709 the United Company received a charter granting it monopoly rights to all English trade beyond the Cape of Good Hope.[1]

In the course of the eighteenth century the Company grew in wealth and power until by the early 1760's it stood with the Bank of England among the most powerful financial organizations of Great Britain. A twenty-four man Court of Directors managed its affairs, nominally subject to the decisions of the General Court, or Court of Proprietors, which consisted of shareholders possessing an investment of at least £500 in Company stock. To facilitate administration of the Company's activities the directors formed themselves into several committees, of which the Committee of Correspondence soon emerged as the most important, serving as an executive board. In charge of Company trade was the Committee of Warehouses. Altogether the directors had little difficulty controlling the affairs of the Company, and only occasionally was their leadership challenged by a revolt of the stockholders meeting in General Court.[2]

Although territorial acquisitions in India would later become a primary source of income and power, in the mid-eighteenth century the Company still depended heavily for profits on its exclusive trading rights. From headquarters at the East India House in Leadenhall Street, London, the Company operated an extensive commercial empire. Here were the directors' offices and meeting-rooms for the committees. Here also the General Court convened to determine policy and sometimes to decide a showdown battle between two factions struggling for control among the direction, as the Court of Directors was referred to. Here also was located the Company's salesroom, where its wares were auctioned by inch of candle. Clustered around East India House, off Lime Street and Fenchurch Street in particular, were the sprawling warehouses, employing hundreds of clerks and laborers to handle the Company's stocks of imports from the East.[3]

By the middle of the eighteenth century tea had become the cornerstone of the East India Company's trade, accounting for over 90 per cent of its commercial profits. As we have already seen, however, the Company in fact sold less than half the total amount of tea consumed in Great Britain each year. For customs and inland duties had climbed so high during the course of the century that smuggling from the Continent amounted to about 7,000,000 pounds annually by the early 1760's. By this means the East India Company lost upwards of £400,000 each year in net profits.[4]

The British-owned Channel Islands provided a convenient route for the smuggler, small vessels running cargoes of tea, brandy, gin, and other goods across the Channel into the ports of Hants, Dorset, and Devon. These ships were heavily armed and well-manned, and more often than not they were successfully brought in past the revenue cutters attempting to intercept them. The Isle of Man, especially before its purchase by Great Britain in 1765, was another den of smugglers, from which cargoes of illicit goods could be landed on the deserted coast of western Scotland with little chance of being apprehended. Once ashore, the smugglers could generally count on the support of the local inhabitants in the event of a showdown with the revenue officers.[5]

Reduction of the inland duty on black and Singlo teas by the Indemnity Act of 1767 improved the Company's competitive position immensely during the five-year duration of the statute. Sales of tea for home consumption increased by 50 per cent to over 6,600,000 pounds a year because of the lower price; exports to Ireland and to the American colonies more than doubled due to a full drawback granted on import duties. But still the Company was far from realizing its potential market for tea. Smuggling into Great Britain persisted during the period of the Act, and when the inland duty was restored to full strength in 1772, illicit traders seemed to grow bolder. Sales for home consumption fell off to 4,000,000 pounds in 1773. Nor was the colonial market more promising for the Company. We have already seen that the Townshend Act quickly snuffed out whatever hope the Indemnity Act offered of kindling a boom in the legitimate importation of tea. With the retention of the Townshend duty after 1770, the Company's tea trade continued to be saddled with an almost impossible burden.[6]

By the fall of 1772 the East India Company was fast approaching a serious financial crisis only partly of its own doing. The Company itself had been pursuing short-sighted policies both at home and in India for some years, and the results of these follies now began to appear. For one thing, the stockholders twice voted to increase the annual dividend, once from 6 to 10 per cent in 1766 and again to 12.5 per cent less than a year later. As a result the Company's deficit for 1767 stood at over £400,000. Although this irresponsibility was caused not so much by greed as by intra-company rivalries, the outcome was the same. Confidence in the East India Company suffered a serious blow, reflected in the immediate passage of an act in Parliament that restricted its dividends to 10 per cent. Although the limit was raised two years later to 12.5 per cent, a pattern of government intervention had been established.[7]

Company stability was further shaken in 1769 by a break in the price of East India stock. Driven up to the level of 280 on a wave of speculation which had begun in 1766, the market price tumbled to 239 by mid-June 1769, following news of a threatened French attack in India. The resulting panic brought turmoil to the internal administration of the Company. The Ministry's interest in Company affairs correspondingly grew, especially in the management of Bengal, over which the Company had increasingly exercised political control since Robert Clive had become Governor in 1765. After his departure from Bengal in 1767 the situation there rapidly deteriorated. A severe famine in 1769-70 made matters worse, and, despite his personal competence, the new Governor, Warren Hastings, could not stem the tide of corruption and inefficiency. A decline in the collection of revenue from India, over-investment in the purchase of goods for the London sales, and unexpected expenditures for military fortifications all contributed to the chaotic situation. The return to England of opulent nabobs like Clive only gave credence to exaggerated tales of extortion and plundering spread by disaffected Company employees. By 1772 it was clear that North's ministry would step in to institute reforms in the Company's administration of Bengal as soon as an opportunity presented itself.[8]

Such an opportunity came in the late fall of 1772. The final crisis resulted through no direct fault of the Company itself. Sudden failure of several important banking houses in the spring had set off a financial panic. The depression that followed stagnated business throughout Great Britain and the Continent for the succeeding twelve months. Receipts from the Company's spring sale failed to come in on schedule, and the September sale was a disaster. By late fall the Company was in serious trouble. Repayment of a short-term loan from the Bank of England for £300,000, customarily borrowed twice a year to carry the Company while waiting for returns from sales, was long overdue. On 29 October the Bank refused to grant another extension.[9]

At the same time the Company owed the government over £1,000,000. One debt, of £203,619, was for duties on tea sold in

March 1772. In addition, the Dividend Act of 1767, as extended in 1769, required the Company to pay £400,000 to the government in any year during which its dividends exceeded 6 per cent. Such a year was 1772, for in March the Company's Treasury Committee recommended and the General Court agreed to continue the current rate, which had been raised the previous spring to the annual rate of 12.5 per cent. Furthermore, in January 1773 the Company would have to pay the Treasury £214,000 for duties on unrated goods sold at the September sale, and an additional £114,000 was due in March on other goods sold. Nor was that the end. In July 1772 the directors voted to indemnify all purchasers of tea who had become liable for the inland duty of one shilling per pound when the 1767 act expired. This would add £117,000 to the deficit by mid-1773. Faced with debts totaling over £1,300,000, the proprietors threatened in September to suspend the regular semi-annual dividend. Alarm spread through London, and in November Parliament was convened to look into the affairs of the East India Company.[10]

While Parliament established a Select Committee under the future general, John Burgoyne, and a Committee of Secrecy to carry on investigations, the Company directors searched about for a solution to their financial problem. They were not completely wrong in considering much of the trouble as temporary, caused by a depression which made the collection of outstanding debts impossible. In January 1773, therefore, they resolved to request a government loan of £1,500,000 to be repaid at 4 per cent interest over a four-year period and also suggested a number of reforms in the administration of Bengal.[11]

The proprietors, however, were now under the leadership of the irascible Duke of Richmond, who sought to embarrass the Ministry. They balked at any concession and reforms. After lengthy consultations among the directors, the proprietors, and Lord North, a compromise petition was drawn up and submitted to the Ministry on 2 March. In requesting the £1,500,000 loan, the Company proposed to limit its annual dividend to 6 per cent until half the loan was repaid; thereafter it would raise its rate to 8 per cent. When full repayment was completed, the Company suggested, any surplus profits over 8 per cent were to be applied to reduction of its bonded debt to £1,500,000. This accomplished, the Company would then split any future surplus profits each year equally with the government. In exchange for the latter arrangement the Company asked that it be released from its obligation to pay the government £400,000 whenever dividends exceeded 6 per cent. Finally, the Company assured Parliament that it would soon thereafter propose some alterations in the administration of Bengal.[12]

These terms, however, were not altogether acceptable to the Ministry. During the course of the next two months Lord North introduced, and the House adopted, a series of resolutions incorporating a number of counterproposals. The loan was to be for £1,400,000, £100,000 less than requested by the Company, and until it was entirely repaid, dividends were to be restricted to 6 per cent. After the bonded debt had been reduced to £1,500,000, the Company would be allowed to raise its dividend to 8 per cent. But the government demanded three-quarters of any surplus profits over that figure, while restricting the uses to which the Company could put the remaining one-quarter. The government proposals, furthermore, implied that the Company's territorial rights in India were temporary, and that henceforth the governor and council of Bengal should be nominated by the government, which after six years would be free to take over full control of administration in India. Still another innovation came with the suggestion that only shareholders owning £1000 worth of stock be allowed to vote in the General Court, instead of the earlier £500 minimum. In a few short weeks the North ministry had laid the basis for a drastic reorganization of the East India Company.[13]

When the Marquis of Rockingham's forces first learned of trouble in the Company's affairs during the fall of 1772, they privately hoped that the Company could save itself without resort to a government loan. By reducing the dividend to 6 per cent the £400,000 obligation could be avoided, and then, perhaps, the Company could hang on until the spring sales of 1773. But such a scheme would depend on

continued extension of the repayment of public and private debts
— an unlikely prospect. At first the Rockinghamites could not agree
on what sort of tactics to pursue when the special session began.
Since there was little hope of defeating any ministerial measures,
some suggested that the most effective means of protesting governmental interference was to secede from that session of Parliament
altogether. This plan was discarded, however, and when North
presented the first of his East India resolutions on 9 March, the
Opposition organized, around William Dowdeswell and Edmund
Burke, a sparkling if futile defense of the Company's rights.[14]

Unable to contradict the charge that Company affairs needed
drastic reformation, the Opposition argued that the government had
no right to force these changes on the Company, for such would
be a violation of its charter. "The despotic Government of France,"
charged Burke, "is the Government of Angels compared to that of
this Country respecting the India Company."[15] The Opposition
particularly denounced the government's assertion that the Company had no permanent right to control the territory of Bengal,
which it had acquired almost entirely through its own effort and
expense. To assert that the public had a legal claim to these territories was absurd and virtually despotic. But the arguments of the
Rockingham forces were in vain. Their concern for the Company's
charter rights, and their fear that North was preparing the way
for a still greater increase of Crown's influence, met with little support either in the House or in the nation at large.[16]

Only the Company's proprietors shared these views. They had
been stunned by the severity and extent of North's proposals. As
soon as the House had adopted the Ministry's resolutions in late
April, the General Court met to draw up an indignant protest.
Its petition charged that the government's limitations of the
Company's dividend rate would bring great hardship to the proprietors. These investors had incurred major expenses in acquiring
and securing the Company's territories in India, while the public
had reaped great advantages from these operations in the form of
dividends, customs duties, and direct payment to the government.

Restricting the expenditure of surplus profits was unwarranted, "a disposal of their property otherwise than by their own consent." And to suggest a six-year limit on the Company's enjoyment of its Indian revenue was an arbitrary violation of its rights.[17]

When North ignored their petition and presented his fully drafted Regulating bill on 18 May, the proprietors were furious. Their position had been made more awkward by the necessity of seeking repeated postponements of their debts to the Treasury. At one point the secretary of the customs threatened to bring suit. Despite this handicap the proprietors fought on, drawing up an even more defiant petition on 26 May. Almost unanimously they charged that the Ministry's plan to appoint the Company's officials in Bengal was a virtual transfer of its powers to the Crown, to the utter destruction of the Company's liberties. Meanwhile the Committee of Correspondence had appealed to the Council of the City of London for support. London was a corporation with a legal status similar to that of the Company, and the Committee pointed out to the Council the common threat. As a result the London Council also petitioned Parliament to reject North's bill; it argued that the bill was "a direct and dangerous attack on the liberties of the people."[18]

George III urged North to stand firm and suggested that Parliament pass an act prohibiting the Company from declaring any dividends for the next three years. "Then they must come on their knees for what they now seem to spurn," he coldly concluded.[19] North did incorporate several compromises in the bill's next version, for he backed down somewhat on his earlier demand that the government appoint the Bengal governor and council. The proprietors staged a last-ditch protest in mid-June by withdrawing their original request for the loan, desperately hoping to straighten out the Company's financial affairs without this assistance. But North amended the bill to make the loan compulsory and at the same time soothed the proprietors' ruffled feelings considerably by striking out all reference to the government's taking three-fourths of the Company's surplus profits. He even removed the passage that suggested that the

Company's rights in Bengal be limited to six years. In this amended form the Regulation bill became law on 21 June. From that day on the East India Company was no longer complete master in its own house.[20]

Lord North was not the only person to suggest a solution to the Company's financial distresses. During the course of the fall and winter of 1772-73 a number of interested people offered alternative proposals. Rockingham, as we have seen, hoped that a reduction of the dividend to 6 per cent would bring a return to solvency.[21] Appended to John Almon's pamphlet, *The Present State of the East India Company's Affairs* . . . , published in late 1772, were several other ideas. George Dempster, M.P., and a director of the Company, put forth a plan similar to Rockingham's. Laurence Sulivan, currently deputy-chairman of the Company, suggested that the necessary funds be raised by an issue of new stocks and bonds to the total value of £1,300,000. Mr. Bosanquet, on the other hand, combined the dividend-reduction scheme with a more modest expansion of stock to arrive at still another solution to the problem. All of these ideas, however, suffered from a similar weakness: they were at best temporary expedients, likely to create equally serious long-run difficulties in their attempt to meet the current crisis.[22]

One plan suggested in *The Present State of the East India Company's Affairs* by Robert Herries was based on a different principle. In modified form it was to play a significant though totally unexpected role in the coming of the American Revolution. Just who Robert Herries was is uncertain. Among the stockholders of the Company as of 1773 were two men named Robert Herries, one designated "Sr.," the other simply as "Esq." Both had become Company proprietors as recently as September 1772, each with the purchase of £500 of stock. Another member of the family, Michael, had owned £1000 in Company shares since July 1769. In 1774 a Robert Herries, "a banker and Colonel of the City Light Horse Volunteers," was knighted. In 1780 Sir Robert Herries, "a London banker," sat for Dumfries, Kirkcudbright, Sanquhar, Annan, and

Lochmaben in the 15th Parliament. He died in 1815 at the age of 85. Perhaps he is the same Robert Herries who made the fateful suggestion in December 1772.[23]

Herries took as his point of departure the fact that the Company had on hand a prodigious surplus of tea, soon to reach an estimated total of 18,000,000 pounds. If the Company could sell this tea on the European continent, a major liability would quickly be converted into a sizable asset. According to his figures English tea could actually undersell that offered by European companies if the government would grant the Company a drawback of all British customs duties on the tea exported. He noted that at the September sale London tea buyers had driven the basic price of Bohea down to 1s. 10d. per pound. At Amsterdam, he asserted, the current price was equal to 2s. 3d. An allowance of 3d. per pound for the cost of shipping English tea to the Continent and selling it there left a small margin for profit. Even by selling this enormous surplus at a loss, Herries pointed out, the Company would at least rid itself of sizable charges for storage, deterioration, and interest on the capital invested.[24]

Herries suggested that the Company retain the equivalent of one year's domestic consumption in the event war should cut off the supply from China. On the 11,500,000 pounds thus made available for sale the Company stood to gain up to £1,425,000 if present prices prevailed. Herries realized of course that dumping this amount of tea in Europe, no matter how carefully planned, would depress prices there. But, he argued, perhaps the Continental companies would be driven out of the tea trade altogether and thus leave the entire market to the English.[25]

Under current law the Company could sell tea only at its wholesale auctions in London. To implement Herries's scheme Parliament would have to grant the Company permission to export abroad and provide a drawback on the customs duties levied upon the tea thus exported. The drawback would not in fact deprive the government of any revenue, Herries contended, since duties were collected only on tea actually sold, and the quantity to be exported was surplus at home. Nowhere in his proposal did Herries mention America as a possible market for the Company's surplus tea.[26]

The directors quickly learned of Herries's proposals and invited him to meet with the Committees of Treasury and Warehouses at India House on 5 January 1773. Thereafter events moved rapidly. On the day following, the directors approved the combined committees' recommendation that the chairman discuss the idea with Lord North. If granted permission, the Company proposed to send a small shipment to Holland as an experiment. On the 7th the General Court wholeheartedly adopted the Herries scheme, recommending that the directors immediately apply to Parliament for an act "to enable the Company to export to Foreign Dominions with an allowance of the Drawback of all the Duties of Customs, a part of their Surplus Quantity of Tea. . . ." The Court then added the suggestion that the directors also seek the removal of the Townshend duty of threepence per pound on tea shipped to America.[27]

On 8 January the Company directors wrote to Hope & Co., a firm of Englishmen doing business in Amsterdam, and, incidentally, one of the major suppliers of Dutch tea to American smugglers. The East India Company sounded out the Hopes on the feasibility of the Herries plan for the sale of English tea on the Continent. At the same time the directors asked whether they would be willing to make any remittance in advance of the projected sale. While awaiting an answer the Company officials conferred on how best to obtain the necessary act of Parliament.[28]

The Hopes returned a discouraging reply on the 12th. They were pleased that the Company had thought of them for the project and were willing to make a modest advance on the tea shipped to them. But if all the tea were to be sold on the Amsterdam market, as apparently the East India Company suggested, then they had to advise against it. The Hopes explained what would happen if the East India Company were to dump any sizable portion of its surplus on Holland: "The Consumption of this country is amply supplied by two ships, we receive Yearly," they pointed out, "[for] the surplus whereof with the supplies we receive from Denmark, Sweden, and France, have no other vent than to the People on the Coasts Dunkirk, etc. for the Smuggling Trade to England. . . ." By sending its surplus to the Continent, they continued, the Company would cause a rise in the price of its tea remaining in England at a time when the price on the Continental market was lowered by the flood of English tea. The resulting price differential would doubly encourage smuggling. In short, the East India Company would find its own tea smuggled back to England, and thus its future sales at home would be materially affected.[29]

The Hopes suggested an alternative plan. Instead of the Company's trying to sell its surplus through Amsterdam, why not let English wholesalers in London handle the exportation? "You will probably make at least as good a price, and save the extra charges." Some procedures could be established to make sure these surpluses actually left the country. The advantage was that by distributing the surplus tea destined for the Continent from London, there was far less danger of flooding any one European market. "Tho there appears great Ingenuity in the Plan which has been transmitted hither," the Hopes concluded, "it fails in the Mode [,] which rests with you and not abroad." [30]

The Company directors also sounded out a Brussels firm, Messrs. Romberg & Co., about the Herries plan, carrying on their negotiations indirectly through Rudolph Valtravers, a minor Company official. Apparently the Rombergs had learned of the alternative suggested by the Hopes, for when they wrote Valtravers in late February, they stated a distinct preference for the original plan. If the Company were to ship tea to Ostend, for instance, "we could distribute it all over the Austrian Netherlands, Luxembourg, Bishoprick of Liege, Germany, and even as far as Switzerland." The Rombergs' enthusiasm for the scheme knew no bounds.[31]

Meanwhile, however, the Hopes' discouraging response had already convinced Company officials that the Herries plan was impractical in its initial form. For some reason they also rejected the alternative of allowing English wholesalers to handle the distribution, probably because one more middleman would reduce the Company's already narrow margin of profit. Instead, the General Court on 17 February decided to ask permission to send a shipment of surplus tea to the British colonies in America. This tea was not likely to be smuggled back into England, the directors presumably reasoned. Nor would it have to compete with tea imported directly from China, as was the case in Europe. There was plenty of illegal Dutch tea on the American market, to be sure. But if the East India Company were to export its surplus directly to the colonies free of all English customs duties and at rock-bottom prices, perhaps Dutch tea could be undersold there.[32]

The prospect of capturing the colonial market must have been most appealing. At any rate on 25 February the General Court voted to petition Parliament "that leave may be given to export teas duty free to America." At the same time they voted to seek permission to export tea to Europe as well, under the original Herries plan, in the event that the Rombergs' optimism was not unfounded. Both requests were simply appended to the petition already in preparation to seek a government loan of £1,500,000. Oddly enough the proprietors did not specifically ask for the removal of the Townshend duty in America, despite their earlier resolution to this effect. It made little difference, however, because the Rockingham forces would make the suggestion on the floor of Parliament anyway.[33]

When the revised petition was submitted to Parliament on 2 March, the Ministry quite naturally concentrated on more pressing features of the East India Company's affairs before considering the propositions relative to the export of tea. It was not until 26 April, therefore, that Lord North finally presented those clauses concerning tea. He explained the advantages of allowing the Company to export some of its immense surplus of tea to America free of all duty, instead of selling it at public auction in London as presently required.[34]

When North had finished introducing the measure, William Dowdeswell took the floor to raise a crucial question. "I observe that the Noble Lord has made no proposition with regard to the duty laid upon teas imported into America," he challenged. It is not the price so much that hinders the regular export of tea to the colonies as it is the duty collected there. Without it the Company might sell up to 2,000,000 pounds a year in America. "I tell the Noble Lord now," he prophetically concluded, "if he don't take off the duty they won't take the tea." [35]

North explained in reply that he had given the matter of the Townshend duty careful consideration and concluded that it had had little effect on the market for English tea in America. To some extent, of course, North was right. The figures showed that the colonists had imported over 600,000 pounds of dutied tea in the two years since the breakdown of non-importation. Then he summarized his position:

> I am unwilling to give up that duty upon America upon which the [costs of Government?] are charged. If the East India Company will export tea to America, they will very much increase that duty, and consequently very much facilitate the carrying of Government in that part. I see no reason to taking it off. I must see a very substantial reason before I part with a fund so applicable to the support of Civil [Government?] [36]

Dowdeswell was far from satisfied. He argued that the Townshend duty had in fact prevented the Company from selling even more tea in America. Furthermore, the duty netted only £400 a year after the costs of collection were deducted. "It is the peppercorn that was so much contended," he sneeringly replied; "for this you risk the export of two million [pounds of tea] to America." North admitted that the Townshend duty had not produced much revenue that year, but he refused to recommend its repeal "till we shall be convinced there is no possibility of having an American [revenue?]. When these two propositions are proved to me, then it may be proper to give it up." [37]

Thanks to Dowdeswell the Townshend duty had quickly become the central issue, and now others joined the debate. Alderman

Trecothick recalled that he had once been commissioned by the colonists to press for a threepence or even sixpence duty payable in England in place of the duty collectable in the colonies. It was not just a political question of Parliament's authority to tax them, he pointed out. The great scarcity of cash in America was a factor too. Mr. Pulteney added that he thought it was ridiculous to hinder the Company's opportunity to sell 2,000,000 pounds a year merely to enhance the revenue. North pointed out in response to the mounting attack that the proposed measure already deprived the Treasury of a considerable revenue by allowing a full drawback of all English duties on the tea to be exported. He simply objected to repealing them both at once, he said.[38]

Dowdeswell saw the opening and leaped to his feet. In place of the Townshend duty, why not retain a proportion of the English duties, equal to 3d. per pound sent to America? he urged. Repeal of the Townshend duty would then cost the Treasury nothing. Taking up the idea, Mr. Cornwall professed to see very little difference between the two methods of raising the necessary revenue. "If there is a dislike in America to the tax," he reasoned, why not replace it as Dowdeswell suggested? Governor Johnstone pressed still further. No speaker in the debate had yet claimed that the *right* to tax Americans was involved in the issue, he pointed out. If those favoring continuation of the duty did so just for the revenue, then the "surest method will be to retain a drawback equal to it in England." [39]

Poultney returned to propose that both duties be given up for two or three years to find out how much tea the Company might sell in America if the trade were totally unencumbered. He regarded the estimated £15,000 annual revenue loss as well worth the knowledge gained. But if one tax must be retained, he concluded, let us give up the Townshend duty. We tried the experiment of the drawback once before, without significant effect. North was now flushed into the open. "No doubt there are political reasons . . . of such weight, and strength," he reluctantly admitted, "that unless I find it is absolutely necessary to take off the duty, I shall be very unwilling to touch that string. I know the temper of the people there is . . . little deserving favour from hence, unless the reasons are very great. . . ." [40]

A stubborn Lord North had unwittingly hammered a nail in the coffin of the old British Empire. For despite the fact that only one member had spoken in his support, the duty was retained. The measures concerning exportation of tea to America were passed without a division as proposed and on 10 May, became the Tea Act of 1773.[41]

Perhaps no bill of such momentous consequences has ever received less attention upon passage in Parliament. "Today [Lord North] confined himself to moving some proposition relative to the permitting the Company to export tea to America," Joseph Yorke reported on the 26th to his patron, Lord Hardwicke. "Tho' the question is interesting to the Company, it would not be very intelligible to you as explained by me. . . ." He did note, however, that "the only question seemed to be whether to take off the duty of three-pence per pound. . . ." [42] Matthew Brickdale omitted the entire discussion from his Parliamentary diary, although he was present that day to record the debate on Wilkes.[43] In his *Parliamentary History* Hansard confined himself to a brief report of Lord North's opening remarks.[44] The London press showed an equal lack of interest. Several newspapers noted that the bill had been discussed, without mentioning America as the tea's destination nor that the Townshend duty had been at issue. When the bill reached the House of Lords, the *Daily Advertiser* merely reported that "Yesterday the Upper Assembly in a Committee went through the East-India Tea Bill. Also the Bill to prevent the murdering or destroying Bastard Children, with Amendments." [45]

The tea bill had scarcely become law before the East India Company began to receive a flood of letters suggesting how to carry out the scheme of shipping tea to the colonies and recommending various American merchants for a share in the undertaking. One of the most influential of these advisers was William Palmer, a London merchant active himself in the tea trade. On 19 May Palmer urged the Company to start planning its exportation and enclosed numerous letters from colonists discussing the enormous consumption of tea there. Palmer concluded that the Company could sell over 3,000,000 pounds a year on the American market. One week later Gilbert Barkley, a Philadelphia merchant, wrote to suggest that the Company establish warehouses in a centrally located colonial city, preferably his own, at which regular sales of tea could be held in the manner of those at India House. Barkley, who estimated American consumption at nearly 6,000,000 pounds per year, humbly offered himself as one of the managers of the warehouses, along with another Philadelphian, John Inglis.[46]

Thomas Walpole, nephew of the famous Robert, and a London merchant-banker, also considered Philadelphia the proper center of distribution for the Company's tea in America. He was at that time associated with Benjamin Franklin, the Whartons, and other prominent Philadelphians in the Vandalia Land Company's plans for the Illinois country. Walpole suggested that about 600 chests be consigned to a reputable firm which would offer them for sale at public auction. If all went well, similar consignments might also be sent to Boston and New York. Walpole urged that the consignees be informed of the shipment enough in advance to engage proper warehouses for it.[47] Palmer submitted a more detailed plan shortly afterwards, in which he suggested that the first teas be sent to consignees in Boston, "as the only considerable mart, where tea from England is at present received without opposition." But before making the shipment, Palmer proposed, the Company should send someone to America to find out more about marketing conditions and whether the dutied tea would be received in New York and Philadelphia.[48] Still another adviser warned against employing anyone in the immediate service of the Crown in connection with the scheme. To do so, he feared, would lead patriots in some provinces to charge that the government was attempting "to establish principle and right to taxation, for the purpose of a revenue. . . ."[49]

Throughout June and July, London merchants nominated various American mercantile firms, generally houses which had been their good customers, to be consignees of the Company's tea. During these weeks the Committee of Warehouses called these advisers together for further discussion of the operation.[50] It is not certain when the Company finally decided to prepare a shipment, but a letter from London dated 17 July and widely printed in America the following autumn clearly shows that the decision was not easily reached:

> Mr. Crabb Bolton, chairman of the India Company carried his point in the India House, a few days ago, when it was determined that tea should be sent to America; he was opposed in very elegant and cogent terms by the Duke of Richmond, who is in highest esteem of the city.[51]

Meanwhile, Messrs. Romberg at Brussels further developed their plans for marketing English tea on the Continent in hope of interesting the Company directors. They forwarded regular accounts of tea prices at the various European sales and concluded that good English Bohea could go off nicely at 2s. 3d. In July they successfully negotiated with the Austrian government for permission to establish special warehouses and for exemption from part of the import duties on foreign tea. Valtravers had to write them in September, however, that the Committee of Warehouses was too busy with other projects to consider their proposals at present. Some Company officials worried that whatever tea they exported to Europe would be smuggled back into Great Britain, he pointed out, while others believed the colonies would eventually absorb the entire surplus anyway. The Rombergs explained in reply that their marketing plan would distribute the tea so widely through the Continent that its return to England would prove too costly. Furthermore, they asked, even if some tea is smuggled back, "is it not better, that English teas should be introduced, rather than those of other Nations?"[52] But the Company officials remained unconvinced, and on 6 October the directors voted that no export of tea be made to the Continent that year. Instead they would await the outcome of their American venture.[53]

By the end of July the Committee of Warehouses had eliminated a number of American firms and their London sponsors from consideration in the plan to ship tea to America. On the 29th it held a final meeting of those sponsors remaining to iron out details. In each of the four ports of Boston, New York, Philadelphia, and Charleston a group of merchants was chosen to act jointly as consignees of the shipment destined for its town. At Boston, for instance, Thomas & Elisha Hutchinson, Richard Clarke & Sons, and Faneuil & Winslow were the three firms selected. Each in turn had been nominated by a London merchant who was prepared to give bond that his American friends would remit the proceeds within four months after the sale. The Company, after all, was about to send tea valued altogether at £61,674 to colonial merchants, most of whom were unknown to its officers. Some guarantee of payment was essential.[54]

After proper notification in the newspapers, the American consignees were to offer the tea for public sale at prices ranging in sterling equivalents from 2s. 0d. for Bohea to 5s. 0d. for Hyson. The buyers were to deposit at least one-eighth the value of their purchase at once, the balance to be due in two months. The Company requested the consignees to make a particular effort to sell the Singlo teas, an inexpensive green tea popular in England, which was priced at 2s. 8d. for the American sale. From the proceeds the consignees were then authorized to deduct all costs, including the Townshend duty and their own commission of 6 per cent, which was to be divided evenly among them. Out of this commission, however, the London sponsors expected a share as compensation for giving security. Abraham Dupuis, for instance, demanded one-third of the net profit accruing to Richard Clarke & Sons.[55]

Net returns to the Company on these sales would necessarily be small. In the case of Bohea, for instance, out of the sale price of 2s. 0d. per pound would come several charges: Townshend duty, 3d.; freight and primage, about ½d.; consignees' commission, 1½d.; and for warehouse and other charges connected with the sale perhaps another ½d. This left a return of only 1s. 6½d. to the Company for tea which it sold in London, when possible, at 1s. 10d. or more. But the fact was, of course, that by the fall of 1773 the Company could not sell its surplus at that price in London.[56]

Even by offering its Bohea at 2s. 0d., the Company would not necessarily have undersold smuggled Dutch tea, as many historians have suggested. For from May 1773 through March 1774 illicit traders could purchase Bohea in Amsterdam for 1s. 9d. per pound. By importing fifty chests of tea at a time, they could reduce shipping costs to 2½d. per pound. Of course the smugglers did not pay the Townshend duty, and had they been willing to limit their profit to the same 6 per cent that the Company allowed its consignees, they could offer Dutch Bohea in New York at about 2s. 1d., coupled, perhaps, with more attractive terms of credit. When the price at Amsterdam dropped to 1s. 7d. in the spring of 1774, the smugglers could in fact have undersold the Company. Naturally they did not welcome the Company's plan, for they were able to get 2s. 7d. per pound for Dutch tea in the fall of 1773, but at any rate they would not necessarily have been driven out of the market by the Company's scheme.[57]

The directors of the East India Company gave final approval to the plan on 4 August. They tentatively decided to send 1700 chests of tea to the four American ports. This figure was later increased to 2000 chests, apparently on the advice of the ubiquitous William Palmer. Now all the Company needed was an export license and the ships to carry the tea to America. Under the provisions of the Tea Act, any three of the Commissioners of the Treasury were authorized to permit the Company to export surplus tea to the colonies. On 20 August, Lord North, Charles Townshend, and Charles James Fox did so. Meanwhile the directors had written to various London merchants to engage shipping space on board the next vessels for America. Jonathan Clarke offered his firm's brig *William*, and George Hayley the American-owned ships *Dartmouth* and *London*, the former destined for Boston, the latter for Charleston. Some captains, including James Scott of Hancock's ship *Hayley* and several New Yorkers, refused to have anything to do with the Company's cargo. But by early September the necessary vessels had been found, and over 2000 chests containing almost 600,000 pounds of tea were ready for shipment.[58]

One major problem remained. The directors realized that payment of the Townshend duties in America might present problems, certainly economic and possibly political as well. Under the current regulations the consignees would have to put up altogether about £7500 before the tea could be landed, unless an alternative procedure could be arranged. In mid-August the directors proposed that the duties be paid by bills of exchange drawn on the Company in London. This would have had a double advantage. Not only could it have avoided the appearance that specie was being drained from the colonies, but also the duties would seem to have been paid in England. In fact, of course, no specie would in any case leave America since the revenue was to be spent there for governors' and judges' salaries. But ultimately these bills of exchange as well as any bills used for the purchase of the tea itself would have represented a balance of trade unfavorable to the colonists.[59]

Lord North apparently endorsed the bills-of-exchange arrangement on the advice of his able secretary, John Robinson. But the London merchant, Richard Reeve, long experienced in the American trade, was worried. "I cannot think that the Americans would be caught with the delusive appearance of the duty being evaded or withdrawn in any shape because it was paid in England," he wrote North on 23 August. "They are, I should imagine, well apprised that all the duties received by the collectors of the several ports, whether paid in bills or otherwise, must center in the American chest." Reeve had an alternative proposal — instruct the Commissioners of Customs in America, with whom the immediate decision lay, not to collect the duties until after the tea had been sold. The consignees could then quietly make payment from the proceeds of the sale.[60] The Company ultimately supported both plans. Writing to the Boston consignees by one of the tea-ships, the directors suggested that they first offer security for a deferred future payment of the duties. If the Commissioners refused, the consignees were next to offer them bills of exchange drawn on the Company. If specie were demanded, however, they were then to try raising it by these bills from private sources.[61]

During the course of late September and early October the tea-ships dropped down the Thames ready for sea. There were the ships

Dartmouth and *Eleanor* and the brigs *Beaver* and *William* for Boston. The ship *London* was cleared for Charleston and *Polly* for Philadelphia. Later the ship *Nancy* would come down for New York. Headwinds held them at Deal until mid-October. Then on the 18th the winds shifted northwesterly, and one by one the tea-ships sailed down-Channel and into the rough swells of the Atlantic, to buck their fateful passages to America.[62]

V

AMERICANS RESIST

THE three years between the final breakup of non-importation
in the autumn of 1770 and the Boston Tea Party in December
1773 have been labeled "the period of calm." Compared with the
turmoil that preceded and the Revolution that followed, these years
certainly appear calm enough. The restoration of Anglo-American
trade brought new prosperity to the seaports, while opposition to
dutied tea all but disappeared in New England and in the southern
colonies. With the end of the boycott on English wares, Americans
imported more than ever before to replenish their depleted stocks.
In fact, in the years 1771-74 inclusive, imports from England were
up 47 per cent from the level reached before non-importation, during
the period 1765-68, and averaged in value nearly £3,400,000 per
year. Furthermore, the North American colonies in the aggregate
remained England's best customer right up to adoption of the Continental Association in December 1774. Because of this increasing
activity most merchants on both sides of the Atlantic fervently hoped
for continued peace between the colonies and the mother country,
although not all of the issues between them had been settled nor the
tea duty repealed.[1]

Even the political arena seemed quiet after the end of non-importation. Writing to Benjamin Franklin in January 1771, Boston's Dr.
Samuel Cooper commented that "there seems now to be a Pause in
Politics. . . . Should [the British] Government be so Temperate
and Just as to place us on the old ground on which we stood before
the Stamp Act, there is no danger of our rising in our demands."

Patriots on the one hand and future Loyalists on the other co-operated in carrying out worthy local projects. At Boston, for instance, the two camps joined to urge moving the powderhouse to a safer location. Many leaders of the patriot cause during the Stamp Act and Townshend duty crises seemed to have retired from politics entirely. Neither John Hancock nor John Adams showed much interest in public affairs after the collapse of non-importation. Hancock, as we noted, allowed his vessels to freight dutied tea for the Hutchinsons and Clarkes and probably imported some himself. After enjoying a cup of green tea at Hancock's home in February 1771, Adams could only hope that it had been smuggled from Holland. A year later Boston's Thomas Cushing ruefully admitted that the people could no longer be depended upon to refrain from consuming dutied articles.[2]

Elsewhere in the colonies the political situation appeared similarly quiet, as the public attention turned to other and less idealistic matters than whether Parliament had a right to tax the colonies. Furthermore, the way in which the non-importation movement had broken up dealt a severe blow to colonial unity. Now quarrels between the colonies threatened to widen the breach. Connecticut and Pennsylvania squabbled over control of the Wyoming Valley in northern Pennsylvania, while New Hampshire challenged New York's claim to the territory later to become Vermont. Violence broke out among people of the same colony too, particularly in the Carolinas. There the Regulators demanded equality of representation in the legislatures and a fairer system of taxation — grievances echoed by backwoodsmen almost everywhere. In Pennsylvania the perennial battle between the proprietors and the legislature flared up anew. The quarrels with Great Britain seemed to many a by-gone issue by the end of 1771.

Writing from England in February 1771, Benjamin Franklin saw a new spirit of conciliation developing in the mother country as well. He reported that the doctrine of Parliament's right to tax the colonies was being abandoned and that the remaining duties might soon be withdrawn. Abusive references to Massachusetts Bay seemed likewise on the wane.[3]

The Ministry had already taken one important step to ease tensions. As far back as the autumn of 1768 government officials had had under consideration a plan to alter the charter of Massachusetts Bay on the grounds that the people there enjoyed too much power. A letter from London in June 1769 reported Lord Hillsborough in favor of changing the charters of several other provinces as well. The plan fell through, but in the fall of 1770 the North ministry revived it. Bernard was heartily in favor of the idea and assisted the Ministry in working out some of the details. Although he agreed with those officials who claimed that the present charter had in effect been forfeited by irresponsible behavior on the part of the General Court, Bernard hoped that any changes would be based simply on the principle of Parliamentary supremacy rather than adopted as punishment.[4]

Subsequent letters from Bernard revealed that it was the popular election of the Governor's Council that the British found particularly intolerable. From their own experience Governor Hutchinson and his predecessor agreed. Bernard pointed out that the authority of Parliament to amend charters had already been demonstrated in a recent case involving the City of London. As the plan evolved in the fall of 1770, the Ministry decided to vest the appointment of the Council in the King, as was the case in other royal colonies, and to alter the method of choosing county jurors to conform with the current British practice of appointment by the sheriffs.[5]

But the breakup of non-importation and the news of Captain Preston's acquittal in the trial following the Boston Massacre made the government reluctant to stir up more trouble. Besides, a crisis with Spain over an incident in the Falkland Islands loomed large at the end of the year, and the proposal was once again laid aside. Bernard was disappointed, but he had no doubt that the Boston patriots would soon provide the Ministry with the opportunity to revive the measure. Within three years they would do so.[6]

Another encouraging sign from England was the resignation of Lord Hillsborough from his post as Secretary of State for the Colonies. Hillsborough had earned the enmity of virtually every

American patriot during his four years in office as much for his haughty attitude toward the colonists as for his preference for strong measures. Even Hillsborough's fellow ministers and the King himself soon tired of him, and he was replaced by the Earl of Dartmouth in August 1772.[7]

Dartmouth had had an unusual political background. Through the remarriage of his mother he became at the age of five the stepbrother of Frederick, later Lord, North. Upon the death of his grandfather in 1750, he succeeded to the title Earl of Dartmouth, taking his seat in the House of Lords four years later. Dartmouth was not an active participant in public affairs, however, until the formation of the first Rockingham ministry in 1765. He then accepted the post of president of the Board of Trade with appointment also to the Privy Council. Dartmouth soon came to favor repeal of the Stamp Act, a stand that endeared him to the colonists, and he remained a Rockingham Whig at least until 1771. His devotion to Methodism gave him an interest in common with many colonists. In 1767 Dartmouth became president of the board of Eleazer Wheelock's Indian Charity School at Lebanon, Connecticut. Two years later the institution was renamed in his honor when it was moved to Hanover, New Hampshire.[8]

Dartmouth's family ties with Lord North drew him away from the Rockinghamites and closer to the King's Friends in the second year of his step-brother's ministry, but his appointment as Secretary of State for the Colonies was nevertheless greeted with enthusiasm by most Americans. Dartmouth brought to the office an interest in the affairs of America and a courtesy toward its representatives rarely shown by his predecessor. In addition to his official contacts with agents in London, he carried on private correspondences with at least two important colonists, Thomas Cushing of Boston and Joseph Reed of Philadelphia. Franklin and other Americans in London felt welcome at his house and spent many pleasant hours in his company. In the Earl of Dartmouth the colonists seemed to have a friend in court.[9]

Despite the highest hopes of Americans like Franklin neither the new spirit of conciliation in England nor the appointment of Lord Dartmouth led to a meaningful redress of colonial grievances. In March 1771 the Assembly of Pennsylvania petitioned the Crown for a repeal of the remaining duty on tea. In July 1772 and again in March 1773 Massachusetts Bay adopted similar measures, but when they were finally shown to him in June 1773, the King took no action. Dartmouth was later to state that repeal would come as soon as the colonists showed a quiet submission to the law and petitioned in "a dutiful and decent manner." There would never be a better opportunity to rescind the law than during the years 1771-73, when Americans *did* submit to the duty on tea and *did* petition for its repeal. But the Ministry was reluctant to make further concessions, and as we have seen, Lord North insisted on its retention in April 1773, when Parliament adopted the Tea Act.[10]

In America, meanwhile, die-hard patriots like Sam Adams, Alexander McDougall, and Charles Thomson struggled to build an organization and to keep the flames of opposition burning. But such efforts were largely futile. Aside from the presence of British troops in Boston there were few issues for the propagandist to take advantage of, and none strong enough to unify the colonists in any case. The patriots made every effort to call attention to what they considered hostile developments, but not even the abuses charged to the customs officers and vice-admiralty courts seemed to have more than momentary appeal, and then only along the seacoast. These issues were of little interest to the vast majority of the Americans living in rural areas. Annual addresses in Massachusetts Bay to remind the citizens of the Boston Massacre "atrocity" also brought little response from people outside the metropolis. Month after month Sam Adams denounced the duty on tea, but Bostonians went right on ordering and drinking the brew. Patriot leaders vehemently denied that the spirit of opposition had entirely receded in America. "Though a high Ferment cannot be expected to continue long among the People and the Irritation into which they were thrown has abated," Boston's Samuel Cooper admitted to former Governor Pownall in November 1771, "yet their inward sentiments are not altered, but by far the greater Part have a settled Persuasion, that we are in a State of Oppression. . . ." As the months of early 1772 slipped by, however, Cooper's argument seemed hollow, for outwardly the colonies remained calm and happy.[11]

Then in June 1772 a mob in Providence broke the peace by boarding the revenue cutter *Gaspée*, wounding its captain, and burning the vessel to the water's edge. Parliament authorized a special commission to make a full-scale investigation. Although the commission could make no headway in the face of the stubborn refusal of witnesses to come forward, the Virginia House of Burgesses saw in the process a serious threat to American liberties. In March 1773 it appointed a standing committee to correspond with the other colonial legislatures on matters of mutual interest concerning their relations with Great Britain. During the spring of 1773 other provinces followed suit, and by autumn a network of communications had been established between the legislatures of all the American colonies.

Meanwhile in Massachusetts another significant development had taken place. In November 1772 a long-smouldering quarrel between Governor Hutchinson and the patriots suddenly flared up again. The British ministry had proposed that a civil list of government officers be established in Massachusetts Bay, their salaries to be paid from customhouse receipts, which would make them independent of the legislature. Since revenue from the tea duty was involved, the dispute threatened to revive the ill-feeling once directed against the Townshend Act. When a Boston town meeting called for an investigation, Hutchinson attempted to squelch the protest. In retaliation, Sam Adams proposed that the town appoint a committee of correspondence to take the issue to the people in other communities in the province. The radicals sent round a bill of particulars that dredged up all the old charges of Parliamentary oppression and suggested that new threats were impending. By early 1773 nearly eighty towns in New England had endorsed the circular letter and some had established committees of correspondence of their own. Samuel Cooper wrote to his friend Pownall of "the Revolution I now see in the Sentiments and Hearts of the People. . . ." Thereafter the propaganda efforts of Adams and his Boston supporters were unceasing.[12]

Governor Hutchinson had made a major contribution to the resurgence of the Boston patriots when he lectured the General Court in January 1773 on the authority of Parliament over the American legislatures, hardly a topic to soothe ruffled feelings. In their rebuttal the patriots virtually denied that Parliament had any authority over the colonies at all. Dartmouth was shocked by these "wild and extravagant Doctrines." Until they were retracted by the General Court, the Secretary saw no chance for a redress of American grievances by Great Britain. In their reply to Hutchinson the patriots also charged that the Governor was a tyrant who had from the beginning favored oppressive measures like the Stamp Act and the Townshend duties. In fact, Hutchinson had opposed both schemes, and at no time did he seem to favor the practice of Parliamentary taxation in America. In the summer of 1773 he wrote Lord Dartmouth: "I have ever endeavoured that the advantages which the Kingdom was entitled to from the colonies might arise from a well-regulated commerce and not from internal or external taxation." But whatever chance Hutchinson may have had to vindicate himself disappeared forever in June 1773.[13]

In England Benjamin Franklin had somehow obtained letters of Hutchinson and the present lieutenant-governor, Andrew Oliver, written years before to English correspondents. In them the two had made uncomplimentary remarks about the patriot leaders, the extent of popular government in Massachusetts, and the necessity for stricter enforcement of the laws. Perhaps to enhance his own reputation among the Boston patriots, Franklin sent them the letters but with strict instructions that they were for private view only. Adams immediately saw their great propaganda value, however, and after presenting them to the General Court engineered a ruse by which they were published. In a flash, copies carefully edited by Adams and others were distributed by the committee of correspondence to the other towns of the province and to most of the colonies as well. By fanning the flames, Adams was able to persuade the General Court to impeach both Hutchinson and Oliver and to draw up petitions for their removal from office. By the autumn of 1773 Hutchinson and the Boston patriots were at sword's points.[14]

The period of calm was over in Boston, but it would take more than a running battle with Thomas Hutchinson to bring about the changes in English policy sought by Sam Adams and the other radical patriots. They knew that as long as Great Britain could treat the colonies as separate entities, cracking down here, making minor concessions there, and setting one against the other, just so long would the patriots have to wait for any real redress of grievances. The committees of correspondence were good for the exchange of ideas, and in time of crisis they would comprise a useful network of communications. But Adams knew that the committees could never of themselves bring about unified national action. Only a congress of delegates from all the colonies, such as that which convened at New York to protest the Stamp Act, could authorize united action. A major crisis was needed to convene a congress, and in the summer of 1773 no such crisis was in sight.

Rumors began circulating in America during the spring of 1773 that the East India Company would soon become directly involved in the colonial tea trade. A report published in the *Boston Post-boy* in April claimed that the Company would receive permission "to send Annually two ships directly from China to America laden with teas, clear of all duties." When a young Boston merchant, Jonathan Williams, Jr., saw the report, he immediately wrote his relative, Benjamin Franklin, to recommend him to the Company as a consignee. Franklin was no help, however, for when he replied in July he had apparently still not heard of the Company's plans, although he had earlier mentioned the fact that tea sent to America was now subject to a drawback. Another Boston merchant, Henry Bromfield, was told about the plan by his brother Thomas in London and was furious to learn that the Clarkes might become consignees.

"I cannot imagine what your reason can be for not applying also," he scolded. He would later have cause to thank his brother for his negligence.[15]

One Bostonian particularly interested in the Company's intentions was Governor Hutchinson. He had been in correspondence with London merchant William Palmer for some months to make arrangements for purchasing a large order of tea at the Company's spring sales. Palmer wrote back in June about the Company's plans. He had already bought the tea for Hutchinson's sons; now he would try to sell it in London instead. Hoping to regain some of his loss, Palmer apparently had suggested the Governor's sons as consignees, for Hutchinson replied in early August, "I wish you may succeed in behalf of my Sons to whom I have given a hint." [16]

During the summer, news of the Company's scheme trickled slowly into American newspapers. From no one source, however, could a reader possibly tell what was in the offing. In late June the *Boston Gazette* reprinted from a London paper, with no further particulars, the fact that the Tea bill had passed the House of Commons. Toward the end of July the *Pennsylvania Gazette* copied from a London journal of 10 May that "the bill to allow a drawback of the duties of the customs on the exportation of teas to any of his Majesty's colonies or plantations in America" had passed the royal assent. No mention was made, however, of the East India Company's role. Rivington's *New York Gazetteer* for 22 July included part of Lord North's speech of 27 April introducing the Tea bill and noted its acceptance by the House, but his account omitted to note that the tea would be sent to the American colonies.[17]

Not until the end of August did the American public get the full story, and even then it was an inaccurate version. On 26 May Frederick Pigou, Jr., one of the East India Company's directors and a prominent London merchant, wrote to the Philadelphia firm of James & Drinker. He reported that the Company planned to send a large shipment of tea from England "duty free" to Boston. To remove any ambiguity concerning the phrase "duty free," Pigou added in a post-script that "the Tea is to be subject to the Duty payable in America." The following day Pigou wrote again, this time to request that his first letter be made public. Both letters were sent via Pigou & Booth, a New York firm whose senior partner was apparently the London Pigou's father. There the letters lay unopened until Benjamin Booth returned from an out-of-town trip in early August. When the letter of 26 May appeared in American newspapers during late August and early September, the post-script about the American duty was strangely missing. New Yorkers willing to read small print and with a flair for understanding the language of British statutes could surmise from their 6 September issue of Gaine's *New York Gazette* that the tea was liable to the Townshend duty, for on that date the full text of the Tea Act appeared in an American newspaper for the first time.[18]

By the end of September more accurate details were rapidly coming in as London merchants advised their American correspondents of the plan. On 4 August, as soon as he had learned of the Company director's final decision, Samuel Wharton sent the news to his brothers in Philadelphia, whom he had successfully nominated as consignees. The Whartons turned the letter over to the editor of the *Pennsylvania Journal*, who printed an excerpt on 29 September:

> The East India Company have come to a resolution to send 600 Chests of Tea to Philadelphia and the like quantity to New York and Boston, and their intention, I hear is to have Warehouses, and sell by public sale four times a year as they do here. . . .

During the next few weeks other papers reprinted the item, and by early October colonists throughout America at last learned of the East India Company's intentions.[19]

First signs of opposition to the Company's plans emanated out of New York. Someone in London had written to a correspondent there to warn him of the scheme, and now the recipient passed the letter along to a friend in Philadelphia, who turned it over to the printer of the *Pennsylvania Journal*. The Londoner warned that several American shipmasters had been approached by the Company to freight the tea to America and had refused. Lord North had rejected a Company plea to repeal the tea duty, he related. "Being a great schemer, [North] struck out the plan of the East India Company's sending this Article to America," he continued, "hoping thereby to outwit us, and to establish that act [The Townshend duty], effectually which will for ever after be pleaded as precedent for every imposition the Parliament of Great Britain shall think proper to saddle us with. It is much to be wished that the Americans will convince Lord North," the letter concluded, "that they are not *yet ready* to have the yoke of slavery rivited [*sic*] about their necks, and send back the tea whence it came." [20]

As this item was being picked up by editors elsewhere in the colonies, more letters from England came in asserting that the British government had adopted the plan to force the colonists to recognize the Townshend Act. "I have told several of the Company that the Tea and Ships will all be burnt," related one, ". . . as I think you will never suffer an Act of Parliament to be so crowded down your Throats; for if you do it is all over with you," he warned. Writing from London to Peyton Randolph and other leaders in Virginia, the merchant John Norton claimed that several Company directors suspected that the government's motives were "to make a cat's paw of the Company, and force them to establish the 3*d*. per pound American duty." Benjamin Hallowell, comptroller of the Boston customhouse, wrote in late September that letters from English merchants had already encouraged plans for preventing the landing of the Company's tea. William Gordon, a minister in Roxbury, Massachusetts, elaborated on the charge in a letter to Dartmouth in December. As provocative reports of the Act's origins and purpose flooded into the colonies and were spread around through the newspapers, a ground-swell of opposition began to mount.[21]

The merchants at New York chosen to be consignees were among the city's most distinguished citizens. Abraham Lott served as province treasurer, and Henry White sat on the Governor's Council. Frederick Pigou and Benjamin Booth, lately from England, formed a strong mercantile partnership. Pigou had once been associated with the East India Company as a supervisor in Canton, while

Benjamin Booth had had long experience as a merchant in London. When the crisis developed, it was Booth who made the most spirited defense of the consignees' rights. As soon as these men learned of their appointment from Frederick Pigou, Jr. in late September, they met together to compare notes. Each expected strong opposition from the smugglers, "who are a formidable body among the mer-chants, and will of themselves be able to raise a considerable mob, including a great number of retainers, such as boatmen, alongshore-men, etc. who are all paid highly for their services," they reported to James & Drinker in Philadelphia. At that time, the New York consignees expected all the tea sent by the Company to come in one vessel, which they hoped would call first at Philadelphia. New York had more smugglers, and if they succeeded in opposing a landing there, it would encourage opposition elsewhere. The consignees therefore proposed to James & Drinker that they share the cost of keeping a small vessel off Sandy Hook to direct the tea-ship first to Philadelphia. For themselves, Pigou & Booth were determined to remain firm, no matter how great the opposition.[22]

On the evening of 7 October the first of many handbills opposing the East India Company scheme circulated through the streets of New York. Entitled *Alarm No. 1*, and appearing over the patriotic signature of HAMPDEN, the broadside exposed the seamier chapters of the East India Company's past history as groundwork for more specific attacks to come. Pigou & Booth reported that opposition to the tea shipment had quickly divided into two themes: (1) if the tea tax is submitted to, other taxes would soon follow; (2) if the East India Company succeeded in establishing a monopoly over trade in one commodity, it would soon monopolize all the foreign commerce of America. Thus the dual bases for opposing the tea scheme were well established by early October. One observer already predicted that if allowed to land at New York at all, the tea would be stored until it could be returned to England. While HAMPDEN hammered away at the monopolistic Company through subsequent numbers of his *Alarm* papers, others concentrated on the issue of the Townshend duty.[23]

The consignees needed all the courage they could muster. On 21 October a particularly threatening letter addressed to them appeared in the *New York Journal* over the signature PHILELI-EUTHEROS. "It will be impossible to shield or screen yourselves from the many darts that will incessantly be levelled against your persons," he warned them. "You cannot become your own cooks, butchers, butlers, nor bakers. You will therefore be liable to be suddenly, and unexpectedly taken off . . . by those whom you may chance to confide in and employ . . . ," he continued. "A thousand avenues to death would be perpetually open to receive and swallow you, and ten thousand uplifted shafts, ready to strike the fatal stroke whenever a favourable opportunity offered for the purpose." [24]

Despite all the patriots' bluster, however, their campaign against the plan made only slow progress at New York. A meeting of merchants in mid-October to praise three local shipmasters who refused to carry the tea on board their vessels met with little enthusiasm. When some of those present attempted to form a permanent committee to organize the opposition, the idea collapsed from lack of interest. Isaac Low, who had been chairman of the merchants' committee during non-importation, refused to reactivate that group to lead a protest movement. The consignees took heart and prepared to launch a counterattack. [25]

Pigou & Booth became the principal spokesmen for all the New York consignees. The partners assumed, probably correctly, that the taxation issue was at the bottom of whatever popular opposition existed. Were that issue somehow removed, they reasoned, smugglers would be isolated in their resistance, for the people would care little about the threat of monopoly if they could be supplied with duty-free English tea at a low price. From their correspondents in London, Pigou & Booth had just learned of the possibility that the Commissioners of Customs might accept payment of the duty by bills of exchange drawn on the Company in London. On 28 October a humorous handbill, purportedly a letter addressed to the agents of the Dutch East India Company at St. Eustatius from the smugglers of New York, appeared on the streets. The smugglers complained bitterly of the English Company's plan, which would permit it to send tea "without paying any duty in America; by which means the people here will have an opportunity of buying good English Tea, for half the price we expected to extort from them for the trash lodged in your hands from Holland." If the consignees did not themselves prepare this piece, at least they knew about it in advance.[26]

The ambiguous language of the Tea Act also played into the hands of the consignees. On 28 October they had Rivington publish in his *Gazetteer* the clause that explained that the teas would be exported to America "discharged from the Payment of any Customs or Duties whatsoever. . . ." Taken alone, this excerpt seemed to imply that the tea would not be subject to the Townshend duty, but other clauses in the act made it perfectly clear that the duties referred to were those collected upon importation into England. Pigou & Booth seemed to admit their game of deception when they wrote James & Drinker late in the month. First they chastised the Philadelphians for supposing that the Townshend duty would be paid in London. "To clear up that point," they said, "we have caused a clause of the late act to be reprinted . . . by which it will appear that the payment of all duties on both sides of the water is as much suspended for the present as if the [Townshend] Act was totally repealed." Perhaps the New York consignees really believed their interpretation to be true. But in August, Benjamin Booth had read Pigou's letter from London which stated specifically that the tea would be subject to the duty in America.[27]

While the consignees congratulated themselves on their apparent victory over the smugglers, the opposition launched a furious attack on their interpretation of the tax issue. Broadsides and letters to the press pounded away on the theme that money for the Townshend duty would ultimately come from America whether actually collected here or not. "Are Americans such blockheads as to care whether it be a hot red poker or a red hot poker which they are to swallow?" asked one New Yorker. On 5 November, Guy Fawkes Day, always an occasion for riotous behavior in colonial America, the patriots staged a demonstration. A handbill circulated at noon bitterly attacked William Kelley, a former New York merchant who had vouched for his partner Abraham Lott as a consignee. Kelley had allegedly boasted in London that New York's Governor Tryon, fresh from his suppression of the Regulators while governor in North Carolina, would have little difficulty strong-arming those opposed to the tea plan. Kelley's effigy was hanged and carted through the streets, a cannister in its hands labeled "Tea three pence Sterling duty." The New York consignees blamed Philadelphia's Colonel William Bradford for organizing the demonstration, but the charge was never proved.[28]

Opponents of the tea plan had another weapon at their disposal. Realizing that because of swift tidal currents the tea-ship could not enter New York without the aid of local pilots, a broadside signed LEGION gave those men due warning. If anyone dared pilot the tea-ship in, "the vengeance of a free people, struggling to preserve their liberties, await and will surely be executed upon you. Bring her to anchor in Sandy Hook Bay, and no further," the author instructed.[29]

As opposition steadily mounted in mid-November the consignees and their friends decided to switch tactics. On 12 November a broadside over the pseudonym POPLICOLA appeared in New York, and Rivington published it in his *Gazetteer* the following week. Here the appeal was to self-interest combined with patriotism. The English East India Company was on the verge of bankruptcy, POPLICOLA pointed out. Were it to fail, all American commerce would feel the effects, and ruin would descend upon us. The Company's troubles, he maintained, could be laid at the door of the smugglers. "Is it the office of a patriot to encourage an unlawful traffic, to the prejudice of the commonwealth . . . and to the support and exaltation of a foreign Company?" he asked. Had POPLICOLA kept to this theme, he might have won some converts. But he could not resist the additional assertion that the tea would be exempt from the Townshend duty. Two weeks later A FARMER defended the plan from a different standpoint. The tea would be sold at vendue and since the city had a 2 per cent tax on such sales, its revenue would be enriched by over £1000 per year.[30]

POPLICOLA's appeal to patriotism went for nought. His broadside was hardly on the streets when A TRADESMAN took him to task for attempting to delude the people with his claim about the Townshend duty exemption. A STUDENT AT LAW produced a four-page, fully documented proof that the Townshend Act had not been repealed, and bitterly denounced POPLICOLA for his fraudulent argument. A MECHANIC added an attack on the East India Company, claiming it had opposed repeal of the Townshend duty on tea and therefore had only itself to blame for its current financial troubles. In his rebuttal, POPLICOLA once more rather stiffly appealed to law and order by concluding that it was the duty of the American colonies to obey Great Britain as a child obeys its parent.[31]

By late November, Pigou & Booth were ready for compromise. "If we do not see clearly that we shall be able to sell the tea without considerable opposition," they admitted to James & Drinker, "we shall give up that point upon condition that it may be stored till we have further instructions from the East India Company." By spring the smugglers would have sold off their teas, the consignees figured, and would not risk sending for more. Thus the market would soon be left free for the English tea. But the patriots relentlessly pressed the advantage. To accept the tea was to accept the duty and therefore enslavement, Z insisted on the 25th. Two days later came a warning from THE MOHAWKS which struck at the consignees' hoped-for compromise. Anyone aiding or abetting the landing or storage of the tea would be paid "an unwelcome visit, in which they shall be treated as they deserve." On the 29th a petition circulated through the town for the establishment of "The Association of the Sons of Liberty of New York," subscribers agreeing to resolve that those having anything to do with the impending tea shipment were enemies to "The Liberties of America." [32]

The consignees at New York had had enough of threats against the tea and against themselves. They had in fact on 25 November and again on the 30th intimated to delegations of patriots calling on them their desire to resign. They agreed that if the tea came subject to the American duty, they would refuse to carry out their commission. On 1 December they petitioned the Governor and his Council, among whom was the consignee Henry White, to assume responsibility for the tea when it arrived, because of "the general and spirited opposition to its being sold subject to the duty." The Council advised Governor Tryon to take the tea under government protection and recommended that he dispatch the warship *Swan* to Sandy Hook to escort the tea-ship into the harbor. Once safely moored under the guns of this vessel, the ship could be unloaded and the tea stored in the lower barracks.[33]

At the beginning of the controversy in New York the consignees had insisted that only smugglers and their apologists opposed the tea plan. Undoubtedly most illegal traders did fear the threat to their exorbitant profits and therefore advanced the argument that the Tea Act created a dangerous monopoly. But the subsequent words and actions of the consignees themselves clearly demonstrated that the decisive opposition was based on the issue of the Townshend duty.

In the first place, the consignees did not give up the fight until they learned from the Company, in late November, what everyone else seemed to know, that the tea would come subject to the duty. With that certainty established, however, they knew there was no hope of landing the tea against the will of the people. In their petition to the Governor and his Council they ascribed the opposition to the tea "to its being sold subject to the duty." In a letter explaining to the Company directors why they had resigned their commission, they stated that the duty was responsible for the difficulties at New York and urged the Company officials to work for its repeal. If the Company could bring about its removal, they went on to suggest, between 1500 and 2000 chests of English tea could be sold in New York each year. The consignees apparently anticipated little opposition to the sale of unduited English tea in America, even by a "monopolistic" company, for they volunteered to act once again as the Company's agents.[34]

In Philadelphia the arguments against the East India Company's plans were virtually the same as those in New York — the tea was subject to a duty and in any case the plan would give the Company a monopoly. Unlike New York, however, the Philadelphia patriots succeeded in staging a mass meeting to demand the resignation of the consignees. The immediate result was to drive a wedge between the two principal firms, and by early December both had capitulated to the demands of the people.

The tea destined for Philadelphia was jointly consigned to James & Drinker, Thomas & Isaac Wharton, Jonathan Browne, and Gilbert Barkley, but the first two partnerships had to bear the brunt of the struggle. Browne was frequently out of town, and Barkley, after having secured a share of the enterprise for himself while in London, had booked passage for Philadelphia on board the ship *Polly*, along with 698 chests of the East India Company's teas. Abel James, Henry Drinker, Thomas and Isaac Wharton were all prominent Quaker merchants. Except for the Whartons' brother Samuel, currently in England, none had had much to do with the tea trade before. But Samuel succeeded in obtaining a commission for his brothers with little difficulty. The James & Drinker firm received its appointment through the good offices of its London friend, Frederick Pigou, Jr. As his own agent in London, Barkley overpowered the Company with ideas that it rejected but finally won a commission for himself. Jonathan Browne was represented by his London-based brother, George.

As soon as James & Drinker received definite word of its role in the undertaking from Frederick Pigou, Jr., on 2 October, the partners met with the Whartons and Browne to discuss plans. There was already talk of opposition in Philadelphia, but the consignees were optimistic. The Whartons even suggested that the Company expand its operations to include shipments of pepper, spices, and silks. James & Drinker found comfort in the recently disclosed fact that since the end of non-importation large quantities of dutied tea had been entered at Boston as well as at many southern ports. To make better use of this information the Philadelphians suggested to Pigou & Booth in New York that "no time should be lost in obtaining from the Custom House books in Boston and Rhode Island a certified account of all Teas imported there from England which have paid the duty. . . . Such an account," they concluded, "will tend much to quiet any opposition that may be made here. . . ."[35]

While the consignees talked over their role in selling the tea, a small band of patriots were summoned to a meeting at Colonel William Bradford's house to lay plans for opposing the scheme. Resolutions were adopted, a meeting of the town decided upon, and then the patriots busied themselves with the task of stirring up public opinion. On 13 October a handbill that had circulated some days before through town over the signature SCAEVOLA now appeared in the *Pennsylvania Journal*. Its author was Thomas Mifflin. He boldly asserted that the tea scheme was simply a trick to enforce the Townshend duty and reminded the consignees of the fate of the stamp-masters eight years before. The weight of Mifflin's argument bore heavily on the theme of taxation, but he also warned that acceptance of the East India Company's tea would open the gate for monopolies in other articles of trade as well. In another broadside, appearing the next day, a COUNTRYMAN from Chester easily explained the origin of the Tea Act. Lord North was disappointed that the Americans had refused to buy dutied tea, and this was his way of persuading them to recognize Parliament's authority to tax the colonies. New duties would surely follow if Americans accepted this one, COUNTRYMAN warned.[36]

Philadelphia patriots, unlike their New York counterparts, did not rely solely on the printed word to rally the opposition. One of them, who had perhaps been at Bradford's house earlier, called for a mass meeting to demand that the consignees resign, and a handbill named Saturday, 16 October, the day. On that afternoon upwards of seven hundred inhabitants gathered at the State House. The resolutions they adopted, apparently without dissent, labeled the tea scheme a plot to enforce the Townshend duty. Anyone aiding its execution was to be considered "an Enemy to his Country." A committee was immediately appointed to call on the consignees for their resignations in order to preserve "the peace and good order of the province." The veiled threat that more forceful measures might come was obvious.[87]

Hoping to make certain that the two firms rebuffed the committee in identical language, Abel James invited Thomas Wharton to bring his family out for Sunday dinner at the James house in Frankfort, where there were "fewer of the Yahoo race," he explained. When the committee members called on each firm separately the next day, the Whartons told them that they had not yet received their commission from the Company and therefore did not know the conditions under which the tea would come. They promised, however, that as soon as they had more details they would "openly communicate the same, and that we would do nothing to injure the property of the India Company or enslave America." James & Drinker had already handed the committee a somewhat less definite statement:

> We have the same Ideas of the American Revenue Act with our Fellow Citizens generally, that we have by four or five lines an Intimation that we are appointed as some of the Commissioners to receive and sell the Tea intended to be sent here by the India Company, that if the Tea should ever arrive and we should be so appointed or have any concern in it, our Conduct will be open to our Fellow Citizens.[38]

When the two statements were read to a small meeting at the Coffee House on the evening of the 18th, however, that of the Whartons was greeted with a loud clap while the James & Drinker reply received "a general Groaning and Hissing." To be sure, the Whartons had shown an explicit concern for the "enslavement" of America, while the James & Drinker statement, that they shared the views of their fellow citizens "generally," was somewhat ambiguous. The committee demanded clarification, and James & Drinker therefore issued another statement insisting they had told the committee at their first conference that *"we neither meant or intended to do anything that would be disagreeable to our fellow citizens, or*

words of this import. . . ." They went on to say it had never occurred to them that their earlier statement could have been interpreted in any other way than to mean that enforcement of the
Townshend Act "would be an infringement of our common rights as
Englishmen." [39]

Still the patriots were not entirely satisfied. James was convinced
that the committee had been against his firm from the start, and he
expected still more trouble from the Sons of Liberty. There was
little question that James & Drinker had been less than co-operative
with the demands of the committee, but then so too had the
Whartons, for neither partnership specifically resigned their commissions, which had been the original goal of those at the mass
meeting. The more favorable reception of the Whartons' statement
may be partly explained by their greater influence in the town at
large. In any case, future attacks on the consignees seemed to
exempt both the Whartons and Jonathan Browne, who signed their
statement upon his return from town and left James & Drinker to
bear the brunt of the ordeal. Hard feelings immediately resulted,
each firm blaming the other for going back on their original agreement to issue similar statements. The Whartons wanted to have
nothing further to do with James & Drinker, while the latter were
convinced they had been deserted under fire by supposed friends.[40]

If the James & Drinker statement was somewhat evasive, at least
the Philadelphians had declined to play the New York consignees'
game of implying that the tea would not be taxed in America.
Opponents of the plan could therefore assume from the start that
the duty was collectable, and they concentrated their attack on this
issue. "The baneful chests [of East India Company tea] contain in
them a slow poison . . . ," wrote Benjamin Rush over the pseudonym HAMDEN [*sic*], "something worse than death — the seeds
of SLAVERY." AN OLD MECHANIC rued the day that tea had
ever become popular in America. He himself had given it up years
before because it affected his mind and nerves. "Tea is now of such
importance," he admitted with disgust, "that our very liberties depend on receiving it, or not receiving it." Other writers pointed out

that even if the Company were to cover the duty in London, colonists
would still pay for it indirectly through higher prices for Company
tea. But Philadelphians themselves could not read the text of the
Act to reach their own conclusions until 3 November. When they
did, opposition became even more clamorous.[41]

As November passed and the day for the tea-ships' arrival drew
near, the James & Drinker firm found itself standing virtually alone.
Quaker meeting had already decided in mid-October to say nothing
at all on the issue, which denied the consignees support from one of
the most important conservative bodies in town. A broadside from
RUSTICUS, datelined Fairview, 27 November, brought another disappointment, for as everyone knew, RUSTICUS could only be
John Dickinson. In the years since his letters of 1767-68, the PENN-
SYLVANIA FARMER had become a spokesman for moderation.
But now in an open letter addressed to "A Gentleman in Philadelphia," he expressed shock and indignation upon learning of the
East India Company's plan. Although he advocated prudence and
spoke warmly of the colonies' union with Great Britain, Dickinson
urged steadfast opposition to dutied tea. He called on the merchants
of Philadelphia to deny the Company use of their wharves and
warehouses, the longshoremen to refuse to unload the tea, and the
shopkeepers to boycott it from their stores. Let the "Watchmen be
instructed as they go their Rounds, to call out every Night, *past
Twelve O'Clock, beware of the East India Company*," Dickinson
concluded.[42]

On the 27th also, ominous warnings to the Delaware River pilots
and to Captain Ayres of the tea-ship *Polly* circulated through town.
The pilot who dared to bring the vessel up the river was threatened
with tar and feathers, while a similar fate awaiting Ayres was spelled
out in more colorful detail: "What think you, Captain, of a Halter
around your Neck, then Gallons of liquid Tar decanted on your
Pate — with the Feathers of a dozen live Geese laid over that to
enliven your Appearance?" The warnings were signed THE COM-
MITTEE FOR TARRING AND FEATHERING, and both had
been printed at William Bradford's shop.[43]

By the end of the month James & Drinker were plainly worried. On the evening of 27 November, they reported, the committee appointed by the October meeting of inhabitants had convened again, this time with members from the merchants' old committee from non-importation days. Another mass meeting was being planned for the day the tea-ship finally arrived. James & Drinker hoped at least to land and store the tea pending further instructions from the Company, but apparently the Whartons were unwilling to commit themselves even to this compromise. The beleaguered firm glumly concluded that the tea-ship would be promptly turned back.[44]

On 1 December the Philadelphia consignees finally received their letter of instructions from the East India Company. In keeping with their promises of 18 October the Whartons, Browne, and James & Drinker jointly informed the people's committee that the tea-ship had left London in mid-September and that the tea would come subject to the Townshend duty. In a separate statement the James & Drinker firm tendered its resignation as consignees on the grounds that the general sense of the people was that the tea should not be received, but at the same time the partners recommended that the tea be landed and stored. No surrender was forthcoming from either the Whartons or Browne, their October statements apparently having been accepted as formal resignations. Nor would an appeal now be made for protection to the Governor, which officer indeed had shown little interest in the consignees' troubles at any time throughout the crisis. The way was now clear for the Philadelphians to return the tea to England.[45]

Opposition to the East India Company's tea at both New York and Philadelphia could be partly attributed to those merchants who had been smuggling Dutch tea in such prodigious quantities for so many years. These men and others undoubtedly considered the Company's plan a serious threat to their livelihood, and numerous writers stressed the danger that such a monopoly entailed. But in both communities it was the issue of the Townshend duty that caught the attention of the general public. In New York the only mass demonstration — on Guy Fawkes Day — focused on the issue of the tax; the resolutions adopted at Philadelphia's mass meeting in mid-October made no mention of the danger from monopoly. To be sure, Bostonians had been tacitly accepting dutied tea since the breakdown of non-importation three years before. But when they concluded that the Ministry was trying to force an overt recognition of Parliament's claim to an American revenue, the Bostonians proved to the world that the issue of taxation mattered very much indeed.

VI

BOSTON PREPARES

B OSTON'S reaction to the East India Company's tea plan differed
somewhat from the reaction in New York and Philadelphia. For
one thing, Thomas Hutchinson, unlike other governors, gave full
and continuing support to the consignees in their efforts to carry
out the plans of the Company. One main reason he did so was that
two of his sons, Thomas and Elisha, were agents appointed by
the Company. Furthermore, young Thomas had married the daughter
of another principal consignee, Richard Clarke, who with his sons
Jonathan and Isaac had been among the major importers of tea in
Boston for the past decade. The other commissioners, Edward
Winslow and Benjamin Faneuil, left the policy-making up to the
Hutchinsons and Clarkes.

Governor Hutchinson could afford to risk supporting the consignees because he felt there were enough soldiers, ships-of-war, and
other Crown officers stationed at Boston to suppress any sort of
uprising or mob violence. Then there was the matter of the Governor's past relations with the Boston patriots. In the Stamp Act
crisis his house had been ransacked, as lieutenant-governor he had
been constantly harassed by Sam Adams and other popular leaders;
more recently the patriots had attempted to smear his character
by publishing some of his private correspondence. Now the General
Court had petitioned the Privy Council that he be impeached and
removed from office.

Hutchinson himself was weary of the punishment he had suffered
almost without interruption since 1765. He had in fact already

requested a leave of absence from his duties as governor and was greatly relieved to learn in the autumn of 1773 that permission had been granted.[1] But like any conscientious, perhaps stubborn, man, he did not want to give the appearance of quitting under fire. He determined to have a final triumph over his adversaries. As the crisis over the East India Company's tea mounted during the fall of 1773, therefore, Thomas Hutchinson's own personal crisis reached a climax too.

Bostonians were particularly upset by the East India Company's plan because two of the principal firms chosen as consignees had long irritated the local patriots. Both the younger Hutchinsons and the Clarkes had been among the last merchants to hold out against the non-importation agreements in 1769. After the boycott had ended in November 1770, the two firms were responsible for a major part of the duties tea entering at the Boston customhouse. Embarrassed by their defiance but powerless to stop it, the patriots resented the merchants concerned more than ever. Unlike their counterparts elsewhere, the Boston consignees had long since become objects of local scorn. The crisis over the East India Company's tea simply gave the Liberty Boys an opportunity to vent their rage.

Despite the fact that rumors of the Company's plans had been drifting around Boston since late spring, the patriots there were among the last to organize any sort of opposition. This lag in response became acutely embarrassing to Sam Adams and his committee of correspondence, who were still prating about judges and governors' salaries while patriots in other colonies had become seriously concerned with the threat posed by the Company's tea. Thomas Hutchinson reported a general calm throughout Massachusetts Bay in mid-September, and the *Boston Gazette* for 27 September contained a letter by an obvious patriot, who saw in the talents and virtues of Lord Dartmouth a good omen for improving relations between England and America. In fact, the first adverse comments in the Boston press about the impending shipment of tea all seems to have been copied from Philadelphia and New York newspapers. Even as late as 21 October the provincial committee of correspondence in a long letter to the committees of other colonies considered the payment of officials' salaries from the King's revenue to be the principal threat to American liberties. The issue of the tea was simply noted in a short final paragraph.[2]

Although several merchants and officials knew of the Company's plans by late September, public opposition did not appear in Boston until mid-October, a week or more after the propaganda campaign had begun in New York and at the time that Philadelphians were preparing for their mass meeting. Years later John Adams allegedly admitted that had resistance not been initiated elsewhere, Boston would probably have accepted the tea, duty and all. Once they had begun, however, the Bostonians made up for lost time by the vehemence of their argument. Henry Bromfield reported the people to be so enraged that he seemed much relieved his brother had not nominated him a consignee after all. As elsewhere, early protests showed concern for the threat of monopoly, which many persons saw inherent in the scheme. Scottish factors for the Company would soon be swarming all over America to drive the legitimate American merchant out of the London trade altogether, A CONSISTENT PATRIOT feared. Company tea should be avoided like the plague, he concluded. JOSHUA, SON OF NUN, considered the Americans' right to free trade at stake, while RECLUSIS objected to the vast amounts of specie that would be drained from Massachusetts to pay for the tea — perhaps as much as £20,000 in Massachusetts currency each year, he estimated.[3]

But at Boston, as at New York and Philadelphia, it was the Townshend duty that caused the greatest opposition. The patriots had long been frustrated in their feeble attempts to stop the importation of dutied tea. Now Parliament and the East India Company gave them another chance. PATRIOT, JOSHUA, and RECLUSIS all showed their resentment toward the tax along with their fear of monopoly. PRAEDICUS was furious at the common rumor that the duty had been repealed and accused Lord North of "low cunning." "Perhaps it is not too late to free ourselves from popes, devils, and locusts. The fifth of November," he noted, "had been for two centuries celebrated in commemoration of such deliverances." Most other writers saw a sinister plot in the plan too. Editorializing in the *Boston Gazette*, Edes and Gill suggested that the consignees themselves be shipped back to England along with the tea. The editors pointed out that the scheme was simply a way to raise enough revenue to render the governor and judges independent of the people. On 21 October the Boston committee of correspondence sent out a circular letter to other towns in the colony, calling attention to the dangers of the tea plan and seeking measures to prevent its taking effect.[4]

The attack on the consignees steadily mounted toward the end of the month. One correspondent noted that the Governor had promised protection to the Clarkes and "the two children," as the young Hutchinsons were generally called. He then queried, "Would his Excellency be certain of protection for himself, should a betrayed people take it upon them to right themselves?" On 23 October patriot members of the North End Caucus, including Joseph Warren and Paul Revere, voted to oppose the sale of Company tea with "their lives and fortunes." Two days later the merchant Henry Bromfield freely predicted that unless the tea were returned, "it will be destroyed by Fire and Water as sure as it comes." The reprinting of Mifflin's SCAEVOLA letter from Philadelphia added to the tension.[5]

The proponents of the tea plan had thus far remained silent in Boston. But at the end of the month two conservative papers, the *Boston Evening Post* and the *Boston Newsletter*, published a long article, signed Z, defending the proposal. The author was in fact one of the consignees, Richard Clarke. He pointed out the evident advantages to the American merchant of buying from Company representatives in America rather than paying for the services of a middleman to make purchases for him at the Company's London sale. If the Company later raised the price at its American sales, as some had predicted, colonial merchants could return to the procedure of buying their tea in London as before. Clarke's attempt to deny that the plan would drain specie from America was less successful, as his argument depended on the currently low price of silver in London. He saved his strongest language to justify the Townshend duty. Have not large quantities of dutied tea been steadily imported into America in recent years? he argued. "What consistency is there in making a Clamor about this small Branch of the Revenue," Clarke concluded, "whilst we silently pass over the Articles of Sugar, Mollasses and Wine, from which more than three-fourths of the American Revenue has and always will arise . . . and the money collected from them are applied to the same Purposes?" [6]

The editor of the *Boston Newsletter* joined Clarke's counterattack by printing the report that the duty on the Company's tea would not be collected in America at all. A shopkeeper related in the same issue that a known patriot had just purchased a pound of English Bohea from him, despite a recent price rise to 4s. 6d. "I shall not only continue to sell that necessary article so long as the Patriotic gentlemen and ladies will buy it of me," he taunted, "but also . . . enquire and take down their names in hopes of being able shortly to furnish you with a pretty handsome list, to be discanted upon the next Town Meeting." [7]

On 1 November PRAEDICUS returned to the columns of the *Boston Gazette* to answer the letter by Z, whom he mistakenly assumed to be Thomas Hutchinson. PRAEDICUS's tirade was a compendium of all the earlier arguments used against the Company's plan, from the charge that tea was poisonous to a condemnation of the Townshend duty. Dealing mostly in personalities, he denounced among others Lord North, customs officers, and the consignees. But Thomas Hutchinson took the worst beating. Perhaps the Governor expected to receive a retirement pension out of the revenue collected, he jeered. Perhaps a fund would be raised to support "*children incapable of any considerable employment in church and state.*" This last barb struck home, for Hutchinson had since summer been writing English officials to find some place in the colonial establishment for his youngest son. But a vigorous stand made against the Tea Act, "this dirty trick," PRAEDICUS called it, would result either in its repeal or in the resignation of Lord North. In the same issue another writer tried to refute Z's claim that Bostonians continued to drink dutied tea by asserting that most New Englanders purchased only Dutch tea smuggled in from the southern provinces.[8]

So far Bostonians had confined their opposition to verbal attacks. Although the newspapers had kept them apprised of activities at New York and Philadelphia, no meeting of merchants or mass protests had yet been organized. On 28 October A MERCHANT expressed his surprise that his colleagues had not yet met to consider the implications of the tea plan. He urged them to do so without delay. But before the other merchants could respond, Boston's radical patriots had decided that the time for action had come. From the first days of November overt threats against the consignees followed each other so rapidly that the moderates were left far behind.[9]

At one o'clock on the morning of 2 November Richard Clarke awoke to a violent pounding on the door of his house in King Street. The moonlight revealed two men in the courtyard who shouted up that they had brought a letter from the country. Instead, the message turned out to be a summons for Clarke's appearance at Liberty Tree on Wednesday noon, the 3rd, "to make a public resignation of your commission." The note was signed O.C. The other consignees received copies that same night. The next morning Bostonians found handbills posted all over town urging them to witness the consignees give up their offices and agree to reship the tea to England. At the bottom of the notice ran the arrogant challenge: "Show me the man that dare take this down." That evening small bands of Sons of Liberty gathered throughout the town, and the committee of correspondence met with the North End Caucus at the Green Dragon Tavern to lay plans for the next day's activities.[10]

Wednesday noon a crowd of about five hundred collected at the flag-bedecked Liberty Tree, summoned by the town crier and the ringing of church bells. Sam Adams, Joseph Warren, John Hancock, the town's selectmen, and other patriot leaders were there, but the consignees failed to appear. They were in fact at that moment conferring in Clarke's store at the foot of King Street, several blocks away. A delegation headed by William Molineux set off to inform them that the people considered their refusal to attend an affront and to demand their resignation. Most of the crowd followed along to Clarke's to see the outcome, and along the way hooted down a justice of the peace who ordered them to disperse. When the consignees replied through the open door that they would pay no attention to the demands of such an illegal gathering, most of the spectators began to drift away. Suddenly a number of them wheeled around and stormed the building before the occupants could bar the way. Wrenching the doors off their hinges, the mob rushed in, flinging stones and mud about as they came. The Clarkes and others fled to the counting-room on the second floor, where a stout door protected them. There they remained for the next hour and a half, until gradually the crowd dispersed. The consignees were later able to walk home without molestation, but they were undoubtedly shaken by their first encounter with a Boston mob.[11]

Only one note in defense of the consignees appeared that Wednesday. In the morning a handbill entitled *Tradesmen's Protest* circulated through the streets, urging the inhabitants not to attend the meeting at Liberty Tree. "AVOID THE TRAP, *Remember the Iniquitous Non-Importation Scheme*," it warned. The tradesmen allegedly supporting the plea argued that the merchants opposed the Company's importation only because the tea would sell at half the price they were now demanding for their stock. The proposed meeting was "illegal and underhanded." The method of its notification was "mean and dispicable, and smells of *Darkness* and *Deceit*. . . ." But the *Protest* had little effect and could not have given much cheer to the beleaguered consignees.[12]

Thursday's edition of the *Massachusetts Spy* brought little comfort into the lives of the Company's agents. Isaiah Thomas printed an extract of a long-delayed letter from Philadelphia that predicted "the most violent convulsions" if the tea were landed at that port. Patriots at New York were also active, the writer reported. Only Boston was in doubt. "Should they be the occasion of repressing the present spirit," he challenged the Bostonians, "it will confirm many prejudices against them and injure the common cause essentially in the future." This kind of letter could only goad the patriots into more vigorous action. Another ominous note was struck by a member of the committee chosen to meet with the consignees the day before. He had since heard criticism from some of the lower class of people that his group had failed to join in the efforts "to bring the consignees to a compliance by force" after the people's demands had been rejected. COMMITTEE MAN agreed that the consignees' action was unjustifiable but pointed out that "there was danger of lives being lost which is not to be ventured upon till the last extremity." If the consignees continued to hold out after this fair warning, however, he concluded, "the world will applaud the spirit that, for the common preservation, will exterminate such malignant and dangerous persons." In another letter CAUSIDICUS all but condoned mob rule whenever the liberties of the people were violated by any member of society. "Such a party openly dissolves the pact of society," he wrote, "turns every member loose into the primitive state of nature, and leaves every one to provide for his own security in the best manner he can." [13]

That evening Benjamin Faneuil found a threatening letter from O. C. at his house on Tremont Street. "Long have this people been irreconcilable to the idea of spilling human blood," the message read, but just recently a common thief had been executed for his crime. "You boldly avow a resolution to bear a principle [sic] part in the robbery of every inhabitant of this country," O. C. continued. The threat against Faneuil's life was but thinly veiled. Encouragements were few and far between for the consignees during these dark days. One of the Clarkes did receive from a Worcester man a letter urging them all to stand fast, but such support was rare indeed.[14]

Meanwhile a number of Bostonians had petitioned the selectmen for a special town meeting to consider what steps to take next. On Friday morning, 5 November, a very full gathering met at Faneuil Hall with John Hancock as moderator. Confusion immediately broke out when someone discovered copies of the *Tradesmen's*

Protest in the Hall. Hancock read the handbill from the chair, and the shopkeepers present, some four hundred in all, unanimously disavowed the tract. When the moderator invited comment favorable to the Company plan, no one stepped forward. Then the town endorsed the resolutions adopted by Philadelphia in mid-October, denouncing the duty on tea and calling for a steadfast opposition to the importation scheme. With that, Hancock and three others were appointed with the selectmen as a committee to demand the resignation of the consignees. After stalling for a while the Clarkes and Faneuil again refused, on the grounds that they had still not learned from the Company the exact terms of the arrangement. They would agree only to give a fuller answer to the town as soon as more complete information arrived. The young Hutchinsons had gone to Milton the evening before to avoid the unpleasantness that Pope Day generally brought. But Sam Adams headed a special committee to track them down, and it finally received a response similar to that of the Clarkes. Town meeting met again on the morning of the 6th, and when the answers were read, they were pronounced "*Daringly Affrontive* to the Town." Earlier the consignees had ignored the demands of small mobs. But now they had taken one further step: they had defied the wishes of a legal town meeting.[15]

The week following was relatively calm in Boston. Provocative letters continued to appear in the newspapers, one claiming that a company of soldiers had been ordered into town in small groups from Castle William. Another letter from Philadelphia reported that the consignees there would soon be compelled to resign, and its author revealed again the fear that Bostonians would not be so firm. Perhaps most disturbing was the publication by someone in the customhouse of figures showing how much English tea had been imported into Boston since the Townshend duty had taken effect in 1768 — over 3000 chests. This item, widely reprinted throughout America, seriously damaged Boston's already tenuous reputation as the seat of patriotism. The radicals knew that only a firm stand could regain the respect of the other colonists. One attempt by the moderate councillor James Pitts to promote a compromise failed to gain any encouragement.[16]

Behind the scenes Thomas Hutchinson prepared for the worst. In his capacity as captain general of the province, he ordered the commanding colonel of his corps of cadets to summon the company into readiness. But the colonel of the corps was John Hancock, who not surprisingly paid no heed to "so extraordinary a Mandate," as Edes and Gill termed the order. Nor could the Governor count on support from his Council. On the day of the riot at Clarke's store he had called a special session to help preserve the peace, but not enough councillors appeared to make a quorum. Rumors flew around town that picked bands would seize the consignees, perhaps to carry out the thinly veiled threat of assassination which O. C. had addressed to Benjamin Faneuil. On the 12th someone told Lieutenant-governor Oliver that such a plot was scheduled for that evening, but nothing came of it. Each night the consignees retired to the greater security of Milton and other neighboring communities. "The wicked fly when none pursue," one Bostonian perversely quoted from the Bible.[17]

On Wednesday, 17 November, Captain James Scott brought John Hancock's ship *Hayley* into Boston harbor from England. Scott was one of the shipmasters who had refused to carry any of the Company's shipment, although he had shown no such reluctance to freight dutied tea on this and numerous earlier voyages. The captain brought news that several vessels laden with East India tea had come down the Channel at the same time as he had, four of which were bound for Boston. *Hayley* carried a provocative cargo of its own in the person of Jonathan Clarke, the young Boston merchant who had worked so hard to secure a consignment of the tea for the family firm.[18]

With the arrival of Captain Scott, Bostonians knew that the tea-ships could not be far behind. Upon a petition of inhabitants the selectmen immediately ordered a town meeting for the next morning, but on Wednesday night, as the Clarkes were celebrating a family reunion at their home in School Street, a small mob called to pay its disrespects. A violent pounding on the door, accompanied by a

cacophony of horns, whistles, and catcalls, sent the ladies scurrying
to the safety of the upper stories. One of the sons went up with a
pistol, threw open a chamber window, and threatened to fire into
the crowd unless it dispersed. Perhaps this was Jonathan, freshly
home from London and unused to the recent insolence of the mob.
Some of the crowd withdrew, but others continued their demonstration. In a fit of exasperation young Clarke discharged his pistol,
fortunately without harm. Thereupon the people below went wild,
smashing in the windows, frames and all. Stones, brickbats, and
other debris flew in through the openings, badly damaging the
furniture and injuring several of the occupants. After holding out
alone for nearly an hour, the Clarkes were joined by a few friends,
who urged them to stand fast. At the height of the battle a gentleman
outside tried to bring about a compromise. The crowd agreed to
disperse if the consignees would promise to appear at the town meeting the following morning. But the Clarkes proudly refused to
bargain with a mob. Gradually the clamor subsided, and the rioters
dispersed. Once more the Clarkes had withstood the frenzy of the
people.[19]

Next morning town meeting appointed still another committee to
demand the consignees' resignation, for they were convinced that the
long-awaited Company orders must have arrived via Jonathan Clarke
the day before. But the consignees again refused. In a public an-
nouncement they released the only information they admitted to
receiving: that their London friends "have entered into Penal Engagements on our behalf, merely of a commercial nature; which puts it
out of our power to comply with the request of the Town." Again
the tea commissioners had stymied the town meeting.[20]

The consignees well knew that they could not hold out alone
much longer. They therefore drafted a petition which was submitted to the Governor and Council on 19 November. First the
agents briefly described the insults and violence they had already
suffered and then expressed their fear that the Company's tea might
be destroyed upon arrival. Finally they suggested a temporary solu-

tion. They would turn over the tea to the Governor and Council, "as the guardians and protectors of the people," so that it might be safely landed and secured. In their first draft the consignees proposed to leave the tea in government custody "in such conditions and during such time as your Excellency and Honors . . . shall direct and advise." But in the final version of the petition they agreed to leave it with the government only "until your petitioners can be at liberty, openly and safely, to dispose of the same," or until they received new instructions from the Company. The difference was important, for, given a free hand, the consignees might well have tried to market the tea as soon as opposition subsided. Hutchinson had already convened the Council on the 19th, and the consignees' petition arrived in the midst of a discussion of the recent tumults and disorders. Although a long debate ensued, the meeting adjourned until the 23rd without reaching a decision. On that day a bare quorum appeared, but action was again postponed, this time until the 27th, when the councillors once more refused to act on the petition.[21]

The Governor's Council of Massachusetts Bay was a peculiar institution. Its twenty-eight members were elected by the General Court, subject to the governor's approval. In most other colonies the Council was appointed by the Crown. After 1766 the Massachusetts Council, under the leadership of merchant James Bowdoin, tended to reflect the political views of its parent body, the lower house. For practical reasons the governor was generally unwilling to act in many important matters without the consent of this advisory body. By taking no action at all, therefore, the Council could effectively bring executive government to a halt. Edes and Gill explained the Council's position in what was probably an accurate reflection of its patriot-members' views. The laws of the province were made for the protection of the people, the editors admitted. Certainly the people would assist in the protection of every individual who was "in the Peace of God and the King." But no man can be said to be in that state "while he is attempting to overthrow the Civil

Constitution." Furthermore, the Council was only one branch of the General Assembly; protecting the people was by no means its sole responsibility. Edes and Gill then concluded:

> Their department by no means admits of their condescending to become the Trustees and Storekeepers of certain Factors for the East India Company. As well might they become the Trustees of all the Individuals, and ex officio be the Storekeepers of every Store in the province; and this it is to be feared would induce such a multiplicity of private Business as to leave them no time to do the duties of their Department, viz. The ordering and directing *the Affairs of the Province*.[22]

Throughout the last weeks of November the Boston press kept up a steady pressure against the planned importation. Letters from London asserted that the Company had millions of pounds of tea rotting in its warehouses. If the present shipment were received, many more were sure to follow. Another correspondent asserted that he would be "less alarmed at the landing of the bedding of those unhappy persons who died at Bagdat [*sic*] of the plague than one chest of the slave making TEA." If the cargo were landed, he warned, Boston's reputation would be ruined throughout the continent. This of course was exactly what Hutchinson hoped to accomplish, he concluded. The Governor came in for a bitter attack at the hands of one E. LUDLOW, who blamed him in part for passage of the Tea Act and for obtaining consignments for his sons. ARGUS cautioned against the compromise suggested by the consignees in their petition to the Council. Once the tea is landed in Boston, he pointed out, certificates would be sent to London and the tribute paid there. As all good patriots knew, this was merely a plot to force Americans into paying the duty indirectly when they purchased the tea. AN OLD CADET wrote in to justify Colonel Hancock's defiance of Hutchinson's orders. The governors of neither New York nor Pennsylvania had had to alert their militia, he twitted.[23]

Meanwhile, in order to broaden the base of opposition, the Boston committee of correspondence had invited the committees from the neighboring towns of Roxbury, Dorchester, Brookline, Cambridge, and later Charlestown, to a meeting. On Monday, 22 November, they all convened at Faneuil Hall to form a joint action committee and to draw up a ringing circular letter addressed to the other towns of the province. Here an interesting new argument was introduced. Because of declining tea sales in America, the East India Company had first tried to bring about a repeal of the duty, the letter asserted. To boost the Company's sagging American sales, North's ministry had instead hit upon the Tea Act. "Now gentlemen," the joint committee reasoned, "if the Company are prevented from reaping the advantages which they expected . . . they must still be obliged to insist upon the total repeal of that unrighteous act, and we are convinced that administration must comply with the demand. . . ." The letter concluded with a summation of all the common arguments against the plan: Parliament taxation, the threat of monopoly, and the drainage of specie from the colonies. The authors somehow estimated the loss of specie at £360,000 annually, enough to pay for about 3,000,000 pounds of tea! The Boston committee's letter brought almost immediate results. In a full meeting on the 26th, Cambridge adopted the Philadelphia resolves. At the same time, that town noted that some of the consignees had recently been retiring into the country towns each night, "where they are treated with respect." A resolution was adopted condemning all those who gave them hospitality.[24]

Worried by the continuing inaction of the Governor's Council, the consignees sounded out the Boston selectmen in an effort to bring about some compromise. Jonathan Clarke requested an appointment for his brother Isaac and himself, and they met on the afternoon of 27 November. Jonathan insisted that he had not sought the consignment of tea for his family's firm, that in fact the arrangement was very disagreeable to him. This was untrue, of course, but Clarke was now desperate. He offered to do almost anything that could in justice be demanded of him. When the selectmen argued that the people would be satisfied with nothing less than a return of the tea to London, however, Clarke objected. He pointed out that both the tea and vessel would become liable for seizure because of the law prohibiting the re-importation of tea into England. The selectmen countered with the suggestion that perhaps the Company and the consignees could protect themselves by proving the reshipment was forced upon them by circumstances beyond their control. The two camps argued back and forth at great length. Finally, Clarke said that the tea-ship would bring its cargo up to town and that it would not be clandestinely unloaded. Furthermore, as soon as he had seen the Company's instructions, Clarke would make new proposals to the selectmen. An uneasy truce had been reached at Boston.[25]

Governor Hutchinson's anxiety deepened each day. "I am in a helpless state," he had written Governor Tryon of New York on 21 November, "no person who shares any part of the Authority of Government concurring with me in Measures for the support of it." On the 24th he reviewed the situation in a letter to a friend, possibly the lieutenant-governor, Andrew Oliver. Town meeting had virtually proposed taking up arms, he claimed; tumultuous mobs freely attacked the King's subjects; others assembled nightly to propose "unlawful measures and very dark proposals." Now the infection was spreading to the neighboring towns, he gloomily pointed out, and still the Council refused to act. Hutchinson wondered aloud if duty did not require him to escape the pressure of the mob by retiring to the safety of Castle William, the island in Boston harbor where the King's troops were stationed. "The event must be left to the great disposer of all events," he concluded with resignation.[26]

On Sunday, 28 November, a bluff-bowed vessel worked its way through the outer islands off Boston and came to anchor in the sheltered waters of the harbor. It was the ship *Dartmouth*, nine weeks from London, with 114 chests of the East India Company's tea on board. Crisis was at hand.

News of *Dartmouth*'s arrival spread rapidly through the town. To the knowledge of Bostonians none of the other vessels had yet reached New York, Philadelphia, or Charleston. What they did in the next few days, they knew, might well influence events in other colonies as well as in their own. The inhabitants' resolution was firm enough — the tea must be returned to England. But Jonathan Clarke had already explained to the selectmen the legal problems involved. No tea once exported from England could be re-entered there — on pain of confiscation. Somehow the patriots would have to overcome this obstacle. Whatever was to be done had to be done quickly. Under a long-standing rule customs officers could seize dutiable goods if payment were not made within twenty days. The deadline would expire for *Dartmouth*'s cargo of tea on 17 December.[27]

To allow the cargo to land under any circumstances was inconceivable. For once the tea was ashore and the duties paid or secured in some fashion, the protest against the tax was a lost cause. The proposal to store the tea in a government warehouse pending further instructions from London was just as unacceptable. Who could trust Hutchinson or the customs officers not to turn it over to the consignees after all? Past events had proved to the patriots' embarrassment that New Englanders could not refrain from the purchase and consumption of tea for long despite their disapproval of the Townshend duty. Now, in the late autumn of 1773, there was not enough tea in Boston to meet the demand, and the price of what there was steadily rose each day. No one could be certain that the people would resist buying the East India Company's inexpensive Bohea under these circumstances.

Sunday, 28 November, was a day of tense activity in Boston. The Board of Selectmen met at noon, an extraordinary procedure for the Sabbath, hoping to head off possible violence by arranging a legal town meeting for the next day. The Board expected new proposals from the consignees, as young Clarke had promised, as soon as they had read their orders. No definite plans could be made for a town meeting until the suggestions were submitted. When no word came, a messenger was sent to Clarke's house, but he was told the consignees were out of town. The selectmen then adjourned for afternoon services and met again at five o'clock. After waiting most of the evening, they reached a relative of the Clarkes, probably

John Singleton Copley, who promised that the proposals would be submitted the next day.[28]

Already the extreme patriots were making their own plans, for the committee of correspondence had also met on Sunday, the 28th. Joseph Warren drew up a letter summoning the neighboring committees to a session at Faneuil Hall at nine o'clock the next morning. William Molineux headed a committee to urge Francis Rotch not to enter the ship *Dartmouth* at the customhouse until Tuesday. Francis was the twenty-three-year-old son of the vessel's owner, Joseph Rotch, formerly of Nantucket but now a wealthy whale-oil merchant of Dartmouth, Massachusetts. Young Rotch agreed to Molineux's demands but said he could delay entering the vessel no longer, for the Townshend Act required shipmasters to report their vessels "directly" upon arrival, although in practice they were often allowed up to forty-eight hours.[29]

Bostonians awoke Monday morning to find notices posted all over town addressed to "Friends! Brethren! Countrymen! The Hour of Destruction or Manly Opposition to the Machinations of Tyranny stares you in the Face." The notices called on all inhabitants to meet that morning at Faneuil Hall. To the pealing of church bells, hundreds and then thousands filed through the narrow streets to jam their way into the building. This was no legal town meeting, convened by a proper notification from the selectmen. In fact, Boston town meeting would not be summoned again until March 1774. This was a gathering at which all the inhabitants of Boston were welcome, and they flocked in from the surrounding towns as well. John Hancock declined serving as moderator because he expected a call at any moment to attend a session of the Governor's Council. Instead, the moderate merchant Jonathan Williams assumed the chair, and William Cooper, long-time town clerk of Boston, took over the role of secretary. Business began with a unanimous resolution that the tea should be returned to the place whence it came. Already Faneuil Hall was filled to overflowing, and as more inhabitants gathered outside, those within voted to adjourn to the larger Old South Meeting House, where more than 5000 people reconvened.

Again the meeting unanimously resolved that the tea should be sent back and without payment of the Townshend duty. It then adjourned till three o'clock to give the consignees time to think matters over.[30]

The afternoon session opened with yet another demand that the tea be returned, this time with the stipulation that it go back in the same vessel that brought it, supposedly to minimize the chance that the cargo might be landed in the process of transfer to another ship. Francis Rotch, who was present along with Captain James Hall, was told not to enter his tea at the customhouse. Rotch objected to the proceedings and announced that he would swear out a legal protest. The meeting then appointed a watch of twenty-five men to protect the cargo and the vessel, now lying at Griffin's Wharf. Ostensibly these men were to discourage mob violence, but they could just as easily be used to block any attempt by Rotch or the consignees to unload the vessel. Reports varied as to whether the men were armed; Hutchinson later insisted that they were, and most contemporary observers agreed. Late in the day the consignees sent word that they needed more time to draw up their proposals, and the meeting agreed to give them until the next morning. Just before adjournment it was learned that the Governor had ordered the justices of the peace to be on guard against tumults that night. In a sensitive mood already, the meeting denounced this act as an insult to the people of Boston. Whereupon the gathering adjourned until the next morning.[31]

Also on 29 November the Governor's Council met to consider the consignees' request for government protection of ten days before. At the last session Hutchinson had appointed James Bowdoin, Samuel Dexter, and John Winthrop a committee to prepare a report on the matter. The authors first traced the controversy over Parliamentary taxation, singling out the Townshend Act's provision for defraying the costs of government as particularly obnoxious. This was a diminution of the colony's charter rights, they claimed. Cast in this light, the Tea Act became a plot to confirm and perhaps to extend Parliamentary taxation. From this beginning Hutchinson had no difficulty guessing what was to come. If the consignees sought personal protection, the report continued, they should apply to the justices of the peace. As to the tea, the committee denied that the Council had any authority to assume responsibility for it. The Council could hardly provide for its landing, for this would violate the General Court's known sentiments in opposition to the duty. The Council of course regretted the recent tumults and advised that the perpetrators (as yet unidentified) be prosecuted.[32]

The Council did recommend that the King's peace officers should be instructed to preserve good order throughout the town. The ten councillors thereupon unanimously adopted the report, and so the Governor and consignees were left to stand alone. In mid-afternoon the two Clarke sons, Benjamin Faneuil, and Thomas Hutchinson, Jr., fled to Castle William for safety. Old Mr. Clarke was apparently in Salem; Hutchinson's other son remained at the lieutenant-governor's home in Middleborough; and the last consignee, Joshua Winslow, was safe at his house in Marshfield. Even Governor Hutchinson found it necessary from 29 November on to stay at his Milton estate whenever possible.[33]

The consignees had sent a letter, apparently before leaving town, to John Scollay, chairman of the Board of Selectmen. Only by returning the tea, they realized, could they satisfy the town, but this they were powerless to do. The consignees did agree, however, to have the cargo stored until they could write the Company and receive further instructions. When the inhabitants met again Tuesday morning, 30 November, Scollay read them the letter. They were angry that the consignees had not communicated directly with them, but Jonathan Clarke's promise was to keep in touch with the selectmen. Suddenly Sheriff Stephen Greenleaf strode in with a message from the Governor. In it Hutchinson denounced the assembly as illegal and ordered those present to disperse forthwith. A loud hiss filled the hall, and the company voted to ignore the Governor's proclamation.[34]

Until then the sessions had been calm, moving in orderly fashion from one motion to the next. But now the hours of frustration had begun to tell, and a restless spirit seemed to sweep through the house. At that point John Singleton Copley spoke up in an attempt to bring about some sort of compromise. Although known to be sympathetic with his in-laws, the Clarkes, the young artist was nonetheless respected as a man of moderation. If he could persuade the consignees to appear at the meeting, he proposed, would those present promise them safety and a fair hearing? The assemblage agreed, and Copley was given two hours to bring the agents in from the Castle. While waiting for his return, the company spent the time presenting still more resolutions. Messrs. Rotch and Hall were again summoned, and this time pledges were demanded that they return the tea to London on board *Dartmouth*. Although they reluctantly agreed, again Rotch announced he would protest the proceedings. Agents for the other tea-ships gave similar assurances for the cargo on board their vessels which had not yet arrived. Plans for continuing the watch were made with warning signals arranged in case of trouble, and experienced riders volunteered to carry the alarm into the countryside if necessary. The inhabitants were preparing against the possibility that Hutchinson would attempt to land the tea by force.[35]

Late that afternoon Copley returned from the Castle, alone. Although the consignees were confident of their safety, he reported, they saw no point in coming before the meeting. As they had said in their letter to Scollay, it was not in their power to return the tea. They did renew their offer to have it stored, however, this time under the inspection of a committee. Copley then made an eloquent appeal to the assemblage. The consignees would be ruined if forced to return the tea, he argued, but they would not interfere if the people themselves sent it back. Nor would they make any attempt to unload the cargo. Copley denied the charge that the consignees were tools of the Governor and were simply following his orders. Few present doubted that the influence of the Governor was strong, however, and later Copley warned the consignees not to discuss the question of tea with Hutchinson even if he joined them at the Castle. Although the meeting voted that the consignees' reply was still unsatisfactory, Copley thought that the feeling against them had moderated somewhat. With one more resolution against the importation of dutied tea and instructions to send a report of their proceedings to the neighboring ports as well as to New York, Philadelphia, and London, the inhabitants of Boston and vicinity adjourned their extraordinary sessions of 29 and 30 November.[36]

These mass gatherings were admittedly not legal town meetings. The patriots called the assemblage "the Body," and when recording the minutes Clerk Cooper had to catch himself several times from using the term "the town." Why did the patriots insist on these sessions instead of settling the question in a regular town meeting? One reason might have been that they considered the town government too cautious. After all, the selectmen were well-established figures, mostly men of considerable means, particularly the merchants John Scollay, John Hancock, and Oliver Wendell. Scollay himself had shown by his efforts to arrange a regular town meeting for the 29th that he preferred to handle matters legally. There is no evidence to indicate, however, that an actual split existed between the radical organization and the selectmen. The committee of correspondence, for instance, regularly held its sessions in the selectmen's room at Faneuil Hall, and many town officers counted themselves in the radical camp.

But a town meeting did have its limitations for the sort of task facing the Boston patriots in late November. In the first place, participation was technically restricted to qualified voters, perhaps about two-thirds of the adult male population. For Boston, with a population of about 20,000 in 1773, this would mean around 2500 men. To be sure, Hutchinson often complained that the legal requirements were regularly ignored. But the consignees had already twice rejected demands from town meeting to resign. On the 28th the selectmen seemed equally powerless to compel a response. A demonstration of grass-roots opposition to the tea plan might be more impressive. By calling a mass meeting the radicals broadened the base of protest to include non-voters and even inhabitants from neighboring towns. Possibly Sam Adams realized he could better manipulate such a gathering.

There was another advantage to an extra-legal meeting. It might be more difficult for the authorities to hold the town of Boston legally responsible if violence resulted. Governor Hutchinson reported, in fact, that "a Lawyer and high Son of Liberty," perhaps John Adams, had advised the earlier town meeting not to meddle with the tea lest it be made liable for the consequences. "[He] left the audience to suppose he thought it a matter more proper to be taken in hand by the people who assembled without colour of Law. . . ." [37]

Despite the fact that over 5000 people attended, the meetings in late November were far from being mob scenes. Observers praised the calm deliberations of the body. Hugh Williamson, a visitor from Philadelphia, reported that a few men made inflammatory speeches but that the leaders present were determined to prevent any measures that would endanger the tea. He would have thought himself to be in "the British Senate . . . were I not convinced . . . that they were not yet corrupted by venality, or debauched by luxury," he added. Even Hutchinson was forced to concede that, although the meetings consisted primarily of "the lower ranks of people . . . , yet there were divers gentlemen of good fortune among them. . . ." Despite its illegality Hutchinson admitted the impossibility of breaking up the meeting. He could have found no justice willing to require the sheriff to raise the posse, and, besides, so many of the townspeople were present that "no other Posse except the meeting itself would have appeared. . . ." [38]

The fact that the consignees at Boston had refused to resign their commissions proved to be of great significance. More important, they were supported in their obstinacy by a governor determined not to give way to popular pressure. In none of the other ports to which the Company's tea was dispatched had the consignees and the government officials combined to offer a united front against the patriots' demands. By 2 December, in the other ports, the Company's agents had all resigned. If a showdown on the tea issue were to come at all, it would have to come at Boston.

VII

THE BOSTON TEA PARTY

WHEN the inhabitants of Boston demanded on 29 November that the ship *Dartmouth* carry its cargo of tea out of the harbor, duties unpaid, they apparently believed that only an order from the owner's representative, Francis Rotch, was necessary to send the vessel on its way. But legal technicalities made the situation far more complicated than the patriots had at first imagined.

Under the terms of the Townshend Act tea become liable to a duty upon importation into America. But what constituted "importation"? Did goods become imported as soon as they arrived in the harbor, or not until they had been entered at the customhouse, or only when they were actually landed at a wharf? The Townshend Act did not deal specifically with this question, but it did incorporate a part of the Sugar Act of 1733 which implied that importation preceded entry — that goods became imported upon arrival.[1]

Even if arrival did not constitute importation, entry at the customhouse evidently did. And by both the Sugar Act and the Townshend Act the master of every vessel arriving in America was required to "come directly" to the customhouse and make entry of his ship and cargo before proceeding to a wharf for unlading. Failure to comply was punishable by a fine of £100. By Massachusetts law, more specifically, incoming masters had forty-eight hours in which to report to the colony's commissioner of impost, and they had to do so before breaking bulk. By an act of Parliament of 1662, made applicable to the colonies in 1696, customs officers could seize goods for which duties had not been paid "within twenty days after the first entry of the ship." "First entry" may have meant entry at the customhouse, although most contemporaries seemed to think it meant "arrival." The law implied, however, that once the twenty-day period did begin, the cargo could neither be landed nor cleared for export until the duties were paid.[2]

The arrival of the ship *Dartmouth* in Boston harbor on 28 November 1773 probably in itself made the tea on board liable to payment of the Townshend duty. Certainly that arrival required Captain Hall to enter his cargo at the customhouse, which in turn definitely made the cargo liable to payment. The only way this liability could have been avoided was for the vessel and its tea not to have legally arrived at all. Writing some years later about the events leading to the Boston Tea Party, Governor Hutchinson made essentially this point. He wrote:

> The Governor, forseeing the difficulty that must attend this affair, advised the consignees to order the vessels when they arrived, to anchor below the Castle; that if it should appear unsafe to land the tea, they might go to sea again; and when the first ship arrived, she anchored accordingly; but when the master came up to town, Mr. [Samuel] Adams and others, a committee of the town, ordered him, at his peril, to bring the ship up to land the other goods, but to suffer no tea to be taken out. The ship being entered, the Custom-house Officers would not clear her out until the duty on the tea was paid.

Hutchinson's statement implied that as long as *Dartmouth* remained anchored "below the Castle," she had not actually arrived in Boston harbor. Its cargo of tea was thus not liable to the duty, and the captain was not required to make an entry at the customhouse. According to Hutchinson it was only when the patriots forced Captain Hall to bring his vessel up to town that entry had to be made and the duties paid. This was a serious charge, for it suggested that Adams had planned from the start to force the detention of *Dartmouth* and thus precipitate a crisis. Writing to former Governor Bernard in early January, Hutchinson in fact suggested that the patriots had planned on the destruction of the tea from the beginning.[3]

A close examination of *Dartmouth*'s journal, however, suggests that Hutchinson's account of what happened during the last days of November was erroneous. Arriving off the harbor at sunset on Saturday, the 27th, Captain Hall brought his vessel to anchor near the lighthouse, and early the next morning a pilot came on board. At 6 a.m. on the 28th *Dartmouth* got under way, "turned up Ship Channel, and came to anchor in King's Road," which de Costa's map of Boston harbor shows to be the area inside Deer Island to the north of Spectacle Island and just below the Castle, now known as President's Road. This maneuver probably took about two hours. *Dartmouth* was now actually within the limits of Boston harbor. As defined by the customs collector in 1768, Boston harbor included all of the area bounded on the north by Point Shirley ("Pudding Point") and Hingham on the south. Both Nantasket and King's Roads were therefore included.[4]

At 11 a.m. on the 28th Hall again got under way and "turned up and came to anchor under the Admiral's stern." According to its log, the flagship *Captain* had been moored since June in the inner harbor, some 400 yards off the Long Wharf. That evening, the journal continues, "two Custom-house Officers were boarded upon us by [i.e., from?] the Castle, we being the first ship ever boarded in this manner, which happened on account of our having the East India Company's *accursed dutiable Tea* on board." Normally a vessel would not be boarded until entry had been made at the customhouse and the ship had been berthed at a wharf. But this was not a normal situation. Captain Hall had no choice of making entry or not, for with customhouse officers on board, his vessel was clearly under the jurisdiction of the port authorities.[5]

According to the ship's journal, *Dartmouth* remained at anchor under the Admiral's stern throughout Monday, the 29th. The report in the *Boston Post-boy* for that date, that on the morning of the 29th the vessel came up and anchored off the Long Wharf, must therefore have been an erroneous account. The ship's journal for the 29th noted that Captain Hall went ashore, apparently for the first time, as there is no earlier entry that he had left the vessel. That night at 9 p.m., the patriots' guard of twenty-five men came on board. On Tuesday, the 30th, after entering his ship at the custom-house, Captain Hall once again weighed anchor and "turned up to Rowe's Wharf," a maneuver that involved passing between Dorchester flats and Fort Hill into what is now Fort Point Channel. On the day following, *Dartmouth* was warped around to nearby Griffin's Wharf, where the sails and cables were put ashore. Hall then began to unload all of his cargo except the tea.[6]

When Captain Hall came up to town on the 29th, therefore, Sam Adams could not have ordered him to bring the vessel in past the Castle. The ship's journal indicates that by that time *Dartmouth* was already in the harbor and under the jurisdiction of the custom-house. Furthermore, the Governor's accusation is wholly unsubstantiated by contemporary evidence. Both Hall and Rotch freely testified before the Privy Council in February 1774, but neither one suggested that the patriots had forced the vessel to enter the harbor. The charge is not to be found in any of Hutchinson's many contemporary letters. Nor is there any evidence to support his claim that he had advised the consignees to hold the vessel below the Castle.

What seems to have happened during those critical days is as follows. By the time the patriots learned on 28 November that *Dartmouth* had arrived, the vessel was already on its way in past the Castle. The committee of correspondence therefore sent a deputation to demand that Rotch postpone reporting the vessel at the custom-house until the last possible moment, Tuesday morning, in order to keep open the possibility of returning the tea to England. For once the ship was legally entered, it was unlikely that the customhouse officers would grant the clearance necessary for its departure until the duties on the tea were paid. Even the fact that the ship was now above the Castle put the patriots in a weak position, for no vessel could run by the batteries of Fort William if the Governor did not wish to grant its owner a pass to depart. But delay in reporting the ship at the customhouse would at least allow enough time for the mass meeting scheduled for the next day to demand that the tea be sent back via *Dartmouth*. Perhaps the consignees and Governor would then accede to the weight of public opinion and agree to its return.

But the consignees had already fled to the Castle, out of the reach of the mob. When they finally sent word to the meeting via John Singleton Copley on the 30th, they refused to order the tea returned. It was already too late anyway, for that morning Hall had had to report his vessel at the customhouse. The patriots now faced a new problem. As long as *Dartmouth* was anchored under the guns of the fleet, it was possible for Hutchinson to request that a detachment of marines overpower the small band of patriots on board and unload the cargo by force. To prevent this the committee of correspondence demanded that Hall bring his vessel "up to town," that is, up to one of the wharves, where the mob could be called upon to help prevent a landing. This was what Jonathan Clarke had told the selectmen would be done when he and his brother had met with them on Saturday, the 27th. In a letter written to Lord Dartmouth in early January, Hutchinson stated that the owners and masters of all the tea-vessels "say they were compelled to bring their ships to the wharves and keep them there." John Rowe, owner of *Eleanor*, noted that on 3 December the committee of correspondence ordered Captain Bruce to bring the vessel up to Griffin's Wharf, giving him "the same Directions as Capt. Hall." [7]

In his testimony before the Privy Council, Hall stated that "upon his arrival he received orders from his owner not to bring his vessel up to town." Rotch at first apparently preferred to leave his vessel under the protection of the fleet. But after making his entry at the customhouse Tuesday morning, Hall complied with the patriots' demand and brought his vessel "up to town" — that is, to Rowe's Wharf. Why he did this is uncertain. If he was threatened with the tar-and-feathers treatment, he made no mention of it in his testimony. It was probably this movement of *Dartmouth* to which Hutchinson referred in his later writings quoted above. With the ship now at Rowe's Wharf, the mob could reinforce the armed guard in preventing a forcible landing of the tea. Admiral Montagu could not use his guns without firing on the town itself. *Dartmouth*'s subsequent move to Griffin's Wharf perhaps took place at the insistence of moderate merchant John Rowe, who hoped to avoid a scene at his wharf.[8]

Rotch may finally have had understandable reasons for agreeing to order *Dartmouth* up to town despite his earlier directions. On board besides the tea was a mixed cargo of winter goods for various Boston merchants. Rotch and Hall were responsible for its delivery. In addition, Rotch was expecting the arrival of some whale oil from southern Massachusetts to be shipped on *Dartmouth*'s return passage to London. He wanted his vessel to arrive there in time to load a cargo of spring goods for Boston. Although Rotch sympathized with the consignees, their dilemma was not his fight. His objective was to clear his vessel for England as soon as possible. Keeping his vessel at anchor out in the harbor was no way to achieve this end. Rotch therefore had good reason to comply with the patriots' demand that *Dartmouth* be brought up to a wharf.[9]

Even without overwhelming evidence that *Dartmouth* was already above the Castle on the 28th, it is unlikely that the patriots would have ordered Hall to bring the vessel into the inner harbor. By the testimony of many witnesses including Hutchinson himself, their intention from the beginning was to force the ship to return its tea to London, an objective made far more difficult if *Dartmouth* had to pass the Castle on its way out. By the same token, however, the Governor and the consignees had good reason to want the vessel inside Castle William, for they obviously wanted the tea landed.[10]

In his *History of Massachusetts-Bay* Hutchinson later noted that in mid-November a member of his Council had told him that "if the ships came into the harbor above the Castle; they could not pass by it again without a permit under his [the governor's] hand." The councillor used this argument in an attempt to persuade Hutchinson to stop the vessels below the Castle so that they could return to England without the necessity of a pass. Despite the Governor's later statement, it is unlikely that Hutchinson would have given in to the patriots as easily as this. He had, after all, ample reason to want a showdown. His correspondence of early December reveals that with *Dartmouth* in harbor he thought he had the advantage over the patriots. In his letter to Governor Tryon written on 1 December he reported that, although Rotch promised the town to send his vessel out with the tea within twenty days, "this cant be done as she can neither be cleared here nor entered in England." He went on to point out that Rotch's agreement with the body should be viewed as "an expedient to gain time, for it is expected the Tea will be sold at New York and that it will make it easier to do it here." At the end of the letter Hutchinson made his own position clear. "I hope the Gentlemen [consignees] will continue firm." In another letter written on the 9th, Hutchinson remained determined to stop *Dartmouth* at the Castle if the vessel attempted to depart without a pass. It was the Governor, in fact, who prepared the way for the consignees' retreat to the Castle, and on several occasions he wrote of his readiness to flee there himself. These are hardly the plans of someone trying to avoid a showdown. Even after the tea was destroyed, Hutchinson expressed satisfaction that he had not given in to the patriots.[11]

With the ship *Dartmouth* safely in port, Hutchinson and the consignees were content to wait out the patriots, for they believed that time was on their side. If the patriots did not back down by 17 December, the customs officers would seize and land the cargo, supported by His Majesty's army and navy if necessary. Or so it appeared to Hutchinson and the consignees.

The patriots also realized that Hutchinson now held the upper hand. The Customs Commissioners and the consignees had safely retired to Castle William, beyond reach of the mob. Threats of tarring and feathering could no longer be relied upon to compel their surrender to the radicals' demands. But the Bostonians' position was not entirely hopeless, for they no longer stood alone in the battle to prevent the landing of the tea. Following the strong resolves of Cambridge on 26 November, other neighboring towns held meetings to join the opposition. Dorchester, Brookline, Roxbury, and Charlestown quickly fell into line. By mid-December, communities as distant as Newburyport, Worcester, and Plymouth had taken firm stands.[12]

The radicals' position within Boston itself was similarly strong. By categorically rejecting all suggestions that the tea be stored, the public meetings at the end of November had squelched whatever chance the moderates had of effecting a compromise. Furthermore, as long as the King's troops remained at the Castle (there was only one regiment there), the patriots ruled Boston's streets and waterfront. *Dartmouth* and its cargo remained under guard at Griffin's Wharf. When the ship *Eleanor* came in on 2 December with more tea, the committee of correspondence ordered its Captain Bruce to bring the vessel to the same wharf, so that a separate watch would not be needed. The brig *Beaver*, the third tea-ship, was reported off Boston on the 7th, but it brought smallpox as well as tea and had to lie below at Rainsford's Island for cleansing and smoking. On the 15th, she too joined her companion vessels at Griffin's Wharf. On the day previous, the committee of correspondence learned from the town of Sandwich that the fourth and last tea-ship, the Clarkes' brig *William*, had come ashore on the back side of Cape Cod, the vessel a total loss but the cargo salvable.[13]

Lest the armed guard prove an insufficient deterrent to the landing of the tea, the patriots issued periodic warnings. Anyone concerned with unloading the vessels would be treated "as Wretches unworthy to live and will be made the first victims of our just Resentment," a notice signed THE PEOPLE proclaimed on 2 December. A RANGER wrote in bellicose language that the Americans were experienced fighters. It would be best to let our enemies from Britain land without opposition, he advised. Then "we can *bush fight* them and cut off their officers very easily, and in this way we can subdue them with very little loss," — the way the Indians ambushed General Braddock, he added unkindly. On the 7th the *Essex Gazette* printed a report that the people in and around Boston, "if opposed in their Proceedings with Respect to the Tea, are determined upon hazarding a Brush." All those willing to help out should get suitably prepared. This item was reprinted in the *Boston Gazette* for 13 December, but the inhabitants there were apparently already making their own preparations. "Twould puzzle any person to purchase a pair of p[isto]ls in town," wrote John Andrews on 1 December, "as they are all bought up, with a full determination to repell force by force." Admiral Montagu, commander of the British squadron lying in Boston harbor, was struck by the military bearing of the patriots' armed guard, which patrolled the waterfront, "like Sentinels in a garrison," he reported.[14]

The radicals were not alone in their efforts to break the impasse. Francis Rotch, owner of the ship *Dartmouth*, wanted to load his cargo of whale oil and clear his vessel outward as soon as possible. Each day the ship lay at Griffin's Wharf with tea in its hold cost him money. Rotch later estimated his loss on this account at a generous £120, which he added to the freight bill submitted to the consignees. The young shipowner decided to cover himself by demanding that the consignees take their tea off his hands. Accompanied by Captain Hall and a notary public to witness the proceedings, he journeyed out to Castle William on 7 December for a confrontation. He was ready to deliver the tea, Rotch told the consignees; were they ready to receive it? To do so was out of their power, they replied, because of the town's resolves against landing the tea and the presence of an armed guard on board. As one of them later put it: "being surrounded with Cannon we have [torn: given?] them such answers as we shou'd not have dared to do in any other situation." Rotch then demanded the bill of lading, to release him from responsibility, and payment for the freight bill, about £69. The consignees refused. Four days later Captain Bruce of the ship *Eleanor* made a similar trip to the Castle, with the same results. Both Rotch and Bruce lodged protests, and Bruce went one step further to protest the committee of correspondence for prohibiting him from landing his tea. At least the record would show that they had both tried to deliver their cargoes.[15]

When Bruce went out to the Castle, he took with him a curious proposal from John Rowe, the wealthy merchant who owned *Eleanor*.

Rowe apparently learned that the Hutchinsons, at least, were unable to raise enough cash to pay their share of the tea duties. Now he offered to lend them the sum needed, "rather then [than] the Affair be kept up in Anger in the Minds of the People." It is difficult to see how payment of the duties could have brought a peaceful settlement to the crisis, unless the consignees were then to permit the ship-owners to carry the tea elsewhere. In any event, nothing came of Rowe's effort at compromise, if that indeed was what the offer was.[16]

Rotch had another dilemma to face. At the November meetings of the body he had been pressured into promising that he would send *Dartmouth* back to England with the tea on board. As the days of early December slipped by, however, it became obvious to all that he would be unable to honor his agreement. On the 9th the committee of correspondence summoned Rotch to explain the delay. Had he requested a permit at the customhouse? he was asked. No, was the reply, but he was satisfied from his conversation with some of the customs officers that a request would be turned down in any case. The committee told him to make the attempt anyway, and to protest the subsequent refusal if necessary. "The sooner these steps were taken by him the better," added the patriots. But Rotch was apparently reluctant to take such measures. On the 11th the committee of correspondence sent him a warning that "the people are greatly alarmed with the reports that he is making no preparation for carrying his Engagements . . . into Execution." Still Rotch refused to confront the customs officials.[17]

As the twenty-day deadline approached, Boston grew tense with excitement. Monday, 13 December, was a critical day. The patriots had already heard that New York's consignees had relinquished all responsibility for the tea expected there, and now they learned by letter from Philadelphia that its consignees had resigned outright. To the Bostonians' knowledge none of the other tea-ships had yet arrived, and so they had no precedents on which to base their actions. In fact, the tea-ship for South Carolina had already entered at Charleston, but Bostonians would not know of the outcome there for two more weeks. The letter from Philadelphia was particularly disturbing, for its author chose this occasion to chide Boston for its past sins of importing duties tea. "You have failed us . . . and we fear you will suffer this [tea] to be landed [also]," he wrote. Even if you allow the vessels to unload the rest of their cargo (as in fact had already been done), "you may depend it will be told in Philadelphia that you smuggled the tea [ashore] too." [18]

Edes and Gill printed other provocative articles in the *Gazette* that day. One writer, over the preposterous signature HONONCHRO-TONTHOLOGOS, described the military preparations allegedly undertaken by the King's forces. Colonel Leslie's soldiers had charged the cannon at Castle William and had even established an artillery battery at Governor's Island, on the other side of the main channel. Admiral Montagu had maneuvered his fleet into an alarming position, the writer continued. Apparently the government was preparing to cram the East India Company's tea down the Bostonians' throats by force. The author was at least partly right. On the 8th Hutchinson had told the Admiral to guard against the possibility that *Dartmouth* would be taken out of Boston harbor without a clearance. Montagu thereupon ordered his warships to block all ship-channels not commanded by the battery at Castle William. [19]

The Boston committee of correspondence had already called a meeting of representatives from the five neighboring towns for Monday, the 13th. The sessions began at nine in the morning, ran through the afternoon, and continued well into the evening. Although the committee minutes reported "no business transacted matter of record," important plans were made that day. The committee called Rotch before it to ask whether he intended carrying out his promise to dispatch *Dartmouth* to London. Now the young merchant stiffened his resistance. He had sought the advice of the best legal counsel — no less than John Adams and Sampson Salter Blowers, in fact. Perhaps the lawyers told him that, if he ordered the ship to depart without a clearance, his vessel would be liable for seizure. Rotch protested that he had earlier acquiesced only because he had been compelled to do so. The committee then decided to call yet another

mass gathering to demand the return of the tea to England. Perhaps the patriots also made tentative plans for their course of
action in the likely event that the meeting failed of its objective.[20]

On Tuesday morning, 14 December, several thousand inhabitants
from Boston and vicinity gathered once more at Old South. Emphasizing the presence of those from neighboring towns, the meeting
chose as its moderator Samuel P. Savage of Weston. Captain Bruce
of the ship *Eleanor* was asked whether he would demand a clearance
for his vessel. Bruce, a hot-headed chap of strong Tory sentiments,
reluctantly said he would, as soon as he had unloaded all his other
cargo. But in response perhaps to a demand that he leave even
without a clearance, he expressed alarm at the presence of 32-pounders
on Castle Island.[21]

When Francis Rotch was summoned before the body, he received
rougher handling for having stalled so long in carrying out the
patriots' earlier demands. He finally agreed to request a clearance
for *Dartmouth*, and a committee of ten, including Sam Adams, went
with him late in the afternoon to the collector's lodgings. That
official, Richard Harrison, had had previous experience with Boston's
patriots. In June 1768 he had accompanied his father, Joseph Harrison, then collector, on the difficult mission of seizing John Hancock's
sloop *Liberty* for a technical violation of the Acts of Trade. A mob
had gathered, and young Harrison was dragged through the streets
and pelted with rocks and filth until rescued by friends. With these
and other memories of rough treatment Harrison was not likely to
sympathize with the patriots' demands that he grant a clearance
for *Dartmouth* and its cargo of tea. Harrison declined giving an
immediate answer but promised to make his decision by the following morning. Upon learning this, the body adjourned until Thursday,
16 December, the last day before the twenty-day period for payment
of the duties expired.[22]

Harrison wished to consult with the comptroller, Robert Hallowell,
before making his decision. The two officials must have discussed the
situation long into the evening. The simple fact of the matter was
that the Townshend Act levied a duty on all teas imported into the

colonies. The tea on board *Dartmouth* had certainly been entered at the customhouse; therefore it obviously had been imported. Furthermore, Collector Harrison probably knew that the tea on board *Dartmouth* could not legally be re-entered in England. Perhaps it seemed beyond his authority to issue a clearance for what in fact would have been an illegal voyage. Even if Harrison thought he had some discretionary powers in the matter, he probably saw no reason why he should give in to the demands of the Bostonians.

Francis Rotch and escorts returned on Wednesday morning, 15 December, to learn Harrison's decision. The shipowner took the opportunity to explain that his demand for a clearance was made under duress. Harrison turned to him. "Then it is you make the demand?" he asked. "Yes," was the reply, "I am compelled at my peril to." Harrison then announced that since *Dartmouth* had entered with dutiable goods on board for which payment had not been made, "it is impossible for me to grant you any clearance for her whatever, it being utterly inconsistent with my duty." He cited no law, no regulation, no precedent for his decision, no reason other than his duty. Possibly Harrison was influenced by the obvious fact that Rotch made his request only under duress. Rebuffed by Harrison, the shipowner next called on the colony's naval officer who was authorized to issue permits allowing outward-bound vessels, once cleared by the customhouse, to pass Castle William. But *Dartmouth* had no such clearance, and the naval officer not surprisingly refused to grant Rotch a let-pass.[23]

On Thursday, 16 December, more than 5000 inhabitants of Boston and vicinity crowded into Old South at 10 a.m. Nearly 2000 had come in from the country towns, and once again Samuel P. Savage presided. Outside a cold rain was falling steadily. Everyone present knew that the next day the customs officers would be free to seize *Dartmouth*'s cargo. No one doubted that the consignees would then gladly pay the duties, and the tea would be landed. What should be done? One observer, signing himself W. T. in a letter to Sam Adams that day, advised the patriots not to obstruct the customs officers but to allow them to land the tea the next day. He pointed out that the patriots would know who bought it at auction and could deal with the purchasers accordingly. Rotch could then be driven out of town, and any owners who dared bring new shipments of tea would be treated as harshly. When word of Boston's opposition reached London, the East India Company would make no further shipments of tea to that port. But to destroy the present cargo would simply bring Boston's enemies down upon it to seek revenge. W. T.'s proposal was of course impractical; the radicals had too often demanded that the tea be returned to back down now. And all observers agreed that the body was unanimous in its intention to prevent its landing whatever the consequences.[24]

Soon after the meeting convened, the hapless Rotch was again called upon to order the departure of his vessel, even without a proper clearance. Once more he explained why he could not do so, and he even refused to lodge a protest against the customhouse. Only one peaceful way out of the impasse remained. The body instructed Rotch to go next to the Governor himself and demand a permit allowing *Dartmouth* to pass safely by the Castle. Hutchinson was at his country place in Milton, seven miles distant, out of reach of the mob. In order to give Rotch time for the journey, the meeting adjourned until 3:00 p.m. Rotch set out to confront Governor Thomas Hutchinson.[25]

Hutchinson had successfully held out against the demands of the patriots throughout the mounting crisis. He had no intention of backing down now. On the 15th he had written Lord Dartmouth that a provincial law of over seventy years' standing prevented him from issuing passes to vessels not cleared by the customhouse. He therefore had his answer ready. When Rotch arrived, the Governor asked what he thought the people were planning to do. The shipowner replied that they still demanded the return of the tea but went on to suggest that some of the patriots might be satisfied if his vessel proceeded as far as the Castle, only to be halted there by a shot across its bow. At least the people could then claim they had made every effort to send back the tea, and they might submit to its seizure by force. Writing to Lord Dartmouth five days before, the Reverend

William Gordon seemed to think the Bostonians would accept such a "solution," provided the tea were then stored in the Castle.[26]

The scheme apparently appealed to Hutchinson as a possible way out of the impasse. He offered to give Admiral Montagu the appropriate instructions for taking the vessel under his protection until it could be made ready for sea. This would involve towing *Dartmouth* back out under the guns of the Admiral's fleet, however, and at that point Rotch balked. It would be impossible to find the men necessary for such a maneuver, he concluded, and, besides, the mob would surely punish him for his treachery. Rotch may have already considered moving *Dartmouth* away from the wharf. Captain Hall later testified that some gentlemen had made the suggestion to him "a short time before the Tea was destroyed." Hall concluded that these men suspected what was about to happen. When Rotch rejected the idea, Hutchinson was left with no alternative. He refused to grant a pass for *Dartmouth* on the grounds that it had not been properly cleared by the customhouse. To permit it to sail out of Boston harbor would be aiding a violation of the Acts of Trade. Wearily the young merchant headed back to Boston and the crowd at Old South.[27]

The body reconvened at 3 p.m. as scheduled, but Rotch had not yet returned from Milton. To keep the people occupied, the leaders proposed resolutions condemning the use of tea as "improper and pernicious," and reiterating the determination to oppose its landing. Adams, Warren, Young, and other patriots spoke warmly on the subject. Then young Josiah Quincy, Jr., rose to address the inhabitants. In the only fragment of his speech remaining, Quincy excoriated Boston's enemies for their "malice, inveteracy, and insatiable revenge." Despite this harsh language, however, his message advised cautious deliberation "before we advance to those measures which must bring on the most trying and terrific struggle this country ever saw." When Rotch failed to return by 5 p.m., the body clamored for action and voted to dissolve the meeting. But the moderates present apparently were apprehensive about what was coming next and pleaded that the company remain until Rotch arrived with the Governor's decision. An hour's extension was reluctantly granted.[28]

When Rotch returned to Old South at 5:45, it was nearly dark. A few candles gave a dim light to the large hall. As Rotch announced that the Governor had refused to grant a pass, cries of "A mob! A mob!" rent the air. Order was quickly restored, and Thomas Young spoke up in defense of Rotch; he pointed out that Rotch had made every effort to comply with the people's demands. Young asked that Rotch's person and property be left unharmed. The shipowner was then asked two final questions. Would he order his vessel back to England with the tea on board? Rotch replied that he could not do so, for it would result in his ruin. Did he intend to unload the tea? He replied that he would attempt to do so only if properly called upon by the authorities and then only to protect himself.[29]

Samuel Adams rose at that point to proclaim that he did not see what more the inhabitants could do to save their country. Perhaps this was a prearranged signal. From the gallery came a war-whoop, answered in kind by a small group at the doorway who were disguised as Indians. Witnesses later recalled some of the shouts that filled the hall: "Boston harbor a tea-pot tonight!" "Hurrah for Griffin's Wharf!" "The Mohawks are come!" "Every man to his tent!" The noise was loud enough to startle John Andrews, a merchant who, ironically, was sipping a cup of tea at his house three blocks away. Andrews hastened to Old South but was unable to get through the crowd at the door. Just then the meeting dissolved. As the throng pushed out, the din reached deafening proportions. "You'd have thought that the inhabitants of the infernal regions had broke loose," recalled Andrews. He himself calmly headed home to finish his tea as other citizens not at the meeting now flocked to the scene. Down Milk Street they swept, and into Hutchinson Street. Finally the crowd reached Griffin's Wharf. Alongside were the ships *Dartmouth* and *Eleanor*, each with 114 chests of tea on board. Anchored nearby was the brig *Beaver*, with 112 chests. Altogether the three vessels held over 90,000 pounds of dutied tea, worth about £9000.[30]

The idea of destroying the East India Company's tea had probably been a last resort in the minds of many patriots ever since the arrival of *Dartmouth* at the end of November. At the meeting on the 29th,

Thomas Young had openly proposed the measure, but more moderate views prevailed for a time. As the deadline for payment of the duties approached, however, the extremists had their way. Tentative plans were probably made at the all-day session of committee of correspondence members from Boston and the neighboring towns, which met at Faneuil Hall on Monday, 13 December. Many members of the Boston committee also belonged to other groups — the North End Caucus, the Long Room Club, and the Grand Lodge of Masons — which may have had a role in the planning as well. The "Big Three" among the patriots, Sam Adams, Joseph Warren, and William Molineux, were all members of the Long Room. These clubs undoubtedly supported the proposed action at their meetings in mid-December, but final responsibility seems to have rested with the committee of correspondence.[31]

Just who took active roles in the Boston Tea Party remains one of the mysteries of American history. A half-century later John Adams wrote that he did not know the identity of a single participant. The unparalleled secrecy which enshrouded their names for years afterwards has inevitably encouraged the growth of family tradition. One list of those active at Griffin's Wharf was supplied by an alleged participant when he was 93 years old; another recorded his reminiscences at the age of 113, seventy-five years after the event. Most of these recollections contain obvious inaccuracies and contradictions. But taken in the aggregate and modified by the more reliable contemporary accounts, they furnish us our only source for surmising what sorts of men took part in destroying the tea that evening.[32]

The decks of the tea-ships were familiar to many of the active participants who had served among the armed bands guarding the vessels since their arrival. Some of these men were members of Hancock's corps of cadets — Hancock himself was seen inspecting the watch on board one of the vessels in early December. Others present that night were Masons, whose organization to this day proudly points to its role in the Boston Tea Party. The Lodge's meeting scheduled for that Thursday evening immediately adjourned "on account of the few members in attendance." Most of the participants, of course, were also members of the loosely organized Sons of Liberty. Some, however, apparently had no prior knowledge that plans had been made to destroy the tea. They simply showed up — for reasons ranging from well-meaning patriotism to the quest for excitement.[33]

And so they gathered along Boston's waterfront. In the van were small groups of men roughly disguised as Indians, in most cases with no more than a dab of paint and with an old blanket wrapped about them. The reason why they dressed this way and called themselves Mohawks is unknown, although they may have learned of the notice signed THE MOHAWKS which had appeared in New York in late November. Others had dabbed soot or dirt on their faces to conceal their identities. They had come from various parts of town. One band allegedly donned its regalia in the back room of Benjamin Edes's house. Another group held its rendezvous in a store on neighboring Fort Hill. The Lebanon Club, seventeen men whose survivors later stated they had come from Maine expressly to destroy the tea, made its preparations at a tavern near the wharf. Others gathered at street corners and private homes.[34]

Family tradition has claimed a role in the Tea Party for men of all ranks. Thomas Melvill, a Princeton graduate with an M.A. from Harvard, was a young businessman in Boston. His presence at Griffin's Wharf was attested to by the tea found in his boots the following morning. Another merchant reportedly active that night was Lendall Pitts, whose brother John served on the committee of correspondence. But most alleged participants were artisans. James Brewer, blockmaker, offered his house on Summer Street as a meeting-place for some of his friends. There Mrs. Brewer helped blacken their faces with burnt cork and sent them on their way. John Crane, Thomas Bolter, and Samuel Fenno, all housewrights, are said to have met at Crane's house on the corner of Hollis and Tremont streets. After joining their neighbors, the Bradlee brothers, they hastened to the waterfront. Some were young apprentices, like Peter Slater and Robert Sessions, who appeared at the wharf when they learned what was going on. Most were Bostonians, but the Party probably included men from many of the neighboring towns and from as far away as Worcester. Best-known among alleged participants were William Molineux, Thomas Young, and Paul Revere. Other patriot leaders like Sam Adams, John Hancock, and Joseph Warren, however, apparently did not go on board any of the tea-ships that night. Their work was already done.[35]

The undertaking had all the signs of a well-planned operation. The merchant Henry Bromfield declared the next day that the whole episode was conducted with such dispatch that there must have been "People of sense and more discernment than the vulgar among the Actors." The rain had stopped, and some people showed up with lanterns to supplement the bright moonlight that now illuminated the scene. Many had hatchets with which to break open the tea chests. Although accounts differ, most witnesses agreed that the active participants numbered between thirty and sixty and were divided into three groups, each with a competent leader. While two parties clambered aboard *Dartmouth* and *Eleanor*, the brig *Beaver*, lying off the wharf, was warped alongside. The customs officers on board each vessel were forced ashore, and the squads began their work. Some men dropped into the hold to attach block and tackle to the heavy chests; others hoisted them to the deck. A third gang broke them open with axes, shoveled and poured the tea over the side, and heaved the chests after it. The tide was nearly low, and the water was only two or three feet deep. Soon the tea began to pile up, threatening to spill back into the vessels. Men pushed it aside as best they could to make room for more.[36]

As work progressed, a large crowd gathered at the wharf to watch the proceedings in silent approval. It was so quiet that a witness standing at some distance could hear the steady whack-whack of the hatchets. By nine o'clock, less than three hours from the time they had begun, the gangs had finished their task. Particular care was taken that no one made off with any of the tea. One fellow had surreptitiously filled the lining of his coat with loose tea, but he was spotted by the others, stripped of his clothing, and given a severe beating as he scampered through the crowd. Despite the precautions a few of the party found bits of tea in their boots and trousers when they reached home, but no sizeable quantity escaped destruction that night. Early next morning when the tide began once more to recede, small boats were launched to break up the long wind-rows of tea which reached far out into Boston harbor.

At no time during the evening did the governmental authorities move to interrupt the proceedings. Colonel Leslie's regiment of troops remained at Castle William. The navy squadron rode at anchor a few hundred yards out in the harbor, but orders to intervene never came. Admiral Montagu witnessed the scene from a house at the foot of Griffin's Wharf. The next morning he allegedly warned members of a crowd that, although they had had their fun, they would soon have to pay the fiddler. Governor Hutchinson was still at Milton, the lieutenant-governor at his home in Middleborough, and the Customs Commissioners at Castle Island along with the consignees. With the throng of onlookers surrounding the wharf, it is doubtful that anything could have been done to save the tea without injury to hundreds. As Montagu explained in his report the following day, "I could easily have prevented the Execution of this Plan but must have endangered the Lives of many innocent People by firing upon the Town." The key to the Boston Tea Party's success, then, was the decision in late November to force the vessels up to Griffin's Wharf. From that time forward the fate of their cargoes was in the hands of the Boston patriots.[37]

"This is the most magnificent Movement of all," wrote John Adams in his diary the next day. "There is a Dignity, a Majesty, a Sublimity in this last Effort of the Patriots that I greatly admire. . . . This Destruction of the Tea," he concluded, "is so bold, so daring, so firm, intrepid, & inflexible, and it must have so important Consequences and so lasting, that I cannot but consider it as an Epocha in History. . . ." Events would soon prove the truth of Adams's eloquent statement.[38]

VIII

IMMEDIATE CONSEQUENCES

WHEN Governor Hutchinson learned of the Boston Tea Party at his home in Milton, he was stunned. This act of violence caught him completely by surprise for several reasons. In the first place, he had moved from Boston in late November and had remained away from the center of activity as much as possible thereafter. Thus it was difficult for him to appreciate the determination of the people from his seat in Milton. Secondly, he was convinced, and rightly so, that the patriots' objective was to force a return of the tea to England. His mistake was to assume that, if the cargo could not be shipped back, the patriots would then have no choice but to permit it to be seized and stored for non-payment of the duty. Hutchinson and the consignees could smell victory as the twenty-day period of grace came to a close in mid-December. They failed to consider the possibility that Adams and his friends would not give in so easily. Finally, Hutchinson was deceived by the presence of so many men of property among the councils of the patriots during the final days, men like Hancock, Rowe, and Dennie, who he thought "would never make themselves liable to pay for [the tea]." [1]

In the weeks that followed the Tea Party the Governor tried to explain to his correspondents that there were no practical means by which the destruction of the tea could have been prevented. The consignees had offered to store the cargo, but the patriots declined. Hutchinson had suggested to Rotch that the vessel be hauled out into the harbor and be placed under the guns of the fleet. Rotch refused. At that point, apparently, the Governor had considered requesting Admiral Montagu to take the vessel under his protection anyway, without the owner's permission. But he was loath to take such serious measures unless supported by the Council, Hutchinson explained, and that body would never agree to such an action—the Council, the selectmen of Boston, the General Court, and the officers of the militia were all against him. "In short, there was no part of the Authority except the Governor himself which was not either favorers of the scheme [to oppose the landing] or affraid to appear against it," he concluded.[2]

Later, in his *History of Massachusetts-Bay*, Hutchinson pointed out why he did not order marines to board the vessels and drive off the patriots guarding them or bring in Leslie's regiment from the Castle. Either action would have brought "a greater convulsion than there was any danger of in 1770 [after the Boston Massacre]," he wrote, and on that occasion the people had succeeded in forcing two regiments out of town. It would have been impossible for Leslie's troops to keep possession of the town for long. Nor did he think such action would have met with the approval of the authorities in London.[3]

The only way he could have prevented destruction of the tea, the Governor concluded, was to have granted a pass for the vessels. To do so would have violated province law and would also have led to a violation of the law prohibiting the return of tea to Great Britain. Besides, Hutchinson was in no mood to give in to the Boston patriots. As he explained to ex-Governor Bernard, who had had ample experience with the Liberty Boys himself, "It would have given me a much more painful reflection if I had saved it by any concession to a lawless and highly criminal Assembly. . . ."[4]

The patriots for their part made every effort to justify the violence which may have surprised some of them as well. The leaders took great pains to point out that the Tea Party came only as a last resort, that there was no other way to prevent the landing of the tea and the eventual payment of the detested duty. Spokesmen for the committee of correspondence placed the blame directly on the consignees for "their aversion to all conciliatory measures," although the only "conciliatory" measure acceptable to the patriots was the return of the tea to England.[5] John Scollay, chairman of the Board of Selectmen, took the same position. He lamented the loss to the East India Company but, without explaining why, concluded that the patriots had acted constitutionally. "I think we have put our Enemies in the wrong," Sam Adams confidently stated to James Warren in Plymouth, "and they must in the Judgment of rational Men be answerable for the Destruction of the Tea, which their own Obstinacy rendered necessary." His legalist cousin John endorsed the proceedings with enthusiasm; he concluded that destruction of the tea was "absolutely and indispensably" necessary to preserve American liberties.[6]

Some commentators were even more specific in their justification of the Tea Party. If the cargo had been allowed ashore, wrote one, who could have trusted the consignees not to pay the duty and surreptitiously take the tea out of the customs warehouse, as the Hutchinsons had done in violation of their agreement during non-importation four years earlier? Nor could the people be trusted not to buy the tea once it was offered for sale, although no one made this argument in writing. Most important, Bostonians knew that their reputation among the other colonists was at stake. To allow the tea to land, one correspondent explained in an open letter to Hutchinson, "would have revived and confirmed a jealousy which would have effectively prevented that union of the colonies which you dread. . . ."[7] Other writers heaped blame for the destruction of the tea on the consignees, for having refused to resign as soon as it was apparent that the community stood virtually united against them. In all events, the Mohawks, whose identities were conveniently unknown to the people as a whole, were merely the instruments of the popular will, forced into action by the stubbornness of the consignees, the customs collectors, and the Governor. The Tea Party was the act of the whole country, wrote one Bostonian to his London correspondent. By "country" he meant the province of Massachusetts Bay. The writer went on to explain his suspicion that Hutchinson intended to land the tea by force upon expiration of the twenty-day period.[8]

On the day following the Tea Party, Hutchinson called a meeting of the Council at Boston, but not enough members appeared to make a quorum. That night he retreated to the Castle on the advice of friends, for spirits in Boston were still high. An attempt to convene the Council at Milton the next day was also unsuccessful. Not until 21 December was the Governor able to gather enough of his advisers together to do business, this time in the comparative safety of William Brattle's Cambridge home. At the rump meeting in Boston on the 17th the Governor had charged that destruction of the tea was nothing short of high treason, and he promised that the attorney-general, Jonathan Sewall, would cite the statutes to prove it. Perhaps on Sewall's advice, however, the Governor soon settled for what John Adams described as "New England Burglary — that is, breaking open a shop or ship . . . ," an offense punishable by branding.[9]

At Cambridge, Hutchinson suggested that the Council issue a proclamation offering a reward for information leading to the conviction of those responsible for the destruction of the tea. But the councillors rejected even this action. Instead, they merely advised the attorney-general to make an investigation and lay his findings before the grand jury for prosecution. No one could expect that body to act on a case which most of its members would not consider an offense.[10]

Despite the Council's refusal to lend its authority to apprehending those responsible for the Tea Party, the committee of correspondence prepared for the worst. Rumors persisted that the patriot leaders were about to be seized and transported to England for trial. On 24 December the committee members with the curious exception of Joseph Warren, pledged in a solemn pact "to support and vindicate each other, and any Person or Persons who may be likely to suffer for any noble Effort *they have made* to serve their Country. . . ."[11] It would appear from this document that the committee members were recognizing their own responsibility for the Boston Tea Party.

Nor did they forget others, for at about the same time the committee prepared a petition to be circulated through the town. Its
signers were to promise "at the hazard of our lives and fortunes [to]
prevent any person from being detained in custody and carry'd out
of the province." There is no evidence, however, that this paper was
actually distributed. Nor, as it turned out, was there any need for
it, for only one man was arrested for suspected participation, a
barber named Eckley, and he was ultimately released for lack of
evidence. Hutchinson had to content himself with his own full
report of the proceedings to the London authorities in hope that
justice would ultimately prevail.[12]

Hutchinson and the consignees did, however, gain one minor
victory. When the Clarkes' brig *William* went ashore at Provincetown on 10 December, the fifty-eight chests of East India Company
tea on board were saved. Rescued from the wreck also were 300 lamps
for Boston's streets which the selectmen had ordered from London.
The patriots expected local "Indians" to confiscate the tea, but young
Jonathan Clarke outwitted them all. Slipping ashore from his asylum
at Castle William when he learned of the disaster, Clarke rode over
a hundred miles to the scene, enlisting the aid of John Greenough,
justice of the peace at Wellfleet, on the way. At Provincetown they
rounded up workers to take out the tea and eventually chartered a
Salem fishing schooner, which had been blown into harbor by the
storm, to carry it to Castle William. There the tea was landed in
early January on orders from Governor Hutchinson himself. Sam
Adams was disgusted. "It is said that the Indians this way, if they
had suspected the Marshpee [Mashpee] tribe would have been so
sick at the knees, would have marched on Snow Shoes . . . to have
done the Business for them." [13]

It is not known whether the consignees ever paid the Townshend
duty on this remnant of the East India Company's consignment or
whether any of it ever reached Boston itself. But at the Cape, Clarke
did sell two chests to Greenough on credit. One of these was turned
over to a Provincetown man for retail sale, but before any customers
appeared, the local patriots put it to the torch. Greenough brought

the other chest back to Wellfleet and sold part of it to Colonel Knowles of Eastham. A local committee confiscated the rest, about 200 pounds. In June 1774 Greenough reported that he somehow had regained his tea from the Wellfleet committee and "sold it there in spright [sic] of all their Malice. . . ." The Clarkes generously allowed him to keep all the proceeds himself. The contents of this chest —perhaps 350 pounds—is the only tea out of the Company's shipment of 600,000 pounds proved to have reached American consumers. Perhaps the patriots could afford this one blemish, for there is no record that the duty on Greenough's tea was ever paid! [14]

The pride of the Boston patriots was obviously stung by Jonathan Clarke's daring exploit to save the tea from his shipwrecked vessel. Greenough suffered constant abuse from his neighbors and did not dare to come up to Boston on business. The owner of the vessel that landed the tea at Castle William was spared a beating from Salem patriots only because he was undergoing inoculation at the smallpox hospital. Boston's consignees were not so fortunate. Except for occasional secret visits ashore, the Clarkes were virtual prisoners at Castle William throughout the winter; although Jonathan managed to get passage aboard a London-bound vessel in late February. In mid-January, JOYCE JR. posted a warning that a coat of tar and feathers awaited any consignee bold enough to return to Boston. Thomas Hutchinson, Jr., escaped to the family home at Milton, while his brother Elisha remained at Middleborough. When he visited his father-in-law in Plymouth, however, Elisha was chased out of town in the midst of a snowstorm. Only the older consignees, Benjamin Faneuil and Joshua Winslow, were left in relative peace. Peggy Hutchinson, young Thomas's wife, expressed their despair in a letter to her sister-in-law. "You may now know how to pity me who have been runing [sic] from a Mob ever since the Year Sixty-five. . . ." At one point the consignees considered petitioning the General Court for a redress of their grievances but were told by Copley that the cause was hopeless.[15]

When the people of Boston recovered from their surprise at the destruction of the tea, they were almost unanimous in their approval of what had happened. Hutchinson confirmed the fact in his letters to Lord Dartmouth. "At and near Boston," he reported, "the people seem regardless of all consequences."[16] Joy seemed to be the most common feeling, as if the inhabitants had just been delivered from the clutches of the Devil. "We are in a perfect jubilee," announced one Bostonian in a letter to his friend in New York.[17] Nor was the response confined to Boston alone. John Adams reported that the inland towns received the news with equal happiness. Those who disapproved or worried about the consequences kept quiet in the days immediately following the Tea Party. John Rowe confined his disappointment to the pages of his diary, while few Tories dared raise their voices in public protest.[18]

In the first of his memorable rides, Paul Revere carried a full report of the Boston proceedings to New York, where it was quickly published and sent on to Philadelphia by another courier. By the beginning of the new year there was hardly an American who did not know of the Bostonians' destruction of the tea. Colonists everywhere were overjoyed. At last the Americans had struck back with a bold blow at tyranny. Now the British ministry would sit up and take notice of the colonists' demands for fair treatment. Throughout America dissenters kept their opinions to themselves.[19]

When Revere returned to Boston in late December he brought with him the news of what had happened at Charleston, South Carolina, earlier in the month. Inhabitants there did not learn of the impending shipment of East India Company tea to that port until mid-November. Then the patriots launched their campaign of opposition in earnest. Two newspaper editors joined in by reprinting many of the scathing denunciations of the plan from northern journals as well as letters of local origin. JUNIUS BRUTUS employed the familiar argument that the scheme was a diabolical plot to establish Parliament's power of taxation over the colonies. He called upon the consignees, Roger Smith and the firm of Leger & Greenwood, to resign their commissions.[20]

Charleston patriots had little time to prepare, for on 2 December the ship *London* arrived with 257 chests of tea and an assortment of other goods on board. Captain Curling duly entered his vessel and all his cargo at the customhouse. On the day following, a mass meeting convened to determine how to handle the situation. Like the inhabitants of Boston, Charlestonians did not have the benefit of precedents from other towns on which to model their actions. The meeting did proceed according to plan. The merchants agreed to import no more dutied tea, and the consignees gracefully refused to accept the shipment just arrived. This left Captain Curling in a quandary. When he asked the meeting what he should do with his cargo, the answer was simply that he should return with it to England.[21]

It was not long before several difficulties arose. For one thing, the planters agreed at a separate meeting to boycott only dutied tea. Many of the merchants who had been importing tea from England demanded that smuggled tea be banned as well, to put all importers on an equal footing. The squabble dragged on until the 17th, when it was agreed that, after the present supply of tea had been used up, in about six months, neither variety would be imported or consumed until repeal of the duty. The ban was put into effect in March 1774. But the argument had split the colony's two groups of leaders, planters and merchants. At the same meeting it was resolved once more that the East India Company's tea should not be landed, but the inhabitants could come to no decision how best to prevent it. Reports later reached northern colonies that the South Carolinians were afraid that violent opposition to the tea would lose them their bounty on indigo and the privilege of exporting rice under license to southern Europe.[22]

Whatever the reason for indecision, the outcome was that nothing at all was done to prevent the landing of the tea, aside from veiled threats which Captain Curling calmly ignored. As a result, when the twenty-day period for payment of the duty expired, the customs officers took swift action. Early on the morning of 22 December, Collector Morris and his men went aboard *London*. With help from the ship's crew, all the tea was ashore by noon, half of it safely stored away in a warehouse under the Exchange. Only a few interested merchants witnessed the proceedings — the inhabitants offered no opposition whatever. The triumph was a hollow one, however, for the tea remained in the custody of the authorities, the duties unpaid. In February 1774 the East India Company requested that the Governor be ordered to sell the tea at auction, but nothing came of it. One report in March declared that the tea was rapidly deteriorating from dampness in the warehouse, "artificially conveyed" the writer suggested. A later account stated that at the outbreak of hostilities in 1775 the tea was sold by the patriots for the benefit of the war effort. The South Carolinians apparently could trust Collector Morris not to allow the tea out of his custody, the resignation of the consignees having already assured that no one would pay the duties.[23]

The situation at New York grew particularly tense during December. When the consignees resigned on 1 December, the patriots gained only a minor triumph, for Governor Tryon and his Council were determined that the tea would be landed by force if necessary and stored in the barracks at the Battery. The patriots could not be sure it would remain there long, however, and the radicals among them argued in favor of blocking its entry altogether. But with the man-of-war *Swan* stationed off Sandy Hook to escort the tea-ship in, the patriots were powerless. Only a strong demonstration of popular opposition could dissuade Governor Tryon from going through with his plans. New Yorkers grew restless as the days slipped by with no sign of the ship. "I wish that when it is about midway of the Atlantic that Old Satan would rigg his Cann Hooks around the Tea and sink it to the Lowermost Horns," wrote one frustrated patriot.[24]

Then the news trickling into New York about resistance in the other colonies began to put a little more starch in the spirits of the inhabitants. First came reports of Boston's strong stand taken at its meetings in late November. The determination of patriots at Philadelphia and Charleston gave the New Yorkers further encouragement. The Governor's Council met on 15 December to reaffirm its intention to land the tea at the barracks in the face of stiffening opposition. A public meeting held two days later drew about a thousand inhabitants, and the mayor, present as an observer, was duly impressed by their staunch resolves against landing dutied tea. When the Association of the Sons of Liberty refused to endorse the plan to store the tea, its moderate members resigned in disgust. The authorities began to waver.[25]

Paul Revere's arrival on 21 December with an account of the Boston Tea Party was the turning-point. New Yorkers greeted the news with high spirits and determined to refuse the tea and to destroy it if necessary. If New York's tea-ship had arrived before Boston's, British General Haldimand later reported to Dartmouth, there would have been little difficulty in getting the cargo ashore. But Revere's dispatches "created such a ferment" that the Governor shortly decided to permit the vessel's return to avoid "dangerous Extremities." Captain Ayscough announced that day, after consulting with Tryon, that he would meet the tea-ship at Sandy Hook and offer its captain the provisions necessary for an immediate return passage to England.[26] The consignees also agreed that an attempt to land the tea would now be unwise. On the 27th they prepared a letter for Captain Lockyer of the tea-ship *Nancy*, to be placed aboard the pilot boat off Sandy Hook. In it they strongly advised him to return with his cargo to England as soon as he had the opportunity to get aboard fresh provisions. "The friends of Government have given up the point," Pigou & Booth wearily reported to James & Drinker in Philadelphia.[27]

By a quirk of nature the New York patriots had to wait four months for their final triumph. On 22 December the ship *Renown* entered from London, having left England in mid-November in company with the tea-ship. But *Nancy* fell behind, and as it approached the American shore, a furious winter storm (perhaps the same one that had wrecked the brig *William* on Cape Cod) drove it off the coast. After a severe battering, Captain Lockyer put into Antigua in early February 1774 for repairs and provisions. While there he learned the fate of the other tea-ships and what was in store for him at New York. With considerable trepidation he decided in late March to try delivering the tea at New York anyway. But by the time he arrived, in mid-April, the attitude of Americans toward dutied tea had become firmer than ever.

Meanwhile, of course, the British ministry had long since learned of the opposition to the other tea-ships and yet took no steps to assure that Lockyer would be able to land his cargo safely in New York. Dartmouth had authorized General Haldimand to use force to protect the flow of commerce, but only upon a request for help from the Governor. But Tryon was not told to demand that the tea be landed when it arrived.[28]

Lockyer anchored off Sandy Hook on 18 April 1774, having passed through another storm, which carried away the ship's mizzenmast and main topmast. There must have been a Jonah on board, suggested one wag. Handbills alerted the public to his arrival, but Lockyer had no intention of forcing the issue. He left his vessel at Sandy Hook, beyond the jurisdiction of the New York customs office, and came ashore to confer with the consignees. A large crowd greeted him at the wharf. Lockyer and the consignees quickly agreed not to land the tea, the shipmaster making first a formal offer of his cargo for delivery. On the 23rd, his vessel being provisioned for the return passage, the captain left the city midst ringing of bells and cheers of the crowd. His crew was not so happy about going back to England, however, and some of them attempted to jump ship by means of a raft, but they were quickly rounded up. The next day, the 25th, *Nancy* sailed for England. New York had been safely delivered from the "odious burden" — dutied tea.[29]

News of the Boston Tea Party reached Philadelphia on 24 December 1773 and was greeted with ringing of bells and celebrations in the coffeehouses throughout town. The editor of the *Pennsylvania Journal* put out an extra edition and headed the story from Boston "CHRISTMAS BOX for the CUSTOMERS of the PENNSYLVANIA JOURNAL." Although some inhabitants were undoubtedly appalled, most of them concluded that the Bostonians had had no other choice. Philadelphians had been in a constant state of suspense all month, for the tea-ship *Polly* had not yet arrived. The consignees had resigned on the 2nd, upon learning from their instructions that the tea would indeed be subject to the Townshend duty. But that triumph, the patriot leaders knew, would be small comfort unless the spirit of opposition continued unabated. Minor irritations became major crises to distract the inhabitants. When a sudden scarcity of smuggled tea encouraged shopkeepers to raise their prices, consumers were outraged. An angry meeting on 4 December appointed a special committee to investigate the matter. Eventually the retailers agreed to ask no more than 3s. 6d. per pound for their tea and to parcel out their stocks in small quantities. Philadelphians could not be expected to go without their Bohea.[30]

Patriot leaders labored hard to keep public attention focused on the East India Company's tea. Letters to the newspapers urged the populace to be watchful. Charles Thomson reported to Sam Adams and John Hancock that he had been circulating handbills "to kindle a flame of resentment against them [the East India Company] as ravagers of Asia, the corrupters of their country, the supporters of arbitrary power, and the patrons of monopoly." The fact that English Whigs under Rockingham had defended the Company as victims of the Crown's arbitrary power was lost on the Philadelphian. "I do not think it unworthy the cause sometimes to borrow aid from the passions," he concluded.[31] The patriots had established their first line of defense at the mouth of the Delaware River, warning the pilots not to bring up the tea-ship when it arrived. But apparently the moderates disapproved of this action, and now a note of uncertainty appeared.[32]

Relations among the consignees steadily worsened. The Whartons urged their London correspondents to have James & Drinker dropped as agents for any future shipment "after the duty is repealed," and to replace them with the firm of Willing & Morris. Thomas Wharton even asked his brother in London to find out in a secret manner what James & Drinker had written to correspondents there. With the consignees hopelessly divided, there was little chance that the tea would even be landed and stored. Besides, the Whartons had no confidence that the colonial government, under the weak leadership of Lieutenant-Governor John Penn, would take any steps to protect the tea if it were brought ashore.[33]

Philadelphians had barely finished celebrating the news of the Boston Tea Party when the report came on the evening of the 25th that *Polly* had been sighted in the river off Chester. In its hold were 598 chests of tea and an assorted cargo of goods, including a handsome chariot which Thomas Wharton had ordered from London. Also on board was Gilbert Barkley, the Philadelphia merchant who had encouraged the Company so strongly to go through with its plans. Captain Ayres had entered Delaware Bay the day before, and when the pilots had refused to assist him, he simply began to follow a vessel of greater draught than his up the channel toward Philadelphia. The patriots had already decided that their best tactic was to persuade Ayres to return to England with the tea. They seemed to realize, however, either from their own knowledge or from the Bostonians' experience, that they would have to prevent the captain from making an entry at the customhouse.[34]

A committee of patriots hastened to Chester the next morning, but by the time the men arrived, *Polly* had already passed on its way upstream. Meanwhile a large crowd had gathered at Gloucester Point, a few miles below the center of the city. When the vessel approached early that afternoon, Ayres was hailed from the riverbank to proceed no further. The Captain brought his ship to anchor and came ashore. He was then escorted by Charles Thomson and other patriots up to town to see for himself the temper of the inhabitants. The next morning, the 27th, a mass meeting convened at the State House. Nearly 8000 appeared, and they had to adjourn to the square in front of the building. There the body resolved that the tea should not be landed, that Ayres should not enter at the customhouse, and that he should return with his cargo to London. A special vote of thanks to the people of Boston "for their resolution in destroying the tea rather than suffering it to be landed" clearly expressed the mood of the gathering. Ayres agreed to allow a pilot to take his vessel sixty miles downstream to Reedy

Island, where it would be safer from the clutches of the custom-house.[35]

After the meeting Ayres went through the formalities of asking the consignees if they would accept the tea. Each declined on the grounds of local opposition to the duty. Although refusing also to pay for the freight, Browne and the Whartons did advance Ayres enough money to purchase provisions for his return. On the afternoon of the 28th, just forty-six hours after he had entered the city, Captain Ayres boarded a pilot boat which took him back to his moored vessel. Accompanying him was Gilbert Barkley, who had joined the other consignees in resigning his commission as soon as he had landed. That evening *Polly* weighed anchor and dropped down the Delaware on its long passage back to England. With the vessel went the East India Company's tea, the assorted cargo of goods, and Thomas Wharton's new chariot.[36]

From the patriots' standpoint the episode at Philadelphia was a remarkably well-managed affair. With the early resignation of the consignees and the unwillingness of the Governor or customs officers to interfere, it remained only to prevent Captain Ayres from making an entry. The long approach by river made interception a comparatively simple matter. Once he saw for himself how determined the inhabitants were, Ayres needed little further persuasion, although *Polly* had anchored within the limits of the port as defined by the customhouse and was thus technically required to make entry. But the patriots saw to it that Captain Ayres left town before the customary forty-eight-hour period of grace expired. Unlike their colleagues at Boston the Philadelphia officials showed no interest in pressing the matter on a technicality.[37]

When *Polly* returned to London in late January, Lord Dartmouth was furious to learn the details of Governor Penn's inaction. In fact Penn had not even bothered to mention the final episode in any of the several letters he had written Dartmouth after the event. The Governor's explanation was revealing. He took no action, he asserted, because neither the consignees, the customs officers, nor Captain

Ayres had requested him to do so. "I was totally ignorant of the Measures taken to prohibit the Entrance of the Vessel 'till after her Departure . . ." he blandly confessed. As for not reporting the matter to Dartmouth, Penn's alibi was equally unimpressive. The tea plan was generally considered a private matter between the Company and the consignees, he said, "in which the Government had no immediate Concern." Had Governor Hutchinson or Lord North's ministry taken a similar approach to the proceedings at Boston, the course of American history might well have been different.[38]

By the beginning of the new year, opposition to dutied tea had begun to spread to all parts of the American continent. The stand taken by the patriots of Boston, New York, Philadelphia, and Charleston during the previous autumn had focused attention on the remaining Townshend duty, which most colonists had condoned not three months before. But it was the unexpected destruction of the tea at Boston that shocked them out of their apathy of over three years' duration. The Boston Tea Party dramatized the radicals' claim that by its tea plan the East India Company supported a grand ministerial conspiracy compelling Americans to recognize Parliament's power of taxation. We consider this scheme so fraught with evil, the Bostonians' action seemed to say, that we will go to any lengths to oppose it. Patriots in other towns awoke from their lethargy and rallied to the cause of American freedom.

The people of Portsmouth, New Hampshire, were particularly concerned about dutied tea in December 1773, for they suspected that a shipment from the East India Company might be planned for their port too. On the 16th they met in town meeting and resolved against receiving the detested cargo. They denounced the "Pensioners, Placemen, and Ministerial Dependants, who like Vultures are preying on the Heart-Strings of their Fellow Subjects." The Portsmouth inhabitants called for "the Union of all the Colonies" as the most effective way of bringing about repeal of the Townshend duty and other revenue measures of Parliament. Governor Wentworth blamed the proceedings on the Boston patriots for having kindled the flame of resentment in neighboring provinces. Other major towns in New Hampshire—Newcastle, Exeter, and Dover among them — followed Portsmouth's lead.[39]

Elsewhere in New England many towns had already taken a firm stand against dutied tea before the Party at Boston. Those that had not, quickly fell into line. Ipswich, Medway, and Brookfield were among the first in Massachusetts Bay to resolve against its use. Lexington and Charlestown went one step further. Each town called upon its citizens to surrender all their tea to a central committee, which then arranged for its destruction in a public bonfire. Other towns took a more sophisticated form of protest. The citizens of Hull, Massachusetts, made it clear that their quarrel was with the duty, not the tea. In late March the town resolved that once the duty was repealed, "we will on equal terms, in [tea] as in all other articles, give the preference to England, whose true interest we have always considered as our own." [40]

Hull's approach, however, was far too rational for most New Englanders. Tea was destroyed wherever it was found, whether it was English or Dutch. A band of patriotic "Indians" seized a parcel from a peddler passing through Shrewsbury and committed it to the flames. A similar fate befell an itinerant tradesman at Lyme, Connecticut, who lost 100 pounds to a mob. Even the cart of a patriotic Boston merchant was searched one night and divested of a small bag of tea found inside. Isaac Jones, an innkeeper at Weston, Massachusetts, paid an even higher price. When the rumor spread that Jones had been selling tea at his tavern, thirty patriots, disguised in the now-familiar war-paint, broke in while the proprietor was away and reduced his inn to a shambles. The mob smashed all the windows, drank all his liquor, and shattered his bowls, mugs, and other china ware. When Jones returned, he tried to explain that he had bought the tea in Albany some months before on the assumption that it had been smuggled. Now he was forced by public resentment to state that it was dutied after all, although this was unlikely, and that he was heartily sorry for his offense. In Newport, Rhode Island, a country man became a laughing-stock when he stepped off a sloop to the wharf with a small bag of tea in his hand, only to miss his footing and fall into the water. "Be careful how you travel with this baneful article about you, for the salt water seems to attract it as a loadstone attracts iron," chided the editor of the *Newport Mercury*.[41]

Patriots applied similar pressure to others who failed to toe the line. When Plymouth town meeting attacked the Company's tea plan in early December, a group of Loyalists headed by Edward Winslow drew up a protest. By the end of the year, however, most of the forty-odd signers were forced to make public recantation. The situation was reversed at Marshfield in late January when the town adopted resolutions denouncing the Boston Tea Party as an unwarranted act of violence. Now it was the patriot minority that adopted a protest, along with accusations that the meeting had been unfairly conducted.[42]

In Boston itself the campaign against dutied tea gained new momentum from the destruction of the Company's shipment. On 18 December some of the town's principal tea dealers met to decide how best to answer a charge that they had instigated the Party themselves as a means of preserving their monopoly of the market. On the 21st a large meeting was called which appointed a committee to ask all the dealers in town to suspend sales of tea, both English and Dutch, after 20 January 1774. Out of an estimated hundred dealers, seventy-nine agreed generally, while nine others wanted to ban the sale of dutied tea only.[43]

The split on the question of selling smuggled tea spread into the Boston press, and for a time the issue threatened to divide an important group of moderates into irreconcilable camps. A TRUE WHIG denounced the recent outbreak of tea-burnings as ridiculous. Tea will continue to be used "by the greater part of the People, some of which are so very fond of it, that they had rather part with any enjoyment in life. . . ." In an open admission that Dutch tea was an available alternative to Bostonians, he wondered why they should not be allowed to buy smuggled tea. The object, after all, in banning English tea was to force a repeal of the Townshend duty. To those who argued that consuming smuggled tea merely enriched the colonies to the south of Boston, A TRUE WHIG asked what was the matter with that? "Are not those Colonies Friends and Brethren? Is not a Union with them one Grand Object . . . ? " [44]

A BATCHELOR wondered what the point was in burning even English tea, since the duty had already been paid, provided no more was to be imported from England while the duty continued. But those advocating the banning of all tea had a strong point in their favor. "If you suffer Dutch Tea, you will soon be over-run with dutied tea under that Name," argued SYDNEY. CONCORDIA and others agreed. An attempt was made at compromise by fixing the wholesale price of Dutch Bohea at 2s. 1½d. per pound. But the argument dragged on. AN ENEMY TO TEA, DUTIED AND UNDUTIED, warned that if Dutch tea were permitted the consignees at the Castle were sure to slip their fifty-six chests of Company tea onto the market. In his rebuttal, A TRUE WHIG pointed out that when AN ENEMY TO TEA could convince the inhabitants of the middle and southern colonies to abandon Dutch tea, he would welcome a similar ban in New England. Until that time, it was cruel to make Boston bear the brunt of the sacrifice. A TRUE WHIG was either a devoted tea drinker, or as his adversaries suspected, an importer of Dutch tea through Rhode Island. Ultimate victory went to those who supported A TRUE WHIG, although evidence indicates that many New Englanders gave up both dutied and undutied tea for the duration.[45]

For the rest of the winter there was very little tea of either variety in the Boston area, the dealers' committee reporting only six chests on hand in early January. Samuel Salisbury wrote from Worcester in the middle of the month that no tea had been available there for nearly two months. Salisbury predicted that, despite all the resolutions against it, he could sell more tea than ever if he had any in stock, and he hoped his brother had not signed the Boston tea-dealers' agreement. So undependable did the patriots consider the general public in the matter of tea-drinking that the newspaper campaign against its use continued unabated. All the old arguments reappeared — tea was a poisonous herb, the East India Company was comprised of men dangerous to the liberties of America, and the duty was unconstitutional. Some new grounds for opposition were also advanced. Tea bred fleas, maintained several writers. One popular rumor, denied by A WOMAN, was that tea was packed into its chests in Canton by Chinese peasants with their dirty bare feet. For herself, though, this lady preferred political arguments to these "scare-crow stories." One result of all this was a boom in coffee sales. The change in consumer habits that by the end of the century would sweep the American continent had thus begun.[46]

Patriots in New England led the way in the latest anti-tea hysteria mainly because citizens there had depended so much on dutied tea. But colonists in other parts of America joined in. One New Yorker took the economic viewpoint: a steady drinker spent almost £7 a year on tea, sugar, butter, and fuel to enjoy his favorite beverage. The writer claimed to have known working families who spent so much of their earnings on tea that their emaciated children soon died of a "marasmus." The New York committee of correspondence revived the monopoly argument in late February and suggested to its counterpart in Boston that English tea be banned until Parliament repealed that part of the Act of 1773 that allowed the Company to send tea directly to the colonies. Boston agreed to join in this goal. The students at Princeton destroyed all the tea they could find at the college in late January and showed sympathy for Boston by burning several effigies of Governor Hutchinson in the process. Further to the south the question of dutied tea was less prominent in the press. Two writers in Purdie's *Virginia Gazette* deplored the destruction of tea at Boston, while others flew to its defense.[47]

The resolution of Boston's patriots not to accept dutied tea was put to the test in early March 1774. The brig *Fortune* arrived in Boston early Sunday afternoon, the 6th, with twenty-eight and one-half chests of tea on board, along with hemp, gunpowder, and other articles. Sixteen chests came consigned to Henry Lloyd from the London firm of Davidson & Newman, while the rest was destined for merchants at Haverhill and Portsmouth. The owners, Thomas Walley and associates, were astounded to discover what their vessel had on board. When the brig had left Boston for London the previous November, popular opposition to the Company's scheme was well known, and the owners instructed Captain Gorham not to return with the Company's tea. Strictly speaking, Gorham obeyed orders, for his cargo was shipped as a private venture between merchants, but the tea was subject nevertheless to the Townshend duty.[48]

Gorham did not enter his vessel and cargo at the customhouse when he arrived Sunday afternoon, perhaps only because it was closed. When the owners learned that tea was on board, they immediately declared their willingness to send the vessel back to London, either with the whole cargo or with the tea alone, and to risk seizure in England under the law prohibiting the re-importation of tea. But they did not count on the obstinacy of Collector Harrison. On Monday morning the owners went to the customhouse. Since *Fortune* had in fact arrived, Captain Gorham was obliged to make entry, but until he had done so, perhaps his vessel would be free to depart. Of course the authorities could easily stop him at the Castle or by a shot from one of Admiral Montagu's warships. The owners asked Harrison to issue "a qualification for the vessel to return with the tea." They noted the strong resolution of the people against dutied tea, the likelihood of its being destroyed, and the fact that the collector in Philadelphia had allowed the ship *Polly* to return unmolested despite having physically entered the boundaries of the customs district there.[49]

Harrison refused Walley's request, for the sole reason that to grant it would be contrary to his duty. Moreover, he pointed out that if Captain Gorham did not report his vessel by two o'clock that afternoon (giving him twenty-four hours instead of the forty-eight granted Captain Hall of *Dartmouth* in late November), the vessel would be seized and the captain fined £100. According to the owners, Gorham then reported his vessel and took out a permit to unload the gunpowder. After doing so, he brought *Fortune* up to Hubbard's Wharf, near Griffin's Wharf. Harrison, in his explanation to the Lords of the Treasury, stated that Gorham reported his vessel and all his cargo late that morning, but whether the tea was actually reported is unclear. The owners implied that it was not. Perhaps they still hoped that *Fortune* would be allowed to depart with the tea after all. But if Harrison was about to change his mind, and there is no evidence to this effect, it was soon too late. The committee of correspondence met that Monday morning, too, and sent an urgent summons to the committees of the neighboring towns to meet the following afternoon. Possibly that was merely a smoke-screen, for Monday evening at 8:30 a band of sixty men disguised as Indians climbed aboard *Fortune,* forced the tidesmen into the cabin, and hoisted the tea over the rail and into the water. Boston had had its second tea party.[50]

Destruction of the tea on board *Fortune* revealed a number of important factors in the situation at Boston. In the first place, there was no question of this tea being sent to establish a monopoly, since it was shipped as a private venture, unconnected with the East India Company's plan, and Bostonians knew this. It was destroyed solely because it came subject to the Townshend duty. In the second place, Collector Harrison's outright rejection of the course of action followed by the Philadelphia collector two months before showed what a stubborn man he could be. He made no mention in his report to the Treasury of his decision not to permit the tea to be returned. It is questionable, in fact, whether Harrison had a right to hold *Fortune* in port, since it had not yet entered at the customhouse and did not need a clearance from him to depart. But the owners understandably had no desire to risk the loss of their vessel as a test of Harrison's decision. Destruction of the tea on board was of little consequence to them as long as the brig remained unharmed. Nor did Thomas Hutchinson show any inclination to compromise on this occasion. Reporting the incident to Lord Dartmouth, the Governor said nothing of the owner's request for permission to depart. Finally, the fact that the patriots acted immediately, not waiting this time for the expiration of the twenty-day period for payment of the duties, showed how far their defiance of authority had progressed since December. There was no sign of remorse for the Boston Tea Party here. It is quite possible that the destruction of *Fortune*'s tea came as a spontaneous act of the people, rather than on orders from the committee of correspondence. If so, the patriot leaders were rapidly losing control of the situation in Boston.[51]

New Yorkers were also given an opportunity for violent resistance to dutied tea. On 22 April 1774, while Captain Lockyer of the teaship *Nancy* was still in the city, James Chambers appeared off Sandy Hook in his ship *London*. Chambers had been one of the New York shipmasters who had refused to take on board any of the East India Company's tea the previous September. New Yorkers were therefore surprised to be told by other captains just arrived from London that Chambers now had dutied tea on board. Chambers did not realize that he had been informed against, and on the strength of his adamant denials of the charge, the pilots consented to bring his vessel into the harbor. As soon as he reached the wharf, a committee of citizens boarded *London* and began questioning the master. After further denials, Chambers finally confessed to having on board eighteen quarter-chests of Hyson tea, which he said he had planned to sell on his own account to several ladies of his acquaintance.

The committee decided to ask the crowd that had gathered what should be done about Chambers's tea. In answer, a number of them climbed aboard and heaved the chests into the water. Captain Chambers managed to slip away during the commotion. Early the next morning, leaving behind his ship and all his personal belongings, he made his way to Lockyer's ship at Sandy Hook. Now that they had had their own tea party, New Yorkers seemed to feel much better.[52]

Before the year 1774 had ended, virtually every colony became the scene of violent demonstrations against dutied tea. In late June the ship *Grosvenor* arrived at Portsmouth, New Hampshire, with twenty-seven chests of tea from England. The cargo was entered at the customhouse, and the owner, Edward Parry, paid the duties, but a committee appointed by a special town meeting persuaded him to ship it out again. Three days later the tea was on its way to Halifax, Nova Scotia, where its reception was more cordial. No sooner had the good patriots of Portsmouth recovered from this threat than thirty more chests arrived to Parry's account in September. This time a small mob assaulted his house, and again he agreed to send his cargo elsewhere.[58]

Other violent demonstrations were held at Greenwich, New Jersey, and York River, Virginia, while a score of communities registered their renewed hatred for dutied tea in more peaceful ways. Perhaps the most serious incident occurred at Annapolis, when the brig *Peggy Stewart* arrived in October. One of the owners, fearful of public criticism, tried to avoid entering the 2000 pounds of English tea on board. The customs officials would not allow a partial entry, however, and the owner thereupon paid the duties on the tea. The local patriots were furious. They forced the owners to make public apology for their effrontery and to burn both the tea and the vessel that had brought it. Joseph Galloway, influential speaker of the Assembly of Pennsylvania, was shocked by the scene, and when he came away he wrote to a friend, "I think Sir I went to Annapolis yesterday to see my Liberty destroyed. . . ."[54]

In none of these demonstrations was the question of the East India Company's monopoly at stake. The events of the previous autumn, and particularly the destruction of the tea at Boston, had awakened the colonists to the fact that English tea was still subject to taxation by Parliament. As a Philadelphian put it:

> There is not an American from New England to South Carolina who would so far shame his country as to accept this baneful diet at the expense of his liberty. Fleets and armies . . . will never subdue the noble spirit of Freedom which fills our breasts. . . . I love Great Britain and rever the King; but it is my duty to hand down Freedom to my posterity, compatible with the rights of Englishmen; therefore no tea duty, nor any unconstitutional tax whatever.[55]

Out of the events of December 1773 and the months that followed came a new spirit of unity in colonial America, recognized by radical Sons of Liberty and Loyalists alike. The patriots' cause was no longer local or provincial, wrote the New York consignees in late December, but continental in scope. "No one circumstance could have taken place more effectively to unite the colonies than this manoevere of the tea," John Hancock reported to his London friends Hayley & Hopkins. Under the pseudonym UNION a writer in the *Boston Gazette* called for a congress of the American colonies. Boston's Thomas Cushing wondered what would happen if the British ministry were to react to the Tea Party by adopting punitive measures. He and his fellow Americans would not have long to wait for their answer.[56]

IX

THE MINISTRY CHOOSES COERCION

EVEN before the East India Company's tea had left London for the voyage to America, many Englishmen had had grave misgivings about the undertaking. William Dowdeswell had predicted that the Americans would not accept dutied tea. The Duke of Richmond attempted without success to use his great influence among the Company's proprietors to block the plan. Governor Pownall had also cautioned the Company that an unfavorable reaction was likely. But these and other warnings from members of the Opposition had little effect on either Company officials or the Ministry.

Many of the English merchants trading with the colonies also expressed doubt of the plan's wisdom. John Norton, a Virginian residing in London, learned of the scheme in early July from some of his friends among the directors of the Company. They suspected that the Ministry was more interested in establishing the power of taxation than in helping the Company. Norton strongly advised them not to go through with the plan. The very fact that the Company tried to arrange an innocuous method for payment of the duties reflected a concern for the scheme's acceptance in the colonies. A rumor appeared in London as early as mid-October that Americans were planning a non-importation agreement against tea until grievances were redressed.[1]

One of the first letters from America reporting opposition to the tea plan was written by Thomas Wharton on 5 October to his brother Samuel. James & Drinker and Pigou & Booth wrote to their correspondents in London the same day, and probably all three letters arrived by mid-November. Thereafter a steady stream of reports brought news of the mounting crisis. In early November, Governor Tryon sent Lord Dartmouth an account of the patriots' attitude at New York and enclosed copies of all five *Alarm* pamphlets.[2]

News of possible trouble seemed to take the Colonial Secretary by surprise. Apparently Dartmouth had not even been informed that the East India Company had in fact shipped its tea to America. Sometime in December his assistant, John Pownall, prepared a letter to the Company secretary inquiring "whether the Company has obtained any Licenses to export Teas on their own account to North America; and if so, what Steps have been taken in consequence thereof." Pownall was somewhat embarrassed for his chief, and the letter was probably never sent. On its wrapper was written in Pownall's hand: "the inclosed letter . . . consequential of the Advices lately rec'd from America is submitted to your Lordship and shall be either sent or suppress'd as you think fit." It seems almost incredible that Lord North, who as one of the Treasury Lords had approved the Company's export license in August, did not inform his Colonial Secretary of the impending shipment. As a result of this apparent oversight not only was Dartmouth totally unprepared, but so too were the colonial governors, none of whom had received either a copy of the Tea Act or advance notice that the tea was coming.[3]

If Dartmouth was long ignorant of the approaching crisis, he very soon became the most informed man in England on the American situation. Colonial governors and other officials kept him posted on the latest developments in their provinces. Letters from American merchants and other inhabitants were forwarded to him or were printed in the London newspapers. One from a Philadelphian complaining about the plan appeared in the *Morning Chronicle* on 29 December. Three days later the editor published a retort from an indignant reader who charged that Americans opposed the scheme only because they preferred to smuggle cheap Dutch tea. "Their whole concern is about themselves, without the least regard for the prosperity of Great Britain," wrote the outraged Londoner. "Here we see the colony patriot without his mask." The first of many British broadsides against the colonies in the final crisis had been fired.[4]

The East India Company was sufficiently alarmed by reports from America to call the directors into special session on 7 January 1774. They decided to instruct the consignees that, if the tea were refused at their respective ports, they were to send it on to Halifax, as the best place from which it could then be sold throughout America. John Butler and John Cochran, merchants there, were chosen as consignees. The next day the directors wrote all the governors concerned to urge them to co-operate with the emergency plan. Except for New York it was of course far too late for such a compromise.[5]

Lord Dartmouth took a more rigid approach to the problem. Writing to General Haldimand at New York on 8 January, he authorized him "upon a proper requisition and in such case only, to protect the King's subjects from insult and oppression, and to remove any unlawful obstruction that may be given to the commerce of this Kingdom." At the same time, Dartmouth wrote Tryon to express his confidence that those opposed to the landing would meet "with Disappointment and Disgrace." To the Governor he also enclosed a copy of his letter to Haldimand, while pointing out "that it is His Majesty's Wish & Intention, that no Requisition should be made by the Civil Magistrate [for military action] upon a slight ground, but only in cases of absolute Necessity when every other effort has failed." As of early January, at least, it was not the King's purpose to cram dutied tea down the throats of the Americans by force of arms if such action could be avoided.[6]

Uncertainty appeared in other government quarters as well. On 14 January the *Morning Chronicle* reported the rumor that Lord North planned "rigorous measures" against the Bostonians as soon as Parliament cleared away its other business. But when King George wrote to Dartmouth on the 19th to say that he was much hurt by Boston's opposition to the tea, he took a more moderate tone. He did, however, fully expect that tea would find its way there eventually. "When Quebec is stocked with that commodity," he concluded, "it will spread Southward." These references to Boston must have been to the behavior of its patriots during November, for no one in Great Britain had yet learned of the Tea Party.[7]

On 20 January 1774 John Hancock's ship *Hayley,* which had left Boston on 22 December, arrived in England. News of the Boston Tea Party spread rapidly through London. By the 22nd most of the major newspapers had reprinted the account which Edes and Gill had published in their *Boston Gazette* of 20 December. It was of course favorable to the patriots, and, perhaps because of this, first reactions in London were mild. The *Public Ledger* introduced its report with a most sympathetic paragraph, describing the Bostonians as people "who have undergone every species of injurious treatment" at the hands of an administration "so infatuated with the idea of despotism as to be qualified only to subvert instead of maintain the liberties of a brave & free people." On 26 January after a fast passage Philadelphia's tea-ship *Polly* reached England. Two days later came news from the consignees at Charleston that their shipment had been seized and stored by the customhouse officers there.[8]

Even after learning the fate of their teas in America, the directors of the East India Company remained surprisingly calm. Every few days they sent to Lord Dartmouth copies of the latest dispatches they had received from the consignees, and when Gilbert Barkley arrived on board *Polly,* they arranged for him to confer with the Colonial Secretary. On 4 February the chairman met with Dartmouth and North to ask for assistance in gaining compensation for the Company's losses, but there were no bitter demands that the Bostonians be punished for the destruction of the tea. The Ministers' response was favorable, and the directors soon after drafted a memorial making a formal request.[9]

Meanwhile Barkley had offered the Company less than £15,000 for the tea returned from Philadelphia, with the thinly veiled intent of selling it to American smugglers at St. Eustatius. The Company had conservatively valued the cargo at over £21,000 and saw no reason to give Barkley bargain rates for such a venture. When the Philadelphian insisted on an allowance in consideration of the losses he sustained by being prevented from selling the tea at Philadelphia, the Company stalled him off for over a year, and finally in March 1775 granted him fifty guineas. What happened to the tea returned to England on board *Polly* is unknown. Technically it should have been seized by the customs authorities for violation of the ban on re-importation, but obviously this did not happen, for the Company had the opportunity to turn down Barkley's offer for it.[10]

Beginning on 29 January, and continuing over several weeks, the British ministry held a series of meetings to decide what action the government should take in response to the Boston Tea Party. The principle of firmness was established at the outset when the ministers agreed that measures should be adopted "to secure the Dependance of the Colonies on the Mother Country." On Friday evening, 4 February, they met again at Lord Rochford's house, where Dartmouth made a significant suggestion. He proposed that the King, on his own authority, direct the Governor of Massachusetts Bay to remove the seat of government to a place in the province least likely to be influenced by the town of Boston. Furthermore, Dartmouth suggested that the King order the removal of the Boston district custom-house to some other port. This proposal did not necessarily mean the closing of Boston harbor, although subsequent action did in fact have this result. The Cabinet unanimously agreed to the scheme. In a note to George III the next day North specifically referred to the proposition as one "for punishing the Town of Boston." The policy of punitive measures had been adopted.[11]

The Cabinet also decided to consult with the attorney-general and the solicitor-general on the legal questions involved, and Dartmouth presented the facts of the Boston Tea Party to them on the day following. The Secretary then asked the legal officers two questions: Did these acts amount to the crime of high treason? If so, who were the persons chargeable and how should they be prosecuted?[12]

The officers replied on 11 February. In their opinion the proceedings at Boston did in fact constitute high treason, namely, "the levying of war against His Majesty." These proceedings, they continued, "are an attempt, concerted with much deliberation and made with open force . . . to obstruct the execution of an Act of Parliament imposing a duty on tea and to put a general restraint upon the exercise of a lawful trade." The report closed with the opinion that the men involved at Boston could be tried either in America or in England.[13]

Already the Ministry was pursuing two policies at once. One dictated the punishment of Boston as a whole; the other attempted to single out guilty individuals and charge them with treason. The Ministry lost no time putting the dual plans into effect. Dartmouth drafted a letter to the Lords of the Treasury on 11 February in which he told them to issue the necessary orders for removing the customhouse from Boston. He had just received an opinion from the legal officers that the King could in fact take this step on his own authority. Two days later North suggested that the Admiralty instruct Montagu to prevent vessels from entering Boston. Here was the first clear indication that the Ministry in fact meant to close Boston harbor altogether. North cautioned Dartmouth that since his letter to the Treasury "is to be enter'd among our Papers, it had better relate only to the removal of the Custom House Officers and be grounded on Reasoning precisely adapted to it." North apparently hoped to avoid any suggestion that the Ministry was embarked on a general policy of punitive action. On the 16th the Cabinet made further arrangements for the arrest of individual patriot leaders and for their removal to England for trial. At the same time, it agreed to send two guard ships with their full complements of marines as reinforcements for Admiral Montagu.[14]

Then on Saturday, 19 February, in a meeting held at Lord Dartmouth's, the Cabinet changed its tactics and made clear its intentions respecting Boston. Although the legal officers had ruled that the King could remove Boston's customhouse on his own authority, the ministers decided to propose a bill in Parliament that would specifically close the port of Boston until the East India Company was indemnified for its losses, either by the town itself or by a committee representing the body of people whose resolutions had led to the destruction of the tea. The change was apparently made because under the previous proposal ships could still have used Boston harbor by entering and clearing at the nearest customhouse. It was Dartmouth's assistant, John Pownall, who suggested that the port be closed by law instead. One result of the switch was to preserve for a few months longer George III's reputation in the colonies as a benevolent sovereign by making Parliament responsible for the Boston Port bill and other coercive measures.[15]

On 19 February, Francis Rotch, Captain Hall, and half a dozen others who had been in Boston during the tea crisis gave their accounts of the events to the Privy Council. None of the witnesses was able, or perhaps willing, to be very specific in linking names with particular actions. This so discouraged the solicitor-general and attorney-general that at the next cabinet meeting held on the 28th they announced that in their opinion no charges of high treason based on the depositions taken at the Privy Council session could be brought against any individuals. The Cabinet thereupon set aside its earlier plans to prosecute individual leaders among the Boston patriots and placed its entire dependence on Parliament for action. Another reason for dropping the scheme of prosecuting individuals was that the Cabinet apparently wanted the legal officers to assume full responsibility for the consequences. George III was annoyed by the change and blamed Dartmouth, but he was pleased with the Cabinet's decision to go ahead with the plans to bring the punitive bill into Parliament.[16]

The reasons why the Ministry adopted a policy of coercion in response to the Boston Tea Party are many and varied. One was the long-standing reputation of Boston as the seed-bed of trouble in the colonies. Ever since the Stamp Act riots of August 1765 Boston had been regarded as the worst among all American communities in defying the authority of Great Britain. Subsequently, it seemed to the Ministry, a procession of insults flowed from the Bay colony. In late January 1774, for instance, the Privy Council was investigating the matter of the Hutchinson letters sent to Massachusetts Bay by its colonial agent, Benjamin Franklin. The Council had before it the General Court's insolent demand that Hutchinson and Andrew Oliver, the lieutenant-governor, be removed from office. Franklin appeared before the Council on 29 January, just one week after news of the Boston Tea Party had reached England. The solicitor-general, Grenvillite Alexander Wedderburn, unleashed an acrimonious attack against Franklin personally and against the colony he represented. The Philadelphian barely controlled his temper as the galleries snickered at Wedderburn's witty and sarcastic onslaught. For Franklin the Boston Tea Party could not have come at a worse moment, and for Boston the province's petition against Hutchinson was equally ill-timed.

One self-styled expert on the Americans wrote Dartmouth in February to pass along his opinion of the Bostonians. "They are not only the worst Subjects, but the most truly immoral Men of any he [the writer] has had to deal with." They did not pay their bills, were religious hypocrites, and possessed "morose and sour" tempers. Finally, this observer charged, Boston was as bad "as Sodom itself was for a Vice which ought not be named." "Treacherous and seditious," wrote another who claimed first-hand experience with Bostonians. Later in the year Richard Champion, the Bristol merchant, recalled that popular anger against Boston was so great after news of the Tea Party had arrived that he scarcely dared speak out in defense of America. "The clamour against the proceeding is high and general," wrote Franklin, as he strongly urged the Bostonians to compensate the East India Company for its loss.[17]

As news came in from the other ports to which the East India Company had sent its cargoes, it soon became apparent that Bostonians stood alone as destroyers of the tea. No matter that only through the inaction of Governor Penn at Philadelphia and contrary winds off New York had the inhabitants there avoided violent measures; no matter that refusal of the tea at those ports cost the Company over £3000 in useless freight charges; Boston's misdeed was monstrous by comparison. Arthur Lee, the Virginian long resident in London, warned Sam Adams that Boston's enemies would take advantage of this situation. And he was correct. Despite the repeated testimony of witnesses that the Bostonians intended only to force a return of the tea, the Ministry was convinced by the mobbing of Clarke's store and house, the illegal meetings, and the armed guard standing watch over the tea-ships that the destruction of the tea was the result of an over-all plan. Although patriots at New York and Philadelphia also obstructed commerce and, along with those at Charleston, prevented the execution of the Townshend Act, the ministers chose to ignore these offenses in view of Boston's long history of defiance. In early March the Lord Chancellor, Lord Apsley, commenting on the proceedings at a cabinet meeting he was unable to attend, noted how important it was "to mark out Boston and separate that Town from the rest of the Delinquents." [18]

In reaching their decision to adopt a policy of coercion, the Ministry was influenced to some extent by the reports and opinions of others. They were of course largely dependent on the letters of Hutchinson, Leslie, Admiral Montagu, and the consignees for information about the events at Boston. While none of these men actually recommended that Boston be punished, their description of conditions there could lead to only one conclusion — that the re-establishment of a firm governmental authority was an urgent necessity. "To concede," explained Hutchinson, "endangers raising the like spirit in other cases of Parliamentary authority." [19]

One of the strongest statements came from General Thomas Gage, recently returned from his post as commander in chief in America. Gage called on the King in early February to confer on American affairs, and George III later reported the conversation to Lord North. "They will be Lyons whilst we are Lambs, but if we take the resolute part they will undoubtedly prove very meek . . . ," Gage had said. The King was in complete agreement with this appraisal, since he himself had lost patience with the colonists. Ever since repeal of the Stamp Act, George called it "that fatal compliance," the Americans had increased their pretensions to the "independency which one state has of another, but which is quite subversive of the obedience which a colony owes to its Mother Country." The grand object of British policy was to bring about this obedience. Concessions had only made matters worse, maintained the King; the time had come for compulsion. And his determination to try coercion was a decisive factor in the formulation of government policy in the early months of 1774.[20]

In taking this stand the King and his ministers were supported by large numbers of his British subjects. Within a few days after news of the Boston Tea Party reached England, America was the leading subject of political conversation throughout London. The question whether the colonists were justified in their conduct was the topic for one of the debates at the famous Robin Hood. (The negative triumphed.) "People talk more seriously than ever about America," acknowledged Gage in early February. And most observers agreed that the balance of opinion was overwhelmingly against the colonists. "There is not a more obnoxious character here at present, than that of a friend to America," admitted one. People in London were so exasperated, reported another colonist there, that one could not even talk with them. Franklin wrote of "a great Wrath" sweeping the country. Arthur Lee went so far as to express concern for the lives of "active Americans here," because, as he explained, "Parliament is equal to any thing." [21]

In February the London newspapers began to receive letters from their readers suggesting appropriate governmental action. Those advocating coercion did so in the common belief that this was the only way to restore Bostonians to a sense of duty. Repeal of the Stamp Act became the common scapegoat, a retreat which many said had been inspired by cowardice and weakness. The Americans, wrote LYCURGUS, "released in a manner from their Allegiance," became virtual rebels, sinking into all sorts of "licentiousness and cruelty, common to a state of anarchy." The Boston Tea Party certainly appeared to substantiate the charge, for all the Bostonians would have had to do to make their protest effective, several correspondents pointed out, was refuse to purchase the dutied tea. What else but a determination to provoke rebellion, "to drive this Country to Extremities," as Dartmouth put it, could explain the mad actions of the Bostonians? Addressing the House of Lords on 1 February, the Earl of Buckinghamshire moved for the immediate punishment of

Massachusetts Bay without further investigation. A fleet of fourteen sail was proposed to stop Boston's commerce and 10,000 troops were to be sent. It was no longer a question of Britain's right to legislate for America. The question was whether Britain should bear all manner of insults and receive laws from her colonies. Dartmouth succeeded in persuading Buckinghamshire to withdraw the motion, but only on the grounds that all the dispatches from America were not yet in.[22]

Some correspondents offered specific cures for the American illness. If Boston succeeded in its aim of becoming independent, Britain would be undone, claimed ANAXAGORAS. He recommended sending over a large body of regular troops to keep "in due subjection . . . those refractory, fierce republicans," whom he somewhat ironically equated with Cromwell's Roundheads. In a more waggish vein another writer submitted a long list of British manufactures which should immediately be shipped to America, "exempt from duty." Included were five or six "large floating castles," 10,000 troops, and artillery well supplied with grapeshot to be crammed down the Americans' throats if they do not agree to drink tea, "and without making damned wry faces" in the process. T. H. had another interesting suggestion. If the Americans found it to their advantage to boycott English tea, would it not be of great benefit both to our health and economy if we vowed not to use any American tobacco?[23]

A number of observers defined the issue dispassionately: either Parliament did or did not have a right to tax the colonies. AN ENGLISHMAN's comments illustrated what a difficult dilemma this problem presented. On the one hand he considered it *unwise* for Parliament to tax Americans, who were not represented in that body. They have been denied "one of the most sacred and valuable privileges" of a free government, he admitted. On the other hand ENGLISHMAN was unwilling to follow his own argument to its logical conclusion that it was therefore *unjust* for the British Parliament to tax Americans. "The Legislature had passed an Act and the grand point to be ascertained is, in what manner obedience to that act is to be enforced." Repeal of the Stamp Act, for instance, to

ENGLISHMAN was an act of lenity, not of justice. Two weeks later, however, he wrote to denounce the suggestion by ANAX-AGORAS that more troops be sent to America.[24]

The prolific Thomas Crowley, writing under the pseudonym AMOR PATRIAE, suggested a compromise at a time when compromise was sought by neither side. The Americans should be granted representation in Parliament with the guarantee that they would be liable only to the same kinds and rates of taxes as were British subjects at home. But in sending a copy of his article to Lord Dartmouth, AMOR PATRIAE took a different tone, recommending that armed sloops and frigates be sent to capture American vessels bound out to foreign ports.[25]

Outright suggestions of conciliation were rare during England's first reaction to the Boston Tea Party. One observer did write directly to Dartmouth when he heard rumors of coercive measures being planned. "There is something so monstrously absurd in such language that I believe it is only propagated as a Libel on the Administration." The Americans have acknowledged Great Britain's authority by their suppliant petitions for a redress of grievances, he went on to say. They wanted only a return to the state they had been in before the Stamp Act. As a starter, this writer suggested, why not remove the duty on tea by a hint to the East India Company that a petition from it to this effect would be granted?[26]

The Reverend William Gordon of Jamaica Plain, near Boston, had made a similar suggestion to Dartmouth in December. In his reply the Colonial Secretary rightly explained that, if he were to propose repeal of the tea duty now, he would be thought as mad as the Bostonians who had destroyed the Company's cargo. Dartmouth considered himself a firm friend of America, and he had once supported a policy of concession by backing repeal of the Stamp Act. But during his first eighteen months in the office of Secretary of State for the American Colonies he was unable to promote repeal of the remaining Townshend duty on tea. Arthur Lee blamed Dartmouth's failure on a lack of will. Perhaps a more determined statesman could have succeeded, but the odds against Dartmouth were great. The seven-member Cabinet, by which major policy decisions were made, was dominated by the Bedfordites Sandwich and Gower, whose faction had always held colonial demands in utter contempt. They were supported by three other advocates of firmness among the ministers: the Earl of Suffolk, the Earl of Rochford, and Lord Apsley. Even Lord North insisted on retaining the tea duty as a means of keeping up Parliament's right of taxation in America. As late as mid-March 1774 Dartmouth still maintained the hope of removing the annoying tea duty. In a chance conversation Shelburne reported the Secretary as stating "his determination to cover America from the present storm to the utmost of his power, even to repealing the Act." [27]

Despite his role in initiating the Port bill, Dartmouth was apparently most reluctant to punish Boston. In early March it was rumored that he was about to resign from the government because of a difference of opinion concerning America. In mid-month American-born William Lee wrote from London that the policy of coercion had been adopted by the Cabinet over the opposition of both Dartmouth and North. This opinion was subsequently shared by the Duke of Grafton, Governor Pownall, and others. Although the Ministry was to show a united front in guiding the Port bill through the House of Commons, when the measure reached the House of Lords, dissension was apparent to many observers.[28]

Why then did Dartmouth contribute to the "present storm" between Great Britain and the colonies by proposing a policy of coercion? In the first place, as he explained in his letter to William Gordon in February, he considered the colonists as subjects whose duty was to submit to the laws of Parliament. If they objected in a dutiful and decent manner to those laws they thought violated their rights, such as the duty on tea for instance, "the Parliament of Great Britain will undoubtedly shew that she looks upon them as her Children and wishes only to treat them as such." Dartmouth could hardly avoid suspecting that the purpose of Boston's opposition to the tea was "to drive this Country to Extremities." If such was the case, all hope of reconciliation was ended, "and both sides must be content to take what follows." Precisely because he considered himself a friend to the colonies, Dartmouth was most deeply disturbed by the Boston Tea Party. The willingness of this usually mild-mannered gentleman to punish all the inhabitants of Boston, guilty or innocent, clearly indicated the depth of his exasperation.[29]

Secondly, Dartmouth was convinced that most Americans would agree that the Bostonians had committed a serious offense and would not oppose the government's efforts to force that town to make restitution for the property some of its inhabitants had destroyed. Finally, Dartmouth realized that the climate of opinion in Great Britain demanded that some sort of firm action be taken in the case, and he undoubtedly shared this viewpoint himself. Nor were his fellow Cabinet ministers likely to accept anything milder than coercion. He was less perceptive of the consequences such a policy would bring about, however, than Chatham, who freely predicted that "if that mad and cruel measure [the Port bill] should be pushed . . . , England has seen her best days." Given the limited vision of Lord Dartmouth, and the pressures put upon him by the other ministers and the country at large, nothing less than the Boston Port bill could have been expected.[30]

As drafted by Attorney-General Thurlow and Solicitor-General Wedderburn, the Port bill declared that because of the destruction of tea at Boston, it was clear that commerce could no longer be safely carried on there nor the duties collected by the customs officers. The customhouse was therefore to be moved to Plymouth, and after 1 June 1774 no vessel engaged in coastwise or foreign trade would be allowed to enter Boston harbor or depart after the 15th. The only exception was for coasters carrying fuel and provisions for the use of Bostonians, such vessels having first to stop at Marblehead for inspection. The seat of government for Massachusetts Bay was transferred to Salem, and the Customs Commissioners were to move there too. The Act was to remain in force until the King was satisfied that full restitution by the inhabitants had been made to

the East India Company and to others who had suffered during the
tea riots. But nothing in the measure in fact bound the King to
reopen the port under these or any other conditions.[31]

The Ministry was ready to present the bill to Parliament shortly
after 1 March, but the House was still engaged in other business.
On the 7th, however, the King's message on the American situation
was read by Lord North. George III called for measures that would
put a stop to the disorders and would secure the dependence of the
colonies on the Crown and Parliament of Great Britain. North then
placed before the House the extensive documentary evidence that
Dartmouth had been collecting since early in the year. Included
was correspondence from the governors, consignees, and others in
America, copies of newspaper articles, handbills, and other inflammatory literature, and the depositions of witnesses to the Boston
meetings and to the destruction of the tea.[32]

Debate on the Boston Port bill opened with its first reading on
14 March. Introducing the measure, Lord North succinctly stated
the Ministry's position. The purposes of the bill were two — to put
an end to disorder and to secure the dependence of the colonies.
Other colonies had also espoused pernicious doctrines, he admitted,
but at Boston they were carried into effect. Commerce was no longer
safe there, North asserted, nor in fact were the customhouse officers.
And three times since 1768 the Customs Commissioners had been
obliged to flee the town. On these grounds, he concluded, the customhouse at Boston should be moved elsewhere. To prevent the smuggling of goods into the harbor in the absence of the officers, the
port would have to be totally closed up by units of the fleet.[33]

Having established this logical basis for the bill's necessity, North
then offered another reason for its passage. "There does result what
will in its consequence be a punishment upon the town of Boston.
I am not sorry for it, Sir; I think the town of Boston has deserved
the animadversion of every part of this c[ountry?]." He hoped in
fact by making an example of Boston to discourage other towns from
following its lead in the future. Anticipating criticism of the bill's
punitive aspects, North said it could not be helped that innocent and

guilty were to be punished together, for the "innocents" had failed to act against the guilty, and so the entire town was responsible for the outcome. North then cited several cases in which English cities had been fined for failure to apprehend murderers and other criminals. The fact that at Boston the mob had destroyed only the tea showed that it was not acting spontaneously but was carrying out the will of what North inaccurately described as the town meeting. Boston was the more culpable for having incited other towns to oppose the tea. It would have been landed without opposition at New York, for instance, had Boston not set a bad example, North charged. Restitution to the Company for its losses would not be enough to reopen the port. The Crown would be in no hurry for that step until the town showed "full signs of a different disposition . . . ," North concluded. Lest anyone think that the Port bill was all the government had in mind for Boston, North assured his listeners that there was more to come, but he refused to discuss the details of the Ministry's other bills.[34]

The Prime Minister then turned to explain why he thought American affairs had come to such a state. Too many concessions in the past were to blame, and North seemed a little embarrassed that he had been the one to propose repeal of most of the Townshend duties. But he was glad he had held the line on the tea duty. Some have said that the present difficulties would have been avoided had the duty been repealed last year, North noted. But he emphatically denied this assertion. The Americans did not mind the tax; it was a submission to the authority of Parliament that they opposed. "If they deny authority in one instance, it goes to all; we must control them or submit to them." Having spoken for over an hour, North then urged unanimity in punishing Boston for its denial of Parliament's supremacy.[35]

Any hope that the bill would be defeated or even watered down by the Opposition was immediately dashed by the speakers who followed North. Many of them were men of moderate views who in earlier times had taken up the American cause. But now they more or less reluctantly came to the support of the Ministry. George

Dempster reminded the House that he had been among the few who had voted against the Stamp Act, but he considered the Boston Tea Party "a very great outrage." Perhaps Dempster was influenced by his position as a director of the Company. Although believing that American happiness depended on Parliament's using its power of taxation gently, he could not bring himself to oppose the Port bill. Rose Fuller, another defender of the colonies, who had moved repeal of the tea duty and would soon do so again, announced tentative support of the measure, although he was concerned about the consequences. Even Thomas Pownall, former governor of Massachusetts Bay and one of America's staunchest friends, fell into line, while insisting that the Bostonians had not intended that the tea be destroyed. Most surprising was the conversion of Colonel Barré, a spokesman for colonial rights of long standing. Barré agreed that Boston deserved punishment and announced his hearty approval of the Port bill.[36]

Other speakers for the bill added more heat than light to North's arguments. Grosvenor underscored the theory that repeal of the Stamp Act had caused all the trouble. Rushout used the old "virtual representation" doctrine to justify Parliamentary taxation of the colonies and concluded that the Americans would not be satisfied until they were wholly independent of Great Britain. Calvert did not think the proposed bill punishment enough. He called for the immediate revocation of the charter of Massachusetts Bay and further demanded that Parliament should "make every ship and fishing boat pay something to those outrages they have committed." [37]

On the first day of debate only two members rose to the defense of Boston. John Sawbridge began a speech denying Parliament's right to tax the colonies, but the King's Friends were seized by such fits of coughing that he had to sit down. When order was finally restored, Sawbridge continued by pointing out flaws in North's argument. Boston's town meeting had never authorized the destruction of the tea. That act was perpetrated by men in disguise, whose connection with the meeting of the town had never been established. "The town of Deal might as well be made answerable for a set of smugglers," he said. Sawbridge then challenged Lord North to seek restitution from Boston first before calling for enactment of the Port bill. As for himself, Sawbridge opposed the further alienation of America and announced he would vote against the measure.[38]

William Dowdeswell then attempted to rally the Opposition. Why should Boston be punished and not the other towns which had also opposed the landing of the tea? he asked. Was not North's game simply to separate one province from another, one town from another? The Port bill was an *ex post facto* punishment, for no law had required Boston to do anything specific about the tea. The cases cited by North concerning London, Glasgow, and Edinburgh were not precedents at all, since the laws involved were different. Was Boston to be convicted without a hearing? Only "more mischief, more folly" could result from such a procedure as proposed by the Ministry. But Dowdeswell and Sawbridge stood alone that first day.[39] It was nearly 8 p.m. when the four-hour debate ended. Later that evening Joseph Yorke reported the proceedings to his patron, the Earl of Hardwicke. North's speech he described as "one of the coldest and unanimated . . . I have ever heard . . . , received as cooly as it was delivered. . . ." On the bill's second reading, Rose Fuller demanded to know what other measures were planned for Boston, but North refused to say, maintaining that the Port bill stood by itself as fitting punishment. "I am for punishing," agreed Rose Fuller.[40]

On 23 March Parliament went into committee for further consideration of the bill. By then Rose Fuller had come to believe that the measure was too severe. If the Bostonians did not submit to it, there was no choice "but to burn their town and knock the people on the head." If troops were sent to enforce the bill, the Americans would unite to crush them, he predicted, pointing out that in America the men all had arms and knew how to use them. Rose Fuller suggested an alternative. First impose a fine, perhaps £25,000, out of which the East India Company would be compensated for its losses. If Boston refused to pay within a specified period, then the port should be closed. But the town should be given the opportunity to make restitution before its harbor was blocked up.[41]

In answer to Rose Fuller, North pointed out that four or five frigates could enforce the act, thus making troops altogether unnecessary. He also maintained that the severity of his original proposal would be felt only if Bostonians refused restitution and continued to defy Parliament. Lenity had only led them to believe we lacked power or resolution, he concluded. Firmness would now convince them that we were in earnest. If rebellion resulted, America alone would be answerable for it. Others joined North in opposition to Rose Fuller's scheme, but his compromise also gained some adherents. In the heat of the debate that followed, Van declared that, if Boston refused to make restitution under the Port bill, the harbor should never be reopened. "*Delenda est Carthago*," he thundered. This outburst was too much for Colonel Barré, who called for a more dispassionate approach to the crisis. But Barré still could not bring himself to support Fuller's motion, and Dowdeswell remained silent. The Opposition's one slim chance to force a compromise had slipped away. When the King learned of the bill's easy progress, he could not restrain his enthusiasm and ascribed its success to "the rectitude of the measure." [42]

Two days later, on 25 March, came the motion for passage of the Boston Port bill. William Bollan, agent for the Council of Massachusetts Bay, petitioned to be heard in behalf of Boston. On the pretext that Bollan was not representing the entire General Court, however, the House voted 170 to 40 not to hear him. The members did agree to hear a petition written by Arthur Lee and signed by twenty-nine "Natives of America" resident in England, that called for defeat of the bill on the grounds it was repugnant to every principle of English law. Then Edmund Burke joined Dowdeswell, Sawbridge, and Rose Fuller to speak in opposition. Burke did not object to punishing the offenders, but to punish innocent people for not preventing a riot was "a devilish doctrine," particularly since Governor Hutchinson himself had failed to call upon the army or the navy to preserve the peace. Burke predicted that the direst consequences would result from the bill and demanded in its place a general review of Britain's over-all policy toward America.[43]

In his final rebuttal Lord North summarized the position of the Ministry. He was confident that the bill would bring about the desired result — the obedience of the Bostonians. If we were to give them a hearing, he argued, we would simply have to listen to their denials of our right to tax them. Firmness was the only policy that could establish our right. Now was the time to be assertive. At a few minutes past 8 p.m. on 25 March the House of Commons passed the Boston Port bill. Although a division was not taken, the fact that only forty members had earlier voted to hear Bollan's petition was indicative of the Ministry's strength. The *General Evening Post* estimated the voice vote to be at least five to one in favor of passage.[44]

When the House of Lords came to consider the Boston Port bill on 28 March, the Opposition made a somewhat better showing. Bollan had asked Lord Dartmouth to support the presentation of his petition, but the Secretary made numerous excuses to avoid the obligation. Only through the friendly offices of Lord Stair was Bollan finally heard, but his appeal was in vain. The petition from the "Natives of America" was also read to the House of Lords. When sympathetic English merchants trading with America tried to circulate a petition among their friends, however, Gilbert Barkley somehow managed to prevent it. Nor would any of the principal English manufacturers raise a hand in opposition to the measure. According to Shelburne, hardly an impartial observer, the original division of opinion among the Ministry revealed itself during the debate, but the bill passed the House of Lords with little trouble. On 31 March George III gave it his royal assent. The policy of coercion had received the overwhelming endorsement of the British government.[45]

Why had Opposition M.P.'s not made a better showing on the question of the Boston Port bill? The most obvious answer is that many of them as individuals could not condone the destruction of property at Boston no matter how sympathetic they had been in the past to the American cause. Chatham, for instance, termed the Tea Party a criminal action and showed no interest in lending his name to Opposition countermeasures. Rockingham was also unable to justify the Bostonians' conduct, although he did feel that they had been sorely provoked. In the second place, a number of Opposition spokesmen believed that the Ministry's reaction to the crisis was rather mild. Colonel Barré, for instance, had told the Earl of Shelburne he was pleasantly surprised by the moderation of North's language in introducing the measure. Shelburne, himself, was impressed by Dartmouth's apparent willingness to support repeal of the tea duty as soon as the present crisis was over. "This, together with Lord North's language . . . ," reported Shelburne to the Earl of Chatham, "leads me to hope the further measures will not be so hostile as was expected." On the other hand Barré condoned his support of the Ministry partly as a means of freeing himself for subsequent opposition, if necessary.[46]

Finally, the Opposition did not have sufficient imagination to offer a sensible alternative of its own. Only Rose Fuller's hastily contrived substitution reached the floor of the House, and the followers of Shelburne, Chatham, and Rockingham, along with the other friends to America, were too disorganized to unite around it. Having seized the initiative, the Ministerial forces had no difficulty in carrying the day. As events of the next two months proved, they had almost the entire country behind them in their belief that coercion was the only way to win American obedience.[47]

If one were to judge by the paucity of public commentary, Britons in general had given little attention to the American colonies since the Townshend Act crisis of 1767-70. To be sure, the burning of the cutter *Gaspée* was reported in many newspapers, and the affair of Hutchinson's letters drew comment, but mainly in terms of the duel it had inspired between John Temple and William Whately rather than the question of Hutchinson's fitness as governor. Even after news of the Tea Party reached England, letters to the press on the colonial situation were surprisingly few in number. But with the introduction of the Boston Port bill in Parliament, interest quickened. From mid-March on, the newspaper columns bulged with letters concerning the immediate issue of the destruction of the tea at Boston and what Great Britain's reaction ought to be.

Comment on the Coercive Acts themselves for the most part reflected what was said in debate on the floor of the Commons. Those that favored the Boston Port bill, for instance, did so largely because they considered the Tea Party a challenge to the authority of Great Britain, a challenge which could only be answered by severe action. One writer declared that on the basis of evidence in the papers laid before Parliament Boston was actually in rebellion, for its people had levied war against the King. In the opinion of governors and others who had reported on the situation, he continued, the colonies would soon be independent unless something were done. In this context LYCURGUS could congratulate Lord Dartmouth on the passage of such a "salutary and lenient law," which would become a monument to Dartmouth's "humane feelings." [48]

Underlying many letters was the attitude seen earlier of utter contempt for Bostonians — "cowards, whimpering wretches," one writer called them; "fraudulent, hypocritical, vindictive, detestable," wrote another. Boston's rebelliousness was attributed by a third commentator to the assertion that three-fourths of them were Scotsmen! One interesting view was that Hutchinson had deliberately refused to call the troops into Boston to see how the inhabitants would behave if no one intervened in the crisis. "Left to the exercise of their own Judgment . . . , they have given all the world an example of it," concluded an observer.[49] It was particularly aggravating to some that Boston's opposition to the tea seemed to inspire the same defiance elsewhere in America. Punish Boston, the wellspring of rebellion, and the other colonists would quickly come to their senses.[50]

Many of those disapproving of the Boston Port bill, on the other hand, saw in its severity rank injustice. One writer asked what London's reaction would have been if its port had been closed in punishment for the Wilksite riots. JUSTICE pointed out how much more severe was the treatment of Boston than of either London or

Edinburgh in the cases cited by Lord North as precedents for the Port bill. Edinburgh had been charged with an overt act of murder and rebellion, yet Parliament had not decided the issue for four months, during which time the city was allowed to present witnesses in its defense. In the end, Edinburgh, was fined £2000. In the case of Boston, however, accused of a trespass and a riot only, Parliament had acted within seventeen days after introduction of the bill, and a spokesman for the town was denied a hearing. Closing their port, JUSTICE estimated, would cost Bostonians £500,000.[51] It was particularly annoying to others that Scottish ministers should accuse the Bostonians of rebellion when their own countrymen had twice within the century borne arms against their British sovereign. The assertion that Scotland went unpunished for its treason made the point doubly sore.[52]

Other objections to the Port bill found their way into print. Writing under the pseudonym FABIUS, Benjamin Franklin pointed out that closing Boston harbor simply made it more difficult for the merchants there to pay their debts to Great Britain. English merchants would be the ultimate sufferers, he warned. BRECKNOCK challenged Parliament's jurisdiction in the matter altogether; as only a civil tort was involved in the destruction of the tea, he claimed, the Company's remedy lay at common law. Subsequently BRECKNOCK came up with a wild theory that ultimately responsible for the Boston Port bill was the present King of Prussia, who stood in line to succeed George III, the writer claimed. The alleged plot included veiled threats and secret letters delivered to Queen Charlotte's private chambers. JUSTICE had a plot of his own, with Thomas Hutchinson cast in the villain's role. Perhaps Hutchinson had hired the men disguised as Indians to destroy the tea at Boston, in the hope that the town would be blamed and punished. Why else did he prevent the tea from being returned and at the same time refuse to call on Admiral Montagu to protect the cargo? JUSTICE queried.[53]

A number of writers criticized Parliament for punishing Boston without first finding out if the town would make amends. The port should be closed only if the restitution were not forthcoming within a reasonable period, Franklin insisted.[54] It was widely reported in London that the Bostonians were already taking steps to pay back the Company for its losses, even before they could have learned of the Port bill.[55] London merchants trading to Boston were confident that the town would make up the damages. A committee headed by Champion & Dickinson, Hayley & Hopkins, and Lane, Son, & Fraser met with North on 18 March. They offered to become answerable to the Company for £16,000, far more than the tea was worth, if the Minister would give them six months to settle with the town before closing the port. North allegedly asked them if they would also become answerable for Boston's conduct if more tea were sent there, a condition which the merchants regarded as absurd and impossible. The Minister then told them to return to their counting-houses and leave politics to his direction. A similar offer by London's Lord Mayor to cover the loss was also rejected. Perhaps the belief that Boston would quickly pay up and that therefore the Port Act would be of temporary duration only persuaded many English moderates not to protest the measure in public. At the same time those writing letters in favor of the Port bill encouraged uncertain members of Parliament to support the government's policy of coercion.[56]

In the end Great Britain accepted the Boston Port Act for a number of reasons. As Edmund Burke explained it, there was in Parliament "a general Notion that, *some Act* of power was become necessary, and that the hands of government ought to be strengthened" by full support of the Ministry's proposals. Although some Britons objected that the measure was too harsh, most seemed to believe that the Bostonians would quickly make compensation to the East India Company for its losses. Having been brought to heel, Boston would then make trouble no longer. Furthermore, most Englishmen assumed that the other colonists in America would show little sympathy for the fate of Boston's inhabitants. Left to suffer alone, the rebellious town would soon be forced to capitulate. Few commentators realized, as Chatham did, that Parliament had just given the American patriots a new cause in which to unite.[57]

X

THE NATION CONSIDERS ITS COLONIES

PASSAGE of the Boston Port Act at the end of March fulfilled the Ministry's determination to punish the town whose inhabitants had destroyed the East India Company's tea. But mere punishment was not enough. The conditions that had permitted such a breakdown of governmental authority in Massachusetts Bay would have to be removed as well. The Ministry therefore laid plans for a reform of the government and administration of justice in that colony. As soon as the Port bill passed the House of Commons at the end of March, Lord North introduced additional legislation intended to improve government in Massachusetts rather than to punish its citizens further.

The Ministry's plans for reform gave the Opposition forces an opportunity to air their views on colonial policy. The Port bill had offered them a poor platform. For Boston had indeed committed an offense, and although one could quibble over details of the punishment, one could not, in view of strong public resentment against the Bostonians, make a successful case for leniency. Moreover, it was difficult to counter the Ministry's charge that opposition to its measures in Parliament only encouraged further rebellion in America. But when the Ministry introduced the first of its reform bills in late March, the halls of Parliament rang with the verbal exchanges of a great debate on the colonies that lasted until the end of May.

In early February 1774 Arthur Lee had warned Sam Adams that the Ministry would probably propose changes in the charter of Massachusetts Bay. The project had been considered and laid aside three years before, but now the Ministry wasted no time in taking advantage of the Boston Tea Party crisis to bring up the idea once again. At a meeting in mid-February the Cabinet discussed the possibility of drafting a bill to alter the government of Massachusetts. At that time the ministers considered deferring its submission to Parliament until the next session, "in order to give an Opportunity to the General Court [of Massachusetts] to show cause . . . why such an Alteration should not be made." At a meeting held on 1 March, however, the Cabinet apparently thought better of this lenient approach and decided to draw up a bill immediately. It was introduced in the House of Commons on 28 March. Another opportunity to combine compassion with coercion was thereby put aside.[1]

The new Massachusetts Government bill incorporated some of the principles that the Ministry had tentatively proposed in 1770. It provided that the King should appoint members of the Governor's Council, tenure to extend during his pleasure, rather than that they be elected annually by the General Court. On the suggestion of Governor Bernard, apparently, the bill proposed that jurors were to be summoned by the county sheriffs, whom the Governor was empowered to appoint or remove without consulting the Council. The governor was also given sole power to select judges of the inferior courts of common pleas and other court officers. Perhaps the most radical alteration of governmental practices in Massachusetts Bay was the provision, also attributed to Bernard's influence, that limited towns to one meeting a year and only then for the purposes of electing officers and making needful rules for local administration. The recent practice of town meetings' resolving to ban importations of British goods, denouncing the customs officers, or denying Parliament's right to tax Americans was to be ended. Only by permission of the governor could a community in Massachusetts Bay now call a special town meeting. Although Dartmouth approved of the change in the Council, the bill's other provisions were adopted over his opposition.[2]

In April, North's government brought in two other measures

designed to strengthen the authority of royal government in Massachusetts Bay. One was the Administration of Justice bill, permitting
the governor to send home to England for trial all government
officers accused of crimes committed in the execution of their official
duties. It was expected that these men could better preserve the
peace and execute the laws if freed from the apprehension that they
would be tried by an American jury whenever they performed their
duties overzealously. This bill was apparently the suggestion of the
Bedfordite ministers in the Cabinet and was unsuccessfully opposed
by Lord Dartmouth. The last of the measures proposed to correct
abuses in the colonial system was the Quartering bill, which authorized the commander in chief of British forces in North America to
seize barns and unoccupied buildings for billeting his troops in the
various towns that had not provided conveniently located barracks.
Although applicable to all of the colonies of North America, the bill
was undoubtedly inspired by the fact that the patriots of Boston had
forced Colonel Leslie's regiment to occupy the barracks on Castle
Island, in the middle of the harbor. The disadvantage of such a
location was made abundantly clear on the night of 16 December
1773.[3]

The implications of these bills were broad indeed. The new
powers of appointment to be granted the governor of Massachusetts
Bay would give him firm control of the entire executive branch as
well as wide influence in the judicial branch. The fact that Thomas
Hutchinson was at the same time to be replaced by Thomas Gage,
commander in chief of the British army in North America, made the
governor's position doubly strong, especially since he would be
specifically authorized by the Quartering bill to billet his troops in
Boston proper. The royal appointees to the Council could of course
be counted upon to co-operate, and in its capacity as the upper
chamber of the legislature, the Council might also check excesses
growing out of the popularly elected House of Representatives.
Depriving the patriots of town meeting as a forum in which to
marshal opposition against British authority would make the governor's task far easier. And now that jury members were no longer

to be chosen by the people, there was some hope that offenders against the peace would be more readily brought to justice. Finally, the bill exempting customs officials and others from prosecution in America for crimes committed in the line of duty would assure a more vigorous execution of the laws. With passage of the so-called Coercive Acts, the inhabitants of Massachusetts Bay would soon know the full meaning of their colonial status as interpreted by Lord North's administration.

Introducing the Massachusetts Government bill, Lord North let the documents placed before the House bear witness to his assertion that executive authority had been undermined in that colony and that "new modelling" the charter was the only remedy. His supporters contented themselves with statements that government there needed strengthening. Lord George Germain contributed the idea for altering the method of selecting jury members and then added rhetorically: "Shall Charters stand in our way, then, to bring Peace and Good Order?" North agreed that they should not.[4]

It was on the question of charter rights that the Opposition forces based their strongest objections to the Government bill. Predictably, William Dowdeswell opened the attack. "You are not now contending for a point of honor," he charged the Ministry; "you are struggling to obtain a most ridiculous superiority. . . ." Sir George Savile picked up the argument three weeks later as the debate was renewed. He had a good excuse to be prejudiced against the Bostonians, for six years earlier the mob protesting the seizure of Hancock's sloop *Liberty* had destroyed a fast sailboat which the customs collector, Joseph Harrison, planned to send as a gift to Saville. Learning of his loss, the M.P. had muttered that it was fortunate repeal of the Stamp Act had already taken place, or else he might have changed his vote. Saville had long since forgiven the Bostonians, however, and now he came to their defense, arguing that charters were sacred, revocable only by due course of law for punishment or for a breach of contract. Welbore Ellis replied on the Ministry's behalf that Parliament could alter or revoke charters as best suited its interpretation of the public good.[5]

The two also exchanged words on the propriety of taking action without giving the colonists a hearing. Ellis referred Savile to the inaction of the provincial Council during the tea crisis as evidence that altering its nature was sufficiently justified. When General Conway protested the Ministry's refusal to hear William Bollan's petition on behalf of Massachusetts Bay, the House shouted him down. In a rebuttal North too ducked the issue of a hearing. Dowdeswell moved to bring up Bollan's petition the next day, but the House voted against the proposal, 95 to 32.[6]

The two former colonial governors then sitting in Commons took up the cause of Massachusetts Bay. Governor Johnstone wondered aloud why Hutchinson had retreated into the country at the height of the crisis. "No man of common sense," he said, could understand such behavior. Thomas Pownall drew on his experience as a governor of Massachusetts Bay to refute charges against the Council. He contended that the charter in no way permitted the Council to block action by the governor, especially when he acted in his capacity as commander in chief. If he had been governor at the time of the Boston Tea Party, Pownall asserted, he would have ordered the military to aid in keeping the peace. Pownall admitted, however, that it was generally wise for the governor to consult with the Council, especially in Massachusetts Bay, and that it was inexcusable for the councillors to withhold their support on this occasion. Perhaps they ought to be censured, but they had surely committed no crime, and their inaction did not suspend the powers of government.[7]

In the bill's final reading, on 2 May, Joseph Dunning spoke for two hours in denunciation of the Ministry's program for Massachusetts Bay. He explained that, when the Port bill stood alone, he did not think it severe enough to oppose, but now that the next two measures were introduced, he wondered at the Ministry's intentions. Dunning was criticizing one of North's shrewdest tactics in managing the Coercive bills through the Commons. The Minister had repeatedly refused to disclose during the debate on the Boston Port bill the nature of the further legislation the Cabinet had in mind. Some members of the Opposition apparently even thought that

North would propose repeal of the tea duty. The total effect of the three measures now before the Commons, said Dunning, was "war, severe revenge, and hatred against our own subjects." Had he and others known of the Ministry's full intentions, perhaps the Opposition could have organized a more effective defense. Most M.P.'s must have suspected what was coming, however, for Arthur Lee seemed to know in early February.[8]

As the debate ran on into the night, others who had supported the Boston Port bill now announced their opposition to the Government bill. Colonel Barré returned from his earlier defection and was joined by a number of moderates whose position on the first measure was never disclosed in debate. But William Meredith, once a staunch Rockinghamite, remained in North's camp and spoke in favor of the Government bill. At three o'clock on the morning of 3 May, the measure passed the House of Commons, 239 to 64.[9]

Debate on the Administration of Justice bill, introduced on 15 April, was at first interspersed between readings of the Government bill until it too was finally passed in early May. Members of the Commons took relatively little interest in the measure, although one of the most notable speeches of the entire session was delivered against it by Isaac Barré. Colonel Barré's behavior during the debates on the Coercive Acts was symptomatic of the dilemma facing the Opposition forces. In their disgust at Boston's destruction of the tea many members of the Opposition had voted for the Port bill, perhaps even expecting any day to learn that the town had made amends for its misbehavior. When they discovered that North had two other bills up his sleeve, however, they suddenly realized that the Ministry's plans were not so moderate as Barré, for one, had thought. Now came the awkward scramble to find a consistent line of counter-attack.[10]

In opposing the bill that permitted accused officials in America to be tried in Britain, Barré first explained that he had supported the Boston Port bill only as "a bad way of doing right." But the present proposal was so unwarranted and so oppressive that he was immediately aroused against it. North had cited no instance of an official's failing to receive justice before an American jury. In contrast Barré made much of Captain Preston's acquittal in the Boston Massacre trial. The retired colonel warned from his own experience that the soldiers stationed in the colonies would abuse their exemption from an American trial and provoke the inhabitants into the very rebellion the bill was supposed to prevent. Put the military beyond the authority of the civil power, and the consequences will be disastrous. "You are becoming the aggressors," Barré concluded, "and offering the last of human outrages to the people of America by subjecting them in effect to military execution." [11]

When debate resumed on the bill in the Commons, only forty-one members were present. Now John Sawbridge pointed out another danger in the measure: it was unfair to expect American witnesses to travel all the way to England at their own expense to testify against an accused official. In most cases the culprit would have to be acquitted. Sawbridge boldly charged that North intended to enslave America, and he went on to suggest that the Minister would enslave England too if given the opportunity. [12]

North turned aside the exaggerated personal attack launched against him and sprang a trump card. He had just learned that Captain Gorham had returned to England in his ship *Fortune* with the report that his cargo of tea had also been dumped into Boston harbor. North seized on this information to ridicule those who had claimed that the Bostonians had seen their error and would voluntarily make restitution to the Company. Although irrelevant to the merits of either the Massachusetts Government bill or the Administration of Justice bill, North's argument was an effective one. In desperation several Opposition speakers suggested that broadening the governor's powers of reprieve would be a wiser means of achieving the same end, but the Ministerial forces showed no interest, despite the fact that they had already instructed Gage to use his pardoning authority when necessary. On 6 May the Commons passed the Administration of Justice bill by the overwhelming margin of 127 to 24. [13]

There was no mistaking that the Opposition had been badly outmaneuvered in the passage of the Coercive bills through the Commons. Rockingham's colleagues could not even make a decent showing against the Port bill in the House of Lords. The Marquis therefore planned a meeting with a few of his friends for 21 April to prepare an attack on the Massachusetts Government bill when it reached the Upper Chamber. The Duke of Manchester had warned him on the 20th that opposition to the measure might not be so popular among the public at large. "The high spirit of the People of England is certainly at this moment irritated against the outrages of the Bostonians," he wrote, "and the doctrine they avow of absolute indepency [sic], leads many moderate men to wish Government may succeed to reduce them within the bounds of Law and Order." Manchester had welcomed what he called Rockingham's original proposal not to oppose government in these measures. Then, he suggested, we could have stepped forward as defenders of American liberty when opinion in England turned against the Ministry's program, but he admitted that the time was still far off. Manchester could not help believing with North that the New England governments did need reformation, although he did not agree with all of the Ministry's proposed changes.[14]

In his reply Rockingham hid whatever disappointment he may have felt in Manchester's acquiesence to the government's policy toward Massachusetts Bay. He denied that his intention was to make no opposition at all but agreed that the people of Great Britain had not yet realized the folly of violent measures. Not so opportunistic as the Duke, Rockingham believed that unless his forces opposed the bills at their passage, silence would be taken as assent. He was determined to make a firm stand against the Massachusetts Government bill — "a Very Very Strong and Arbitrary Measure" — which he likened to the proceedings against the East India Company of the previous year.[15]

When the Massachusetts Government and Administration of Justice bills reached the House of Lords, Rockingham's small band did the best it could against overwhelming odds. As in the case of the Port bill, the Upper Chamber agreed to hear William Bollan's petition in behalf of the accused. The struggle was not entirely in vain, for out of it came three notable declarations in support of American rights. The first was the speech delivered by Lord Camden on 11 May against the Government bill. Admitting that the Port Act had some shadow of right because of Boston's violent resistance to law, Camden saw no such justification to abrogate the colony's charter. "I look upon such a step as tyrannical; I think resistance in such a case is lawful. . . ." Camden would not go so far as had the Duke of Richmond, who several days before had declared that, if it came to armed rebellion, he wished to see America prevail against Great Britain. Camden was too much of an Englishman not to support his country, he admitted, "let her cause be good or bad." But the present bill, he said, would produce either war or slavery, each of which depended on violence for its support. "You made the colonies free," Camden concluded. "You cannot now rob them of their liberty." [16]

On 11 May he Opposition also drew up a formal Protest against the Ministry's American policy, which summarized most of the objections made during the long debates on the Coercive Acts. Acting against Massachusetts Bay in haste and without a hearing was entirely unjustified, the minority proclaimed. The protestors criticized the content of the Government Act as well. Giving the King authority to appoint the councillors would upset the equilibrium of government in Massachusetts Bay. In many ways the governor and the Council there were made more powerful than the King and Privy Council in Great Britain. "The lives, liberties, and property of the subject are put into their hands without controul." The Opposition also objected to the policy of colonial taxation that these measures were intended to support. All our present difficulties, said the protestors, have stemmed from attempts to enforce this unwise policy. They called for a return to those principles upon which repeal of the Stamp Act had been based. [17]

One week later the Opposition presented a second protest — this one against the Administration of Justice Act. Only eleven Peers signed the first document and nine the second, although twenty-

four had voted against one or more of the Coercive Acts. At least
the protests deprived the Ministry of the claim to unanimity that
it so badly wanted at the outset of the debates. Already criticized for
a want of patriotism, Rockingham and his supporters would receive
still greater abuse for their opposition. They had taken their stand
against policies they feared could only result in disaster, but in the
spring of 1774 they stood virtually alone.[18]

In the debates on the Ministry's program for Massachusetts Bay,
members of Parliament often discussed the more theoretical aspects
of the relations between Great Britain and her American colonies.
Contributors to the London press pursued these broader questions
with even greater thoroughness, as did pamphleteers later in the
year. Almost all observers seemed to agree on the supremacy of Great
Britain over the colonies. But from this starting-point they fell into
disputes on the origin of this supremacy, whether it resided in the
Parliament or in the Crown only, whether it could be better maintained by lenient or coercive measures. Virtually all discussions
seemed to lead ultimately to the question that both Britons and
Americans considered basic: did Parliament have the right to tax
the Americans?

In introducing the Port bill to Commons Lord North noted that
one of the purposes of the measure was "to secure the just dependence
of the colonies on the Crown of Great Britain." As the debate on
that and subsequent bills continued, however, it became clear that
what most government supporters were concerned about was the
dependence of America not on the Crown but on Parliament. As
Solicitor-General Wedderburn put it: "The Americans do not attack
the law, otherwise than attacking the legislature that made it. . . .
They say that no laws shall be put in force there; you [Parliament]
say, all laws shall." In fact no member of Parliament who spoke in
debate during the spring of 1774 denied the right of that legislature
to govern America. Even Edmund Burke, in his famous speech
on repeal of the tea duty, noted that one of Parliament's duties was
to "superintend all the several inferior legislatures . . . , to coerce
the negligent, to restrain the violent, to aid the weak and de-

ficient. . . ." In Burke's concept of the Empire, as in North's, Parliament's powers over the colonies were unlimited. They disagreed only in the exercise of these powers.[19]

The colonists' common assertion that they owed allegiance to the Crown rather than to Parliament was in fact particularly annoying to many Britons. Mr. Welbore Ellis, for instance, in supporting the Massachusetts Government bill, explained that although it was the King who originally granted the charter of Massachusetts Bay, "it was the Legislature's duty to correct the errors that have been established in the infancy of that Constitution. . . ."[20]

Parliamentary supremacy was endorsed by many contributors to the English press, some of whom equated the colonists' opposition to Parliamentary authority with traditional Tory support for the King's prerogatives. In the Revolution of 1688 and in the Act of Settlement the English people "disposed of the Crown as they thought proper," wrote one. Thereafter the Crown's title to American land was by gift.[21] A common argument was that sovereignty in England had been delegated by the people to "the King, Lords and Commons in Parliament assembled." The King therefore had no right to act alone in colonial affairs, and by inference the colonists were wrong to recognize only his authority. HAMPDEN argued that in accepting the Navigation Acts, the colonists had in fact accepted the authority of the House of Commons alone, where those bills had originated.[22]

Behind the specific assertion of Parliamentary supremacy was a more general attitude shared by most Britons toward the colonies. Benjamin Franklin succinctly described it in 1767. "Every man in England seems to consider himself as a piece of a sovereign over America; seems to jostle himself into the throne with the King, and talks of *our subjects in the Colonies*."[23] In opposing colonial requisitions as an alternative to Parliamentary taxation, Richard Rigby considered it undignified for Great Britain "to go cap in hand" to request financial aid from the colonies. The most common figure of speech describing the relationship was that of parent and children.

COLUMBUS probably spoke for thousands of his fellow Britons when he wrote:

> Is it not rather a Duty incumbent on the Parent when every lenient every soothing Expedient has been tried in vain, to bring [their children] back to their Allegiance by a gentle Correction? *Spare the Rod and spoil the Child*, is an Adage perfectly applicable in the present Instance.

Even William Dowdeswell referred to the colonists as children, but as he did so, he reminded Parliament that just as there were "forward children" so too were there "peevish parents." The more often parents demanded "You shall do it," the more likely children would answer "I won't." [24]

Those who maintained that Americans owed a filial duty to Great Britain commonly based their argument on the historical assertion that the mother country had founded the colonies, and had nurtured, supported, and defended them at great sacrifice to itself in blood and money. LYCURGUS, for instance, claimed that from the infancy of the colonies, Parliament had promoted the efforts of the "primitive wanderers," and that only under its benevolent care had the settlements in America become wealthy and flourishing.[25]

Others used history to launch a devastating attack against the Americans. Their ancestors had fled from England when the cause of freedom was threatened by the Stuarts and had sought refuge from that oppression "which they had not courage enough to resist at home." [26] At every danger the Americans had come whimpering to England for help, most recently involving the mother country in a ruinous war with France that had resulted in an enormous debt. Now that their safety was assured, "they shamelessly tell us they are NOT ENGLISH SUBJECTS . . . !" [27] In a series of letters SAGITTARIUS gave vent to particularly bitter feelings against the New England Puritans, who by hangings and persecutions had denied to others that liberty that they had claimed in England. Their descendants, like their forebears, were "factuous [sic] and turbulent and ever in opposition to legal government." [28]

Defenders of the colonies also appealed to history for support of their own arguments. In an open letter to Lord North a writer who identified himself as an American stated that when Britons migrated to Ireland and America, they continued within the King's allegiance, but, "ceasing to participate or enjoy the legislative power of this realm, the operation of this power over them necessarily terminated." Denying this contention, LYCURGUS claimed that the British subjects who planted the colonies "carried with them their allegiance, an indelible mark of their subjection to a British Parliament. . . ."[29]

The battle over historical interpretation raged on. AN OLD ENGLISH MERCHANT, B.T. A PLAIN CITIZEN, and FABRICIUS all maintained that the Americans had pushed back the wilderness and established thriving communities largely by their own efforts. Major John Cartwright, over the pseudonym of CONSTITUTIO, argued that whatever aid Great Britain gave the colonies was for its own selfish purposes of extending its commerce, and the Americans were therefore under no obligation in receiving it. Others picked up this theme to emphasize the great economic benefits which England and other parts of the Empire derived from the North American settlements. But some commentators denied the importance of these blessings altogether. When the Robin Hood society debated "whether Europe in general or England in particular had reaped any advantage from the discovery of America," only one speaker argued in America's favor, and the body agreed almost unanimously that the New World had been on the whole prejudicial to the interests of the Old.[30]

One popular defense of the colonists advanced by numerous writers emphasized the major contributions Americans had made since 1690 to British military and naval successes in the New World. Most commonly cited, of course, was colonial support to invasions of French Canada, and particularly the capture of Louisbourg by forces from Massachusetts Bay in 1745. Also noted were the defense of Jamaica in 1703, the attack on Cartagena in 1739, and the reduction of Havanna in 1762, in all of which campaigns Americans had participated. In rebuttal it was asserted that since the colonists fought only for their own welfare, they deserved no special credit for their efforts.[31]

No Englishman went further in renouncing the authority of Parliament than did John Cartwright, who in his pamphlet *American Independence the Interest and Glory of Great Britain* asserted that Great Britain should declare the colonies independent of Parliament but not of the Crown. A.B. summed up the pro-American argument when he asked how the people of England as represented in Parliament obtained the sovereignty over the colonies claimed for them. It was certainly not by concession of the Americans nor by the spirit of English laws which they had carried with them to the New World. The Americans were subjects of the King, but they could not also be subjects of the King's own English subjects.[32]

If almost all Britons agreed that Parliament enjoyed legislative authority over the American colonies, they disagreed over the best means by which to exercise this authority. Among members of Parliament coercion was obviously the more popular method of handling disobedient colonists, as evidenced by the overwhelming adoption of the Ministry's program for Massachusetts Bay. One of the most common arguments heard on the floor of the Commons was simply that lenient measures in the form of repealing the Stamp Act and most of the Townshend duties had already been tried. Since colonial agitation against Parliamentary authority had continued, it was time to change to a policy of severity. This contention was put in its most extreme form by Charles Van, the member who had called out *"Delenda est Carthago,"* in his enthusiastic support of the Boston Port bill. Later he urged that if the inhabitants of Massachusetts Bay were to oppose the three measures then under consideration:

> I would do as was done of old in the time of ancient Britons,
> I would burn and set fire to all their woods, and leave their
> country open, to prevent that protection they now have; and
> if we are likely to lose that country, I think it is better lost
> by our own soldiers, than wrested from us by our rebellious
> children.[33]

Other members of Parliament were more restrained in their advocacy of coercion. But many feared that the situation in America would steadily worsen unless decisive action was taken against Massachusetts Bay. The colonists there had tarred and feathered citizens, attacked customs officers, destroyed private property, and denied the authority of Parliament. "We must risk something," as North put it; "if we do not, all is over." To do nothing would simply invite further disobedience in both New England and the other colonies. "We are now to establish our authority or give it up entirely," North concluded at the end of the debate on the Government bill, and 239 members of Commons agreed with him.[84]

Members of Parliament who favored a lenient policy toward the colonies explained their position primarily in terms of expediency. Unable to condone the recent misbehavior of Bostonians, they argued instead that coercion would make matters worse and that only leniency could regain American respect for the mother country. Among the advocates of the latter policy were several of those M.P.'s who had served as military or civil officers in America. Colonel Barré told the Commons that the Americans "may be flattered into anything, but they are too much like yourselves to be driven. Have some indulgence for your own likeness," he urged; "respect their sturdy English virtue." Governors Johnstone and Pownall, along with native Americans living in London, agreed that coercion would only goad the Americans into further disobedience.[85] Outside of Parliament, however, most civil and military officers with experience in America apparently predicted that the colonists would submit to the Ministry's program of coercion.[86]

Numerous letters calling for severe countermeasures against the Bostonians appeared in the London press. Some writers recommended a policy of retribution such as might be pursued against defeated aggressors or traitors, and they pointed out that Great Britain would never permit a foreign country to insult the nation as the Bostonians had. Others followed out the parent-child theme in calling for paternal chastisement. Those who advocated a shift toward severity did so mainly out of impatience for the lenient policies of earlier years. As in Parliament, Britons in general seemed to share a strong belief that repeal of the Stamp Act had caused the current alienation of colonial affections. One commentator, who signed himself PERIANDER, claimed to have voted for repeal while in Parliament. But the Boston Tea Party had so angered him that he labeled the Bostonians parricides and called for rigorous punishment.[37]

Compared to some of the plans suggested by newspaper contributors, the Ministry's program for Massachusetts Bay seemed moderate indeed. MERCATOR AMERICANUS proposed that all the inhabitants there be prohibited from building ships, from engaging in foreign and coastwise trade, and from the fishing banks of Newfoundland. Then, by some sort of loyalty oath apparently, the submissive citizens would be granted a general pardon, while those refusing to sign would be treated as rebels. Another writer suggested that "about one hundred of these Puritanical Rebels in Boston" ought to be hanged. COLUMBUS proposed that if Massachusetts Bay continued its disobedience its charter should be annulled and half the province be added to New York and the other half to Nova Scotia.[38]

Most of those advocating severity agreed that the Bostonians, at least by the Tea Party, were in an actual state of rebellion and that the situation therefore demanded prompt military attention. MERCATOR AMERICANUS proposed dispatching a sizable fleet and army. CRITO suggested 6000 or 7000 men and a train of artillery. The next cargo sent to Boston should be gunpowder tea, one wag offered.[39] Readers were assured that the Bostonians would cower before a display of strength from the mother country. "The Boston Rioters will scamper behind their counter . . . ," wrote one observer, "then assume an affecting hypocritical air, clasp their hands, cast up their eyes to Heaven, [and] wonder if the King knows their oppressed condition." [40]

Despite the vehemence of these writers, however, the Opposition was not without support for its policy of leniency. Not only was this approach more likely to regain the affections of the Americans, many Britons believed, but the precedents set by the adoption of harsh measures seemed dangerous. If Parliament could remove Boston's customhouse to another town, it could do the same with London's. Others also thought they saw in the Ministry's American policy a premeditated attack on the liberties of all Britons, which merely reflected the whole course of the North administration. To a number of commentators, the American question was obviously little more than a political football in the warfare between the King's Friends and the Opposition.[41]

Only occasionally did commentators show a real understanding of British-American relations as they actually were in the 1770's. With a rare sense for the concept of historical development, one writer explained that, although the colonies were Britain's children, they had now grown up. "When [the child] is become in turn a man, he does not cease for that to be a son, but he is a competent judge of his own actions; he still owes to his father respect and deference, but no longer a blind obedience." Few Englishmen were willing, or able, to see the basic truth of this statement from their limited observation-post.[42]

In the great debate on colonial policy all arguments ultimately led to the question of Parliamentary taxation of America. Members of the House of Commons had the opportunity to discuss the issue when on 19 April Rose Fuller moved to repeal the tea duty. Fuller himself said little in support of his own motion other than to assert that without an olive branch in one hand in the form of repeal Parliament could not expect its coercive measures to succeed.[43]

George Rice, on the other hand, expressed the fear of many members when he asserted that repeal of the tea duty would be interpreted by the colonists as a surrender of Parliament's right to tax them. If one concession were made, there would be no end to their demands for more. Charles Cornwall, once a dependable supporter of Rockingham but now a convert to the Ministerial forces, pursued this theme at greater length. The colonists had not been contented by repeal of the Stamp Act. They would be content only when Britain has given up its authority over them altogether. Thus was the issue joined.[44]

The principal speaker on repeal of the tea duty was Edmund Burke. Burke's long political career had begun less than ten years before, when he accepted the post of private secretary to the Marquis of Rockingham in the summer of 1765. In January of the following year Burke took a seat in Parliament, where he fought hard for repeal of the Stamp Act. After the Rockingham ministry fell from power, Burke continued to support his patron's policies with great skill. He opposed the Townshend duties in 1767, defended the East India Company in 1769 (he was a stockholder), and was a champion of Wilkes. In 1770 he became the agent for the colony of New York. Over the years Burke's sharp tongue had won him the grudging respect, though not the affections, of most members of Parliament. In the spring of 1774 he had already spoken against North's proposals for punishing Massachusetts Bay when he rose on 19 April to deliver his famous speech subsequently published under the title *On American Taxation*.[45]

Burke opened his argument by attacking those who asserted that repeal of the Stamp Act had encouraged the Americans to greater obstinacy and that to rescind the tea duty would have the same undesirable result. If repeal of Parliamentary taxation would lead to further American disobedience, as some contended, then why had the North administration rescinded the other Townshend duties in 1770? Burke asked. Not because those duties were "uncommercial," the justification offered by the Ministry at the time. Rather it was because, as Hillsborough had said in his circular letter of 1769, repeal would be the means "of re-establishing the confidence and affection of the colonies." This reason was, and remained, equally valid for the repeal of the remaining duty on tea.[46]

Burke then traced in detail the development of British colonial policy from the first Navigation Act in 1660 to the year 1764. By the principles thus established the colonies contributed to the Empire through their commerce. During that period direct revenue was never contemplated by Parliament. Even Governor Bernard referred to Parliamentary taxation in 1765 as an innovation, Burke noted. The Americans accepted the arduous terms of the original system through habit and because they prospered under it. Burke admitted that the Navigation Acts had been evaded in America, but their validity had never been denied. After all, Britons at home evaded unpleasant laws of trade as well. But the Americans did complain when a new system of internal revenue was combined with the familiar system of commercial monopoly, for in the opinion of Burke the product was rank slavery.[47]

Burke blamed passage of the Townshend Act in 1767 for all the current difficulties with America. Declared to be an act to raise a revenue in America, it had not done so since partial repeal in 1770. The duty on tea that remained served only to provoke the colonists into further acts of violence. Burke urged the Commons to repeal it. To do so would not in any way reduce the revenue of the Empire or the power of Parliament, he argued. Left to tax themselves for the common supply, the colonists would do so, as they had done under the old system. If they refused, Parliament then might step in to tax them itself. But return to the old system first, Burke begged his colleagues. Until you do, there will be no peace for England.[48]

When Burke had finished, others rose to support his arguments. Both Charles Fox and Thomas Townshend agreed that repeal of the duty would restore tranquility in America. Barré and Dowdeswell could foresee only more violence if the Coercive Acts were sent to America unaccompanied by conciliatory measures of any kind. But the opponents of Fuller's motion returned to their argument that repeal would be regarded in America as a sign of weakness. Neither Wedderburn, Beauchamp, Burgoyne, nor North was dissuaded by Burke from their conviction that repeal implied giving up a right and would encourage the colonists to greater assertions of independence. When division came on the question at 11 p.m., the majority supported North, and the motion was rejected, 182 to 49. This was the highest proportion of votes gained by the Opposition forces during the course of the debates on American policy. But the margin was still nearly four to one against them. Yet another opportunity for conciliation had passed by.[49]

As in the case of other topics on colonial policy debated that spring, commentators in the press seemed to be more interested in the theoretical basis for Parliament's claim to the power of taxation than were the members of Parliament themselves. This was mainly because few of the latter doubted that power. They were more concerned with the practical effects of retaining or repealing the duty on tea.

The American contention that Parliament had no right to tax the colonies was supported on a variety of grounds. AMICUS noted that the original charters vested the colonists with the privilege of taxing themselves and exempted them from taxes levied by bodies other than their own assemblies. In answer to the common assertion that Parliament had the power to legislate for the colonies and therefore the right to tax them as well, Benjamin Franklin wrote to the *Public Ledger* under the psuedonym RATIONALIS. He pointed out that in Great Britain taxation was actually separate from the legislative power. While the governing power rested with both Houses of Parliament jointly, taxes were a voluntary grant of the Commons alone from the property of those represented by that body. The assertion that Parliament had legislative authority over the colonies, therefore, gave no support to the contention that the Commons had authority to tax the Americas. This was Chatham's basic position, and it was endorsed by a number of other commentators.[50]

One writer pointed out that the House of Commons based its exclusive right to tax Britons without concurrence of the Lords on the claim that only the Lower House was representative. How, then, could that House tax Americans, whom it did not represent at all? Many contributors regarded taxation by one's representatives as an old English principle, founded on the rock of Magna Carta, fought for by Hampden in the ship-money controversy, and continued as an integral part of a Briton's liberties. Although a number of writers exhumed Grenville's old "virtual representation" arguments, others quickly refuted the theory.[51]

Defenders of the Ministry's policy did not forget that the debate over the colonies had broad political implications at home. None of the Rockingham forces could sensibly have expected immediate profit from opposing North's program, because they realized how popular it was among the people. As Burke had made clear at the end of his speech on taxation, the road followed by Rockingham, Dowdeswell,

and himself was not the road to the assumption of office — at least
not until the Ministry's policies were proved wrong by the events of
history. Meanwhile the Opposition members were vulnerable to every
charge by Ministerial spokesmen that they were giving aid and comfort to rebellion abroad and were obstructing an obviously popular
policy at home. When Rose Fuller admitted in Commons that the
nation fully endorsed the Administration of Justice bill, he was
chided for opposing the will of the people.[52]

Part of the difficulty facing the Opposition lay in the nature of its
argument. The Ministry was faced with long-term disobedience in
the colonies, which had culminated in what nearly all Britons seemed
to agree was an inexcusable act of violence in Boston. Its proposed
response, punishment of Boston and reforms in the government of
Massachusetts Bay, perfectly conformed with the widely accepted
attitude that the colonies were Britain's children and therefore owed
the parent a dutiful submission. When one punished his disobedient
child at home, the youngster was generally brought to his senses and
reminded of his filial duty. It was simple logic that such a salutary
outcome would result from the Ministry's program for Massachusetts
Bay.

To answer this contention the Opposition had to assert instead that
in response to the punishment of Boston the colonies would unite in
open rebellion and that as a result the nation would be ruined. But
this argument faced several difficulties. First, it ran counter to experience: chastised children generally did not rebel; secondly, few
Britons thought the other colonies would come to Boston's aid;
thirdly, the argument implied that Great Britain, with the world's
most powerful fleet, would be unable to cope with a rebellion if it
did come; finally, predictions of impending disaster always appear
implausible to a people as happy and prosperous as were most Britons
in the 1770's.

The Opposition had no other recourse, however, than to play
Cassandra to a nation of optimists. In the Commons virtually all its
spokesmen foretold a national tragedy. Fuller summed it up just
before passage of the Administration of Justice bill. "You will com-

mence your ruin from this day if you do not repeal the tax which has created all this disturbance. . . . If ever there was a nation running headlong to its ruin, it is this." [53]

A few voices among the people joined those raising the alarm in Parliament. Some correspondents to the press predicted that the Americans would quickly adopt economic reprisals against the mother country. Their debts to British merchants would go unpaid, the West Indian islands would be cut off from necessary provisions, and British manufactures would be boycotted by another non-importation agreement.[54] Accounts filtered into London throughout the spring that the wool trade of Norwich, Chippenham, and Devizes had come to a virtual standstill because the Bristol merchants had placed no orders for the American trade. MYRIAD claimed that there were 10,000 men out of work in the Devizes area alone and that emigration to North America or to recently discovered New Zealand was being considered by some. Liverpool and Manchester reported a similar depression. In most of the towns of northern England, the *London Packet* asserted, "the people murmur about the measures . . . against the Americans." [55]

It was the possibility of a military showdown with the colonies, however, that troubled many observers. In the first place these writers freely expected that the punishment of Boston would result in uniting all the colonies against the mother country to uphold the cause of that martyred town. Already letters from America reprinted in the London press seemed to substantiate the prediction.[56] Extraordinary accounts of the military potential of the colonies filled the newspapers, one common report being that New England alone could raise 140,000 men in less than a week, all trained and equipped. An observer in Boston wrote that teen-aged lads could use their muskets with surprising proficiency and that there was not a man in the neighborhood who did not allot some part of the day for military drill. "They will resist to the last drop of their blood," he predicted.[57]

America was a rapidly expanding country, several writers noted, and was seemingly marked out as the future seat of a great empire. The only way to cope with the situation there, facetiously remarked

Benjamin Franklin, writing as A FREEHOLDER OF OLD SARUM, was to send a company of sow-gelders along with Gage's army to castrate all the males in America. The managers of the opera would be saved a considerable expense and the Levant trade encouraged by supplying the Grand Signior with eunuchs for his seraglio.[58]

To those who saw the possibility of foreign intervention into Britain's quarrel with the colonies, the situation was even more alarming. One of the letters from Boston claimed that overtures had been made to the patriot leaders there "by a neighboring nation" but were rejected with contempt. France and Spain were the obvious threats, especially after the death of Louis XV, but B.T. A PLAIN CITIZEN suggested the possibility that Ireland would rebel in sympathy with the colonists in the event of an American war.[59]

Ministerial writers, on the other hand, were confident that the other colonies would leave Boston to its just deserts. It was foolish to think that America was the future seat of empire, scoffed BRITTANICUS, even if all the colonies did unite in support of Massachusetts Bay. And of course to the intelligent Briton who had observed the quarrelsome way that the non-importation movement had broken up, who knew the distances separating the colonies, and who was aware of the religious, cultural, and economic differences among their inhabitants, the threat of an American war seemed absurd indeed. That most of the Opposition's predictions would in time come true was beside the point. To the overwhelming majority of Britons in the spring of 1774 the possibility was remote indeed.[60]

XI

THE PERFECT CRISIS

DURING the months immediately following the Boston Tea Party colonial patriots took advantage of the brief lull in the struggle with Great Britain to build for the future. New committees of correspondence sprang up in towns and colonies alerted for the first time by the tea crisis to alleged threats to their freedom. Another step toward unity was the plan for a continental post office to be run by the colonists themselves. William Goddard of Philadelphia laid the groundwork by a journey through the principal towns north of his home city, where the plan received the blessings of the local committees of correspondence. The necessity for some means of communication safe from the interference of British authorities was apparent to the patriots. Besides, as Sam Adams pointed out, the present system was supported by taxes raised without the colonists' consent. Joseph Reed complained to Lord Dartmouth that postal rates were high and that the revenue was not spent to build bridges and improve roads as it should have been. By late summer the American post office was a reality in the northern colonies.[1]

In Boston the patriot leaders had lost none of their resolve to resist the authority of Great Britain wherever it irritated the sensitive American skin. Hancock's fiery oration on the anniversary of the Boston Massacre left no doubt of that. And there were plans for the future too. "When we have settled the present momentous affair," wrote Thomas Young in mid-March, "our next attack will be on the Customs House." Young claimed that the Crown had no right to appoint customs officers in Massachusetts Bay, and the patriots intended to prosecute each one in court for robbery. Reed reported a proposal to harass the admiralty courts. America's British friends who argued that repeal of the tea duty would restore the colonies to tranquility would have been dismayed to learn of the patriots' real intentions.[2]

During the last weeks of winter Bostonians showed remarkably little apprehension over the possible reaction in Britain to their Tea Party. Despite rumors current in London during March that the town had agreed to pay for the cargoes destroyed, no organized effort to this end was in fact seriously considered by any group responsible to the community.[3] The destruction of Captain Gorham's cargo on 7 March 1774 and the continued harassment of the consignees made it clear that Bostonians showed no remorse for the December Tea Party.

First word concerning England's response gave no indication of impending reprisals. A vessel arriving in New York in late March brought the misleading report that the American attitude toward the tea was much applauded, and that, although Britons agreed someone would have to pay for the cargoes destroyed at Boston, Parliament would probably repeal the duty on tea during its coming session.[4] Ships reaching Baltimore, Norfolk, and other ports carried similar news, and patriot editors throughout the colonies were quick to print the optimistic reports.[5] One popular story had Lord North receiving the account of "the Mischief" at Boston "with the utmost insensibility," and telling the Company to seek redress itself from the Americans if it wanted compensation for its losses.[6] Thomas of the *Massachusetts Spy* picked up the item from the *Public Ledger* praising the Americans for sustaining injuries with such patience, and Edes and Gill enjoyed reprinting the London report that Bostonians were now complaining that their fish tasted like tea. John Adams did not believe that there was enough spirit among either Americans or Britons to bring about a showdown. "We shall oscilate like a pendulum and fluctuate like the ocean, for many years to come," he concluded in April.[7]

By mid-April, however, grimmer news began to arrive in letters written from London during February. Arthur Lee gave Sam Adams an account of the Earl of Buckingham's speech in the House of Lords, and a similar report appeared in the *Pennsylvania Packet* for 25 April.[8] Franklin wrote of the great resentment in England and of violent countermeasures under consideration there.[9] The *Boston Gazette* printed a long report from London on 25 April about the possibility of Boston harbor's being blocked up.[10]

Then on 2 May a vessel which had left London on 16 March arrived in Boston with a sketchy account of the Port bill as introduced to Parliament by Lord North two days before. Even so, Bostonians were not alarmed. The report was looked upon "as a mere hum," John Scollay later recalled. No one imagined Parliament would be so "infatuated" as to pass such a measure. In the meantime weather conditions in the North Atlantic had improved, enabling vessels leaving England after the bill became law in early April to reach America within four or five weeks. Boston therefore received the full text of the measure on Tuesday, 10 May, New York on the 12th, and Philadelphia two days after that. From these three centers the news of Parliament's first retaliatory Act spread rapidly through the American continent.[11]

Already some people had begun to suggest that the best policy for patriots was to close the ports throughout America in sympathy with Boston.[12] The first specific offer to this effect came from a group of merchants in Newburyport. Meeting on the 12th they agreed, if the other ports of Massachusetts Bay would concur, to suspend all foreign commerce after 14 June, the last day that vessels would be allowed to clear from Boston under the terms of the Port Act. Such a plan would be far more sweeping than the non-importation agreements of five years before. Now the West Indies would be deprived of necessary supplies and no trade whatsoever would be carried on with the mother country. Although it would be many months before the colonists finally adopted such a sweeping economic boycott, the lines had been drawn within forty-eight hours after news of the Port Act had arrived.[13]

Meanwhile, the patriots' organization at Boston had already swung into action. The committee of correspondence called a meeting with its counterparts from eight neighboring towns for 12 May. The Boston committee met again at noon that day and appointed Sam Adams the head of a group to draft a circular letter to the other colonies. When representatives of the neighboring towns gathered at Faneuil Hall that afternoon, they accepted a strong report drawn up by Joseph Warren denouncing the Port Act and pledging support to Boston. The meeting then adopted Adams's draft of the circular letter. In it the patriots outlined the details of the Port Act, suggested that similar treatment was in store for other ports, and called upon Americans everywhere "to consider Boston as now suffering in the common cause." Finally, it proposed that trade with Great Britain be suspended in protest to the Act. As Adams later explained, "Our business is to make Britain share in the miseries which she has unrighteously brought upon us." [14]

In two letters Adams referred to the joint-session of the committees on the 12th as a town meeting.[15] Perhaps the inhabitants were spectators, but in fact the town did not meet formally until the day following, when the citizens adopted resolutions calling on the other colonies to suspend their commerce with Great Britain and all the West Indies. On the 14th copies were dispatched as far south as Philadelphia by Paul Revere, who also carried with him a letter from the committee of correspondence. Adams and Warren were never more eloquent than in these appeals for an immediate cessation of trade with Great Britain. The fate of their beloved Boston depended on the favorable response of the other colonies, for without support they knew that resistance could not long continue. Many patriots would agree with Thomas Young when he wrote to a correspondent in New York: "At length the perfect crisis of American politics seems arrived and a very few months must decide whether we and our posterity shall be slaves or freemen." [16]

The response from some communities was astounding. Inhabitants of Middletown, Connecticut, for instance, were indignant at Parliament's action. A resident there reported to Samuel P. Savage that "even the old Farmers who were So Sorry that So much Tea should be wasted Sometime Since, Now Say that they will Stand by the Bostonians and do everything in their power to Assist them." [17] In Farmington, Connecticut, a copy of the Port Act was publicly burned before a crowd estimated at nearly a thousand people. Afterwards a stirring set of resolves was passed, denouncing the "pimps and parasites" who had advised King George to adopt such a measure.[18]

Messages of sympathy came in from all quarters of New England, but the seaports were less than unanimous in their willingness to suspend trade with Great Britain. By the end of May the merchants of Newburyport could still be counted on, and the towns of Salem, Providence, Newport, and Westerly endorsed the idea, although probably without much enthusiasm from the merchants. New London, New Haven, and Portsmouth, New Hampshire, however, made no reference to a suspension of trade in their general resolutions. News from other colonies would at first prove even more discouraging.

Despite the fact that Boston town meeting had adopted Adams's no-compromise stand without dissent, a number of inhabitants there felt that the town should pay for the tea destroyed in December. In a letter written to the leaders of Boston on 2 February, Franklin had strongly advised immediate repayment to the Company as the only way of gaining the opinion of Europe in the event Great Britain used military force against the colonies. Upon its receipt Sam Adams suppressed its contents, allegedly commenting that, while Franklin was a great philosopher, he was a poor politician. In all likelihood this letter had arrived before news of the Port Act. Had the moderates and conservatives of Boston known of Franklin's advice, they might have been encouraged to press the matter of compensation. But once Bostonians learned of the Port Act's terms, repayment became a ransom for the restoration of the harbor privileges. A policy of conciliation was virtually hopeless, because the harsh terms of the Port Act converted many moderates to the patriots' cause and drove others to silence. John Rowe, for instance, thought the tea ought to be paid for but also believed that "the revenge of the ministry was too severe." His was the dilemma of many moderates.[19]

The merchant John Amory had proposed repayment at town

meeting without much encouragement, but Loyalists did not abandon the project immediately. George Erving offered to contribute £2000 sterling, nearly a quarter of the necessary total, if others would join in.[20] Governor Hutchinson sent word from his refuge at the Castle that if only the prime cost of the tea were met, he would make every effort upon his arrival in England to bring about the reopening of the port. But response was not enthusiastic.[21] At the end of the month five gentlemen met with Gage to find out how much money was expected and how to go about repayment, but the new Governor responded in vague language. Apparently only an application from town meeting or from the General Court would be considered, a strict interpretation of the Act's requirement that the money be given by or on behalf of the inhabitants of Boston.[22]

The question of repayment received surprisingly little attention in the local press. An item in the *New Hampshire Gazette*, picked up by a correspondent to the *Boston Post-boy*, suggested that all the colonies except Georgia and Nova Scotia should contribute to a repayment fund. A letter from Philadelphia criticized Boston for its immoderate attitude and asserted that the town would receive little support from other colonies until its inhabitants learned "a little wisdom." Elsewhere repayment was apparently not given serious consideration.[23]

Resentment in Boston was too strong for compromise. One commentator in reviewing the tea crisis pointed out that opposition to the Company's shipments had begun with the English merchants and was adopted in Philadelphia and New York before Boston had decided to resist. Now the Ministry was making an example of the town because its efforts to return the tea had been successfully blocked. Bostonians, he claimed, had expected a demand for repayment with time allowed to raise the necessary sum. "Instead of this, vengeance in the highest extreme immediately falls upon us. . . ." The writer suspected that only "the hypocritical, smiling, ambitious, avaricious *Hutchinson*" could have planned such an edict.[24] Another observer pointed out that even if the tea were paid for, the Act still required in vague terms that "reasonable satisfaction" be made of those who had suffered during the tea crisis the previous autumn. Nor could Bostonians know how to give assurances that "peace and obedience to the laws" had been restored to the town, as the Ministry also required. The town would have already lost the profits of the summer trade anyway, he emphasized, before the King could know of the town's submission, so that there was no advantage to making immediate compensation.[25]

As Bostonians were reaching their decision to resist the terms of the Port Act, they received advice from numerous friends in England. Most of those letters from which excerpts were taken for publication in the Boston press naturally encouraged the inhabitants to stand fast. One writer endorsed the claim that the present crisis was the result of a plot. "This *accursed Tea* is the very *Match* that is appointed to set fire to a *Train of Gunpowder* that has been long, tho' secretly, laid by *our Ministry and your Governor. . . .*" Their purpose was to destroy the liberties of Americans. Another correspondent made a similar charge.[26]

A private letter to Sam Adams later published in Boston came from someone signing himself "America's Friend." He urged Bostonians to hold out for only six months, by which time "England will rise on the occasion. . . ." Perhaps he was only predicting that the King's Friends would be overthrown in the next Parliamentary election, although this same writer reported that if the Port bill had not been introduced secretly, "the Parliament house would [have been] destroyed. . . ."[27] These letters, along with those to Americans in other colonies that were reprinted in Boston, supported the patriots' campaign to rally the inhabitants behind a policy of resistance.[28] By the end of May, John Scollay reported, citizens throughout Massachusetts Bay, "from the cobbler up to the Senator," realized that they would all be affected by the closing of the harbor. For the other ports depended upon Boston as a market place for most of their own imports, and of course the inland towns were accustomed to sell their surplus produce there. Lord North would soon discover he had "overshot his mark," Scollay predicted.[29]

Meanwhile, the inhabitants of Boston steeled themselves for existence under the Port Act. General Gage had been received politely but with little public enthusiasm when he ceremoniously entered the town on 17 May, four days after his arrival at the Castle.[30] Hutchinson sailed for England on 1 June with several addresses of praise signed by local Loyalists and moderates to console him. That was the day for the closing of the port to incoming vessels, although ships already in the harbor were allowed an additional two weeks in which to clear outward. On 1 June also the customhouse was moved to Plymouth and the seat of government to Salem, twenty miles away. Boston greeted these procedures with resignation, the bells tolling solemnly and the inhabitants appearing on the streets in mourning.[31] On Boston Common a regiment of British troops staked out their tents; out in the harbor frigates patrolled the channels leading to the port.[32] Gage, however, showed judicious caution. When the provincial treasurer refused to comply with his order to move the colony's funds to Salem, the Governor did not press the matter. Nor did he attempt to round up suspected ring-leaders of the Tea Party for trial. Dartmouth's instructions had in fact given the new Governor wide discretion and urged him to make every effort to calm the people.[33]

The debate on whether Boston should pay for the tea reached a climax in mid-June. Patriots argued that it had been criminal for the Company to send the tea, for the purpose of the scheme from the beginning had been to enslave America. Furthermore, since all the colonies were now involved in the issue, only a general congress ought to decide the question of repayment.[34] But moderates and conservatives replied that the same justice that Americans demanded from Great Britain required that the Company be compensated for its loss. Friends in England and the other colonies expected Bostonians to show this much respect for private property, some of them argued.[35]

A town meeting was called in Boston for 17 June to settle the matter. Joseph Warren wrote Sam Adams, then in Salem for the sessions of the General Court, and urged him to attend, but Adams had more important work to do. His absence was hardly noticed, however, as John Adams assumed the duties of moderator, and patriot speakers led the argument against repayment. One of them skillfully employed his mentor's favorite weapon. Insinuating that anyone favoring repayment was thereby endorsing the Boston Port Act, he declared that the debate would show "our friends from our foes." The ground crumbled beneath the moderates. No one dared speak in favor of repayment, and the battle went to the patriots by default. Although the discussion continued in the press intermittently throughout the rest of the summer, the issue of repayment was effectively settled on 17 June.[36]

The patriots had already begun their campaign of retaliation against Great Britain. On 5 June the Boston committee of correspondence adopted a plan drafted by Joseph Warren for circulation through all the towns of Massachusetts Bay. Called "the Solemn League and Covenant," it pledged its subscribers to suspend all trade with Great Britain, to stop purchasing English goods imported after 31 August, and to boycott anyone who refused to sign. In addition it encouraged the development of home industries. Since Boston harbor was already closed, the appeal was of course mainly directed to the inhabitants of other towns. The Solemn League combined many features of previous non-importation and non-consumption agreements. But these earlier boycotts had been authorized by the joint action of town meetings. The new plan originated with the extra-legal committee of correspondence in Boston and was communicated to the citizens of the province by that group, by-passing the legal town government altogether.[37]

In publicizing the Solemn League the patriots of Boston attempted to use the technique of the self-fulfilling prophecy by announcing that thousands had already signed with the first week of circulation. But just as quickly the conservatives launched their counterattack. P.R. asserted that the Solemn League was an illegal combination supported only by those who could afford to suspend their trade or by those with no property to lose. Besides, he argued, such a policy would simply make repeal less likely and conditions in Massachusetts Bay more uncomfortable.[38] In early June some of the Boston merchants had already decided to continue their commerce with Great Britain through Salem and other ports. Among those moving temporarily to the North Shore community was the firm of Richard Clarke & Sons, whose partners had finally considered it safe to return to the mainland from their island sanctuary. At a meeting on the 15th nearly 800 tradesmen of Boston refused to agree to the Solemn League, much to Joseph Warren's disappointment. The patriots' campaign had stalled by the end of the first week.[39]

But patriots struck back. Town meeting on the 17th instructed the committee of correspondence to inform all the colonies that the farmers of Massachusetts Bay were supporting a non-consumption agreement with enthusiasm, although in fact the plan had not yet become popular in the inland towns. Worcester town meeting had drawn up a similar covenant, but about fifty influential inhabitants immediately signed a vigorous protest. Letters for and against the boycott continued to flood the Boston press. Proponents stressed the economic self-sufficiency that the Covenant would encourage. In emphasizing the ineffectiveness of the measure, foes pointed out that orders for fall goods had already gone out, that no other colonies showed interest in joining, and that enforcement was impossible. Strongest of all was the argument that the committee of correspondence had no constitutional basis for existence and that its pet project was thus every bit as tyrannical as it claimed the Coercive Acts to be.[40]

The showdown in Boston came at a town meeting on 27 June. The day was hot, and so many inhabitants attended that the meeting had to be shifted from Faneuil Hall to Old South Church. John Amory moved for the conservatives that the committee of correspondence be censured for misconduct in proposing the Covenant and be immediately dissolved. Sam Adams stepped down as moderator to fight for the life of his revolutionary committee. The debate continued all afternoon, and the meeting adjourned until the next morning, when the motion was finally defeated by a four-to-one margin. In its place town meeting gave the committee of correspondence an overwhelming vote of confidence. The minority had to settle for circulating a protest of the proceedings, which gained the signatures of 129 men, most of whom were thereafter stigmatized as Loyalists.[41]

Then on 29 June, Governor Gage made a grave tactical blunder when he issued a proclamation labeling the Covenant a "traitorous combination" to destroy Great Britain's trade with the colonies. The public was warned not to sign it, and anyone encouraging its circulation or signing it himself was to be arrested. From that day on the agreement, in either its original Boston form or the less drastic Worcester version, began to make headway in Massachusetts. James Warren reported from Plymouth on 1 July when he learned of the proclamation that "we have been embarrassed with a division about the Covenant but I think this will remove the difficulties. . . ." On the day following, Plymouth town meeting adopted it by a large majority. Throughout the summer several other towns in Massachusetts Bay followed suit, while similar covenants circulated through communities in New Hampshire and Connecticut.[42]

A plan of non-importation for the whole continent, however, needed the full support of New York and Philadelphia in order to succeed. From New York the patriot leaders Isaac Sears and Alexander McDougall wrote Sam Adams on 15 May, shortly after they had received news of the Port Act from England. Appreciating the impending distress facing Boston, the New Yorkers urged that the town stand firm. "We have stimulated the merchants to appoint a meeting tomorrow evening [the 16th] to agree upon a general non-importation and non-exportation. . . ." They proposed that the committees of correspondence from all the colonies meet in a congress at New York to establish the grounds for redress of American grievances. When Adams released excerpts of this letter for publication in the *Boston Gazette,* he altered the text to read "the merchants are to have a meeting . . ." and omitted reference to the suggestion of a congress altogether. Perhaps these changes were made for the sake of brevity, or perhaps Sam was somewhat jealous of the initiative of Sears and McDougall.[43]

As events developed, however, the New York patriots had little success. At the merchants' meeting on the 16th moderates and conservatives appeared in great numbers, forcing a move from Fraunces' Tavern to the Exchange. According to McDougall, leaders of the De-Lancey faction had summoned "every tool who was under their influence" to attend. Gouverneur Morris later admitted that the take-over was a prearranged trick to keep affairs out of the hands of the radicals. The result was a victory for moderation. Isaac Low was elected to head a new committee of correspondence, the old group having considered its work done with the departure of the tea-ship in April. The meeting decided that the committee should have fifty-one members, large enough, one of its conservative members later suggested, to prevent the radicals from dominating it. Although all shades of political opinion were represented, the balance went against the Sons of Liberty. McDougall and Sears were included, but so too was Benjamin Booth, late consignee of the Company's tea. Some conservatives who had opposed the establishment of any committee at all were made members.[44]

The committee membership was confirmed by a meeting of inhabitants on the 19th, at which time Low called for unity among New York's feuding factions and cautioned the gathering against overzealousness in support of a good cause. When Sears tried to read the letters calling for non-importation which had just been brought by Paul Revere from Boston, Low managed to block the effort. The next day a group of merchants and mechanics friendly to the patriot cause agreed to close ranks and give the new committee a fair trial.[45]

Low's group, now known as the Committee of Fifty-one, met on 23 May to answer Boston's request that all shipping be drawn up in protest to the Port Act. Although McDougall was put on the drafting committee, he was unable to make much headway against the moderates. That evening, after first overcoming the obstructionist tactics of several conservative members, the full committee adopted a cautious statement. The New Yorkers agreed that Boston's plight was the cause of all America, but they did so in a manner totally unexpected to the Bostonians. "The cause is general and concerns a whole continent. . . ," the report read, "and we foresee that no remedy can be of avail unless it proceeds from the joint act and approbation of all. . . ." The letter called for an immediate convening of a congress to adopt "unanimous resolutions." It was therefore premature for

New York to consider a suspension of trade. In the eyes of many moderate New Yorkers, a congress was seen as the best way to hold the radicals in check by requiring a consensus of support throughout the colonies for any retaliatory measures. The tea consignee, Benjamin Booth, in fact had previously described New York's idea of a congress as a meeting of delegates from neighboring colonies, except Massachusetts Bay, to advise the Bostonians what to do or not to do in their predicament.[46]

New York was badly divided as the summer of 1774 approached. Differences of opinion concerning Anglo-American relations were made far worse by the bitter political warfare that had long been waged between the DeLanceys and the Livingstons. In 1769 McDougall had gone to jail as a result of a libel against the DeLancey faction, and although the Livingstons were hardly radical in their attitude toward British policy, the patriot leader favored them in the internecine battles within New York. In mid-May McDougall suspected that the DeLanceys hoped to seize credit for whatever patriotic measures resulted from the city's discussion of Boston's situation. But when the Committee of Fifty-one took a weak stand, he blamed it on an attempt by the DeLanceys to ingratiate themselves with the authorities in order to attain places in the government. The efforts of the patriots had become hopelessly tangled in the web of local politics.[47]

Despite his hatred of the DeLanceys McDougall admitted privately that most New Yorkers were not yet ready for bold action. On 28 and 29 May, William Goddard arrived to discuss his plans for a colonial post office. But McDougall, Sears, and other patriot leaders could give Goddard no encouragement at that time for fear that the issue would further split the city. McDougall could only hope that the people "would become more animated from the Zeal of the Southern colonies." He was badly stung when Goddard threatened to tell the Bostonians that New York would give them no assistance.[48]

Philadelphians first learned of the Boston Port Act on 14 May from New York. Immediately a struggle ensued between the patriots and conservatives to influence the city's official reaction. As in the case of New York, political lines had long since been drawn in Philadelphia — not between feuding family factions but between the Quakers on the one hand and the Presbyterians on the other. But the alignment was further complicated by the endless battles between the proprietary party — those supporting the Penn family's special claims — and men like Joseph Galloway and Benjamin Franklin, who spoke for the rights of the Pennsylvania Assembly. Neither of these divisions, however, conformed exactly to the patriot and Loyalist camps. Although the Penns could be counted on to support the Crown, and the Quakers were inherently conservative in their politics, the Quakers opposed the claims of the proprietors. Towering above these factions was John Dickinson. His Quaker heritage gave him the respect of that group, while his politics earned the support of the patriots. Without Dickinson's endorsement no policy of firm action toward Great Britain could possibly be adopted in Pennsylvania.

In the first days after arrival of the Port Act the battle in Philadelphia was waged behind the scenes. Only one letter appeared in the press, an inflammatory prediction that New York, Philadelphia, and Charleston would soon share the fate of Boston. The patriots talked of an immediate non-importation agreement, but the merchants remembered with continuing resentment Boston's alleged violations of the 1768-70 pact.[49]

Meanwhile, the patriots laid careful plans for supporting Boston. After issuing a call for a public meeting for the evening of 20 May, Thomas Mifflin, Charles Thomson, and Joseph Reed traveled out to Dickinson's magnificent estate to enlist his aid. Dickinson admitted that some sort of opposition to the Port Act was necessary, but he was by nature a man of great caution and timidity who would rather write closely-reasoned arguments than take part in public meetings. He finally agreed, however, to a plan suggested by the patriots. At the meeting that evening Mifflin, Reed, and Thomson would demand an immediate non-importation, after which Dickinson would propose instead that the Governor be asked to call the Assembly into special session to decide what policy Pennsylvania should adopt. This suggestion would appear so moderate by contrast to non-importation that all factions would quickly unite behind it.[50]

The meeting at City Tavern went according to plan. Nearly 300 inhabitants had already crowded into the Long Room when Dickinson and the others arrived. Mifflin called for vigorous measures in support of Boston. Thomson rose to second the motion but soon fell in a dead faint from the heat and accumulated fatigue of two sleepless nights. When Dickinson suggested the petition to the Governor instead, he was joined by Thomas Wharton and others, whom Wharton later described as men "who had never before met at any of [the] meetings. . . ." None of the conservatives had any idea of the prearrangements made by the patriots; they were probably too preoccupied with their own scheme of packing the meeting with their friends to notice. Dickinson's proposal was adopted with enthusiastic relief, and after the appointment of a carefully balanced committee of correspondence, the meeting adjourned. The next day a moderate letter was sent to the Bostonians suggesting that a general congress of all the colonies should first be called to petition the King for a redress of grievances. Suspension of trade should follow only if the petition failed. The letter even went so far as to suggest that Boston might consider paying for the tea destroyed there.[51]

The conservatives came away convinced they had won a great victory, and in the immediate sense, of course, they had. The first wave of patriotic indignation over the Port Act had been weathered without the adoption of a non-importation agreement. The reply to Boston was cautiously non-committal. "We think much time will be taken before any plan is form'd. . . ," wrote James & Drinker. "The men who have an Itch to be doing and to keep up a Bustle . . . have not succeeded in one instance that we can learn. . . ."[52]

The patriots made no attempt to explain the intricacies of these procedures to the outsiders. And perhaps they themselves were disappointed by the outcome of the meeting. Writing to Sam Adams, Thomas Mifflin defended the Philadelphians' preference for a congress to appeal to the King before direct action was taken. He added the optimistic prediction that the very idea of a congress would persuade Great Britain to rescind the Port Act. Charles Thomson wrote almost apologetically to Adams. Recalling that Philadelphia had once before come late into a non-importation agreement, he pointedly reminded the Bostonian that "none were more steady once they were engaged."[53]

The patriot forces had only one immediate triumph at Philadelphia. Plans were laid for a general suspension of business on Wednesday, 1 June, in sympathy with the closing of Boston port that day. One or two Quakers apparently supported the idea, but at a Friends' meeting on 31 May they were repudiated as spokesmen for the Society as a whole. Nevertheless, on the appointed day many inhabitants closed their shops, church bells tolled with muffled ring, and ships in the harbor flew their colors at half-mast. "Sorrow mixed with indignation seemed pictured in the countenances of the inhabitants," noted the Quaker merchant Christopher Marshall. Although Boston needed more than sympathetic mourners to rescue it from its plight, the Philadelphia patriots had planned well for the future. John Dickinson was now on their side.[54]

As in the northern communities, first reaction in southern colonies of news of the Boston Port Act took a variety of forms. At Annapolis, Maryland, inhabitants met on 25 May to consider the crisis. Here for once the radicals outmaneuvered their opponents and controlled the proceedings from the start. It was unanimously agreed that the colonies should join in an immediate cessation of all commerce with Great Britain until the Port Act was repealed. No mention was made that such a decision should await a general congress. Annapolis was ready to cut off its trade as soon as the other colonies agreed to follow suit. In addition, the meeting proposed that no lawyer in Maryland bring suit for recovery of any debt due an inhabitant of Great Britain until the harbor of Boston was reopened.[55]

Conservative residents of Annapolis were in an uproar when the resolves were announced. They issued an immediate call for another meeting of the inhabitants, particularly of those who dissented from the resolutions. On the 27th they convened once more, and the decisions of the previous meeting were presented for confirmation. Again the inhabitants overwhelmingly agreed to join an immediate cessation of trade if supported by a majority of the other colonies. The real controversy came on the suggested suspension of debts, but a motion to expunge that clause was defeated, reportedly by a vote of 47 to 31.[56]

Despite their defeat on the debt question, by the end of the month Annapolis conservatives managed to obtain 162 signatures to a petition protesting that decision. The dissenters emphasized the bad faith entailed in the proposal and the catastrophic effect such a proceeding would have on the colony's good name. Daniel Dulany, Jr., one of the signers, was convinced that such an unjust act would do immeasurable harm to the American cause, but he admitted he would have agreed to it if the ban had excluded as well the collection of debts by American merchants.[57]

Elsewhere in Maryland reaction to the Boston Port Act came almost as quickly as at Annapolis. Queen Anne's County met on the 30th and endorsed the capital's demand for an immediate cessation of trade. Baltimore agreed in principle when its inhabitants met on the day following. They proposed to enter into "an Association" with the other colonies and pledged to suspend exportations to Great Britain and the West Indies after 1 October and importations after 1 December, the first mention of specific dates by any community. The Baltimore resolutions suggested that such an association could best be organized at a continental congress.[58]

When news of the Port Act reached Virginia, the House of Burgesses was in session at Williamsburg. On 24 May the delegates voted to set aside 1 June as a day of "Fasting, Humiliation, and Prayer" throughout the colony, and Governor Dunmore dissolved the House in retaliation. But on 27 May eighty-nine delegates under the leadership of Peyton Randolph met in the Long Room of the Raleigh Tavern. There they formed themselves into an association and drew up a resolution asking Virginians to boycott all East India goods, especially dutied tea. They also recommended that a congress of deputies from all the colonies meet annually to discuss matters of common interest. When the letters from Boston, Philadelphia, and

Annapolis arrived, Randolph brought together those delegates still in town. Only twenty-five attended, however, and further action was postponed until 1 August, when representatives from the counties were expected to adopt a non-importation agreement.[59]

By the end of May all of the major colonies save South Carolina had had the opportunity to consider the significance of the Boston Port Act. In the weeks to come a new wave of resentment toward Great Britain swept through America, more widespread and at the same time more intense than ever before. The issue was no longer confined to that of Parliament's claim to the right of taxing Americans. In the Port Act the colonists now had before them an example of naked tyranny. Furthermore, the Massachusetts Government Act suggested to all Americans that the charters of their own colonies could be changed at the whim of Parliament. The threat to colonial rights was thus brought home to the inhabitants of inland towns as well as of the seaports for the first time since the Stamp Act crisis nearly a decade before. Finally, the effect of the Coercive Acts on those moderates who had disapproved of Boston's destruction of the tea was particularly significant. As George Washington explained in early June: "The cause of Boston[,] the despotick Measures in respect to it I mean[,] now is and ever will be considered as the cause of America (not that we approve their conduct in destroy[in]g the Tea)." [60]

Although most local patriots were unable to secure immediate adoption of non-importation in protest to the Coercive Acts, New England's demand for such action served a useful purpose. For as those communities rejected the extremists' proposal, they came to endorse the idea of a general congress of delegates from all the colonies. No matter at the moment if conservatives in New York saw a congress as a means of holding the radicals in check. No matter if Philadelphians felt that the congress ought first to petition for a redress of grievances before considering direct action. By early June the idea of a congress had been adopted by many cities and towns throughout the continent and in the weeks to come would be endorsed by twelve of the thirteen colonies. The call for a congress had emerged as the moderates' answer to the radicals' demand for immediate retaliation on the one hand and to the conservatives' hope for no action at all on the other. But translating the idea of a congress into actuality was not a simple matter.

XII

THE COLONIES UNITE

SAM ADAMS received the news of proceedings in other colonies with mixed feelings during the late spring of 1774. He was naturally disappointed that the suggestion of an immediate non-importation agreement met with so little enthusiasm. Now the New England towns that had conditionally supported the plan would consider themselves released from their pledges, and Boston would be isolated. Perhaps the conservatives could then force the town to capitulate to the Port Act before a congress could convene. Adams did not abandon hope that some of the other colonies would join in a boycott before it was too late. In reply to a letter from Charles Thomson he again urged that Philadelphia immediately suspend its commerce, but he knew that ultimate colonial unity was far more important than prompt retaliation against England. The idea of a congress had long been cherished by Adams, and he had been writing openly of it since January 1773. He and his followers therefore pursued a dual policy in the months to come. While pushing on with a plan of economic retaliation in New England, they encouraged everywhere the movement toward a continental congress.[1]

On 7 June a committee of the Massachusetts General Court was appointed with Sam Adams at its head to consider the state of the province. All of its members were patriots except Daniel Leonard, a conservative lawyer from Taunton. The majority was afraid that if strong countermeasures to the Port Act were discussed, Leonard would report the matter to Gage, who would promptly dissolve the

General Court. Elaborate precautions were therefore adopted. By day the committee talked seriously of paying for the tea, and Sam Adams was the model of cautious moderation. But after adjournment each evening, when Leonard had left, the committee joined with other representatives behind closed doors to plan quite another course of action. During these nightly sessions the patriots decided in favor of a continental congress and drew up a slate of five men as delegates. In order for the legitimate committee to adopt the proposal safely, however, Leonard had somehow to be removed from the scene. Robert Treat Paine therefore suggested that the two ride down to Taunton to attend the Court session in Leonard's home district. Leonard agreed, apparently confident that the committee would continue to discuss only moderate measures.[2]

During their absence, Adams and the other patriots worked fast. On 17 June the committee reported out to the General Court resolutions calling for a continental congress to meet on 1 September. Samuel and John Adams, James Bowdoin, Thomas Cushing, and Robert Treat Paine were nominated as delegates. Adams had ordered the doors locked and had instructed the keeper to let no one enter or leave while the matter was on the floor. As the question came to vote, however, one conservative was allowed to depart on plea of illness. He hurried to inform the Governor, who immediately dispatched the province secretary, Thomas Flucker, with an order to dissolve the assembly. But Flucker could not gain entrance to the chamber. He contented himself with reading the proclamation to the crowd that had gathered around the door while inside the Court voted to adopt the committee's resolutions. As soon as the business was done, the Court acceded to Gage's demand. But a crucial step had been taken toward making the congress a reality.[3]

With payment for the tea rejected, a delegation for congress chosen, and the Solemn League and Covenant circulating through the province, patriots of Boston turned to the more practical problem of feeding and clothing the thousands of inhabitants who were thrown out of work by the closing of the port. Morale remained high, but some sort of relief program was necessary. Ambitious projects like hiring unemployed workers to build a bridge to Charlestown were considered but rejected. Instead, a committee was appointed under the chairmanship of Sam Adams to request the sending of provisions to the Bostonians. Beginning in July towns as far away as Charleston, South Carolina, responded to the appeal by making donations of grain, flour, sheep, fish, rice, and money for the relief of the town. Here was an opportunity for the farmer to participate in the cause of liberty. By donating a lamb or an ox, by cutting a cord of wood, or by grinding a bag of flour, the country man could for the first time make a direct contribution to the struggle.[4]

So strictly did the authorities enforce the Port Act that none of these goods could enter Boston by water. Even vessels carrying firewood had to stop in Marblehead and completely unload for inspection before being allowed to proceed to Boston. Cumbersome building materials could not be sent by water from one wharf to another within the harbor itself; no new vessels could be launched; everything had to enter the town by wagons, which soon became known to the inhabitants as "Lord North's Coasters." The more desperate grew Boston's plight, the more its inhabitants became martyrs to a common cause. During the summer of 1774 the beleaguered Bostonians, with five regiments of troops in their midst and a fleet blocking their harbor, stood for all America as victims of British tyranny. Throughout their ordeal the inhabitants were sustained by one hope — that the continental congress would give them full support in their determination not to pay for the tea as demanded by the Port Act.[5]

Sam Adams could do little more to bring about a continental congress; patriots in the other colonies had to wage their own battles to maintain public interest in the idea and to secure the selection of delegates who would be willing to take a firm stand against Great Britain. The congress could not have taken place without a hardcore group of men in each town or county throughout America urging fellow citizens that the time had come for action. For the movement toward a congress consisted of decisions made on the local level. Through the colonial press and private correspondence

each community learned of the resolutions reached in town meetings and county conventions elsewhere. Although local resolves were
phrased in similar language, each was the result of separate local
conditions. In some colonies like Rhode Island the patriots had no
trouble at all bringing about approval of their proposition; in other
colonies like New York the final resolves were the product of many
weeks of compromise. By the end of August, however, all the continental colonies save Georgia had chosen delegates to the meeting at
Philadelphia.[6]

Just what the forthcoming congress would be like was of course
unknown to the colonists during the summer of 1774 because there
had never been one quite like it before. The Stamp Act Congress
of 1765 served as a model for some, but that gathering had confined
itself to adopting a set of resolutions. Many patriots saw a wider role
for the Philadelphia congress. Another question was whether delegates should be chosen by the colonies only or whether towns and
counties could also send representatives. Would delegates selected
by provincial conventions be acceptable or had they to be chosen
by the legislatures? Should they be bound by instructions or left
free to vote as their consciences directed? Answers to these questions
varied, but all patriots recognized the importance of sending delegates
firmly dedicated to the cause of American liberty.

The most important practical question to be discussed during the
summer of 1774, other than the decision to call a congress at all,
was whether action should be taken against Great Britain in retaliation for the Coercive Acts. Should congress immediately draw up a
non-importation agreement, or should it be delayed until Britain
could reply to a petition for the redress of grievances? Perhaps a
cessation of trade should not be considered at all. A related issue was
when and to what extent exports from America should be stopped,
if ever. Ought the West Indies to be included in any trade stoppage?
Some colonies would answer these questions for themselves and
instruct their delegates to vote accordingly. Others would decide to
leave them up to the congress and agree to abide by that body's
decision. Gradually through the summer, plans for the congress took

concrete shape as thousands of Americans decided what they expected from their leaders.

The first colony to take action was Rhode Island, where the patriots had little difficulty achieving their ends. At a meeting on 15 June the General Assembly approved the idea of a congress and appointed two delegates, Stephen Hopkins and Samuel Ward, to represent the people of the colony. They were authorized to consult and agree upon a petition and remonstrance to the King for a redress of grievances and to discuss other lawful measures to be taken for the protection of American liberty. But no specific mention was made of a non-importation agreement, although the three major ports of Rhode Island had sanctioned such a plan within the last month. Rhode Island did suggest, however, that the congress meet annually to consider the affairs of the colonies.[7]

Massachusetts Bay selected its delegates on 17 June, while the two remaining New England colonies made their choices one month later. The House of Representatives in Connecticut had approved the principle of a congress in early June but had left the selection of delegates up to the committee of correspondence. This group met at New London on 13 July and chose five candidates. When three of them later dropped out, Roger Sherman and Joseph Trumbull were elected to join Eliphalet Dyer and Silas Deane of the original delegation. Some communities in Connecticut had already expressed interest in a non-importation agreement, but the committee of correspondence apparently did not think it necessary to bind the delegation with special instructions.[8] In New Hampshire deputies from the several towns met at Exeter on 21 July to choose John Sullivan and Nathaniel Folsome as representatives to the upcoming congress. But as in the case of Connecticut no mention was made of non-importation in the instructions.[9]

Patriots faced a major struggle in New York. After the Committee of Fifty-one had sent its moderate reply to Boston on 23 May, it took pains to correct a misinterpretation by the committee of correspondence there that the city had agreed to an immediate cessation of trade. The New Yorkers wrote the Bostonians on 7 June to emphasize their determination to leave such decisions up to the congress.[10] It was not until the end of June, however, that the Committee began to consider the selection of congressional delegates for the city and county of New York. On 29 June Alexander McDougall suggested that the group nominate five people and submit their names to the Committee of Mechanics for approval. McDougall of course hoped to assure the selection of a slate favorable to the patriots' cause. The Committee postponed the question until 14 July, when McDougall's proposal was rejected, 24 to 13. Then Philip Livingston, John Alsop, Isaac Low, James Duane, and John Jay were nominated as delegates, with the provision that a meeting of inhabitants be summoned shortly to concur in these choices or to choose others.[11]

McDougall was highly dissatisfied with these proceedings. For one thing, he had little confidence that the delegates nominated would take a firm stand at Philadelphia unless prodded by a strong expression of public opinion. For the Committee of Fifty-one had not yet published any resolutions condemning the Port Act or pledging support to Boston. Perhaps McDougall was angered at having been left off the list himself. He realized that the packet for London was about to depart and that New York's failure to support Boston would surely be interpreted in England as a weakness to be exploited. The patriots therefore took matters into their own hands and called a meeting of the inhabitants for the evening of 6 July. A large crowd gathered at the Fields to hear McDougall attack those whom he said sought to divide the people. He then offered a series of resolutions condemning the Port Act, calling for a cessation of trade with Great Britain, and instructing the New York delegates to agree to whatever reasonable plan congress proposed to that end. The gathering adopted each resolution in turn without dissent and ordered the proceedings to be published so that a copy could immediately be sent to England.[12]

On the following evening the Committee of Fifty-one met to discuss this extraordinary event. The majority was furious at McDougall and voted to renounce the proceedings at the Fields by a margin of 21 to 9. As the meeting broke up and most of the patriots had left the room, those members remaining decided that the disavowal should immediately be published. On the 8th McDougall and ten other members of the Committee resigned in protest. Now New York was more deeply divided than ever.[13]

Completely dominated by moderates and conservatives, the Committee next called a public assembly for 19 July at which the names of the proposed delegates were to be submitted along with several resolutions offering support for Boston. McDougall's supporters, however, succeeded in dominating the sparsely attended meeting. Both the candidates and the resolutions suggested by the Committee were summarily rejected. One resolve, vaguely implying that the Bostonians were wrong to have destroyed the tea, was singled out for particular denunciation. Instead, the gathering appointed its own committee to draw up new resolutions and to suggest another means of choosing delegates. Isaac Low and several other moderates from the Committee of Fifty-one were included in this group, but they refused to serve, leaving control firmly in McDougall's hands. The next day the patriots drafted strong resolves, although no mention of a non-importation agreement was made, and proposed that the city choose delegates to the congress in precinct elections.[14]

All was confusion in the moderates' camp. Alsop, Low, and Jay tentatively withdrew as candidates, and what remained of the Committee of Fifty-one met on 25 July to reconsider its earlier proposals. The ambiguous resolve about the Boston Tea Party was amended and a new plan for the choice of delegates drawn up. The Committee suggested a citywide election in which all tax-payers were invited to participate, with representatives from both the Committee and the Mechanics to watch the polls. On the eve of the election the Committee's candidates were asked whether if chosen as delegates they would endeavor to bring about a non-importation agreement at the congress. Four of the nominees replied that they now considered that such a plan, "faithfully observed, would prove the most efficacious means to procure a redress of our grievances." On the 28th the five men originally nominated by the Committee of Fifty-one,

Philip Livingston, John Alsop, Isaac Low, James Duane, and John Jay, were unanimously elected by the inhabitants. The moderates had their candidates, but they had been forced into a public statement supporting a non-importation agreement.[15]

In Pennsylvania the patriots faced even stronger opposition to their efforts to elect firm delegates to congress and to commit the province to a policy of non-importation. In the end they failed of both objectives. On 7 June Governor Penn rejected Philadelphia's petition, suggested by Dickinson, that he convene the Assembly. For many weeks the patriots were uncertain how next to proceed. Throughout the rest of June and into the month following, a debate between radicals, moderates, and conservatives raged in the city's newspapers. At the same time various groups of citizens met to express their opinions of the situation. Not until mid-July could the issue of selecting delegates be considered.

The moderates were particularly strong in Philadelphia. The idea that congress should first petition for a redress of grievances before considering a cessation of trade seemed to have wide support. Some inhabitants still urged Boston to pay for the tea as a first step toward reconciliation. Others looked further, toward the establishment of a constitutional union with Great Britain similar to the plan of union that Joseph Galloway would submit to congress in October. Although no one spoke out against the convening of a congress, Galloway and several others insisted that only the colonial legislatures could properly elect representatives. By this standard, delegations from many of the colonies would be considered illegitimate.[16]

Against the preponderant strength of the moderates and conservatives the patriots worked hard to promote their own plans for an active resistance to the policies of Great Britain. On 8 June more than a thousand Mechanics from Philadelphia and vicinity met at the State House. Letters from the Mechanics of New York were read and a committee of correspondence was elected "to strengthen the hand of the merchants' committee," as the one chosen on 20 May was labeled. Apparently this session prodded the original committee into action, for it met on 10 and 11 June. In a series of resolutions the regular committee condemned the Port Act and laid plans for the relief of the Bostonians. Other resolves suggested the appointment of a new committee of correspondence, called for a congress to seek redress of colonial grievances, and urged Joseph Galloway, as speaker of the House, to call that body into special session to appoint delegates. But nothing was said about non-importation.[17]

On 18 June a large number of inhabitants convened in Philadelphia to discuss the proposed resolves. Moderates Thomas Willing and John Dickinson served as joint chairmen, and the Reverend William Smith made a pointed plea for temperate proceedings. The inhabitants then adopted most of the resolutions suggested by the old committee, including the election of a new committee of correspondence with forty-four members, ranging in political sentiment from Charles Thomson and Thomas Mifflin to John Dickinson and Thomas Wharton. Instead of demanding that Pennsylvania's delegates be chosen by the Assembly, however, the meeting decided to leave that matter up to the committee. The patriots had gained a minor point in principle, but much work remained to be done if their hopes for vigorous action were to be realized.[18]

Meanwhile, the patriots in the important farming county of Lancaster were faring somewhat better. On 15 June a meeting there called for an immediate and complete cessation of trade with Great Britain and expressed a willingness to join with Philadelphians in a solemn agreement to that purpose. Edward Shippen, chosen a member of Lancaster's committee of correspondence, explained his convictions on the matter to a friend. Some have said that a cessation of trade would put Pennsylvania in the same distressed condition as the Bostonians, Shippen wrote, "but whoever will scrutinize the late Act of Parliament may plainly discover that we are all included . . . the words Rhode Island, Connecticut, New York, etc. . . . are written in lime juice and want only the heat of the fire to make them legible. . . ." In mid-July Joseph Reed reported to Lord Dartmouth that sentiment for non-exportation as well as non-importation was particularly strong among inhabitants of inland counties.[19]

The patriots of Philadelphia argued their cause in the press and on the streets. "Many zealous men are preparing the minds of the people by speaking and writing of a non-importation agreement," explained James & Drinker to their London correspondents.[20] MARCUS BRUTUS bitterly attacked all Britons, including those members of Parliament who had defended the colonies, because even they seemed to agree that Parliament had at least the right to pass the Port Act. Another writer sharply criticized the moderate author of the letters entitled *Political Reflections*, which had been appearing in the Philadelphia papers. He demanded instead an immediate cessation of trade, particularly of exports to the West Indies, with the hope of putting pressure on Parliament through the planters who sat in the House of Commons and through the important English firms trading with the Caribbean.[21] Others joined in the attack on moderation. On 11 July a meeting of tradesmen in Philadelphia recalled the success of the earlier boycott of British goods and hoped that congress would draw up a uniform agreement that all colonies would sign.[22]

Pennsylvanians finally agreed to a convention of deputies from all the counties to discuss the crisis facing America. They met in Philadelphia on 15 July, with Thomas Willing in the chair. The meeting immediately proceeded to adopt a series of resolutions condemning as unconstitutional the Declaratory Act of 1766 and all the Coercive Acts. The deputies agreed that a congress should be convened to bring about a redress of grievances. Then they unanimously declared that, although a suspension of trade would bring great hardship, nevertheless they were willing to make that sacrifice for the preservation of American liberties. Out of regard for the welfare of both Britons and Americans, however, they hoped that congress would first state the colonists' grievances and seek redress. But by a majority vote the convention agreed to join a total cessation of trade with Great Britain if congress decided upon such a plan.[23]

John Dickinson had already been at work on an *Essay of Instructions* to the Pennsylvania Assembly. Governor Penn had finally agreed to convene that body, and it met at Philadelphia before the county convention broke up. During the sessions of the special convention Dickinson's draft had been polished up with the help of a committee and was adopted by the whole group. After a brief opening section outlining colonial grievances, the *Instructions* called on the Assembly of Pennsylvania to appoint delegates to congress. Then followed an *Argument* surveying the recent disputes between Great Britain and the colonies. In a series of lucid notes the author ranged through the classics, English constitutional law, and modern history to buttress his case against Parliament. As in his *Farmer's Letters*, Dickinson singled out for particular attack Britain's policy of colonial taxation. But now he carried the battle much further. At the end, he had stripped Parliament of all its claimed authority over the colonies except for the right to regulate the trade of the Empire. The special convention decided to omit Dickinson's *Argument* from the *Instructions* proper as too cumbersome, but recognizing the importance of that part of the document, the deputies ordered it to be published for the perusal of all Americans.[24]

The *Instructions* drafted by Dickinson and his committee were hardly less extraordinary than the *Argument*. The men to be chosen as Pennsylvania's congressional delegates were told to strive for a renunciation on the part of Great Britain of all power of internal legislation, from revenue laws to the statutes giving special powers to the courts of admiralty in America, and of course the Coercive Acts were included. In exchange for this abandonment of authority by Parliament, Dickinson urged the congress to compensate the East India Company for its losses, to offer an annual supply to the King, subject to the control of Parliament as were all revenue grants, and to reaffirm the principles of the Navigation Acts. The *Instructions* permitted the delegates to accept minor modifications of these terms if proposed by congress.[25]

Dickinson hoped that a delegation would be sent to England to press all these claims before further action was taken. If congress decided upon an immediate cessation of trade, however, the *Instructions* authorized the Pennsylvanians to concur, provided the pact were binding on all the colonies. Dickinson further reminded the delegates-to-be that the province approved only a stoppage of trade with Great Britain, but if relations deteriorated, an extension of the ban to cover other parts of the Empire might be justifiable. Dickinson saw American trade as a strong bargaining power, however, and suggested that it be restricted only in proportion to Britain's refusal to accede to the demands of congress for a general redress of grievances.[26]

Governor Penn had ostensibly called the Assembly into session because of a threatened Indian war in western Pennsylvania. But when the House met on 18 July it promptly added to its agenda the selection of representatives to the forthcoming congress. On the 22nd the House chose seven of its own members — Joseph Galloway, Samuel Rhoads, John Morton, George Ross, Edward Biddle, Charles Humphreys, and Thomas Mifflin. Of the group, only Ross, Morton, and Mifflin could be counted on as staunch friends of the patriots. On the day following, the House instructed the delegates to try to obtain a redress of grievances but to avoid "every thing indecent or disrespectful to the mother country." [27]

The patriots' fears that the Assembly would undermine their campaign were justified after all. The convention of county deputies, still in Philadelphia as the House made its decisions, had suggested Thomas Willing, John Dickinson, and James Wilson as congressional delegates. But these men were not members of the House and were passed over. Worse, Dickinson's *Instructions* were totally ignored. Galloway's conservatives had won a considerable victory. One factor contributing to this turn of events was the appearance of a stinging letter signed A FREEMAN, which was circulated among the representatives the evening before they were to elect their slate of delegates. Condemning the convention of county deputies as illegal, the writer pointed out that these men were a threat to the assemblymen's positions of authority. It would be tantamount to a dissolution of the provincial charter to accept their *Instructions,* drawn up, he asserted, "by a zealous partisan, perhaps by a fiery spirit, ambitiously solicitous of forcing himself into publick notice. . . ." The rise of the local committees that arranged this convention was "THE BEGIN-

NING OF REPUBLICANISM . . . Nip this pernicious weed in
the bud, before it has taken too deep root." By thus inciting the
jealousy of the representatives, A FREEMAN helped hold the line
for the conservatives in Pennsylvania, at least temporarily. Whether
this defeat would damage the patriot cause at the congress remained
to be seen.[28]

While patriots struggled against the moderates and conservatives
in the key provinces of New York and Pennsylvania, their colleagues
elsewhere were achieving one success after another. In Maryland
the demand for immediate cessation of trade was already strong on
the local level, where county conventions had come into firm resolves.[29] Therefore, at a meeting of delegates from all the counties at
Annapolis on 22 June, patriots had little difficulty securing the acceptance of a resolution recommending that the congress adopt a commercial boycott. The convention agreed to join in an association to
stop all exports as well as imports to the West Indies, if necessary,
as well as to Great Britain. Even the exportation of tobacco was
included, provided Maryland, Virginia, and North Carolina, the
principal producers of that commodity, were allowed to work out
the details of the plan themselves. On the 25th the convention
chose Matthew Tilghman, Thomas Johnson, Jr., Robert Golds-
borough, William Paca, and Samuel Chase to represent the colony in
congress.[30]

South Carolina was one of the last colonies to learn of the closing
of Boston but was the first outside New England to come to the aid
of the distressed inhabitants there. Arrangements were made in
June to send off a shipment of rice with more to follow. To help
raise the money necessary a group of young men in Charleston
proposed a benefit performance of "Busiris, King of Egypt," a play
described as representing "an injured gallant people struggling against
oppression . . . wading through a dangerous bloody field in search
of freedom." For admission rice was as acceptable as money.[31] In
a series of letters to the press A CAROLINIAN called for a total
cessation of commerce with both Great Britain and the West Indies,
including the export of indigo and rice, after 1 February 1775. He

was seconded by NON QUIS SED QUID.[32] The sense of crisis was heightened in late June when a vessel arrived in Charleston with two chests of tea. After all efforts to force its return had failed, the cargo was ultimately left to be confiscated by the customs officers for non-payment of duties. The captain of the vessel barely escaped from an angry mob by taking refuge aboard a British frigate in the harbor.[33]

Deputies from the counties, as well as large numbers of inhabitants, convened at Charleston on 6 July. Although the idea of a congress was unanimously endorsed, the assemblage was not willing to commit the colony in advance to a cessation of trade. Assurances were given by several prominent merchants, however, that they would support the plan if proposed by congress. For the sake of unity the matter was not pressed. The inhabitants then elected Henry Middleton, John and Edward Rutledge, Christopher Gadsden, and Thomas Lynch as delegates, with a free hand to act as they thought best in congress.[34] The South Carolina Assembly was scheduled to meet on 2 August. Ostensibly because of the excessive heat the members assembled that morning at 8 o'clock instead of the usual 10 or 11 o'clock hour. By prearrangement the proceedings of the meeting at Charleston were ratified, the congressional delegates confirmed, and £1500 voted from provincial funds for their expenses before Lieutenant-Governor Bull could discover what was up and prorogue the session. In his report to Lord Dartmouth, Bull pointed out by way of explanation that "you will see by this instance with what perseverence, secrecy, and unanimity they form and conduct their designs." [35]

New Jersey and Delaware followed in rapid succession with their choice of representatives. At New Brunswick on 23 July deputies from the various counties of New Jersey elected five delegates to congress — James Kinsey, William Livingston, John Dehart, Stephen Crane, and Richard Smith. The meeting also recommended that congress adopt a plan of non-importation and non-consumption.[36] On 2 August delegates from the three Delaware counties adopted similar resolves, including a call for a complete cessation of trade with Great

Britain, and chose Caesar Rodney, Thomas McKean, and George Reed to represent them in congress.[37]

The last major colony to take action on the crisis facing America was Virginia. But the delay had nothing to do with a reticence to propose drastic measures. When the House of Burgesses broke up in late May, plans had already been laid for a convention of representatives from the counties to meet in Williamsburg on 1 August. During June and July inhabitants met in their towns and counties to prepare the way. In almost every case some sort of restriction on trade with Great Britain was urged.[38]

One notable exception was the county of Middlesex. There the Boston Tea Party was roundly denounced. The convention instructed its representatives to oppose all measures that might result in another dissolution of the House of Burgesses. It cited the threat of Indian warfare, the disruption of the courts, and the non-payment of government debts as having stemmed from the previous dissolution. In particular, the people of Middlesex condemned an unlimited cessation of trade. They proposed instead a selective ban on the importation of British luxury goods and most East India commodities.[39] But this action was more than offset by the resolves of counties like Albemarle, where Thomas Jefferson drafted resolutions denying Parliamentary authority in America altogether. In Fairfax County George Washington presided over a convention proposing a boycott of most articles from Great Britain to become effective on 1 September and for an end to the "wicked, cruel, and unnatural" slave trade as well. The exportation of all commodities including tobacco was to stop by 1 November 1775, unless grievances were redressed before that date.[40]

By the time the special convention met at Williamsburg on 1 August the patriots' work was nearly done. Almost without change the delegates endorsed the strong resolutions of Fairfax and other counties. Even the prohibition of the slave trade was adopted. But these were not mere recommendations to congress. The Virginians planned to form their own association, ending importations by

1 November 1774 and exportations by mid-August following, and to boycott all merchants, traders, and planters who refused to adhere to its provisions. A distinguished congressional delegation was then chosen, headed by Peyton Randolph and including Richard Henry Lee, George Washington, Patrick Henry, Richard Bland, Benjamin Harrison, and Edmund Pendleton. They were instructed to urge the adoption by congress of Virginia's association as the best means of bringing about a just settlement of the dispute with Great Britain.[41]

In addition to the precedents established in the various county conventions, the delegates assembling in Williamsburg had the benefit of Thomas Jefferson's thoughts concerning the crisis. Unable to attend himself because of illness, Jefferson forwarded copies of his *Summary View of the Rights of British America.* A brilliant survey of the relations between Great Britain and the American colonies, this document was the most revolutionary yet published by a responsible colonist. From an exhaustive study of British statutes and history, Jefferson concluded that Parliament had no authority over the colonies whatsoever, not even the right to regulate imperial trade. Jefferson even criticized the conduct of the King, an unprecedented step. By referring to him as "the Chief Officer of the People," Jefferson reduced the stature of his office to that of a man whose job was "to assist in working the great machine of Government." Not even the fiery Patrick Henry was ready to accept such doctrines, however, and the assembly made no effort to endorse them. But as his colleagues were preparing the way for the first step toward an independent America, Jefferson was laying the groundwork for the last step.[42]

By the last week in August, when North Carolina held its belated convention, twelve colonies had chosen delegates to attend the congress in Philadelphia. Only Georgia, with a population well under 50,000 whites, and still economically undeveloped, failed to participate. By translating the idea of a congress into a reality, the colonists had achieved a truly remarkable accomplishment. The decision was reached by thousands of inhabitants meeting in their towns and counties to elect deputies to special conventions or to urge their regularly chosen representatives to send a delegation to Philadelphia.

Futhermore, most of the Americans taking part in these proceedings had decided what they wanted their congress to do. First, they expected congress to support the Bostonians in rejecting the terms of their punishment for the Tea Party. In the second place, they instructed their delegates to state the rights of the colonists as they saw them and to petition for a redress of grievances. Finally, most of them recommended that congress exert some sort of economic pressure on Great Britain, by a cessation of trade or the threat of it, in order to force an acceptance of colonial demands. The delegates from at least eight of the colonies were either specifically instructed to support a commercial boycott or at least personally favored such action themselves.

On 6 September delegates from twelve American colonies assembled in Carpenter's Hall, Philadelphia, for the first business session of the Continental Congress. Any doubt that the patriots would have their way was dispelled in less than two weeks. Massachusetts Bay's Suffolk County, in which Boston was located, had held a convention early in the month. There a set of resolutions drafted by Joseph Warren were adopted. Paul Revere brought them to the Congress on 16 September. The Suffolk Resolves denounced the Coercive Acts as patently unconstitutional and recommended that the people commence military training and that an immediate cessation of trade with the British Empire be adopted by the other counties. The Suffolk delegates agreed to confine themselves to defensive measures, "so long as such conduct may be vindicated by reason and the principles of self-preservation and no longer." When the Congress unanimously endorsed these principles on 18 September, the determination of the assemblage to take firm action was established.[43]

The conservatives made only one major effort to stem the tide toward the adoption of radical measures. On 28 September Joseph Galloway submitted his comprehensive Plan of Union for consideration by the delegates. In his introductory remarks the Pennsylvanian rejected the patriots' contention that Parliament had no authority over the internal affairs of the colonies. He did admit, however, that it was unjust for Americans to be taxed by a body in which they had no representatives and that it was impractical for colonists to sit in Parliament. As an alternative, Galloway suggested the establishment of a Grand Council in America, in which all the colonies would be represented. This Council, together with a president-general appointed by the King, would govern the American colonies. Although its acts would be subject to approval by the British Parliament, it would enjoy a similar veto power over bills of that body that affected the American colonies.[44]

Galloway's plan had merit as a means of restoring harmony within the Empire and establishing a permanent federation between the colonies and the mother country. But his Grand Council was admittedly a body inferior to and dependent upon the Parliament at Westminster, and by the autumn of 1774 the thinking of most patriot leaders had gone far beyond the point where such a principle was acceptable. To be sure, none of them knew what sort of permanent relations with the mother country they did want, but they agreed that Galloway's scheme would not do. By great effort the patriot leaders succeeded in postponing further discussion of it indefinitely. Contributions from the conservatives were thereafter brushed aside in the deliberations of the Congress.[45]

Congress had already adopted, on 27 September, a resolution banning importations from Great Britain and Ireland after 1 December 1774. Three days later the body resolved, after the hardest debating of the Congress, that, unless American grievances were redressed by 10 September 1775, exportations from America to Great Britain, Ireland, and the West Indies should stop. On 20 October the delegates signed the Continental Association, committing their colonies to the policy of commercial retaliation and establishing procedures for its enforcement throughout America.[46]

Meanwhile, on 14 October, the delegates had accepted a series of resolutions that came to be known as the Declaration of Colonial

Rights and Grievances. Here the patriots stated the rights to which they thought the colonists were entitled "by the immutable laws of nature, the principles of the English constitution, and the several charters or compacts." Among them was a clause written by John Adams, asserting the colonists' right to self-government in matters of taxation and internal law. The resolution did grant that by consent, not by right, Parliament might regulate the commerce of the Empire to the advantage of the mother country, provided no attempt were made to raise a revenue thereby. Consistent with this statement, the Declaration ruled that all existing acts of Parliament that taxed the colonists, including of course the remaining Townshend duty on tea, were infringements on American rights. Finally, the delegates called for the repeal of the Coercive Acts, the Quebec Act, and several other laws deemed unconstitutional. The patriots had made their demands; they had adopted a policy of commercial warfare to coerce Great Britain into compliance; all that remained was to rally public opinion behind their cause.[47]

Addresses were prepared and adopted which were directed to the King, to the people of Great Britain, to the inhabitants of Quebec, to the other continental colonies not represented at the Congress, and, finally, to the people of America who had sent delegates to Philadelphia. Each of these addresses stated the rights of the colonists and catalogued their grievances as seen by Congress. In each were assurances that the patriots considered themselves loyal subjects of George III. But in each was the demand that the colonies be returned to that freedom from interference that they had enjoyed in the years before 1763. Nor were these addresses written in the language of compromise, for a just cause could not admit of compromise.[48]

On 26 October the Continental Congress adjourned, but its members had already taken the historic step of providing for another Congress to be convened in May 1775, unless the colonists' grievances were redressed before that date. That possibility was not considered likely, however, for the resolution urged all colonies to choose their delegates as soon as possible. Having achieved their long-sought

Congress, and pleased by its achievements beyond their wildest hopes, the patriots were not about to permit the apathy of others to smother the gains they had made in less than two months at Philadelphia.

The American colonies now stood united, not only in their determination to back Boston's resistance to the Coercive Acts but also in their decision not to wait for possible redress of grievances before launching their program of economic retaliation. More important, the colonists' demands had become more sweeping than ever before. No longer did they simply deny Parliament's claim to the right of taxation, as in the days before the Boston Tea Party. Now their delegates united behind the contention of Sam Adams, John Dickinson, and Thomas Jefferson that Parliament had no authority to legislate for the colonies in any case whatsoever. The gulf between Great Britain and America had widened to a point that made reconciliation virtually impossible.

XIII

THE ROUTE TO REVOLUTION

IN three shorts hours on a cold December night in 1773 a small band of men precipitated a reaction that led with little pause to the Declaration of Independence. Perhaps some other event might have had the same result. We will never know. But we do know that the Boston Tea Party had just those characteristics necessary to change the course of history. As American colonists went about their daily affairs in September 1773, almost all of them ignored the desperate efforts of a few radical patriots to keep alive the spirit of resentment that had swept through the colonies in the years from 1765 to 1770. In September 1774 these radicals succeeded in bringing about a congress of representatives from all the major colonies. Furthermore, they succeeded in committing those delegates to a position of defiance few of them would have accepted twelve months earlier. For such a reaction to take place in so short a time required a catalyst precisely suited to the conditions around it. The Boston Tea Party was such a catalyst.

In the period 1770-73 a number of issues remained unsettled between the colonies and the mother country. There was, for instance, the question concerning payment of governors' salaries out of the King's revenue, a procedure that rendered them independent of the colonial legislatures. But this was a point of dispute in only two or three colonies. There were numerous questions involving the enforcement of the Acts of Trade, particularly the abusive conduct of several customs officials, the jurisdiction of the vice-admiralty courts, and the functions of the Commissioners at Boston. But these issues primarily concerned inhabitants of the northern seaports. Colonists elsewhere showed little interest in the subject. British restrictions on western migration and settlement was a third troublesome topic, but, likewise, comparatively few Americans considered it one of fundamental or immediate importance. Another concern was the possibility that the Anglican Church would establish an episcopate in the colonies, but it had not yet done so, and the danger was therefore remote to most inhabitants. There were also many general questions concerning the imperial constitution, particularly the extent to which Parliament had the right to make laws for America. But in 1773, with the Stamp Act and Townshend Act crises receding into the past, this topic seemed too theoretical to trouble more than a few colonists. Those who worried about these problems at all for the most part worried alone, for the patriots were too disorganized in the period 1770-73 to evoke much support from the great mass of Americans, most of whom seemed content with the *status quo*.

Any change in this *status quo* on the part of Great Britain, however, might well have serious consequences. An overly vigorous campaign against smuggling, or further restrictions in the West, or the establishment of an American bishopric could each precipitate another crisis. Potentially the most dangerous question was the right claimed by Parliament to colonial taxation, for this was an issue that affected all inhabitants. It had aroused American resentment once before, in the period 1765-70 and might well do so again.

In 1773 several British statutes in fact still provided for a revenue from colonial trade, among which were duties on foreign wines and molasses. But these acts had long been accepted by most Americans as regulatory even though their preambles revealed their true purpose. Only the Townshend duty on tea reminded the colonists of Parliament's claim of taxation. But in September 1773 the tea-duty question must have seemed rather unpromising to even the most optimistic of radical patriots. Duted tea was regularly imported into both New England and the southern colonies, where it was openly sold and consumed. In the middle colonies tea smuggled from

Holland was so common that virtually none had been imported from England in nearly five years, and therefore the Townshend duty was largely a theoretical threat. Resentment over Parliament's asserted right to tax the colonies seemed to have died out altogether. Or so Lord North and his supporters thought when they adopted the Tea Act in May 1773 and refused to rescind the Townshend duty in the process.

Opposition to the East India Company's tea plan was based almost entirely on the issue of the tax. To be sure, the smugglers in New York and Philadelphia supported the campaign because their lucrative trade was endangered. But the threat of monopoly was of secondary importance, too remote to concern most Americans. Not so the question of taxation, however, for this was an issue long familiar to all colonists in the fall of 1773, and it was potentially explosive. Besides, agitation during the non-importation period had concentrated on tea as the most common of the dutied articles. Its consumption would imply acquiescence to Parliamentary taxation. No matter that many inhabitants had in fact drunk dutied tea before. For now the issue had a new aspect to it.

What made the plan to send dutied tea to the colonies particularly ominous was the nature of the arrangement itself. Earlier shipments had been sent by private English merchants mainly in response to orders from America. But now the East India Company was to send 600,000 pounds of low-priced tea under a license authorized by Act of Parliament. Patriots were quick to maintain that the plan was a conspiracy between the Ministry and the Company to force American recognition of Parliamentary taxation. Letters from Americans in Britain and from English merchants who resented the scheme for their own selfish reasons added credibility to the charge. Most important, however, was the fact that the colonists were willing to endorse the accusation. Americans had long subscribed to a devil theory of the universe. If a belief in the literal existence of Satan had died out with the witchcraft mania at the beginning of the century, the Devil's political cousin remained to haunt Americans of later generations. In short, the Company's cheap tea was bait for a trap set by the enemies of America. To accept these shipments was to admit the right of Parliament to tax the colonists.

Writing from London, Arthur Lee referred to the plan as a "ministerial trick." Virginia's Edmund Pendleton labeled it a "preconcerted scheme." In New England, town after town adopted resolutions attacking the Ministry for its "crafty manner," "Diabolical Designs," "allureing [sic] Snares," and "artfull contrivance." Once popular resentment had been aroused, resistance to the Company's tea was accomplished with comparative ease. For in most American seaports mob violence had been a commonplace since 1765. Harassment of stamp distributors, of merchants violating nonimportation agreements, and of overzealous customs officials met with little effective opposition from governmental authorities. In the autumn of 1773 the mere brandishing of a tar brush was generally enough to persuade the most stubborn "enemies of the people" to mend their ways. Such was the case with the tea consignees at New York and Philadelphia. But at Boston the situation was different. There the conspiracy theory seemed particularly plausible, since several of the consignees were related to the governor, and a diabolical governor at that. The refusal of the consignees to resign their commissions and the governor's refusal to let the ships depart with the tea could only be ascribed to motives of the basest kind. Unwilling to permit the cargo to be landed, the patriots destroyed the tea.

Had the Tea Party occurred at New York or Philadelphia instead, as might well have happened under slightly different circumstances, it is questionable whether the same reaction would have followed in Great Britain. The fact that the tea was destroyed at Boston made the deed doubly offensive in the minds of Britons, for Boston had long been regarded as the seat of American agitation. When Rhode Islanders burned His Majesty's cutter *Gaspée* in 1772, an offense at least as serious as the destruction of the East India Company's tea, Parliament investigated but took no action. But that was in Rhode Island. Boston was different. There the Stamp Act riots had been particularly vicious. There the Customs Commissioners had been driven to refuge on Castle Island more than once. There British troops were met with open hostility. Even as news of the Tea Party reached England, the Privy Council had before it the impertinent demand from Massachusetts Bay that its governor be removed from office. So bad was the town's reputation at home that many Britons attached undue significance to the spotty evidence that Bostonians were equally hated throughout the colonies. This assumption was a fatal misunderstanding, for it led the Parliament to believe that the town could be punished without arousing the sympathy of the other colonists.

English resentment over the Boston Tea Party was so strong that caution was thrown aside. When the East India Company had fallen into financial straits in 1772, Parliament had appointed two special committees to consider the crisis. The Company was given opportunity to be heard, and legislative action came only after nearly five months of investigation and discussion. Had the government shown this care in formulating its policy toward Boston in 1774, perhaps its program would not have been so disastrous. As it was, however, the Opposition's words of caution went unheeded. Although there is some evidence to suppose that public opinion demanded even harsher measures than those adopted, the fact remains that the Coercive Acts were enough to produce precisely the result that the Ministry most hoped to avoid — the union of the American colonies.

Word of Parliament's action had no sooner reached America than the cause of Boston became the common cause. That town, thought many, was being punished for its resistance to a wicked scheme that colonists elsewhere had also opposed. The spirit of unity that erupted in the late spring of 1774 had its immediate roots in the common agitation of the previous autumn. The patriots of New York, Philadelphia, and Charleston had taken action at that time along with Bostonians to oppose the landing of dutied tea. Now they came to the aid of their colleagues. The enormity of the Coercive Acts quickly overshadowed the violence of the Boston Tea Party, which had been a source of embarrassment to many moderates. The issue of Parliamentary tyranny took on a new dimension; one no longer had to condone the destruction of private property in order to defend American liberty.

The Coercive Acts had moved the dispute onto new grounds. It was now a question of whether the colonists had any rights at all in the face of Parliamentary oppression. The Port Act punished all Bostonians, innocent and guilty alike, without a hearing and without an opportunity to make restitution before the harbor was closed. The Massachusetts Government Act did violence to the sacrosanct charter itself, for it virtually destroyed three basic institutions of self-government: the popular Council, the elected jurymen, and the town meeting. In short, the Coercive Acts were a display of naked power. There was no pussy-footing about virtual representation now, no attempt to make the bitter pill more palatable. Troops and frigates made such legal niceties unnecessary.

The Coercive Acts confirmed for many Americans the suspicions that the British government was in the hands of diabolical men. What happened in Massachusetts Bay would happen one by one in the other colonies as well. The alteration of one provincial charter made it more plausible that changes in others were soon to follow. In the absence of a single act demonstrating their good will, the Ministry and Parliament became conspirators against the rights of all Americans. For the first time in the struggle between Great Britain and the colonies a crisis had come that seemed to threaten freedom throughout the country. The rights of inhabitants in rural towns and counties were threatened along with those of the seaport dwellers. And now for the first time country folk could take concrete action in defense of American liberty. Hundreds, perhaps thousands, showed their sympathy for the martyred Bostonians by donations from the produce of their farms. This action gave many people living in areas remote from the seacoast their first real sense of commitment to the cause.

That this spirit of unity was transformed into the fact of union was due partly to several important conditions separate from the issues themselves. Communication among the colonies had undergone significant improvement in the ten years since the Stamp Act crisis. Better roads meant faster travel for post-riders and special couriers. Furthermore, the number of newspapers in the colonies had increased from twenty-three in 1764 to thirty-eight by the spring of 1775, while total circulation had probably doubled. Editors, most of whom were staunch patriots, habitually reprinted entire sections from newspapers of other colonies, so that in a few weeks' time the resolutions of every town and county were available for all to read. Establishment of formal committees of correspondence was of course a significant step, but their exchanges were supplemented by an even wider private correspondence between patriot leaders of different colonies. Many of these letters both public and private were turned over to local editors for publication. By the summer of 1774 Americans everywhere knew that their fellow colonists were ready for common action.

A continental congress was the logical means by which to take this action. Inhabitants throughout the colonies had the opportunity to express their views in the resolutions adopted by virtually every local governing body. It was not surprising that a firm policy toward Great Britain gained broad endorsement, for the Coercive Acts had all but destroyed conservative alternatives. One could not convincingly argue that Boston should make restitution for the tea, since that was no longer the main issue. Rather, the question was how best to avert the threat represented by the Coercive Acts. With no concrete evidence to support their belief that the rulers of Great Britain were men of good will, the Loyalists soon lost the uneven debate. By summer's end the idea of adopting a plan of commercial retaliation to force a redress of grievances had won wide approval, and many of the delegates assembling at Philadelphia brought this mandate with them.

Many colonies chose moderate men as their representatives in Congress, but almost all of them seemed to vote like radicals, once they settled down to business. A cautious procedure such as postponing non-importation until Parliament could respond to its threat was never seriously considered. The dispute over non-exportation sprang from the clash of self-interest rather than from a difference in policy. One clause in the Declaration of Colonial Rights was a particularly daring innovation — that the colonies would accept only by consent, not by recognition of a Parliamentary right, Parliament's regulations of the Empire's commerce. Even this principle was accepted by the majority, although after considerable debate. New York conservatives, who had struggled hard to choose what they considered a safe delegation, agreed afterwards that they might as well have sent Alexander McDougall himself. If the men who gathered at Philadelphia came close to representing the opinions of their constituents, and an examination of local resolutions offers convincing evidence that they did, there was little chance that Americans would take the first step toward reconciliation.

Perhaps, as most colonists hoped, Great Britain would make some move toward compromise upon receiving the results of the Continental Congress. But events proved otherwise. Several Americans resident in England had expected that the colonial crisis would return a more conciliatory Parliament to power in the elections held during the autumn of 1774. Franklin even predicted that the North ministry would be obliged to resign if the Continental Congress took a firm stand. But these observers were wrong on both counts.

The Opposition nevertheless desperately attempted to stave off disaster. The Earl of Chatham introduced a sweeping plan for imperial reform to the House of Lords on 1 February 1775. He proposed that in exchange for an agreement by the colonists to make voluntary grants toward their own support and for an explicit recognition of its theoretical supremacy, Parliament should withdraw all troops from America, give up the power of internal legislation there including that of taxation, and repeal all statutes relating to the colonies that had been enacted since 1763. Franklin thought the plan had possibilities, and Jefferson later wrote that he was much impressed by its terms, but the House of Lords voted it down by a margin of more than two to one. A much more limited proposition suggested by Lord North was adopted by Parliament in March

1775. But by the time the Continental Congress considered the proposal, hostilities had already broken out, and it was summarily rejected.

Within twelve months after the Boston Tea Party the colonists had become convinced that their very freedom was at stake, and the rulers of Britain concluded with equal conviction that the Americans were in rebellion. As George III said of the New England colonies in November 1774, "blows must decide whether they are to be subject to this country or independent." With both sides more willing to fight than to retreat, war became inevitable.

Given an enlightened colonial policy on the part of Great Britain, American aspirations to self-government might well have been achieved within a revised imperial structure. Although a handful of men could envision such an empire, only a few members of Parliament at the time understood the need for such a change. Furthermore, the Boston Tea Party destroyed whatever chance there was that a federal empire would gradually evolve through peaceful means. The violence at Boston forced the Ministry to retaliate with its own show of force. The Coercive Acts, like the decision to ship dutied tea to America, only drove the colonies closer together in their determination to resist the mother country.

That American independence ultimately came by revolution instead of by evolution was largely determined by the events and attitudes in the months following the arrival of the East India Company's dutied tea. The American nation was to be born in war rather than in peace, and this fact has had a profound influence on its development ever since.

NOTES

List of Abbreviations Used in Footnotes and Bibliography

AAS	American Antiquarian Society, Worcester, Massachusetts
APS	American Philosophical Society, Philadelphia, Pennsylvania
BM	British Museum, London
BPL	Boston Public Library, Boston, Massachusetts
Bristol	Bristol University Library, Bristol, England
Columbia	Columbia University Library, New York
EI	Essex Institute, Salem, Massachusetts
Harvard	Harvard's Houghton Library, Cambridge, Massachusetts
HBS	Harvard Business School Library, Cambridge, Massachusetts
HL	House of Lords Record Office, London
HSP	Historical Society of Pennsylvania, Philadelphia, Pennsylvania
LibCo	Library Company, Philadelphia, Pennsylvania
Liverpool	Liverpool Public Libraries, Liverpool
MHS	Massachusetts Historical Society, Boston, Massachusetts
NEHGS	New England Historic and Genealogical Society, Boston, Massachusetts
NYHS	New-York Historical Society, New York
NYPL	New York Public Library, New York
PRO	Public Record Office, London
Sheffield	Sheffield City Libraries, Sheffield, England
WSL	William Salt Library, Stafford, England
Yale	Yale University Library, New Haven, Connecticut

CHAPTER I

1. *The Works of Samuel Johnson* (12 vols., London, 1806), II, 390.
2. William Milburn, *Oriental Commerce* . . . (2 vols., London, 1813), II, 528; Kristof Glamman, *Dutch-Asiatic Trade, 1620–1740* (Copenhagen and The Hague, 1958), pp. 215–16, 230–34; Earl H. Pritchard, *The Crucial Years of Early Anglo-Chinese Relations, 1750–1800* (Pullman, Washington, 1936), pp. 186–7.
3. Milburn, *Oriental Commerce*, II, 524–5; Glamman, *Dutch-Asiatic Trade*, pp. 213–14; Pritchard, *The Crucial Years*, pp. 164–5.
4. Glamman, *Dutch-Asiatic Trade*, pp. 214–15, 231–3, 240–41; Pritchard, *The Crucial Years*, pp. 116, 133–40, 152–4; Milburn, *Oriental Commerce*, II, 526–7.
5. Milburn, *Oriental Commerce*, II, 534, 538; Pritchard, *The Crucial Years*, pp. 395, 396.
6. The duties as of 1767 were as follows: the "old subsidy" of 5 per cent *ad valorem*, 12 Car. 2, c. 4 (1660); the "new subsidy" of 5 per cent *ad valorem*, 9 & 10 Gul. 3, c. 23 (1698); the "one-third subsidy," 2 & 3 Ann, c. 9 (1703) and the "two-thirds subsidy," 3 & 4 Ann, c. 5 (1704) together adding another 5 per cent *ad valorem*; the inland duty of 25 per cent *ad valorem* plus 1 shilling per pound, 18 Geo. 2, c. 26 (1745); a customs duty of 5 per cent *ad valorem*, 21 Geo. 2, c. 2 (1747); and a further customs duty of 5 per cent *ad valorem*, 32 Geo. 2, c. 10 (1759). Because of the complicated formula by which it was computed, the customs duty on tea actually amounted to 23.9 per cent *ad valorem* by 1759. For a convenient guide through the labyrinth of statutes see Samuel Baldwin, *A Survey of the British Customs* . . . (London, 1770). For the price of Bohea tea at the East India Co. sales in 1772: *An Account of Tea Delivered from East India Co. Warehouses* . . . Add. Ms. 8133B, ff. 326–7 (BM).
7. Nicholas W. Posthumus, *Inquiry into the History of Prices in Holland* (Leiden, 1946), I, lxii, 189–90; [William Richardson?], paper dated 6 February 1783, Add. Ms. 8133B, ff. 312–14 (BM); one authority estimated in 1772 that English smugglers could count on a profit of up to 2s. 6d. per pound of Dutch tea: *The Present State of the East India Company's Affairs* . . . (London, 1772), p. 53.
8. 7 Geo. 1, sess., c. 21, sec. 9. For a comprehensive view of English exports of tea to America, see Appendix, Table I.
9. Timothy Pitkin, *A Statistical View* . . . (New Haven, 1835), pp. 250–51; the average annual consumption of coffee increased from 379,358 pounds (.19 lbs. *per capita*) in 1768–72 to 6,641,935 pounds (1.41 lbs. *per capita*) in 1790–99. (About four times as much coffee by weight is required for a cup as of tea.) Customs 16/1 (PRO).

10. *An Estimate of Tea, Sugar, and Molasses illegally imported into the Continent of North America in One Year* [n.d.: 1763?], Add. Ms. 38334, 243 f. (BM); [George Grenville], *The Regulations Lately Made . . .* (London, 1765), pp. 92, 93; George Spencer to Lords Commissioners of His Majesty's Treasury, 8 January 1766, T. 1/445 (PRO); William Bollan to Lord Dartmouth, 22 December 1772, Dartmouth Papers, II–483 (WSL); Samuel Wharton, *Observations upon the Consumption of Teas in North America,* 19 January 1773, Wharton Correspondence, 1771–1830 (HSP); "Alarm No. IV," [Rind's] *Virginia Gazette,* 25 November 1773; Sir Jeffrey Amherst to Lord Dartmouth, 9 March 1774, Dartmouth Papers, II–852 (WSL); William Cobbett, *The Parliamentary History of England . . .* (London, 1803), XVII, 1233; Customs 3/67 (PRO).

11. In 1723 earlier drawbacks of customs duties for exported tea were rescinded (10 Geo. 1, c. 10), because they had encouraged the clandestine re-importation of the same tea into England. When in 1745 the inland duty of 25 per cent *ad valorem* plus 1s. per pound was enacted, Parliament failed to provide for a drawback upon exportation, ostensibly for the same reason (18 Geo. 2, c. 26). Complaints by the East India Company and London merchants brought the desired provision in 1748 (21 Geo. 2, c. 14). The same statute required that tea be exported in the same package in which it was imported. In addition it reaffirmed an act of 1723 (11 Geo. 1, c. 30), to the effect that under no circumstances could tea once exported to the colonies (or anywhere else) be landed again in England. As a guarantee that the tea would in fact be exported, the British merchant posted a bond which was canceled only upon presentation of a certificate attesting to its arrival in America. For comparative tea prices see Appendix, Table II. Note that all prices in this book have been converted to sterling values.

12. Customs 16/1 (PRO); Richard Clarke & Sons Invoice Book, 1767–75 (NEHGS); Gerard G. Beekman (New York) to Henry Lloyd (Boston), 19 April 1756, Philip L. White, ed., *The Beekman Mercantile Papers, 1746–1799* (3 vols., New York, 1956), I, 279; Isaac Adolphus (New York) to Michael Gratz (Phila.), 30 December 1765, McAllister Mss., No. 2 (LibCo); Henry Lloyd (Boston) to John Fillis [Halifax?], 18 March 1766, Henry Lloyd Letterbook, 1765–67 (HBS). See Appendix, Table II, for comparative tea prices at Boston, New York, and Philadelphia.

13. Governor Clinton (New York) to the Lords of Trade (London), 4 October 1752, *Documents Relative to the Colonial History of the State of New York . . .* (15 vols., Albany, 1856–87), VI, 765; John Kidd (Phila.) to Rawlinson & Davison (London), 28 January 1757, John Kidd Letterbook, 1749–63 (HSP); Sir Charles Hardy (Halifax) to the Lords of Trade (London), 10 July 1757, *N.Y. Col. Docs.,* VII, 271–2, 273; Governor Bernard (Boston) to the Earl of Halifax (London), 17 May 1764, in Bernard Papers, Sparks Ms. 4, III, 21620 (Harvard). It is possible, though not likely, that the Governors deliberately exaggerated the extent of smug-

gling within their own jurisdictions; Lieut.-Gov. Colden (New York) to the Lords of Trade (London), 12 October 1764, *N.Y. Col. Docs.*, VII, 666; Andrew Brown [New York?] to Lords Commissioners of H.M. Treasury (London), 21 January 1768, T. 1/465 (PRO); Brown was looking for a job as enforcement officer and probably inflated the figures somewhat. But even 40 vessels averaging 20 chests each meant nearly 300,000 pounds a year. Memorial of the Commissioners of Customs at Boston to the Lords of the Treasury, 12 February 1768, Secy. of State In-Letters, C.O. 5/226 (PRO).

14. Thomas Hancock (Boston) to Capt. Simon Gross, 20 December 1743, Domestic Letters, Thomas Hancock Papers, 1 (HBS); Thomas & Adrian Hope (Amsterdam) to Thomas Hancock (Boston), 8 August 1745, Foreign Letters, Thomas Hancock Papers, 7 (HBS); Thomas Hancock (Boston) to Thomas & Adrian Hope (Amsterdam), 24 November 1751, 14 January 1754, Thomas Hancock Letterbook, 1750–62 (HBS); Thomas Hancock (Boston) to Simon Gross, 23 September 1754, Domestic Letters, Thomas Hancock Papers, 1 (HBS); Invoice of Schooner *Lydia's* cargo to the West Indies, September 1754, Foreign Letters, Thomas Hancock Papers, 7 (HBS); *Portlidge Bill for Schooner "Lydia"* . . . , Shipping Bills, Thomas Hancock Papers, 4 (HBS); Thomas Hancock (Boston) to Kilby & Barnard (London), 17 April 1755, and to Thomas & Adrian Hope (Amsterdam), 17 April 1755, Thomas Hancock Letterbook, 1750–62 (HBS).

15. John Ludlow (New York) to Capt. Richard Jeffrey, 6 April 1755, to Capt. Jeffrey, Jr., 13 October 1755, to John DeNeufville (Amsterdam), 5 January 1756, and John Ludlow, Elias Desbross, John Waddell, William Ludlow, and Richard Jeffrey to Capt. Jeffrey, Jr., 8 January 1756, all in John Ludlow Letterbook, 1752–63 (Columbia).

16. Papers relating to voyage to Amsterdam, 1763, Meletiah Bourne Papers, III (HBS). Landing costs included the following item: "Thomas Flucker entry . . . £15 [L.M.]," apparently a bribe to the future Secretary of the Province.

17. *Account of Sales . . . by the General Amherst*, 29 November 1759, and *Sales of 10 chests Bohea Tea imported from Hambro* . . . , February–April 1760, Shaw Collection (Yale); Richard Sonerstrom (Boston) to Christopher Champlin (Newport), 9 February 1764, Letters of Boston Merchants Coastwise to Newport, 1732–66 (HBS); William Gough (Phila.) to John Kidd (London), 3 October 1754, John Kidd (Phila.) to Rawlinson & Davison (London), 24 March 1761, and 10 October 1762, all in John Kidd Letterbook, 1749–63 (HSP); Tench Francis's Invoice Book, 1759–63 (HSP).

18. Thomas Wharton (Phila.) to John Waddell (New York), Thomas Wharton Letterbook, 1752–59, *passim* (HSP); John Waddell (New York) to Thomas Wharton (Phila.), Wharton Correspondence, 1679–1756, *passim* (HSP); Henry Lloyd (Boston) to Aaron Lopez (Newport), 22 March

1756, in Letters of Boston Merchants Coastwise to Newport (HBS); and Henry Lloyd (Boston) to Aaron Lopez (Newport), 3 April and 3 May 1756, in *Commerce of Rhode Island 1726–1800* [*Collections* of MHS vol. 69] (2 vols., Boston, 1914), I, 65–7.

19. William Cunningham (New York) to Martin Kutckran Alierop (London), 27 October 1756, Greg & Cunningham Letterbook, 1756–58 (NYHS).

20. Duke of Grafton to Earl of Chatham, 8 January 1767, in William S. Taylor and John H. Pringle, eds., *Correspondence of William Pitt, Earl of Chatham* (4 vols., London, 1838–40), III, 163–6; the Indemnity Act is 7 Geo. 3, c. 56; for importations, see Customs 16/1 (PRO).

21. Customs 16/1 (PRO).

CHAPTER II

1. The well-known studies by Sir Lewis Namier, *The Structure of Politics at the Accession of George III* (London, 1929) and *England in the Age of the American Revolution* (London, 1930) are invaluable for an understanding of eighteenth-century English politics. The lectures by Richard Pares, published under the title *King George III and the Politicians* (Oxford, 1953), are useful interpretative essays. For particular reference to the colonial crisis, see Charles R. Ritcheson, *British Politics and the American Revolution* (Norman, Okla., 1954).

2. Ritcheson, *British Politics*, pp. 5–67.

3. Ritcheson, *British Politics*, pp. 68–71; for a detailed study of Chatham's administration see John Brooke, *The Chatham Administration, 1766–1768* (London, 1956).

4. Grafton to Chatham, 28 February 1767, Taylor and Pringle, *Correspondence of Chatham*, III, 224–5.

5. Lord Edmond Fitzmaurice, ed., *Life of William, Earl of Shelburne . . .* (3 vols., London, 1876), II, 37–48; Shelburne to Chatham, 1 February 1767, Taylor and Pringle, *Correspondence of Chatham*, III, 182–8; Charles Garth (London) to Committee on Correspondence of South Carolina, 31 January 1767, *South Carolina Historical Magazine*, XXIX (April 1928), 128–32; Ritcheson, *British Politics*, pp. 79–83, 87–96; William S. Johnson (London) to Jonathan Trumbull (Conn.), 14 March 1767, "The Trumbull Papers," *Colls.* MHS, 5th ser., IX (1885), 484–8.

6. Fitzmaurice, *Shelburne*, II, 55–8; Thomas Bradshaw to the Duke of Grafton, 14, 16 May 1767, Sir William R. Anson, ed., *Autobiography and Political Correspondence of Augustus Henry, Third Duke of Grafton, K.G.* (London, 1898), pp. 127, 176–81; Denis Le Marchant, ed., *Memoirs of the Reign of King George III by Horace Walpole* (4 vols., London, 1845), III, 23–40; William S. Johnson (London) to William Pitkin (Conn.), 16 May, 9 June, 13 July 1767, in "The Trumbull Papers," *Colls.* of MHS,

5th ser., IX (1885), 228–43; *Journals of the House of Commons*, XXXI, 394–5, 398, 406–7, 408, 412, 414; Ritcheson, *British Politics*, pp. 86–101.

7. Fitzmaurice, *Shelburne*, I, 259.

8. Albert H. Smyth, *The Writings of Benjamin Franklin* (10 vols., New York, 1907), IV, 424; see also Edmund S. and Helen M. Morgan, *The Stamp Act Crisis* (Chapel Hill, N.C., 1953), pp. 273–6.

9. Shelburne to Chatham, 31 January 1767, Fitzmaurice, *Shelburne*, II, 38–9.

10. Jenkinson: Ritcheson, *British Politics*, pp. 18–19, 19n.; Spencer: George Spencer to Lords Commissioners of the Treasury, 8 January 1766, T. 1/445 (PRO). There was one important difference between Spencer's proposal and Townshend's ultimate plan: Spencer suggested that the duty be collected in England upon exportation of the tea rather than in America upon its importation.

11. Charles Garth to Committee on Correspondence of Charleston, S.C., 17 May 1767, in "Garth Correspondence," *S.C. Hist. Mag.*, XXIX (July 1928), 223–32 (italics mine). See also, William S. Johnson (London) to William Pitkin (Conn.), 9 June 1767, in "Trumbull Papers," *Colls.* MHS, 5th ser., IX (1885), 236–8; for progress of Indemnity bill through Parliament, *Journals of the House of Commons*, XXXI, 394–5, 401, 403, 410, 412–13, 417; for the actual effect these acts had on the price of tea in America see Appendix, Table II. Max Farrand, "The Taxation of Tea, 1767–1773," *Amer. Hist. Rev.*, III (January 1898), 266–9, attempts to clarify the problem with only partial success.

12. The Revenue Act was 7 Geo. 3, c. 46 (1767); Thomas Cushing (Boston) to Dennys DeBerdt (London), 9 May 1767, in *Colls.* MHS, 4th ser., IV (1858), 347–9, outlines some of these grounds for objection; for a fuller discussion of the Revenue Act and the actual uses of its proceeds, see Oliver M. Dickerson, "Use Made of the Revenue from the Tax on Tea," *New Eng. Quar.*, XXXI (April 1958), 232–43.

13. John Hancock (Boston) to William Reeve (London), 3 September 1767, and to George Hayley (London), 2 November 1767, John Hancock Letterbook, 1762–83 (HBS).

14. Governor Bernard to the Earl of Halifax, 14 November 1767, Letters from the Governors of Massachusetts Bay, C.O. 5/756 (PRO), and to the Earl of Shelburne, 21 November 1767, C.O. 5/757, Pt. 1 (PRO).

15. James Parker (New York) to Benjamin Franklin (London), 24 December 1767, Franklin Papers, II, 1, 106 (APS); Thomas Wharton (Phila.) to Benjamin Franklin (London), 17 November 1767, Franklin Papers, II, 1, 101 (APS); for Massachusetts petitions see Harvey A. Cushing, *The Writings of Samuel Adams* (4 vols., New York, 1904), I, 134–77; for Philadelphia, see R. L. Brunhouse, "The Effect of the Townshend Acts in Pennsylvania," *Penna. Mag. Hist. & Biog.*, LIV (October 1930), 355–6.

16. Charles M. Andrews, "The Boston Merchants and the Non-Importation

Movement," *Publications* of the Colonial Society of Massachusetts, XIX (1916–17), 191–8.

17. Governor Francis Bernard (Boston) to Lord Barrington (London), 4 March 1768, in Edward Channing and Archibald C. Coolidge, eds., *The Barrington-Bernard Correspondence, 1760–1770* (Cambridge, Mass., 1912), 147; Thomas Cushing (Boston) to Dennys DeBerdt (London), 18 April, 6 June 1768, *Colls.* MHS, 4th ser., IV (1858), 350–52; Governor Bernard to the Earl of Shelburne, 21 March 1768, C.O. 5/757, pt. 2 (PRO); Memorial from Commissioners of Customs (Boston) to Lords of the Treasury, 28 March 1768, Secretary's In-Letters, C.O. 5/226 (PRO); Richard Clarke & Sons (Boston) to Peter Contincen (London), 10 May 1768, Richard Clarke Letterbook, 1767–69 (NEHGS); Andrews, "Boston Merchants," *Pubs.* Col. Soc. Mass., XIX (1916–17), 201–2.

18. *New York Journal,* 2, 14, 21 April 1768; *Penna. Chronicle,* 18 April, 30 May 1768; *Penna. Journal,* supplement [25 April 1768?]; Andrews, "Boston Merchants," *Pubs.* Col. Soc. Mass., XIX (1916–17), 202–4; Brunhouse, "The Effect of the Townshend Acts," *Penna. Mag. Hist. & Biog.,* LIV (October 1930), 360.

19. *Boston Gazette,* 15 August 1768; Boston Committee of Merchants to Phila. Committee of Merchants, 11 August 1768, in Mss. Relating to Non-Importation Agreements, 1766–75 (APS); Governor Bernard to Earl of Hillsborough, 9 August 1768, Bernard Papers, Sparks Ms. 4, VII, 23–4 (Harvard); *A copy of the resolves subscribed by the merchants in New York,* 27 August 1768, in Mss. Relating to Non-Importation Agreements, 1766–75 (APS); *New York Journal,* 8 September 1768; Andrews, "Boston Merchants," *Pubs.* Col. Soc. Mass., XIX (1916–17), 204–8.

20. John Fothergill (London) to Israel Pemberton (Philadelphia), 5 July 1768, Pemberton Papers, II, Etting Collection (HSP); "Extract of a letter from London, dated 6 July 1768," in *Penna. Chronicle,* 19 September 1768; John Reynell (Phila.) to Mildred & Roberts (London), 25 August 1768, to Welch, Wilkinson, and Startin (London), 5 November 1768, and to his brother [London?], 2 February 1769, all in John Reynell Letterbook, 1767–69 (HSP); for a particularly bitter attack on Philadelphia, see *New York Journal,* 24 October 1768. A copy of the Philadelphia merchants' petition to London merchants is in Mss. Relating to Non-Importation Agreements, 1766–75 (APS); Dennys DeBerdt (London) to Thomas Cushing (Boston), 1 February 1769, Albert Matthews, ed., *Letters of Dennys DeBerdt, 1757–1770* (Cambridge, Mass., 1911), pp. 355–6; "Letter from a Committee of Merchants in Philadelphia to the Committee of Merchants in London," 8 April 1769, *Penna. Mag. Hist. & Biog.* XXVII (January 1903), 84–7; see also, Andrews, "Boston Merchants," *Pubs.* Col. Soc. Mass.; XIX (1916–17), 208–11; and especially Arthur L. Jensen, *The Maritime Commerce of Colonial Philadelphia* (Madison, Wisc., 1963), pp. 174–80; Brunhouse, "Effect of Townshend Acts," *Penna. Mag. Hist. & Biog.,* LIV (October 1930), 360–66.

21. *Boston Gazette*, 31 July, 14, 28 August 1769; Thomas Hutchinson to Earl of Hillsborough, 8 August 1769, C.O. 5/758 (PRO). Hillsborough's circular letter of 13 May 1769 suggesting that repeal was imminent served as a legitimate basis for the rumors.

22. Philadelphia Committee of Merchants to Boston Committee of Merchants, 21 September 1769, Sparks Ms. 62, 200–201 (Harvard); Thomas Hutchinson to the Earl of Hillsborough, 20 October 1769, C.O. 5/758 (PRO); *Boston Gazette*, 23 October, 4 December 1769; Boston Committee of Merchants to Salem Committee of Merchants, 10 November 1769, Sparks Ms. 10, New England Papers III, 52 (Harvard), to Norwich, Conn., Committee of Merchants, 7 December 1769 (BPL), and to Benjamin Franklin (London), 29 December 1769, Franklin Papers II, 2, 210 (APS); Cadwalader Colden to Earl of Hillsborough, 4 December 1769, C.O. 5/1101 (PRO); John Dickinson, however, agreed with the Bostonians that the colonists should demand the repeal of all revenue acts; John Dickinson (Phila.) to Arthur Lee (London), 25 November 1769, Richard H. Lee, ed., *Life of Arthur Lee* (2 vols., Boston, 1829), II, 299.

23. *Boston Chronicle*, 17, 21 August 1769; Mein's list of importations is recapitulated in the *Boston Chronicle*, 22 January 1770; see also *Boston Gazette*, 1 January 1770, for other violations.

24. Stephen Salisbury (Worcester) to Samuel Salisbury (Boston), 25 December 1769; see also his letters of 3, 6, 7 January 1770, and Samuel Salisbury (Boston) to Stephen Salisbury (Worcester), 2, 3, 16 January 1770, Salisbury Papers (AAS).

25. Stephen Salisbury (Worcester) to Samuel Salisbury (Boston), 11 January 1770, Salisbury Papers (AAS).

26. Stephen Salisbury (Boston) to Samuel Salisbury (Worcester), 31 [*sic*] April 1770, Salisbury Papers (AAS).

27. Philadelphia Committee of Merchants to New York Committee of Merchants, 21 October 1769, Sparks 62, 202 (Harvard); *Boston Gazette*, 25 December 1769, 30 April 1770; *Narrative of Occurrences in Boston, 25 April to 14 May* [1770], Sparks Ms. 10, New England Papers III, 77 (Harvard); John Hancock (Boston) to Hayley & Hopkins (London), 18 May 1770, John Hancock Letterbook, 1762–83 (HBS); the Act of Parliament, 2 Geo. I, c. 30, sec. 8, is mentioned in an "Extract of a letter from a principal merchant in Boston to his friend in New York, 26 June [1770]," *New York Journal*, 5 July 1770; at least one other merchant understood why tea could not be returned to England: Stephen Salisbury (Boston) to Samuel Salisbury (Worcester), 31 [*sic*] April 1770, Salisbury Papers (AAS). This fact was probably common knowledge among Bostonians, for none of the patriots there insisted on return of the tea.

28. William S. Johnson (London) to William Pitkin (Conn.), 9 June 1767, "Trumbull Papers," *Colls. MHS*, 5th ser., IX (1885), 236.

29. *Penna. Journal*, 12 November 1767, 28 April 1768; *New York Gazette*,

25 April 1768; poem as quoted from the *Boston Post-boy*, 16 November 1767, by Arthur M. Schlesinger, *The Colonial Merchants and the American Revolution, 1763–1776* (New York, 1918), p. 108.

30. *Boston Gazette*, 9 November 1767, 11, 25 January, 29 August 1768; *Penna. Journal*, 12, 26 November 1767; *Boston Chronicle*, 4 April 1768; *New York Gazette*, 25 April, 1 September 1768.

31. *Penna. Journal*, 12, 26 January 1768; *Boston Chronicle*, 2 March 1768; *Boston Gazette*, 8 January 1770; *Penna. Chronicle*, 5 February 1770.

32. *Boston Gazette*, 15 August 1768.

33. *Boston Gazette*, 29 August 1768.

34. *Penna. Chronicle*, 28 December 1767; *New York Journal*, 24 December 1767, 23 January 1768; *Penna. Journal*, 14 January 1768; *Boston Gazette*, 5, 9 May, 21 November 1768.

35. *Boston Gazette*, 15 February, 24 October 1768; *New York Journal*, 7 July 1768, 11 May 1769.

36. *New York Journal*, 3 November 1768; *Penna. Journal*, 29 December 1768; *Boston Gazette*, 8 May 1769; for Newburyport incident, see my *Patriots and Partisans: the Merchants of Newburyport, 1764–1815* (Cambridge, Mass., 1962), p. 24.

37. Unsigned and undated paper from America, c. 1769, concerning effects of Townshend duties, Liverpool Papers, Add. Ms. 38340, f. 135 (BM).

38. *Boston Gazette*, 5, 12, 19, 26 February, 26 March, 2 April 1770; *A Narrative of Proceedings at Boston from February 7th to March 14th, 1770*, Sparks Ms. 10, N.E. Papers, III, 70 (Harvard); [Names of those refusing to sign against . . . tea in Newburyport], Eben F. Stone Papers (EI); see also my *Patriots and Partisans*, pp. 25–6.

39. "Extract of a Letter from London," *Boston Chronicle*, 14 June 1770.

40. Customs 3/67 and 3/68 (PRO); Customs 16/1 (PRO).

41. Customs 16/1 (PRO).

42. Richard Clarke Invoice Book, 1767–75 (NEHGS); Richard Clarke & Sons (Boston) to Peter Contincen (London), 23 August 1768, Richard Clarke Letterbook, 1767–69 (NEHGS).

43. Richard Clarke & Sons (Boston) to Peter Contincen (London), 21 October 1768, 21 January, 18 February, 2 March, 9 May, 9 August 1769, Richard Clarke Letterbook, 1767–69 (NEHGS).

44. Richard Clarke Invoice Book, 1767–75 (NEHGS); Richard Clarke (Boston) to Buckeley Emerson (Newburyport), 3, 10 April, 31 July, 17 August 1769, and to Thomas Robie (Marblehead), 25 April, 13 June, 17 August 1769, Richard Clarke Letterbook, 1767–69 (NEHGS).

45. Richard Clarke & Sons to Peter Contincen (London), 19 August 1769, Richard Clarke Letterbook, 1767–69 (NEHGS).

46. [Importation of dutied tea into Boston, 1769], *Boston Chronicle*, 22 January 1770, in which editor John Mein lists twenty vessels that brought nearly 100,000 pounds of tea into Boston in 1769, along with the names of the importers and the number of chests on which they paid duties.

An account of what Tea has been Imported into Boston, since the year 1768 . . . , Ms.L (MHS), seems to have been partly compiled from John Mein's list. Here the owners of the vessels are listed along with the total amounts of tea in their cargoes for the years 1769–72.

47. *Boston Gazette,* 4, 11, 18 September, 9 October 1769, 22, 29 January 1770; Thomas Hutchinson to the Earl of Hillsborough, 5 October 1769, C.O. 5/758 (PRO); George Mason (Boston) to [Joseph Harrison (London?)], 24 January 1770, Sparks Ms. 10, New England Papers, III, 63 (Harvard); Thomas Cushing, *et al.* (Boston Committee of Merchants), to Dennys DeBerdt (London), 30 January 1770, Misc. Bound Mss. (MHS); Henry Pelham (Boston) to Charles Pelham (Newton), 1 May 1770, Copley-Pelham Correspondence, C.O. 5/39 (PRO).

48. John Powell (Boston) to Christopher Champlin (Newport), 23 October 1769, in *Commerce of Rhode Island,* I, 294–5.

49. Customs 16/1 (PRO).

50. Thomas Hutchinson to Earl of Hillsborough, 27 April 1770, Sparks Ms. 10, New England Papers III, 78 (Harvard).

51. *Boston Gazette,* 10 July, 28 August, 23, 30 October, 20 November, 4 December 1769; Samuel Salisbury (Boston) to Stephen Salisbury (Worcester), 4 August 1769, Salisbury Papers (AAS).

52. Thomas Robie (Marblehead) to Richard Clarke & Sons (Boston), 13 January 1770, Misc. Bound Mss. (MHS); *New York Journal,* 1 March 1770; *Penna. Journal,* 12 April 1770.

53. Customs 16/1 (PRO); *Account of Goods which pay a duty in the Unity, Capt. Enoch Story,* [Phila.] Custom House Papers, IX (HSP).

54. *List of Ships . . . that have sailed from the Muse or Goerée . . . 1768,* Letter from British Consul in Amsterdam, 26 December 1768, Extract of Advices from Amsterdam, 6 April 1769, all in T. 64/312 (PRO); *New York Journal,* 31 May 1770; Sailing Orders for Captain Hammond, 6 June 1770, in *Commerce of Rhode Island,* I, 332–3.

CHAPTER III

1. Ritcheson, *British Politics,* pp. 102–9, 118–22.

2. Dennys DeBerdt (London) to Thomas Cushing (Boston), 27 June, 29 July 1768, in "Letters of Dennys DeBerdt," *Pubs.* Col. Soc. Mass., XIII (March 1911), 332–3, 336–7; William S. Johnson (London) to William Pitkin (Conn.), 23 July, 10 October 1768, 3 January 1769, "Trumbull Papers," *Colls.* MHS, 5th ser., IX (1885), 289–300, 305; Charles Garth to Committee on Correspondence of South Carolina, 10 December 1768, *S. C. Hist. Mag.,* XXX (October 1930), 233–5.

3. "Extract of a letter from a Gentleman in London to his friend in Virginia, dated November 9, 1768," *Penna. Chronicle,* 27 March 1769; for

North's and Hillsborough's attitude: "Extract of a Letter from a Gentleman in London to his Friend in [Annapolis], dated November 18, 1768," *Penna. Journal,* 9 February 1769; William S. Johnson (London) to William Pitkin (Conn.), 18 November 1768, 3 January 1769; in "Trumbull Papers," *Colls.* MHS, 5th ser., IX (1885), 302–3, 304–6; William Strahan (London) to David Hall (Phila.), 10 November 1768, "Correspondence between William Strahan and David Hall," *Penna. Mag. Hist. & Biog.,* X (October 1886), 463–4.

4. Dennys DeBerdt (London) to Thomas Cushing (Boston), 1 June 1769, "Letters of Dennys DeBerdt," *Pubs. Col. Soc. Mass.,* XIII (March 1911), 374–5; Hillsborough to King, 15 February 1769, Sir John Fortescue, ed., *The Correspondence of King George III* (6 vols., London, 1927), II, 81–5.

5. For a report of Barré's speech, William S. Johnson (London) to William Pitkin (Conn.), 9 February 1769, "Trumbull Papers," *Colls.* MHS, 5th ser., IX (1885), 313–14; for Richmond and Dartmouth, Richmond to Rockingham, 12 December 1768, Rockingham Papers, R 1-1129, and Dartmouth to Rockingham, 13 December 1768, Rockingham Papers R 1-1132 (Sheffield); for Rockingham quote, Rockingham to Joseph Harrison (Boston), 19 May 1769, Rockingham Papers, R 1-1186 (Sheffield).

6. "Extract of a letter from London, dated November 17, [1768]," *Boston Chronicle,* 19 January 1769; "Extract of a letter from a Gentleman of Distinction in London, dated February 5, 1769," *Boston Gazette,* 10 April 1769; William S. Johnson (London) to William Pitkin (Conn.), 25 May 1769, "Trumbull Papers," *Colls.* MHS, 5th ser., IX (1885), 353–4.

7. *Parliamentary History,* XVI, 610–22; William S. Johnson (London) to William Pitkin (Conn.), 26 April 1769, "Trumbull Papers," *Colls.* MHS, 5th ser., IX (1885), 334–40.

8. The events of the Cabinet Meeting are recounted by Grafton in Anson, *Grafton,* pp. 229–30; for the King's position: Fortescue, *Correspondence of George III,* II, 84–5. In September 1774 the King was still insisting that the tea duty be retained so that there would "always be one tax to keep up the right." King to North, 11 September 1774, Fortescue, *Correspondence of George III,* III, 130–31.

9. Anson, *Grafton,* pp. 230–34; Dennys DeBerdt to Thomas Cushing, 1 June 1769, and to Caesar Rodney, *et al.,* 13 June 1769, "Letters of Dennys DeBerdt," *Pubs. Col. Soc. Mass.,* XIII (March 1911), 374–5; Jonathan Carver (London) to Edmund Quincy (Boston), 10 June 1769, Adams Papers, IV, 344 (MHS).

10. William S. Johnson (London) to William Pitkin (Conn.), 25 May, 5 December 1769, in "Trumbull Papers," *Colls.* MHS, 5th ser., IX (1885), 346–55, 384; Francis Bernard to Thomas Hutchinson, 19 September 1769, Bernard Papers, Sparks Ms. 4, VIII, 9 (Harvard); "Extract of a Letter from London, October 4, 1769," *Penna. Journal,* 7 December 1769; "Extract of a letter from a merchant in London to his Correspondent in

Boston, November 1, 1769," and "Extract of a letter from a Gentleman in London to his Friend in Boston, November 3, 1769," *Boston Chronicle*, 8 January 1770; Francis Bernard to Thomas Hutchinson, 16 November 1769, Bernard Papers, Sparks Ms. 4, VIII, 17–18 (Harvard); Charles Steuart (London) to John Swift (Phila.), 3 January 1770, Custom House Papers, XII (HSP); "Extract of a letter from London, January 16, 1770," *Penna. Journal*, 3 May 1770; "Extract of a letter from London, February 8, 1770," *New York Journal*, 3 May 1770; Mildred & Roberts (London) to Reynell & Coates (Phila.), 8 February 1770, in Reynell & Coates Correspondence, 1769–71 (HSP); Francis Bernard to Thomas Hutchinson, 14 February 1770, Bernard Papers, Sparks Ms. 4, VIII, 62–3 (Harvard); Richard Champion (Bristol) to Caleb & John Lloyd (Charleston, S.C.), 16 July 1770, in G. H. Guttridge, ed., *The American Correspondence of a Bristol Merchant* (Berkeley, 1934), pp. 19–21.

11. *Petition of the Merchants and Traders of the City of London Trading to North America* [n.d.], Liverpool Papers, Add. Ms. 38340, f. 192 (BM).

12. Francis Bernard to Lord North, 22 February 1770, Bernard Papers, Sparks Ms. 4, VIII, 67–8 (Harvard); Dennys DeBerdt (London) to Thomas Cushing (Boston), 2 February 1770, "Letters of Dennys DeBerdt," *Pubs. Col. Soc. Mass.*, XIII (March 1911), 396–7.

13. *Parliamentary History*, XVI, 853–4; Henry Cavendish, *Debates of the House of Commons, 1768–1771* (2 vols., London, 1841–43), I, 483–500.

14. *Parliamentary History*, XVI, 853–4; J. Yorke to Lord Hardwicke [n.d.], Hardwicke Papers, Add. Ms. 35609, f. 282 (BM); Francis Bernard to Thomas Hutchinson (Boston), 7 March 1770, Bernard Papers, Sparks Ms. 4, VIII, 70–72 (Harvard).

15. *Parliamentary History*, XVI, 855–70; Charles A. W. Pownall, *Thomas Pownall . . .* (London, 1908), p. 227.

16. *Parliamentary History*, XVI, 871–4.

17. *Parliamentary History*, XVI, 874. Soames Jenyns to Lord Hardwicke, 6 March 1770, Add. Ms. 35631, f. 85 (BM); Francis Bernard to Thomas Hutchinson, 7 March 1770, Bernard Papers, Sparks Ms. 4, VIII, 70–72 (Harvard); the Repeal Act was 10 Geo. 3, c. 17. One commentator favorable to the colonies attributed the failure of total repeal to the vigorous measures adopted by the Americans: Alexander Mackay (London) to James Bowdoin (Boston), 7 April 1770, "Bowdoin- Temple Papers," *Colls. MHS*, 6th ser., IX (1897).

18. Lady Chatham to Rockingham, March 1770, Rockingham Papers, R 1-1290 (Sheffield).

19. *Parliamentary History*, XVI, 928–9; Marquis of Rockingham to Lord Dartmouth, 9 April 1770, Dartmouth Papers II-322 (WSL); J. Harris to Lord Hardwicke, 10 April 1770, Hardwicke Papers, Add. Ms. 35609, ff. 176–7 (BM). Trecothick's motion was "better supported than many expected," reported William Bollan to Samuel Danforth, 10 April 1770, Bowdoin-Temple Papers," *Colls. MHS*, 6th ser., IX (1897), 172–3.

20. William S. Johnson (London) to Jonathan Trumbull (Conn.), 2 January, 3 February 1770, "Trumbull Papers," *Colls.* MHS, 5th ser., IX (1885), 394–5, 406–7; "Extract of a letter from London, dated February 2," *Boston Chronicle*, 23 April 1770.

21. William S. Johnson (London) to Jonathan Trumbull (Conn.), 6 March 1770, "Trumbull Papers," *Colls.* MHS, 5th ser., IX (1885), 423; reports of the alleged bargain also appeared throughout the spring in American newspapers: *Boston Gazette*, 30 April, 21, 28 May 1770; *New York Journal*, 24 May 1770; *Boston Chronicle*, 14 June 1770; see also Francis Bernard (London) to Thomas Hutchinson, 7 March 1770, Bernard Papers, Sparks Ms. 4, VIII, 70–72 (Harvard).

22. George Grenville to Thomas Pownall, 17 July 1768, Grenville Papers, Add. Ms. 42086 (BM); Francis Bernard (London) to Lord North, 22 February 1770, and to Thomas Hutchinson, 7 March 1770, Bernard Papers, Sparks Ms. 4, VIII, 67–8, 70–72 (Harvard); "Extract of a Letter from London, 12 February 1770," *Boston Gazette*, 23 April 1770; Benjamin Franklin (London) to ———, 18 March 1770, Smyth, *Franklin Writings*, V, 251–4.

23. *Boston Gazette*, 30 April 1770; *New York Journal*, 3 May 1770; William Jones (Bristol) to John Hancock (Boston), 14 April 1770, Boston Private and Business Papers, II (1770–83) (BPL); *Penna. Chronicle*, 21 May 1770; Edmund Boehm & Sons (London) to Reynell & Coates (Phila.), 6 June 1770, Reynell & Coates Mss., I (HBS); "Extract of a letter from London, June 11 [1770]," *Boston Gazette*, 3 September 1770; Thomas Harris (London) to James Beekman (New York), 7 July 1770, in White, ed., *Beekman Mercantile Papers*, II, 810; Thomas Cushing (Boston) to Stephen Sayre (London), 6 November 1770, *Colls.* MHS, 4 ser., IV (1858), 356–8.

24. Lieutenant-Governor Colden to Earl of Hillsborough, 16 May 1770, *N.Y. Col. Docs.*, VIII, 214; *New York Journal*, 24 May, 7, 21, 24 June 1770.

25. *Boston Gazette*, 11, 25 June 1770; *Penna. Journal*, 28 June 1770; *Notice Published in New York*, 9 July 1770, C.O. 5/1101 (PRO); Lieutenant-Governor Colden to Earl of Hillsborough, 7, 10 July 1770, and Alexander Colden to Anthony Todd, 11 July 1770, *N.Y. Col. Docs.*, VIII, 216–21.

26. Isaac Stroud (London) to Henry Drinker (Phila.), 25 August 1770, Drinker Papers, 1739–79 (HSP); Thomas Hutchinson to [the Earl of Hillsborough], 26 July 1770, C.O. 5/759 (PRO); *Penna. Journal*, 12 July 1770 (postscript); *Boston Gazette*, 23, 30 July, 6 August 1770.

27. John Penn to Earl of Hillsborough, 19 May 1770, C.O. 5/1283 (PRO); Richard Waln (Phila.) to Harford & Powell (London), 11 May 1770, Waln Letterbook, 1766–69 (HSP); John Reynell (Phila.) to [his brother], 14 May 1770, to Thomas Rutter [London?], 16 May 1770, to Thomas Greer, [London?], 12 June 1770, to Robert & Nathaniel Hude (London), 22 September 1770, Reynell Letterbook, 1769–70 (HSP); Humphrey Marshall (Chester) to Benjamin Franklin (London), 28 May 1770, Ben-

jamin Franklin Papers, III, 1, 16 (APS); Thomas Irving (Boston) to John Swift (Phila.), 5 June 1770, Custom House Papers, X (HSP); James & Drinker (Phila.) to Lancelot Couper (Bristol), 17 July 1770, James & Drinker Letterbook, 1769–72 (HSP); *Penna. Gazette*, 7, 28 June, 19 July, 20, 26 September 1770; "Extract of a letter from Phila., July 16 [1770]," *Boston Gazette*, 30 July 1770; Samuel Coates (Phila.) to William Logan (London), 26 September 1770, Samuel Coates Letterbook, 1763–81 (HSP); Jensen, *Commerce of Philadelphia*, pp. 187–95.

28. Samuel Salisbury (Boston) to Stephen Salisbury (Worcester), 23 May 1770, Salisbury Papers (AAS).

29. Samuel Prince (Boston) to Dr. Isaac [W. Clarke?], 28 July 1770, Misc. Bound Mss. (MHS).

30. *Boston Gazette*, 28 May, 11, 18, 25 June, 30 July, 13 August, 3, 10 September, 15 October 1770; Thomas Hutchinson to Earl of Hillsborough, 26 July 1770, C.O. 5/759 (PRO); Samuel Salisbury (Boston) to Stephen Salisbury (Worcester), 10 October 1770, Salisbury Papers (AAS); Samuel Cooper (Boston) to Governor Pownall (London), 12 October 1770, King's Mss., 203 (BM); Samuel Adams (Boston) to Stephen Sayre (London), 16 November 1770, Harry A. Cushing, ed., *The Writings of Samuel Adams* (4 vols., New York, 1904), II, 58; John Dickinson (Phila.) to Arthur Lee (London), 31 October 1770, and Arthur Lee to Samuel Adams, 10 January 1771, Lee, *Life of Lee*, II, 302–3, 248–51; Joseph Palmer (Bristol) to Thomas Flucker (Boston), 30 July 1771, Adams Papers, IV, 344 (MHS).

31. Alex. Mackraby (Phila.) to Sir Philip Francis, 9 November 1770, Joseph Parkes, *Memoirs of Sir Philip Francis* . . . (2 vols., London, 1867), I, 448–9; George Mason to ———, 6 December 1770, Kate M. Rowland, *The Life of George Mason, 1725–1792* (New York, 1892), pp. 148–51.

32. Samuel Salisbury (Boston) to Stephen Salisbury (Worcester), 14 November 1770, Salisbury Papers (AAS).

33. *An Account of what Tea has been Imported into Boston, since the year 1768* . . . [through 1772], Ms.L (MHS); Customs 16/1 and Customs 3/70–73 (PRO); *Penna. Gazette*, 17 November 1773.

34. Richard Clarke Invoice Book, 1767–75 (NEHGS); Buckley Emerson (Newburyport) to Richard Clarke (Boston), 7 May 1773, Misc. unbound Mss. (MHS).

35. Stephen Salisbury (Worcester) to Samuel Salisbury (Boston), 14 March 1771, 18 January, 14, 19 May 1772, 3, 14 April, 16 August 1773; Samuel Salisbury (Boston) to Stephen Salisbury (Worcester), 12 May 1772, 23 June 1773; Abraham Dupuis (London) to Samuel & Stephen Salisbury (Boston), 5, 19 June, 29 September 1773, Salisbury Papers (AAS); Jonathan Jackson (Newburyport) to Oliver Wendell (Boston), 11, 14 December 1770, Oliver Wendell Papers (MHS); miscellaneous bills, *passim*, Caleb Davis Papers (MHS); *An Account of what Tea has been imported into Boston since the year 1768* . . . [through 1772], Ms.L (MHS); Hayley & Hopkins (London) to John Hancock (Boston), 22 July 1772, Foreign

Letters, John Hancock Papers, vol. 27, and John Hancock (Boston) to Hayley & Hopkins (London), 4 November 1772, John Hancock Letterbook, 1762–83 (HBS).

36. Customs 16/1 (PRO); *An Account of the Tea that has been imported into the several ports of North America from the Commencement . . . of 7 Geo. III to 1 December, 1770, An Account of the Tea that has been imported into the Several Ports of North America since the partial repeal of . . . 7 Geo. III . . .*, and *An Account of Duties received on Tea in America* [1770–1773], T.1/505 (PRO); Earl of Hillsborough to Dunmore, 16 June 1770, C.O. 5/1101, and two letters to the Lords of the Treasury, 7 December 1770, C.O. 5/759 (PRO).

37. Governor Hutchinson to the Earl of Hillsborough, 26 July 1770, Sparks Ms. 10, New England Papers IV, 8 (Harvard).

38. Commissioners of Customs (Boston) to John Swift, *et al.* [General Letter No. 1], 17 January 1771, and John Swift (Phila.) to Commissioners of Customs (Boston), 31 January 1771, [Phila.] Custom House Papers, XI (HSP).

39. Customs Commissioners (Boston) to Collector of Customs (Salem), 23 January 1772, Salem Custom House Records (EI).

40. Charles Wharton Cash Book, 1765–71 (HSP); Customs 16/1 (PRO); Richard Waln (Phila.) to Elijah Brown (shipmaster), 26 May 1770, Richard Waln Letterbook, 1766–99, and Elijah Brown (St. Eustatius) to Richard Waln (Phila.), 19 July 1770, Richard Waln Foreign Correspondence, 1763–90 (HSP).

41. *Observations on the Trade and Revenue of North America, with some Hints for the improvement of Both, and A Plan for the Prevention of Smuggling* [n.d.: 1772?], Dartmouth Papers, II-500 (WSL); Governor Tryon's response to King's Questionnaire, 11 June 1774, C.O. 5/1105 (PRO).

42. Governor Bernard to Lords of the Treasury, 28 April 1766, T.1/452 (PRO); the clause was 4 Geo. 3, c. 15, sec. 42 (1763).

43. Governor Bernard to Lords of the Treasury, 28 April 1766, T. 1/452 (PRO).

44. John Swift (Phila.) to Custom Commissioners (Boston), 25, 30 November 1771, [Phila.] Custom House Papers, XII (HSP).

45. John Robinson (Treasury) to Grosvenor Bedford (Phila.), 8 November 1770, *A Case* [1772], [Phila.] Custom House Papers, XII (HSP); Papers relating to the *Speedwell*, 5 February–30 April 1771, T. 1/485 (PRO); John Swift (Phila.) to Capt. Dudington (Wilmington), 16 January 1771, [Phila.] Custom House Papers, XI (HSP).

46. John Swift (Phila.) to John Robinson (Treasury), 30 April 1771, [Phila.] Custom House Papers, XI (HSP).

47. Unsigned and undated paper from America, *c.* 1769, *re* Townshend Act, Liverpool Papers, Add. Ms. 38340, f. 135 (BM).

48. Specialists will note that I disagree with some of the conclusions drawn

by Oliver M. Dickerson in *The Navigation Acts and the American Revolution* (Philadelphia, 1951). Dickerson suggests (p. 91), "...there is little evidence that there was any extensive direct importation of tea from Holland or other sources in violation of the trade acts after 1765." Reports to the contrary "were rumors . . . industriously circulated by the partisans of administration...." But the Americans did continue to consume tea in vast quantities after 1765, and most of it could only have been smuggled. In his effort to emphasize customs racketeering in the period 1768–72, as a cause of the Revolution, Dickerson gives us only one side of the picture. American merchants had regularly violated the laws of trade for years, at least as far as tea was concerned, and continued to do so after 1765. Customs officers who stood in the way of their illicit profits were intimidated, mobbed, or made the victims of false testimony in court, time after time. Racketeering there was, as Dickerson ably demonstrates, but the onus of first transgressors rests with the Americans.

CHAPTER IV

1. Lucy S. Sutherland, *The East India Company in Eighteenth-Century Politics* (Oxford, 1952), pp. 1–5; F. P. Robinson, *The Trade of the East India Company: from 1709 to 1813* (Cambridge, 1912), pp. 1–30.
2. Sutherland, *East India Company*, pp. 7–13; Robinson, *Trade*, pp. 46–8.
3. Robinson, *Trade*, pp. 30, 48–9.
4. Pritchard, *The Crucial Years*, p. 163.
5. William Wood (Custom House, London) to John Cleveland (Admiralty), 3 November 1757, Adm. 1/3866 (PRO); John Read and J. Wilkinson to Lords of the Treasury, 6 August 1764, John Snaffield & Robert Poulden to [Lords of the Treasury], 25 August 1764, and ——— Onslow to Lords of the Treasury, 16 December 1764, T.1/433 (PRO); Charles Lutwidge (Isle of Man), *Proposals for Suppressing the Present Illicit Trade carried on from Foreign Parts into Great Britain and Ireland ...*, 20 November 1766, T.1/455 (PRO).
6. *An Account of Tea Delivered from East India Company Warehouses...* [1763–1778], Add. Ms. 8133B, ff. 326–7 (BM). See Appendix, Table III, for comprehensive figures.
7. Sutherland, *East India Company*, pp. 54, 146, 171–2, 184–5; *Report from the Committee of Proprietors, Appointed the 1st of December, 1773...., To Enquire Into The Present State and Condition of the Company's Affairs* (London, 1773), pp. 18–23.
8. Sutherland, *East India Company*, pp. 190–93, 205, 225–7.
9. Sutherland, *East India Company*, pp. 222–4.
10. East India Co. Miscellanies (Home letters sent out), vol. 20, ff. 76–7, 85,

131–2, 163–4, 192–3; Committee of Correspondence Reports, vol. 10, ff. 118–19; E.I. Co. Court Minutes, vol. 4, ff. 17, 23, 36, 51, and vol. 81, f. 96 (Commonwealth Relations Office).

11. E.I. Co. Court Minutes, vol. 81, ff. 394–5 (Commonwealth Relations Office); Sutherland, *East India Company*, pp. 249–50.

12. E.I. Co. Court Minutes, vol. 81, ff. 471–6, 486 (Commonwealth Relations Office); *Parliamentary History*, XVII, 799–800; Sutherland, *East India Company*, pp. 251–2.

13. *Parliamentary History*, XVII, 805–6, 813–14, 831; Sutherland, *East India Company*, pp. 248–54.

14. Rockingham to Edmund Burke, 28 October 1772, Duke of Portland to Rockingham, 21 November 1772, Rockingham to William Dowdeswell, 30 November 1772, Rockingham Papers, R1-1408, 1413, and 1415 (Sheffield).

15. Matthew Brickdale's Parliamentary Diary, VIII, 11–12 (Bristol). Brickdale was M.P. for Bristol. His diary, covering the years 1770–74, includes key phrases from many major speeches.

16. *Parliamentary History*, XVII, 813–37.

17. E.I. Co. Miscellanies, vol. 20, ff. 240–43 (Commonwealth Relations Office); *Parliamentary History*, XVII, 848–50.

18. E.I. Co. Miscellanies, vol. 20, ff. 253–4, 266–7, 269–70, 278, E.I. Co. Court Minutes, vol. 82, ff. 146–7, 165–7, 184–8; Committee of Correspondence Reports, vol. 11, ff. 9–13 (Commonwealth Relations Office); *Parliamentary History*, XVII, 887–90.

19. King to North, 15 May 1773, Fortesque, *Correspondence of George III*, II, 484.

20. E.I. Co. Court Minutes, vol. 82, f. 213; Committee of Correspondence Reports, vol. 11, ff. 18–19; E.I. Co. Miscellanies, vol. 20, ff. 298–300 (Commonwealth Relations Office); *Parliamentary History*, XVII, 887–917; Sutherland, *East India Company*, pp. 259–65.

21. Rockingham to Burke, 28 October 1772, Rockingham Papers, R1-1408 (Sheffield).

22. *The Present State of the English East-India Company's Affairs...*, (London, [1772?]), pp. 27–45, 59–64.

23. *The Present State*, pp. 46–58; *List of ... Proprietors of East India Company Stock* ... (London, 1773), pp. 28–9; Francis Townshend, *A Catalogue of Knights from 1660 to 1760* ... (London, 1833), p. 31; Robert Beatson, *A Chronological Register of ... Parliament, from ... 1708 ... to ... 1807 ...* (3 vols., London, 1807), II, 411.

24. *The Present State...*, pp. 46–58. In the autumn of 1772 tea actually was selling in Amsterdam for 2s. 3d. But this was its highest level in eight years and by the following May it had returned to a more normal level of 1s. 9d. See Appendix, Table II.

25. *The Present State...*, pp. 56–8.

26. *The Present State...*, pp. 50–53.

27. E.I. Co. Miscellanies, vol. 20, f. 156; Committee of Correspondence Reports, vol. 10, ff. 195–6; E.I. Co. Court Minutes, vol. 81, ff. 378–9, 383–4 (Commonwealth Relations Office). The important tea merchant William Palmer objected to the Herries plan from the start.

28. Hope & Co. (Amsterdam) to [E. I. Co.], 12 January 1773, E.I. Co. Miscellaneous Letters Received, vol. 57 (Commonwealth Relations Office).

29. Hope & Co. (Amsterdam) to [E. I. Co.], 12 January 1773, E.I. Co. Miscellaneous Letters Received, vol. 57 (Commonwealth Relations Office).

30. Hope & Co. (Amsterdam) to [E. I. Co.], 12 January 1773, E. I. Co. Miscellaneous Letters Received, vol. 57 (Commonwealth Relations Office).

31. Messrs. Romberg (Bruxelles) to Rodolph Valtravers (London), 23 February 1773, (Copy), Dartmouth Papers, V, 298 (WSL). How copies of this correspondence found their way into the Dartmouth Papers is uncertain.

32. E.I. Co. Court Minutes, vol. 81, ff. 471–6 (Commonwealth Relations Office).

33. E.I. Co. General Court Minutes, vol. 4, ff. 118–19; Court Minutes, vol. 81, ff. 489–92; Miscellanies, vol. 20, ff. 189–90 (Commonwealth Relations Office).

34. Cavendish Debates, Egerton Ms. 246, pp. 1–3 (BM). Henry Cavendish was Member for Lostwithiel and spent almost his entire time in Commons from 1768 to 1774 recording debates *verbatim* in shorthand. He trained a clerk to transcribe his notes, but the final version has many gaps resulting from difficulties of deciphering. Two volumes, covering the period 1768 to March 1771, were published by John Wright. The rest of the notes are in the British Museum except for several missing books. *Parliamentary History*, XVII, 840–41.

35. Cavendish Debates, Egerton Ms. 246, pp. 4–5 (BM).

36. Cavendish Debates, Egerton Ms. 246, p. 6 (BM).

37. Cavendish Debates, Egerton Ms. 246, p. 7 (BM).

38. Cavendish Debates, Egerton Ms. 246, pp. 7, 9 (BM).

39. Cavendish Debates, Egerton Ms. 246, pp. 10–11, 13 (BM). Johnstone later claimed that the Company specifically requested that the Townshend duty be replaced by a 6d. duty collectable on tea upon export. *Parliamentary History*, XVIII, 178.

40. Cavendish Debates, Egerton Ms. 246, pp. 14–16 (BM).

41. 13 Geo. 3, c. 44.

42. Joseph Yorke to Lord Hardwicke, 26 April 1773, Hardwicke Papers, Add. Ms. 35375, ff. 77–8 (BM).

43. Matthew Brickdale's Parliamentary Diary, VIII, 27 (Bristol).

44. *Parliamentary History*, XVII, 840–41.

45. *Daily Advertiser*, 27, 28 April, 6, 8, 11 May 1773; *Morning Chronicle*, 27, 28 April, 6, 8, May 1773; *Lloyd's Evening Post*, 28 April, 7 May 1773; *London Chronicle*, 29 April, 6 May 1773.

46. William Palmer to the Directors of the East India Company, 19 May 1773; E.I. Co. Court Minutes, vol. 82, ff. 146–7 (Commonwealth Relations

Office); Francis S. Drake, *Tea Leaves* . . . (Boston, 1884), pp. 189–98; The Memorial of Gilbert Barkley . . . to the Hon'ble the Court of Directors of the East India Company, 26 May 1773, Drake, *Tea Leaves*, pp. 199–202. Reliance on Mr. Drake for these and subsequent letters raises a difficult problem for the historian. It is obvious from internal evidence that these letters were addressed to the Committee of Warehouses of the East India Company. A careful search of the extant files of the Company at the Commonwealth Relations Office during the summer of 1962 failed to reveal any trace of that Committee's records. And yet except for obvious errors in dating, and the annoying omission of signatures and addresses, the papers seem to be completely reliable. The present author is grateful they have been preserved, by whatever circuitous route, in Mr. Drake's volume.

47. "A Proposal for sending tea to Philadelphia, received from the Hon'ble Mr. Walpole," [n.d.], Drake, *Tea Leaves*, pp. 203–5.

48. "[Mr. Palmer's] Outlines of a Plan...," [n.d.], Drake, *Tea Leaves*, pp. 205–7.

49. "Some thoughts upon the East India Company's sending out Teas to America," [n.d.], Drake, *Tea Leaves*, p. 221.

50. E.I. Co. Miscellanies, vol. 20, ff. 281–2 (Commonwealth Relations Office); Letter from Committee of Warehouses to Brook Watson, *et al.*, 25 June 1773, Drake, *Tea Leaves*, p. 215; [Letter from the Committee of Warehouses] to Brook Watson, *et al.*, Drake, *Tea Leaves*, p. 235.

51. *Penna. Gazette*, 6 October 1773. Johnstone charged that the Company adopted the plan only after "intrigues, solicitations, and counter-solicitations" by the Ministry. Johnstone ignored the fact that the Company made the original proposal. *Parliamentary History*, XVIII, 178.

52. *Abstract of Rodolph Valtravers' Negociation between the Hon'ble Brittish East India Company & Messrs. Romberg at Bruxelles in 1773...*, 15 April 1774, Romberg to Valtravers, 8 June, 1773; Julius Hieronymus Zollikoffer (Switzerland) to Valtravers, 11 August 1773, Valtravers to Romberg, 3 September 1773, Romberg to East India Company, 10 August, 27 September 1773, Rodolph Valtravers to [Committee of Warehouses, E.I. Co.], 5 October 1773, copies all in Dartmouth Papers, V, 298 (WSL).

53. E.I. Co. Court Minutes, vol. 82, f. 424 (Commonwealth Relations Office).

54. E.I. Co. Court Minutes, vol. 82, ff. 313, 330–31 (Commonwealth Relations Office); Committee of Warehouses to Walter Mansell, *et al.*, 29 July 1773, Drake, *Tea Leaves*, p. 237; miscellaneous letters to sponsors, 4–5 August 1773, Drake, *Tea Leaves*, pp. 238–40; Agreement between Abraham Dupuis & Co. and Richard Clarke & Sons [November 1773], Edes Papers (MHS).

55. E.I. Co. Court of Directors to Thomas & Isaac Wharton, *et al.* (Phila.), 1 October 1773, Papers relating to the shipment of tea . . . (HSP). Despite their alleged eagerness to sell Singlo tea in America, Company officials included only 22,500 pounds in their shipment. Agreement between Abra-

ham Dupuis & Co. and Richard Clarke & Sons [November 1773], Edes Papers (MHS).

56. E.I. Co. Court of Directors to Thomas & Isaac Wharton, *et al.* (Phila.), 1 October 1773, Papers relating to the shipment of tea . . . (HSP); see Appendix, Table III, for details of the Company's plans.

57. John C. Miller, *Origins of the American Revolution* (Boston, 1943), p. 339, Schlesinger, *Colonial Merchants,* p. 264, Edmund S. Morgan, *The Birth of the Republic, 1763–1789* (Chicago, 1956), p. 59, John R. Alden, *The American Revolution, 1775–1783* (New York, 1953), pp. 6–7, for the view that the Company would undersell smugglers. My calculations for determining potential shipping costs of smuggled tea are based on the mercantile papers cited in Chapter I. Reduction of the price of Dutch tea in Boston to 2s. 1½ d. was proposed in January 1774: *Boston Gazette,* 17 January 1774.

58. E.I. Co. Court Minutes, vol. 82, ff. 330–31 (Commonwealth Relations Office); Petition of the United Company to the Lords Commissioners of His Majesty's Treasury, 19 August 1773, Drake, *Tea Leaves,* pp. 246–7; E.I. Co. Miscellanies, vol. 20, ff. 340–41 (Commonwealth Relations Office); "Licence to Export Tea," 20 August 1773, Drake, *Tea Leaves,* pp. 250–51; Jonathan Clarke, 5 August 1773, George Hayley, 10 August 1773, Lane, Son, & Frazer, 6 August 1773, John Blackburn, *et al.,* 26 August 1773, Pigou & Booth, 31 August 1773, all to William Settle (Committee of Warehouses), Drake, *Tea Leaves,* pp. 243–6, 251–4; "Mr. Palmer's Assortment of Teas for America," Drake, *Tea Leaves,* p. 245. See Appendix, Table IV, for a full accounting of the tea sent to America.

59. Richard Reeve to Lord North, 23 August 1773, T. 1/501 (PRO), hints at the Company's proposal.

60. Richard Reeve (London) to Lord North, 23 August 1773, and John Robinson to Lord North, 26 August 1773, T. 1/501 (PRO).

61. E.I. Co. Miscellanies, vol. 21, f. 2 (Commonwealth Relations Office).

62. *Middlesex Journal,* 21 September 2, 7, 9, 12, 14, 16, 19, 21 October 1773.

CHAPTER V

1. Customs 3/65–3/68, 3/71–3/74 (PRO).

2. Samuel Cooper (Boston) to Benjamin Franklin (London), 1 January 1771, King's Mss. 203 (BM); Petition to Town Meeting, 29 January 1771, in Copley-Pelham Correspondence, C.O. 5/39 (PRO); Lyman H. Butterfield, ed., *Diary and Autobiography of John Adams* (4 vols., Boston, 1961), II, 5; Thomas Cushing (Boston) to Roger Sherman (New Haven), 21 January 1772, *Colls.* MHS, 4th ser., IV (1858), 358–9.

3. Benjamin Franklin (London) to Thomas Cushing (Boston), 5 February 1771, Smyth, *Writings of Benjamin Franklin,* V, 292–6.

4. "Extract of a letter from London, dated 7 June 1769," *Boston Gazette,* 21 August 1769; Bernard to Hutchinson, 9 October 1770, Bernard Papers, Sparks Ms. 4, VIII, ff. 133–4 (Harvard); William S. Johnson (London) to Jonathan Trumbull (Conn.), 15 November 1770, "Trumbull Papers," *Colls.* MHS, 5th ser., IX (1885), 466.

5. Bernard to Hutchinson, 6, 10 November 1770, Bernard Papers, Sparks Ms. 4, VIII, ff. 138–42, 148–9 (Harvard); Thomas Pownall (London) to James Bowdoin (Boston), 14 July 1770, "The Bowdoin-Temple Papers." *Colls.* MHS, 6th ser., IX (1897), 197–8; see also Francis G. Walett, "The Massachusetts Council, 1766–1774," *William and Mary Quarterly,* 3rd ser., VI (October 1949), 605–27.

6. Bernard to Hutchinson, 22 December 1770, Bernard Papers, Sparks Ms. 4, VIII, f. 153 (Harvard); Benjamin Franklin (London) to Samuel Cooper (Boston), 30 December 1770, Smyth, *Writings of Benjamin Franklin,* V, 285–6; William S. Johnson (London) to Jonathan Trumbull (Conn.), 2 January 1771, "Trumbull Papers," *Colls.* MHS, 5th ser., IX (1885), 470–71; Arthur Lee (London) to Samuel Adams (Boston), 10 June 1771, in Lee, *Life of Arthur Lee,* I, 215–19.

7. Benjamin Franklin (London) to William Franklin (New Jersey), 17 August 1772, Smyth, *Writings of Benjamin Franklin,* V, 410–11.

8. Historical Manuscripts Commission, 14th Report, Appendix, Part X, *The Manuscripts of the Earl of Dartmouth* (London, 1895), II, iv-xi.

9. Benjamin Franklin (London) to Thomas Cushing (Boston), 3 September, 4 November, 2 December 1772, to William Franklin (New Jersey), 3 November 1772, in Smyth, *Writings of Benjamin Franklin,* V, 435, 448, 448–51, 444–6.

10. Pennsylvania's Petition, 5 March 1771, Charles J. Stillé, ed., *The Writings of John Dickinson* (2 vols., Philadelphia, 1895), II, 451–2; Dickinson said the petition underwent "much pruning" before being sent: John Dickinson to Arthur Lee, 21 September 1771, Lee, *Life of Arthur Lee,* II, 303–4; Massachusetts petition of 14 July 1772 and 6 March 1773, Papers of the Committee of the House of Lords inquiring into the Boston Riots, April 1774 (HL); for Dartmouth, Dartmouth to Thomas Cushing (Boston), 19 June 1773, in Benjamin F. Stevens, *Facsimiles . . . Relating to America,* No. 2028, and to J. Thornton, Esq., 12 February 1774, Dartmouth Papers, II–827 (WSL).

11. CANDIDUS, *Boston Gazette,* 10 June, 19 August, 9 September, 9, 23 December 1771, 20, 27 January 1772, in Cushing, *Writings of Samuel Adams,* II, 172–5, 198–212, 287–93, 297–306, 313–26.

12. CANDIDUS, *Boston Gazette,* 7 October 1771; VALERIUS POPLICOLA, *Boston Gazette,* 5 October 1772, in Cushing, *Writings of Samuel Adams,* II, 246–50, 332–7; *A Report of the Record Commissioners of the City of Boston . . .,* vol. 18: *Boston Town Records, 1770–77,* pp. 90–108; Samuel Cooper (Boston) to Thomas Pownall (London), 25 March 1773, King's

Mss. 203 (BM); Oliver M. Dickerson, "Use Made of the Revenue from the Tax on Tea," *New Eng. Quar.*, XXXI (June 1958), 232–43.

13. *Speeches of the Governors of Massachusetts Bay* (Boston, 1839), pp. 337–64; Cushing, *Writings of Samuel Adams*, II, 401–26, 431–54; Thomas Cushing (Boston) to Arthur Lee (London), 22 April 1773, in Lee, *Life of Arthur Lee*, II, 234–5; Dartmouth to Thomas Cushing (Boston), 19 June 1773, in Stevens, *Facsimiles*, No. 2028; Hutchinson to Dartmouth, 2 July 1773, C.O. 5/762 (PRO).

14. "Tract Relative to the Affair of Hutchinson's Letters," Smyth, *Writings of Franklin*, VI, 258–89.

15. *Boston Post-boy*, 12 April 1773; Jonathan Williams, Jr. (Boston) to Benjamin Franklin (London), 21 April 1773, Benjamin Franklin Papers, XXXVII, 20 (APS); Benjamin Franklin (London) to Jonathan Williams, Jr. (Boston), 7 July 1773, Franklin letters to Jonathan Williams, 5 (APS); Benjamin Franklin (London) to Thomas Cushing (Boston), 4 June 1773, Smyth, *Writings of Franklin*, VI, 56–7; Henry Bromfield (Boston) to Thomas Bromfield (London), 4 September 1773, Henry Bromfield Letterbook, 1773 (NEHGS).

16. Thomas Hutchinson (Boston) to William Palmer (London), 26 June, 7 August 1773, and to East India Co. Directors, 19 December 1773, Hutchinson Letterbooks, XXVII, 499, 523, 597–9 (MHS transcripts of originals in Mass. Archives).

17. *Boston Gazette*, 28 June 1773; *Pennsylvania Gazette*, 21 July 1773; *New York Gazetteer*, 22 July 1773.

18. Frederick Pigou, Jr. (London) to James & Drinker (Phila.), 26, 27 May 1773, Drinker Papers, 1739–79 (HSP); *Connecticut Journal*, 3 September 1773; *New York Gazette*, 6 September 1773.

19. *Penna. Journal*, 29 September 1773; *New York Journal*, 7 October 1773; *Conn. Journal*, 8 October 1773; *Boston Gazette*, 11 October 1773.

20. "A Letter from New York, September 27," *Penna. Journal*, 29 September 1773; *Boston Gazette*, 11 October 1773; paraphrased also in *New York Journal*, 7 October 1773.

21. "Extract of a letter from London," *New York Journal*, 7 October 1773, (which issue also refers to "several letters," from England warning of the plan), *Boston Gazette*, 18 October 1773; John Norton (London) to Peyton Randolph, *et al.*, 6 July 1773 (Copy), Sparks Ms. vol. 71, Mss. of Virginia, 11 (Harvard); Benjamin Hallowell (Boston) to John Pownall (London), 29 September 1773, Dartmouth Papers, II-712 (WSL); Rev. William Gordon (Roxbury) to Dartmouth, 11 December 1773, Dartmouth Papers, II-754 (WSL).

22. Pigou & Booth (N.Y.) to James & Drinker (Phila.), 4 October 1773, Drinker Papers, 1739–79 (HSP).

23. "Alarm Nos. I, II, III," *New York Journal*, 14, 21, 28 October 1773; Pigou & Booth (N.Y.) to James & Drinker (Phila.), 8 October 1773, Drinker Papers, 1739-79 (HSP); Arthur M. Schlesinger, "The Uprising

Against the East India Company," *Pol. Sci. Quar.*, XXXII (March 1917), 60–79, emphasizes the monopoly issue.

24. *New York Journal*, 21 October 1773.

25. Pigou & Booth (N.Y.) to James & Drinker (Phila.), 18 October 1773, Drinker Papers, 1739–79 (HSP); [Rivington's] *New York Gazetteer*, 21 October 1773.

26. *To the Agents of their High Mightinesses, the Dutch East-India Company, at St. Eustatius*, New York, 28 October 1773, C.O. 5/1105, f. 21 (PRO); Pigou & Booth (N.Y.) to James & Drinker (Phila.), 27 October 1773, Drinker Papers 1739–79 (HSP).

27. [Rivington's] *New York Gazetteer*, 28 October 1773; Pigou & Booth (N.Y.) to James & Drinker (Phila.), 28 October 1773, Drinker Papers, 1739–79 (HSP).

28. A CITIZEN, *New York Journal*, 4 November 1773; CATO, [Rivington's] *New York Gazetteer*, 4 November 1773; "Extract of a letter from New York, dated November 3," *Penna. Journal*, 8 November 1773; *To the Friends of Liberty and Commerce*, New York, 5 November 1773, C.O. 5/1105, f. 23 (PRO); LEGION, [Rivington's] *New York Gazetteer*, 11 November 1773; "Alarm No. V," *New York Journal*, 18 November 1773; Pigou & Booth (N.Y.) to James & Drinker (Phila.), 10 November 1773, Drinker Papers, 1739–79 (HSP).

29. "To the Stated Pilots...," signed LEGION, [Rivington's] *New York Gazetteer*, and *New York Journal*, 18 November 1773.

30. POPLICOLA, [Rivington's] *New York Gazetteer*, 18 November 1773; A FARMER [possibly Samuel Seabury], [Rivington's] *New York Gazetteer*, 2 December 1773.

31. A TRADESMAN, [Rivington's] *New York Gazetteer*, 18 November 1773; *Fellow Citizens, Friends to Liberty and Equal Commerce*, signed A STUDENT AT LAW, New York, 19 November 1773, C.O. 5/1105, ff. 29–32 (PRO); *To the Worthy Inhabitants of New York*, signed A MECHANIC, New York, [n.d.], C.O. 5/1105, ff. 35–8 (PRO).

32. Pigou & Booth (N.Y.) to James & Drinker (Phila.), 24 November 1773, Drinker Papers 1739–79 (HSP); Z, *New York Journal*, 25 November 1773; THE MOHAWKS, New York, 27 November 1773, in [Rivington's] *New York Gazetteer*, 2 December 1773; "The Association of the Sons of Liberty of New York," New York, 29 November 1773, printed in *New York Journal*, 16 December 1773.

33. *New York Journal*, 2 December 1773; *The Memorial of Henry White, et al* . . . , and Minutes of the Governor's Council, C.O. 5/1105 (PRO); [Rivington's] *New York Gazetteer*, 12 May 1774.

34. *The Memorial of Henry White, et al.* . . . , C.O. 5/1105 (PRO); Henry White *et al.*, to Directors of the East India Company, 1 December 1773, C.O. 5/133, ff. 24–5 (PRO); Benjamin Booth (New York) to James & Drinker (Phila.), 7 January 1774, Drinker Papers, 1739–79 (HSP).

35. James & Drinker (Phila.) to Pigou & Booth (N.Y.), 29 September, 3

October 1773, Henry Drinker Letterbook, 1772–84 (HSP), 5 October 1773, Drinker Papers, 1739-79 (HSP), and to Pigou & Booth (London), 5 October 1773, Drinker Foreign Letters, 1772–85 (HSP); Thomas Wharton (Phila.) to Thomas Walpole (London), 5 October 1773, in Drake, *Tea Leaves*, pp. 274-5, and to Samuel Wharton (London), 5 October 1773, in Drake, *Tea Leaves*, p. 273.

36. Benjamin Rush (Phila.) to William Gordon (Roxbury), 10 October 1773, and to John Adams, 14 August 1809, Lyman H. Butterfield, ed., *Letters of Benjamin Rush* (2 vols., Philadelphia, 1951), I, 81–2, 82 *n*; SCAEVOLA, *Penna. Journal*, 13 October 1773; this item was widely reprinted in other colonies during the month of October; *To the Freeholders and Freemen of Pennsylvania...*, signed A COUNTRYMAN, Chester, Penna., 14 October 1773, Evans, No. 13039.

37. CASSIUS, *Penna. Journal*, 13 October 1773; *Inhabitants of Pennsylvania ...*, Philadelphia, 13 October 1773, Evans, No. 12940; resolutions of the meeting are in *Penna. Journal* and *Penna. Gazette*, 20 October 1773.

38. Abel James (Frankfort) to Thomas Wharton (Phila.), 16 October 1773, Wharton Correspondence, 1771–1830 (HSP); *Report of the Committee appointed to Wait on the Tea Commissioners*, 17 [18?] October 1773, in Mss. Relating to Non-Importation Agreements, 1766–75 (APS).

39. "Extract of a Letter from Philadelphia, October 19," *Boston Evening Post*, 1 November 1773; James & Drinker (Phila.) to Pigou & Booth (New York), 19 October 1773, and Statement of James & Drinker, 22 October 1773, Drinker Papers, 1739-79 (HSP).

40. *Report of the Committee appointed to Wait on the Tea Commissioners*, 17 [18–23] October 1773, in Mss. Relating to Non-Importation Agreements, 1766–75 (APS); James & Drinker (Phila.) to Pigou & Booth (N. Y.), 19 October 1773, Committee's response to James & Drinker statement, 23 October 1773, Drinker Papers, 1739–79 (HSP); James & Drinker (Phila.) to Pigou & Booth (London), 30 October 1773, Drinker Foreign Letters, 1772–85 (HSP).

41. HAMDEN, and AN OLD MECHANIC, *Penna. Journal*, 20 October 1773; for identification of HAMDEN, see Benjamin Rush (Phila.) to William Gordon (Roxbury), 10 October 1773, Butterfield, ed., *Rush*, I, 81–2; MUCIUS, *Penna. Packet*, 1 November 1773; TAMMANY, and Y.Z. (John Dickinson), *Penna. Journal*, 3 November 1773; for text of the Tea Act, *Penna. Journal* and *Penna. Gazette*, 3 November 1773; "Extract of a Letter from New York, November 3," in *Penna. Journal*, 8 November 1773; *Penna. Packet*, 15 November 1773.

42. James Pemberton (Phila.) to John Fothergill, *et al.* (London), 30 October 1773, Pemberton Papers, vol. 34, f. 169 (HSP); *A Letter from the Country to a Gentleman in Philadelphia*, signed RUSTICUS, Fair-View, 27 November 1773, Evans, No. 12751.

43. *To the Delaware Pilots...*, Philadelphia, 27 November 1773, Evans, No. 12942; Irving Brant, *James Madison: The Virginia Revolutionist* (Indianapolis, 1941), pp. 137-8.

44. James & Drinker (Phila.) to Pigou & Booth (N. Y.), 20, 30 November 1773, Drinker Papers 1739–79, (HSP); and to Pigou & Booth (London), 30 November 1773, Drinker Foreign Letters, 1772–85 (HSP).
45. *Statement of Philadelphia consignees to the Committee*, 2 December 1773, in Mss. Relating to Non-Importation Agreements, 1766–75 (APS); James & Drinker Statement, 2 December 1773, and James & Drinker to Pigou & Booth (N. Y.), 4 December 1773, Drinker Papers, 1739–79 (HSP).

CHAPTER VI

1. Thomas Hutchinson to the Earl of Dartmouth, 15 November 1773, Hutchinson Letterbooks, XXVII, 570–71 (Mass. Archives, MHS transcripts).
2. A., in *Boston Gazette*, 13 September 1773; W., *Boston Gazette*, 27 September 1773; Hutchinson to Dartmouth [n.d., September 1773], Hutchinson Letterbooks, XXVII, 542–4 (Mass. Archives, MHS transcripts); see Phila. and New York items in *Boston Post-boy, Boston Gazette,* and *Boston Evening Post*, 11 October, and *Boston Newsletter*, 14 October 1773; Massachusetts Committee of Correspondence, 21 October 1773, *Proc.* MHS, XIII (1873–75), 161–3.
3. Henry Bromfield (Boston) to Thomas Bromfield (London), 14 October 1773, Henry Bromfield Letterbook, 1773 (NEHGS); Benjamin Rush to John Adams, 14 August 1809, Butterfield, *Benjamin Rush,* II, 1113–14; A consistent PATRIOT and JOSHUA, SON OF NUN, both in *Massachusetts Spy,* 14 October 1773; RECLUSIS in *Boston Evening Post,* 18 October 1773.
4. PRAEDICUS and Edes's and Gill's editorial, *Boston Gazette,* 18 October 1773; Boston Comm. of Corresp. Circular Letter, 21 October 1773, in Boston Comm. of Corresp., General Correspondence, 1772–75 (NYPL).
5. *Massachusetts Spy,* 21 October 1773; "Proceedings of the North End Caucus," in Elbridge H. Goss, *The Life of Colonel Paul Revere* (2 vols., Boston, 1891), II, 641; John Cary, *Joseph Warren* (Urbana, Ill., 1961), p. 130; Henry Bromfield (Boston) to Thomas Bromfield (London), 25 October 1773, Henry Bromfield Letterbook, 1773 (NEHGS); SCAEVOLA, *Boston Gazette,* 25 October 1773.
6. Letter signed Z., *Boston Evening Post,* 25 October, and *Boston Newsletter,* 28 October 1773. For author's identification see Richard Clarke & Sons (Boston) to Abraham Dupuis (London), November 1773, in Drake, *Tea Leaves,* p. 281.
7. *Boston Newsletter,* 28 October 1773.
8. PRAEDICUS in *Boston Gazette,* 1 November 1773; for Hutchinson's attempts to find a place for his son see Hutchinson to Lord North, to Lord Dartmouth, and to the Duke of Grafton, 20 August 1773, Hutchinson

Letterbooks, XXVII, 529 (Mass. Archives, MHS transcripts); for reference to smuggled tea, see *Boston Gazette*, 1 November 1773.

9. *Massachusetts Spy*, 28 October 1773.

10. Richard Clarke & Sons (Boston) to Abraham Dupuis (London), November 1773, in Drake, *Tea Leaves*, pp. 282–3, Hutchinson to Dartmouth, 4 November 1773, Papers relating to the Boston Tea Party (HL); Boston Comm. of Corresp. Minutes, 2 November 1773 (NYPL); "Proceedings of the North End Caucus," Goss, *Revere*, II, 641–3.

11. Richard Clarke & Sons (Boston) to Abraham Dupuis (London), November 1773, in Drake, *Tea Leaves*, pp. 283–6; Hutchinson to Dartmouth, 4 November 1773, and statements of witnesses present, Papers relating to the Boston Tea Party (HL); Governor Hutchinson to Governor Tryon (New York), 21 November 1773, Hutchinson Letterbooks, XXVII, 572–4 (Mass. Archives, MHS transcripts); "Extract of a letter from Boston to Watson & Rasleigh (London), 4 November 1773," in Drake, *Tea Leaves*, p. 262; *Boston Newsletter*, 4 November 1773; Henry Pelham (Boston) to Charles Pelham (Newton), 5 November 1773, *Copley-Pelham Letters*, pp. 200–202; in the *Boston Gazette*'s account, 8 November 1773, the only comment on the mob activities was that some people present had "shewed marks of their resentment."

12. "Tradesmen's Protest against the Proceedings of the Merchants...," reproduced in *Copley-Pelham Letters*, p. 203.

13. *Massachusetts Spy*, 4 November 1773.

14. Benjamin Faneuil (Boston) to Brook Watson (London) [n.d.: November 1773], in Drake, *Tea Leaves*, pp. 292–4; William Paine (Worcester) to Isaac W. Clarke (Boston), 3 November 1773, Misc. Bound Mss. (MHS).

15. *Boston Town Records*, 1770–77, pp. 141–6; "Proceedings of the Inhabitants of the Town of Boston on the 5th and 6th November 1773," in Drake, *Tea Leaves*, pp. 295–303; *Boston Gazette*, 8 November 1773; *Boston Newsletter*, 11 November 1773.

16. DETERMINATUS, *Boston Gazette*, 8 November 1773, "Extract of a Letter from a Gentleman in Philadelphia," *Massachusetts Spy*, 11 November, and *Boston Gazette*, 15 November 1773; the report of tea importations first appeared in Draper's *Boston Newsletter*, 11 November 1773; Proposition of James Pitts for a Meeting on the Subject of the East India Company's Tea, 8 November 1773, Price Papers (MHS).

17. For Hutchinson's order to Hancock and his reported response, see *Boston Gazette*, 15 November 1773; Thomas Hutchinson to Lord Dartmouth, 15 November 1773, Hutchinson Letterbooks, XXVII, 570–71 (Mass. Archives, MHS transcripts); for rumors of impending harassment and the consignees' nightly flights see Benjamin Faneuil (Boston) to Brook Watson (London) [November 1773], Drake, *Tea Leaves*, pp. 292–4; Hutchinson to William Tryon, 21 November 1773, Hutchinson Letterbooks, XXVII, 572–4 (Mass. Archives, MHS transcripts); "Extract of a Letter from Boston, 15 November," *Penna. Journal*, 24 November 1773.

18. *Boston Newsletter*, 18 November 1773; *Boston Post-boy*, 22 November 1773; "Extract of a Letter from Boston, 18 November," *Penna. Journal*, 1 December 1773.

19. Hutchinson to William Tryon, 21 November 1773, Hutchinson Letterbooks, XXVII, 572–4 (Mass. Archives, MHS transcripts); *Boston Post-boy*, 22 November 1773; *Boston Newsletter*, 26 November 1773; see *Boston Gazette*, 13 December 1773, for a version more favorable to the patriots.

20. *Boston Town Records*, 1770–77, pp. 147–8; *Boston Gazette*, 22 November 1773.

21. The draft of the consignees' petition is in Edes Papers (MHS); the final version is printed in Drake, *Tea Leaves*, pp. 309–10; for Minutes of the Council Meetings, see Drake, *Tea Leaves*, pp. 310–15.

22. *Boston Gazette*, 22 November 1773; Walett, "Massachusetts Council," *Wm. & Mary Quarterly*, 3rd ser., VI (October 1949), 605, 609.

23. London Letters and AN OLD CADET in *Boston Gazette*, 22 November 1773; the others are in *Massachusetts Spy*, 26 November 1773.

24. Boston Comm. of Corresp. Minutes, 16, 22, 23 November 1773 (NYPL); for Cambridge resolutions, *Boston Gazette*, 29 November 1773, *Boston Newsletter*, 2 December 1773.

25. *A Report of the Record Commissioners of the City of Boston...*, vol. 23: *Selectmen's Minutes, 1769–1775* (Boston, 1893), pp. 202–3; John Scollay (Boston) to Arthur Lee (London), 23 December 1773, *Colls.* of MHS, 4th ser. IV (1858), 381–2.

26. Hutchinson to Tryon, 21 November 1773, and to [Andrew Oliver?], 24 November 1773, Hutchinson Letterbooks, XXVII, 572–4, 574–5 (Mass. Archives, MHS transcripts).

27. 13 & 14 Car. 2, c. 11, sec. 4 (1662), made applicable to the colonies by 7 & 8 Gul. 3, c. 22, sec. 6 (1696).

28. John Scollay (Boston) to Arthur Lee (London), 23 December 1773, *Colls.* of MHS, 4th ser., IV (1858), 382; *Boston Selectmen's Minutes*, 28 November 1773, p. 203.

29. Boston Comm. of Corresp. Minutes (NYPL); John M. Bullard, *Joseph Rotch in Nantucket and Dartmouth*, Old Dartmouth Historical Society (1932), 14–16; for regulation regarding time limit on reporting, see 7 Geo. 3, c. 46, sec. 9 (1767).

30. "Minutes of the Tea Meetings, 1773," *Proc.* of MHS, XX (1882–83), 10–11; John Scollay (Boston) to Arthur Lee (London) 23 December 1773, in *Colls.* of MHS, 4th ser., IV (1858), 383–4; "Proceedings of the Town of Boston on the 29th and 30th November 1773," Drake, *Tea Leaves*, pp. 320–21; (Copy), Information of Hugh Williamson, M.D., Miscellaneous Papers of the Revolution, pp. 182–3, Sparks Ms. 52, III (Harvard).

31. "Minutes of the Tea Meetings, 1773," *Proc.* of MHS, XX (1882–83), 10–11.

32. Minutes of the Governor's Council, 29 November 1773, Drake, *Tea Leaves*, pp. 315–20.

33. Minutes of the Governor's Council, 29 November 1773, Drake, *Tea Leaves*, pp. 315–20; Thomas Hutchinson (Milton) to Elisha Hutchinson (Middleborough), 30 November 1773, Hutchinson Papers, Egerton Ms. 2659, f. 50 (BM).

34. "Minutes of the Tea Meetings, 1773," *Proc.* MHS, XX (1882–83), 11–12; John Scollay (Boston) to Arthur Lee (London), 23 December 1773, in *Colls.* of MHS, 4th ser., IV (1858), 383–4.

35. "Minutes of the Tea Meetings, 1773," *Proc.* MHS, XX (1882–83), 12–13; John Scollay (Boston) to Arthur Lee (London), 23 December 1773, in *Colls.* of MHS, 4th ser., IV (1858), 383–4.

36. "Minutes of the Tea Meetings, 1773," *Proc.* MHS, XX (1882–83), 13; John Scollay (Boston) to Arthur Lee (London), 23 December 1773, in *Colls.* of MHS, 4th ser., IV (1858), 384; J. S. Copley (Boston) to Jonathan and Isaac W. Clarke (Castle William) [1 December 1773], in *Copley-Pelham Letters*, pp. 211–13.

37. Hutchinson to Dartmouth, Private letter, 2 December 1773, Hutchinson Letterbooks, XXVII, 578–9 (Mass. Archives, MHS transcripts).

38. J. S. Copley (Boston) to Messrs. Jonathan & Isaac W. Clarke, 1 December 1773, *Copley-Pelham Letters*, pp. 211–13; Information of Hugh Williamson, M.D., Miscellaneous Papers of the Revolution, Sparks Ms. 52, III, 182–3 (Harvard); "Letter from a Visitor to Boston" [Hugh Williamson?], *Boston Gazette*, 20 December 1773; John Scollay (Boston) to Arthur Lee (London), 23 December 1773, *Colls.* of MHS, 4th ser., IV (1858) 383; Hutchinson to Dartmouth, 2 December 1773, Hutchinson Letterbooks, XXVII, 577–8 (Mass. Archives, MHS transcripts).

CHAPTER VII

1. Townshend Act: 7 Geo. 3, c. 46, sec. 4 (1767); Sugar Act: 6 Geo. 2, c. 13, sec. 2 (1733) reads: "that upon the importation of such goods . . . an entry or entries shall be made . . . in the port or place where the same shall be imported."

2. Townshend Act: 7 Geo. 3, c. 46, sec. 9 (1767); Sugar Act: 6 Geo. 2, c. 13, sec. 2 (1733); Province Laws 1770–1771, ch. 2, sec. 3; 13 & 14 Car. 2, c. 11, sec. 4 (1662) made applicable in America by 7 & 8 Gul. 3, c. 22, sec. 6 (1696); see also Kinvin Wroth and Hiller B. Zobel, eds., *The Legal Papers of John Adams* (2 vols., Cambridge, 1964), II.

3. Peter O. Hutchinson, ed., *Diary and Letters of Thomas Hutchinson* (2 vols., London, 1883), I, 100–101; see also, Lawrence S. Mayo, ed., *The History of the Colony of Massachusetts Bay by Thomas Hutchinson* (3 vols., Cambridge, 1936), III, 308, where it is implied that the alleged confrontation took place on the same day as the mass meeting—29 No-

vember. Bernard Knollenberg has pointed out some of the weaknesses in Hutchinson's statement in "Did Samuel Adams Provoke the Boston Tea Party . . . ? " *Proceedings* of the Amer. Antiq. Soc., LXX (1960), 493–9; see also Hutchinson to Bernard, 1 January 1774, Hutchinson Letterbooks, XXVII, 609 (Mass. Archives, MHS transcripts).

4. "Extract of the Journal of the ship *Dartmouth,* from London to Boston 1773," [Benjamin B. Thatcher], *Traits of the Tea Party; Being a Memoir of George R. T. Hewes* . . . (New York, 1835), pp. 259–60; for boundaries of Boston harbor see George G. Wolkins, "The Boston Customs District, 1768," *Proc.* MHS, LVIII (June 1925), 421.

5. "Extract of the Journal of the ship *Dartmouth,*" *Traits of the Tea Party,* p. 260; for *Captain's* anchorage, Adm. 57/158, Captain's Log;—1681, Master's Log (PRO). I am indebted to Cmdr. P. K. Kemp, Librarian of the Admiralty Library, London, for locating this information.

6. "Extract of the Journal of the ship *Dartmouth,*" *Traits of the Tea Party,* p. 260; *Boston Post-boy,* 29 November 1773.

7. Hutchinson to Dartmouth, 4 January 1774, Papers relating to the Boston Tea Party (HL); Cunningham, *Diary of John Rowe,* pp. 256–7.

8. Information of James Hall before the Privy Council, 19 February 1774, C.O. 5/763 (PRO).

9. Protest of Francis Rotch, *et al.,* 10 December 1773, C.O. 5/763 (PRO), printed in Drake, *Tea Leaves,* pp. 353–4, for an account of the whale-oil cargo.

10. Hutchinson to ————, 30 December 1773, and to Bernard, 1 January 1774, Hutchinson Letterbooks, XXVII, 608, 609 (Mass. Archives, MHS transcripts).

11. Mayo, ed., *Hutchinson's Diary,* III, 305; Hutchinson to Tryon, 1 December 1773, to William Palmer (London) [9 December 1773?], and to Bernard, 1 January 1774, Hutchinson Letterbooks, XXVII, 576, 584–5, 609 (Mass. Archives, MHS transcripts).

12. *Boston Gazette,* 6, 13, 20 December 1773; *Boston Newsletter,* 9, 16 December 1773.

13. *Boston Newsletter,* 9 December 1773, for arrival of *Eleanor. Beaver's* status is traced in *Selectmen's Minutes, 1769–1775,* pp. 204–6; the fate of *William* is first reported in a letter from the Sandwich Comm. of Corresp., 13 December 1773, Boston Comm. of Corresp. Minutes (NYPL).

14. THE PEOPLE, *Boston Post-boy,* 6 December 1773; A RANGER, *Boston Evening Post,* 6 December 1773; *Essex Gazette,* 7 December 1773, and *Boston Gazette,* 13 December 1773; John Andrews (Boston) to William Barrell (Phila.), 1 December 1773, *Proc.* MHS, VIII (1864–65), 325; Admiral Montagu to Phillip Stevens (London), 8 December 1773, Dartmouth Papers, I, ii, 942 (WSL).

15. Questions proposed by Francis Rotch . . . , 7 December 1773, Questions

Proposed by James Bruce..., 11 December 1773, Drake, *Tea Leaves*,
pp. 344–8; Protests of Rotch and Bruce, Drake, *Tea Leaves*, pp. 353–8.

16. John Rowe to Messrs. Hutchinsons, "Saturday" [11 December 1773?],
Hutchinson Papers, Egerton Ms. 2659, f. 58 (BM).

17. 9, 11 December 1773, Boston Comm. of Corresp. Minutes (NYPL).

18. "Extract of a letter from Phila., December 4, 1773," *Boston Gazette*, 13
December 1773.

19. HONONCHROTONTHOLOGOS, *Boston Gazette*, 13 December 1773;
Hutchinson to Dartmouth, 15 December 1773, C.O. 5/763 (PRO); Mon-
tagu to Customs Commissioners, 16 December 1773, T. 1/505 (PRO);
Hutchinson to Israel Mauduit, December 1773, *Proc*. MHS, XIII (1873–
75), 170–71; Hutchinson to East India Co. Directors, 19 December 1773,
Hutchinson Letterbooks, XXVII, 599 (Mass. Archives, MHS transcripts).

20. Boston Comm. of Corresp. Minutes, 10, 13 December 1773 (NYPL); Account of the Boston Tea Party, *Penna. Gazette*, 24 December 1773 (postscript). This was the account carried as far as New York by Paul Revere;
Rotch's bill to the consignees, 31 December 1773, Drake, *Tea Leaves*, pp.
351–2. The bill included £7 4*s*. o*d*. [L.M.] to Adams and Blowers "for
advice."

21. "Minutes of the Tea Meetings," *Proc*. MHS, XX (1882–83), 15.

22. For the episode of June 1768, see Joseph Harrison to Marquis of Rockingham, 17 June 1768, Rockingham Papers, R 63–1 (Sheffield), printed in
William and Mary Quarterly, XX (October 1963), 587–95; "Minutes of the
Tea Meetings," *Proc*. MHS, XX (1882–83), 15; *Boston Post-boy*, 20 December 1773.

23. R. A. Harrison and Robert Hallowell to Customs Commissioners, 16 December 1773, T. 1/505 (PRO); "Minutes of the Tea Meetings, 1773,"
Proc. MHS, XX (1882–83), 15–16; Hutchinson to Dartmouth, 17 December
1773, Hutchinson Letterbooks, XXVII, 589 (Mass. Archives, MHS transcripts).

24. "W.T." to [Samuel Adams], 16 December 1773, Samuel Adams Papers
(NYPL).

25. "Minutes of the Tea Meetings, 1773," *Proc*. MHS, XX (1882–83), 16.

26. Hutchinson to Dartmouth, 15 December 1773, C.O. 5/763 (PRO); Province Laws 1700–1701, Ch. 7, sec. 4; Hutchinson to Israel Mauduit, December 1773, *Proc*. MHS, XIII (1873–75), 170–71; Hutchinson to East
India Co. Directors, 29 December 1773, Hutchinson Letterbooks, XXVII,
599 (Mass. Archives, MHS transcripts); William Gordon (Jamaica Plain)
to Dartmouth, 11 December 1773, Dartmouth Papers, II–754 (WSL).

27. Hutchinson to Israel Mauduit, December 1773, *Proc*. MHS, XIII (1873–
75), 170–71; Hutchinson to Dartmouth, 17 December 1773, and to East
India Co. Directors, 19 December 1773, Hutchinson Letterbooks, XXVII,
589, 599 (Mass. Archives, MHS transcripts); Informations of Francis
Rotch and of James Hall, 19 February 1774, before the Privy Council, C.O.
5/763 (PRO); a naval officer was told that Admiral Montagu offered to

protect the tea-ships but was turned down: "Extract of a Letter from Boston from an Officer Aboard the *Active*," 6 December 1773 (postscript), Dartmouth Papers, II–752 (WSL). One commentator claimed that Hutchinson had often made exceptions in granting passes to uncleared vessels: AN IMPARTIAL OBSERVER, *Boston Gazette*, 20 December 1773.

28. "Minutes of the Tea Meetings, 1773," *Proc.* MHS, XX (1882–83), 16–17; Drake, *Tea Leaves*, pp. lix-lx, for Quincy's speech; Informations of William Turner and of William Tyler before the Privy Council, 19 February 1774, C.O. 5/763 (PRO).

29. Hutchinson to Mauduit, December 1773, *Proc.* MHS, XIII (1873–75), 170–71; to Dartmouth, 17 December 1773, Hutchinson Letterbooks, XXVII, 589 (Mass. Archives, MHS transcripts); "Minutes of the Tea Meetings, 1773," *Proc.* MHS, XX (1882–83), 16.

30. Henry C. Watson, *The Yankee Tea Party* . . . (Boston, 1851), 18–21; "Minutes of the Tea Meetings, 1773," *Proc.* MHS, XX (1882–83), 16; Andrews to Barrell, 18 December 1773, *Proc.* MHS, VIII (1862–65), Information of John D. Whitiworth, 19 February 1773, before the Privy Council, C.O. 5/763 (PRO).

31. Evidence for Young's statement is in Informations of Capt. James Hall, of Nathan Frazier, and of Andrew MacKenzie before the Privy Council, 19 February 1774, C.O. 5/763 (PRO); Drake, *Tea Leaves*, pp. xxiii-xxiv, lxvi-lxvii.

32. Edward L. Pierce, "Recollections as a Source of History," *Proc.* MHS, XXX (1895–96), 475–80; John Adams to Hezekiah Niles, 10 May 1819, Charles F. Adams, ed., *The Works of John Adams* (10 vols., Boston, 1850–56), II, 334n.

33. Drake, *Tea Leaves*, pp. lxvi-lxvii.

34. Drake, *Tea Leaves*, p. lxxvii; Watson, *Yankee Tea Party*, pp. 18–21.

35. Drake, *Tea Leaves*, pp. xcv-clxxii.

36. Henry Bromfield (Boston) to Messrs. Flight & Halliday (London), 17 December 1773, Henry Bromfield Letterbook, 1773 (NEHGS); Protest of Alexander Hodgdon, James Bruce, and Hezekiah Coffin, 17 December 1773, C.O. 5/137 (PRO); Memorials of Samuel Hunt and Thomas Dade, Thomas Kirk and George Lewis, and William Elliot and George Lilley (Tidesmen on board the tea-ships), T. 1/505 (PRO); Informations of William Rotch, James Hall, Hugh Williamson, and John D. Whitiworth before the Privy Council, 19 February 1774, C.O. 5/763 (PRO); *Boston Gazette*, 20 December 1773; *Penna. Gazette*, 24 December 1773 (postscript); Drake, *Tea Leaves*, pp. lxviii-lxxxii.

37. For Montagu's retort, see Hutchinson to Col. Williams, 23 December 1773, Israel Williams Papers, II (MHS); Watson, *Tea Party*, pp. 21-2; Leslie to Barrington, 17 December 1773, T. 1/505 (PRO); Montagu to Lords of the Admiralty, 17 December 1773, Secretary of State for the Colonies In-Letters, C.O. 5/247 (PRO). Hutchinson's failure to call for assistance gave support to the belief that he wanted the tea destroyed.

See *N.Y. Journal*, 30 December 1773, and *Boston Newsletter*, 20 May 1774, for accusation of Hutchinson.

38. Butterfield, ed., *Diary of John Adams*, II, 85-6.

CHAPTER VIII

1. Hutchinson to Montagu, 28 December 1773, to ————, 30 December 1773, to Bernard, 1 January 1774, Hutchinson Letterbooks, XXVII, 603, 608, 609 (Mass. Archives, MHS transcripts); quotation from Hutchinson to Israel Mauduit, December 1773, *Proc.* MHS, XIII (1873-75), 170-71.

2. Hutchinson to Montagu, 28 December 1773, to ————, 30 December 1773, Hutchinson Letterbooks, XXVII, 603, 608 (Mass. Archives, MHS transcripts), and to Israel Mauduit, December 1773, *Proc.* MHS, XIII (1873-75), 170-71.

3. Mayo, *Hutchinson's History of Massachusetts-Bay*, III, 313-14.

4. Hutchinson to Bernard, 1 January 1774, Hutchinson Letterbooks, XXVII, 609 (Mass. Archives, MHS transcripts).

5. Thomas Cushing, *et al.*, to Arthur Lee, 21 December 1773, *Colls.* MHS, 4th ser., IV (1858), 377-8.

6. John Scollay to Arthur Lee, 21 December 1773, *Colls.* MHS, 4th ser., IV (1858), 385; Samuel Adams to James Warren, 28 December 1773, *Warren-Adams Letters* (Boston, 1917), I, 19-20; Butterfield, *Diary of John Adams*, II, 86.

7. *Mass. Spy*, 23 December 1773.

8. MARCHMONT NEDHAM, *Boston Gazette*, 20 December 1773; MENTOR, *Mass. Spy*, 23 December 1773; Excerpt from a letter dated Boston, 27 December 1773, in [London] *Gazetteer*, 22 February 1774; A COUNTRYMAN, *Boston Gazette*, 17 January 1774.

9. Mayo, *Hutchinson's History of Massachusetts-Bay*, I, 314-15; Minutes of the Governor's Council, 21 December 1773, enclosed in Hutchinson to Dartmouth, 24 December 1773, Papers relating to the Boston Tea Party, (HL); *Boston Gazette*, 27 December 1773; John Adams to James Warren, 22 December 1773, Adams, *Works*, IX, 334-5.

10. Minutes of the Governor's Council, 21 December 1773, enclosed in Hutchinson to Dartmouth, 24 December 1773, Papers relating to the Boston Tea Party (HL).

11. *Agreement not to be recorded, 24 December 1773*, Boston Comm. of Corresp., General Correspondence, 1772-1775 (NYPL).

12. *Copy of an Association to bear* [?] *harmless* [?], *left for the Committee to peruse, December 1773* (*not to be rec[orde]d*), Boston Comm. of Corresp., General Correspondence, 1772-1775 (NYPL).

13. *Boston Gazette*, 20 December 1773, 17 January 1774; Jonathan Clarke

(Provincetown) to Richard Clarke, *et al.* (Castle William), 31 December 1773, Misc. Bound Mss. (MHS); Hutchinson to Dartmouth, 4 January 1774, Papers relating to the Boston Tea Party (HL); Samuel Adams to James Warren, 10 January 1774, Warren-Adams Papers, I, 20 (MHS).

14. John Greenough (Wellfleet) to Richard Clarke & Sons (Castle William), 26 March 1774, Misc. Bound Mss. (MHS); Richard Clarke & Sons to John Greenough (Wellfleet), 30 March 1774 (BPL); John Greenough (Boston) to Richard Clarke & Sons ("Merchants at Salem"), 2 June 1774, Misc. Bound Mss. (MHS).

15. Thomas Hutchinson, Jr. (Milton) to Elisha Hutchinson (Middleborough), 9 January 1774, Hutchinson Papers, Egerton Ms. 2659, f. 59 (BM); to Jonathan Clarke (Castle William), 20 January 1774, Misc. Bound Mss. (MHS); to Elisha Hutchinson (Middleborough), 21 January and 4 February 1774, Hutchinson Papers, Egerton Ms. 2659, ff. 63 and 70 (BM); *Boston Gazette*, 17, 24 January 1774; *Boston Evening Post*, 14 February 1774; Richard Clarke (Castle William) to Henry Bromfield (Boston), 9 May 1774, Misc. Bound Mss. (MHS); the quotation is in Peggy Hutchinson (Milton) to Polly Hutchinson (Middleborough), printed in *Diary and Letters of Hutchinson*, p. 108; J. S. Copley to [Richard Clarke] *c.* 15 February 1774, *Copley-Pelham Letters*, pp. 213–14.

16. Hutchinson to Dartmouth, 21 December 1773, Dartmouth Papers, I, ii, 921 (WSL).

17. "Extract of another letter [from Boston]," *New York Journal*, 23 December 1773.

18. John Adams (Boston) to James Warren (Plymouth), 22 December 1773, Warren-Adams Papers, I, 17 (MHS); Cunningham, *Diary of John Rowe*, 16, 18 December 1773, pp. 257–8.

19. *Boston Gazette*, 3 January 1774.

20. [Timothy's] *South Carolina Gazette*, 15, 22 November, JUNIUS BRUTUS, 29 November 1773.

21. Leger & Greenwood to East India Co., 4 December 1773, T.1/505 (PRO); [Timothy's] *South Carolina Gazette*, 6 December 1773.

22. Leger & Greenwood to East India Co., 18 December 1773, T.1/505 (PRO); [Timothy's] *South Carolina Gazette*, 20 December 1773; reports of concern over bounty in TACITUS, *New York Journal*, 3 January 1774, and Thomas Wharton (Phila.) to Samuel Wharton (London), 4 January 1774, Wharton Letterbook, 1773–84 (HSP).

23. John Morris to Corbyn Morris, 22 December 1773, Drake, *Tea Leaves*, p. 342; and to Lords of the Treasury, 24 December 1773, T.1/505 (PRO); Governor Bull to Lord Dartmouth, 24 December 1773, Drake, *Tea Leaves*, pp. 339–41; *South Carolina and American General Gazette*, 24 December 1773; [Timothy's] *South Carolina Gazette*, 27 December 1773; Petition to the Lords of the Treasury, 16 February 1774, East India Co. Miscellanies, vol. 21, ff. 75–6 (Commonwealth Relations Office); "Extract of a letter

from a gentleman in Charleston to his friend in New York," *Penna. Journal,* 16 March 1774 [suppl.]; Richard Walsh, *Charleston's Sons of Liberty: A Study of the Artisans, 1763–1789* (Columbia, S.C., 1959), p. 60.

24. Matthew Bowne to Reynell & Coates, 4 December 1773, Reynell & Coates Papers (NYPL); Gov. Tryon to Dartmouth, 1 December 1773, C.O. 5/1105 (PRO).

25. Alexander McDougall to Boston Comm. of Corresp., 13 December 1773, Boston Comm. of Corresp. Minutes (NYPL); New York Council Minutes, 15, 17 December 1773, Papers relating to the Boston Tea Party (HL); BRUTUS, [Rivington's] *N.Y. Gazetteer,* 12 May 1774, in recapitulating these events, claimed there were 2000 present at the meeting. The mayor had estimated the crowd at 800; Pigou & Booth (N.Y.) to James & Drinker (Phila.), 20 December 1773, Drinker Papers, 1739–79 (HSP); *New York Journal,* 23 December 1773.

26. General Haldimand to Dartmouth, 28 December 1773, Papers relating to the Boston Tea Party (HL); *Boston Newsletter,* 30 December 1773.

27. Henry White, *et al.,* to East India Co., 27 December 1773, and to Captain Benjamin Lockyer, 27 December 1773, Papers relating to the Boston Tea Party (HL); [Gaine's] *New York Gazette,* 27 December 1773; Pigou & Booth (New York) to James & Drinker (Phila.), 31 December 1773, Drinker Papers, 1739–79 (HSP).

28. [Rivington's] *N.Y. Gazetteer,* 23 December 1773, 7 April 1774; *N.Y. Journal,* 21 April 1774; Dartmouth to Haldimand (New York), 8 January 1774, C.O. 5/243 (PRO), and to Tryon, 8 January 1774, C.O. 5/1105 (PRO).

29. [Gaine's] *New York Gazette,* 25 April 1774; *Boston Newsletter,* 25 April 1774; Lockyer to Consignees, 20 April 1774, and Consignees to Lockyer, 20 April 1774, Drake, *Tea Leaves,* pp. 359–60; [Rivington's] *N.Y. Gazetteer,* 28 April, 12 May 1774.

30. "Extract of a letter from Philadelphia, dated 28 December 1773," *Boston Gazette,* 24 January 1773; *Penna. Journal,* 24 December 1773; Joseph Reed (Phila.) to Dartmouth, 27 December 1773, in W.B. Reed, *Life and Correspondence of Joseph Reed* (2 vols., Phila., 1857), I, 54–6; Philadelphia Comm. of Corresp. to Boston Comm. of Corresp., 25 December 1773, Boston Comm. of Corresp. Minutes (NYPL): *Penna. Packet,* 6, 13 December 1773; *Penna. Gazette,* 8 December 1773.

31. *Penna. Gazette,* 8 December 1773; Charles Thomson to Sam Adams and John Hancock, 19 December 1773, Samuel Adams Papers (NYPL).

32. Joseph Reed to Lord Dartmouth, 22 December 1773, Dartmouth Papers, I, ii, 923 (WSL).

33. Thomas Wharton to Samuel Wharton (London), 30 November 1773, and to Thomas Walpole (London), 24 December 1773, Wharton Letterbook, 1773–84 (HSP).

34. George Clymer and Thomas Mifflin to Samuel Adams, 27 December 1773,

Samuel Adams Papers (NYPL); *Captain Ayres' Protest,* 27 December 1773, Papers relating to the Shipment of Tea . . . (HSP); James & Drinker (Phila.) to Pigou & Booth (New York), 28 December 1773, Drinker Papers, 1739–79 (HSP); *Penna. Gazette,* 29 December 1773.

35. Thomas Wharton (Phila.) to Thomas Walpole (London), 27 December 1773, Wharton Letterbook, 1773–84 (HSP); George Clymer and Thomas Mifflin (Phila.) to Samuel Adams (Boston), 27 December 1773, Samuel Adams Papers (NYPL); *Captain Ayres' Protest,* 27 December 1773, in Papers Relating to the Shipment of Tea . . . (HSP); John Patterson (Collector of Phila.) to Customs Commissioners, 20 December 1773, T. 1/505 (PRO); *Penna. Packet,* 27 December 1773; for size of meeting see *Penna. Packet,* 3 January 1774; the resolution of thanks is found in *Penna. Gazette,* 29 December 1773.

36. *Captain Ayres' Protest,* 27 December 1773, Papers relating to the Shipment of Tea . . . , (HSP); Thomas Wharton (Phila.) to Thomas Walpole (London), 27 December 1773, Wharton Letterbook, 1773–84 (HSP); George Clymer and Thomas Mifflin (Phila.) to Samuel Adams (Boston), 27 December 1773, Samuel Adams Papers (NYPL); *Penna Packet,* 27 December 1773, 3 January 1774; *Penna. Gazette,* 29 December 1773.

37. For boundary of customhouse district commencing at the Delaware border, see John Swift (Phila.) to Customs Commissioners (Boston), 20 January 1768, Custom House Papers, VII (HSP); Capt. Ayres was in Philadelphia for forty-six hours according to the *Penna. Packet,* 3 January 1774.

38. Dartmouth to Penn, 5 February 1774, and Penn to Dartmouth, 3 May 1774, C.O. 5/1285 (PRO).

39. *Boston Gazette,* 20 December 1773; resolves printed in *New Hampshire Gazette,* 24 December 1773; Wentworth to Dartmouth, 24 December 1773, C.O. 5/938 (PRO); other towns: *New Hampshire Gazette,* 7, 14 January 1774; *Boston Newsletter,* 20 January 1774.

40. *Boston Gazette,* 20 December 1773, 3, 17 January 1774; *Boston Newsletter,* 6 January 1774; Hull resolutions in *Boston Gazette,* 4 April 1774.

41. *Boston Gazette,* 14 February 1774; *Connecticut Journal,* 25 March 1774; Cyrus Baldwin (Boston) to Comm. of Corresp. of Charlestown, 25 January 1774, Misc. Bound Mss. (MHS); for Jones, *Mass. Spy,* 17 March 1774; *Boston Evening Post,* 4 April 1774; *Boston Post-boy,* 4 April 1774; his confession is in *Mass. Spy,* 7 April 1774. The Newport incident: *Newport Mercury,* 14 February 1774.

42. For Plymouth: *Boston Gazette,* 27 December 1773, 7 February 1774; James Warren (Plymouth) to John Adams (Boston), 3 January 1774, *Warren-Adams Letters,* I, 23–4; General Haldimand took special care to send Lord Dartmouth a full account of the Plymouth proceedings: Haldimand to Dartmouth, 5 January 1774, Papers relating to the Boston Tea Party (HL). For Marshfield: *Mass, Spy,* 24 February 1774; *Boston Gazette,* 7 February 1774.

43. *Boston Gazette*, 20 December 1773; Minutes of a Meeting of Boston Tea Dealers, 21 December 1773 (BPL); *A List of the Principal dealers in Tea lately applied to . . .*," Ms.L (MHS).

44. A TRUE WHIG, *Boston Evening Post*, 10 January 1774.

45. Samuel Salisbury (Boston) to Stephen Salisbury (Worcester), 3 January 1773 [*sic*: 1774], Salisbury Papers (AAS); A BATCHELOR, *Boston Evening Post*, 17 January 1774; SYDNEY, *Boston Evening Post*, 17 January 1774; CONCORDIA, *Mass. Spy*, 13 January 1774; fixing price of Dutch tea: *Boston Gazette*, 17 January 1774; AN ENEMY TO TEA, *Boston Evening Post*, 7 February 1774; A TRUE WHIG, *Boston Evening Post*, 14 February 1774; Joseph Babcock (Westerly) to Benjamin Franklin (London), 15 February 1774, Franklin Papers, IV, 1, 8 (APS).

46. Stephen Salisbury (Worcester) to Samuel Salisbury (Boston), 16 January 1774, Salisbury Papers (AAS); MILLIONS, *Mass. Spy*, 23 December 1773; AN AMERICAN, *Boston Evening Post*, 3 January 1774; A WOMAN, *Mass. Spy*, 23 December 1773; for coffee: *Boston Gazette*, 20 December 1773, 14 February 1774.

47. *New York Journal*, 13 January 1774; New York Comm. of Corresp. to Boston Comm. of Corresp., 28 February 1774, Boston Comm. to New York Comm., 24 March 1774, Boston Comm. of Corresp., Other Colonies (NYPL); for the Princeton episode, *Boston Gazette*, 14 February 1774; for the south: [Purdie's] *Virginia Gazette*, 13 January, 10 February, 3 March 1774; "Extract of a Letter from a Gentlemen of Distinction in North Carolina, dated 18 February 1774," *Boston Gazette*, 28 March 1774.

48. *Boston Gazette*, 7, 14 March 1774; "Extract of a Letter from Boston, 7 March 1773," *Penna. Journal*, 16 March 1774; Nathaniel Taylor (Boston) to Isaac Clarke (Castle William), 8 March 1774, Misc. Bound Mss. (MHS); Thomas Walley, Peter Boyer, and William Thompson [owners of *Fortune*], *Boston Newsletter*, 10 March 1774.

49. Thomas Walley, Peter Boyer, and William Thompson [owners of *Fortune*], *Boston Newsletter*, 10 March 1774.

50. PHILANTHROP, *Mass. Spy*, 17 March 1774; Report of the Collector, 10 March 1774, T. 1/505 (PRO); Boston Comm. of Corresp. to those of Roxbury, Brookline, Dorchester, Newton, Cambridge, and Charlestown, 7 March 1774, Boston Comm. of Corresp., General Correspondence, 1772–75 (NYPL); John Adams knew ahead of time that the tea would be destroyed that evening, Butterfield, *Diary of John Adams*, II, 91; Benjamin Gorham's Protest, 8 March 1774, Affidavit of Benjamin Clark and Hammond Green (tidesmen), 10 March 1774, and protest of Benjamin Gorham, *et al.*, all in T. 1/505 (PRO); *Boston Gazette*, 14 March 1774.

51. Report of the Collector, 10 March 1774, T 1/505 (PRO); Hutchinson to Dartmouth, 9 March 1774, List of Papers Relating to the Disturbances at Boston (HL).

52. *New York Gazette*, 25 April 1774; "Extract of a Letter from New York,

25 April 1774," *Penna. Journal*, 27 April 1774; *Penna. Packet*, 2 May 1774; Petition of James Chambers to Treasury, 15 April 1776, T.1/545 (PRO).

53. Collector of Customs, Portsmouth, to Lords of the Treasury, 30 June, 12 September 1774, T. ⁞/⁝⁝ (PRO); *New Hampshire Gazette*, 1, 8, 22 July, 19 August 1774; Governor's Council Meeting at Exeter, New Hampshire, 9 September 1774, in Emmet Papers, 316 (NYPL).

54. *Maryland Gazette*, 20, 27 October, 3, 11 November 1774; "Account of the Destruction of the Brig *Peggy Stewart*, at Annapolis, 1774" in *Penna. Mag. of Hist. & Biog.*, XXV, No. 2 (1901), 248–52; William Aitchison to —— Parker, 14 November 1774, Parker Family Papers, PA 6.2 (Liverpool).

55. "Letter from Philadelphia, dated 25 December 1773," in [London] *Morning Chronicle*, 1 February 1774.

56. Henry White, *et al.*, to East India Co., 27 December 1773, Papers relating to the Boston Tea Party (HL); John Hancock (Boston) to Hayley & Hopkins (London), 21 December 1773, John Hancock Letterbook, 1762–83 (HBS); UNION, *Boston Gazette*, 27 December 1773; Thomas Cushing (Boston) to Arthur Lee (London), 23 January 1774 (BPL).

CHAPTER IX

1. John Norton (London) to Peyton Randolph, *et al.*, 6 July 1773, Francis N. Mason, ed., *John Norton & Sons, Merchants of London and Virginia* (Richmond, Va., 1937), pp. 336–7; Report from London, 13 October 1773, in *Boston Newsletter*, 9 December 1773.

2. Thomas Wharton (Phila.), to Samuel Wharton (London), 5 October 1773, Drake, *Tea Leaves*, p. 273; Tryon to Dartmouth, 3 November 1773, *N.Y. Col. Docs.*, VIII, 400–401.

3. John Pownall to Peter Michell (E.I. Co. Secretary), December 1773, Dartmouth Papers, II-760 (WSL); Tryon to Dartmouth, 3 November 1773, *N.Y. Col. Docs.*, VIII, 400–401; William Knox verifies the fact that Dartmouth and the Governors did not know the tea had been sent: Historical Manuscripts Commission, *Report on Manuscripts in Various Collections*, vol. VI (London, 1909), 269.

4. *Morning Chronicle*, 29 December 1773, 1 January 1774.

5. East India Co. Court Minutes, 7 January 1774, vol. 82, ff. 678–9 (Commonwealth Relations Office); Directors to Governors, 8 January 1774, Dartmouth Papers, I, ii, 936 (WSL); and C.O. 5/133, f. 5 (PRO).

6. Dartmouth to Haldimand, 8 January 1774, C.O. 5/243 (PRO), and to Tryon, 8 January 1774, *N.Y., Col. Docs.*, VIII, 408–9.

7. *Morning Chronicle*, 14 January 1774; George III to Dartmouth, 19 January 1774, Dartmouth Papers, IV (WSL).

8. *Hayley's* departure: *Boston Newsletter*, 23 December 1773; its arrival,

Morning Chronicle, 21 January 1774; quote from *Public Ledger*, 21 January 1774, as reprinted in *Mass. Spy*, 14 April 1774. The original of this issue could not be located. News from Philadelphia and Charleston, E.I. Co. Court Minutes, 26, 28 January 1774, vol. 82, f. 717, and vol. 81, ff. 735–6 (Commonwealth Relations Office).

9. E.I. Co. to Dartmouth, enclosing American dispatches, 10, 21, 26 January, 2 February 1774, C.O. 5/133, 5 ff., 28, 32, 46, and 47 (PRO); request for assistance: 4 February 1774, E.I. Court Minutes, vol. 82, f. 756; petition: 16 February 1774, E. I. Co. Miscellanies, vol. 21 (Commonwealth Relations Office).

10. Directors to Barkley, 26 January 1774, E.I. Co. Miscellanies, vol. 21, f. 63; Barkley's offer: 31 January 1774, E.I. Co., Miscellaneous Letters Received, vol. 57; Company's refusal: 2 February 1774, E.I. Co. Court Minutes, vol. 82, f. 743; Barkley's request for compensation and Company's grant: 9 March 1774, E.I. Co. Court Minutes, vol. 82, f. 829, and 10 March 1775, vol. 83, f. 486 (all in Commonwealth Relations Office).

11. Minute of the Cabinet Meeting of 29 January 1774, Dartmouth Papers, II–799, of 4 February 1774, Dartmouth Papers, II–817 (WSL); North to King [n.d. 5 February 1774], Fortesque, *Correspondence of George III*, III, 55. Fortesque misdates this letter as January 1774, but it was in fact written the day after Dartmouth's proposition to the Cabinet.

12. Dartmouth to the Attorney-General and Solicitor-General, 5 February 1774, C.O. 5/160, ff. 1–12 (PRO).

13. Report of the Attorney-General and Solicitor-General, 11 February 1774, C.O. 5/160, ff. 40–42 (PRO).

14. Dartmouth to Lords of the Treasury (draft), 11 February 1774, C.O. 5/160, f. 46 (PRO); Solicitor-General and Attorney-General to Dartmouth, 11 February 1774, C.O. 5/159 (PRO); North to Dartmouth, 13 February 1774, Dartmouth Papers, II–828 (WSL); Minute of the Cabinet Meeting, 16 February 1774, Dartmouth Papers, II–832 (WSL).

15. Minute of the Cabinet Meeting, 19 February 1774, Dartmouth Papers, II–834 (WSL); "Minutes of a Conversation with Lord Dartmouth," Hist. Mss. Comm., *Report on the Manuscripts of the Marquess of Lothian* (London, 1905), 290–91; William Knox's notes, Hist. Mss. Comm., *Report on Various Collections*, VI, 257.

16. Informations of William Rotch, *et al.*, before the Privy Council, 19 February 1774, Papers relating to the Boston Tea Party (HL); Minute of the Cabinet Meeting, 28 February 1774, Dartmouth Papers, II–839 (WSL); George III to Dartmouth, 1 March 1774, Dartmouth Papers, IV (WSL); Minute of the Cabinet Meeting, 1 March 1774, Dartmouth Papers, II–842 (WSL). William Knox's notes, Hist. Mss. Comm., *Report on Various Collections*, VI, 270; George III to North, 14 March 1774, Fortesque, *Correspondence of George III*, III, 80–81.

17. *Remarks of a Merchant who makes an annual Progress through the Colonies . . .* , February 1774, Dartmouth Papers, II–840 (WSL); *Morning*

Chronicle, 23 February 1774; Richard Champion (Bristol) to Willing & Morris (Phila.), 30 September 1774, Guttridge, *Correspondence of a Bristol Merchant*, pp. 29–33; Benjamin Franklin (London) to Thomas Cushing (Boston), 2 February, 22 March 1774, Smyth, *Writings of Franklin*, VI, 179, 223.

18. Arthur Lee (London) to Samuel Adams (Boston), 8 February 1774, Samuel Adams Papers (NYPL); Lord Chancellor to Dartmouth, 5 March 1774, Dartmouth Papers, II–849 (WSL).

19. Hutchinson to Dartmouth, 21 December 1773, Dartmouth Papers, I, ii, 921 (WSL).

20. King to North, 4 February 1774, Fortesque, *Correspondence of George III*, III, 59.

21. *Morning Post*, 2 February 1774; *Morning Chronicle*, 19 February 1774; Thomas Gage to Thomas Hutchinson, 2 February 1774, Hutchinson Papers, Egerton Ms., 2659, f. 68 (BM); "Extract of a Letter from London dated February 14," *Penna. Gazette*, 4 May 1774; see also "Extract of a Letter from London, dated February 2," *Penna. Packet*, 25 April 1774; Benjamin Franklin (London) to J. Kinsey and T.P. Hewlings (New Jersey), 18 February 1774, Franklin Papers, XLV, 77 (APS); "Extract of a Letter from London dated February 17," *Penna. Journal*, 27 April 1774; Benjamin Franklin (London) to Joseph Galloway (Phila.), 18 February 1774, Smyth, *Writings of Franklin*, VI, 195; Arthur Lee (London) to Joseph Warren (Boston), 20 February 1774, in Lee, *Life of Arthur Lee*, I, 265–6.

22. *Morning Chronicle*, 2 February 1774; LYCURGUS, *Middlesex Journal*, 25 January 1774; *Whitehall Evening Post*, 25 January 1774; *Morning Chronicle*, 2 February 1774; Buckingham's motion is commented upon in "Extract of a Letter from London dated 2 February 1774," *Penna. Packet*, 25 April 1774, and Arthur Lee to Samuel Adams, 8 February 1774, Samuel Adams Papers (NYPL); Earl of Shelburne to the Earl of Chatham, 3 February 1774, Taylor and Pringle, *Correspondence of Chatham*, IV, 323–4.

23. *Gazetteer*, 4 February 1774; *Middlesex Journal*, 10 February 1774; T.H., *Gazetteer*, 14 February 1774.

24. ENGLISHMAN, *Middlesex Journal*, 29 January 1774; *Gazetteer*, 14 February 1774.

25. AMOR PATRIAE, *Public Ledger*, 5 February 1774; also published in *St. James Chronicle*, 10 February 1774, and *London Evening Post*, 11 February 1774.

26. ———— to Dartmouth, February 1774, Dartmouth Papers, II–841 (WSL).

27. William Gordon (Jamaica Plain, Mass.) to Dartmouth, 11 December 1773, Dartmouth Papers, II–754 (WSL); Dartmouth to J. Thornton, Esq., 12 February 1774, Dartmouth Papers, II–827 (WSL): (Thornton was the go-between for Dartmouth's correspondence with Gordon); Shelburne to Chatham, 15 March 1774, Taylor and Pringle, *Correspondence of Chatham*, IV, 334–6.

28. *Middlesex Journal*, 8 March 1774; William Lee (London) to Richard H.

Lee (Virginia), 17 March 1774, Worthington C. Ford, ed., *Letters of William Lee, 1766–1783* (2 vols., Brooklyn, N.Y., 1891), I, 83; Anson, *Grafton*, pp. 266–7; Pownall and others as reported by Benjamin Franklin, "An Account of Negotiations in London," Jared Sparks, ed., *The Works of Benjamin Franklin* (10 vols., Chicago, 1882), V, 32–3; see Ritcheson, *British Politics*, pp. 158–9; Shelburne to Chatham, 4 April 1774, Taylor and Pringle, *Correspondence of Chatham*, IV, 339.

29. Dartmouth to J. Thornton, Jr., 12 February 1774, Dartmouth Papers, II-827 (WSL).

30. Chatham to Shelburne, 20 March 1774, Taylor and Pringle, *Correspondence of Chatham*, IV, 336–8; Ritcheson, *British Politics*, pp. 158 ff.

31. For authorship of the bill's final version, see A. Francis Steuart, *The Last Journals of Horace Walpole* (2 vols., London, 1910), I, 314; the Port bill is 14 Geo. 3, c. 19.

32. *Parliamentary History*, XVII, 1159; Papers relating to the Boston Tea Party (HL).

33. *Parliamentary History*, XVII, 1163–4; Cavendish Debates, Egerton Ms. 254, ff. 86–8 (BM); Matthew Brickdale's Parliamentary Diary, X, 10 (Bristol).

34. Cavendish Debates, f. 89; Brickdale Diary, X, 17; *Parliamentary History*, XVII, 1164–6; Cavendish Debates, ff. 89–100; Brickdale Diary, X, 17.

35. *Parliamentary History*, XVII, 1166–7; Cavendish Debates, ff. 103–11; quote from Brickdale Diary, X, 18; *Morning Chronicle*, 15 March 1774.

36. *Parliamentary History*, XVII, 1167–9; Cavendish Debates, ff. 115–16, 121, 126–7, 133, 144–7; Brickdale Diary, X, 19–20, 21, 23.

37. *Parliamentary History*, XVII, 1167; Cavendish Debates, ff. 113–14, 151–2; Brickdale Diary, X, 23.

38. *Parliamentary History*, XVII, 1167–8; Cavendish Debates, ff. 117–20; Brickdale Diary, X, 19.

39. *Parliamentary History*, XVII, 1168; Cavendish Debates, ff. 121–5; Brickdale Diary, X, 20.

40. Yorke to Hardwicke, 14 March 1774, Hardwicke Papers, Add. Ms. 35375 (BM); Cavendish Debates, ff. 185–8.

41. *Parliamentary History*, XVII, 1170; Cavendish Debates, ff. 235–9. The transcription of the Cavendish Notes breaks off toward the end of Rose Fuller's speech, and his clerk merely copied the shorthand itself. This has been deciphered by an expert for the Parliamentary History Project, and I am indebted to Mr. John Brooke of the Institute for Historical Research for allowing me to see this transcript.

42. *Parliamentary History*, XVII, 1171–3, 1173–9; Cavendish Debates, ff. 242–8; Brickdale Diary, X, 38–43; King to North, 21, 23 March 1774, Fortesque, *Correspondence of George III*, III, 81–2, 84.

43. *Parliamentary History*, XVII, 1179–85, 1189; Bollan's petition: "Bowdoin-Temple Papers," *Colls.* MHS, 6th ser., IX (1897), 364–5. For authorship of American petition, see Lee, *Life of Arthur Lee*, I, 207n; Brickdale Diary, X, 44–7; *London Chronicle*, 29 March 1774.

44. *Parliamentary History*, XVII, 1186-9; Brickdale Diary, X, 51-3; *Morning Chronicle*, 26 March 1774; *General Evening Post*, 26 March 1774.
45. William Bollan to John Erving, *et al.*, 1 April 1774, Misc. Bound Mss. (MHS); Shelburne to Chatham, 4 April 1774, Taylor and Pringle, *Correspondence of Chatham*, IV, 339-41; Petition of William Sayre, *et al.*, 28 March 1774 (HL).
46. Shelburne to Chatham, 15 March 1774, Chatham to Shelburne, 20 March 1774, Taylor and Pringle, *Correspondence of Chatham*, IV, 334-8; Rockingham to Burke, 30 January 1774, Lucy S. Sutherland, ed., *The Correspondence of Edmund Burke, 1768-1774* (Cambridge, Eng., 1960), II, 516.
47. *General Evening Post*, 17 March 1774.
48. Henry Ellison (London) to ———, 13 March 1774, Ellison Family Papers (Columbia); *Morning Post*, 12 March 1774; LYCURGUS, *Morning Chronicle*, 4 April 1774.
49. *Morning Chronicle*, 14, 16, 25 March 1774; *Lloyd's Evening Post*, 16 March 1774.
50. *Middlesex Journal*, 17 March 1774; *General Evening Post*, 5 April 1774; MERCATOR AMERICANUS, *Gazetteer*, 10 March 1774; A PATRIOT, *Gazetteer*, 11 March 1774; *Morning Chronicle*, 12 March 1774.
51. *Morning Chronicle*, 16 March 1774; JUSTICE, *Public Advertiser*, 5, 8 April 1774.
52. *St. James Chronicle*, 31 March 1774; CUSHING, *Public Ledger*, 4 April 1774.
53. FABIUS, *Public Advertiser*, 9 March 1774: for identification as Franklin, see Verner W. Crane, *Benjamin Franklin's Letters to the Press* (Chapel Hill, N.C., 1950), pp. 249-52; BRECKNOCK, *Morning Chronicle*, 1, 6 April 1774; JUSTICE, *Public Advertiser*, 30 March 1774.
54. Henry Ellison (London) to ———, 28 March 1774, Ellison Family Papers (Columbia); FABIUS (Benjamin Franklin), *Public Advertiser*, 2 April 1774; CIVIS, *Morning Chronicle*, 2 May 1774.
55. *Middlesex Journal*, 17, 29 March 1774; *Morning Chronicle*, 21, 29 March 1774; *Lloyd's Evening Post*, 28 March 1774.
56. Merchants' Offer to Compensate the East India Co., 1774, Chatham Papers, 30/8/97 (PRO); *General Evening Post*, 19 March 1774; *Morning Chronicle*, 5 May 1774.
57. Burke to N.Y. Comm. of Corresp., 6 April 1774, Sutherland, *Burke Correspondence*, II, 528; Arthur Lee (London) to Richard H. Lee (Virginia), 18 March 1774, Lee, *Life of Arthur Lee*, I, 208; Chatham to Shelburne, 6 April 1774, Taylor and Pringle, *Correspondence of Chatham*, IV, 342.

CHAPTER X

1. Minute of the Cabinet Meeting, 19 February, Dartmouth Papers, II-834 (WSL), and 1 March 1774, Dartmouth Papers, II-842 (WSL).

2. Arthur Lee (London) to Samuel Adams (Boston), 8 February 1774, Lee, *Life of Arthur Lee*, I, 240–42; the Massachusetts Government bill was 14 Geo. 3, c. 45 (1774); William Knox's notes, Hist. Mss. Comm., *Report on Various Collections*, VI, 257.

3. 14 Geo. 3, c. 39 (1774); 14 Geo. 3, c. 54 (1774); for authorship of the Administration of Justice bill, see Ritcheson, *British Politics*, p. 161. On the Massachusetts bills generally, see Jack M. Sosin, "The Massachusetts Acts of 1774: Coercive or Preventive?" *Huntington Library Quarterly*, XXVI (May 1963), 235–52.

4. *Parliamentary History*, XVII, 1192–7; Brickdale Diary, X, 57.

5. Dowdeswell: *Parliamentary History*, XVII, 1198–9; Saville: 1277–8; Ellis:

6. *Parliamentary History*, XVII, 1278–80, 1289–91; Brickdale Diary, XI, 36–40; *Morning Chronicle*, 29 April 1774. According to Governor Hutchinson, the Council's inaction during the tea crisis was the primary argument for adoption of the Government bill: Thomas Hutchinson (London) to Thomas Hutchinson, Jr. (Milton), 4–6 July 1774, Hutchinson Papers, Egerton Ms. 2659, ff. 82–3 (BM).

7. *Parliamentary History*, XVII, 1281, 1285–6.

8. *Parliamentary History*, XVII, 1300–1302; Burke to New York Assembly, 4 May 1774, Sutherland, *Burke Correspondence*, II, 533.

9. *Parliamentary History*, XVII, 1302–16; *Morning Chronicle*, 3, 4 May 1774; *London Chronicle*, 5 May 1774; *General Evening Post*, 5 May 1774; *Public Ledger*, 9 May 1774.

10. *Parliamentary History*, XVII, 1199–1201.

11. *Parliamentary History*, XVII, 1201.

12. *Parliamentary History*, XVII, 1274.

13. *Parliamentary History*, XVII, 1274–7, 1288–97, 1316–20; *General Evening Post*, 10 May 1774.

14. Dowdeswell to Rockingham, 8 April 1774, Rockingham Papers, R1–1482 (Sheffield); Duke of Manchester to Rockingham, 20 April 1774, Rockingham Papers, R1–1486 (Sheffield); Rockingham to Manchester, 20 April 1774, Rockingham Papers, R1–1487 (Sheffield).

15. Rockingham to Manchester, 20 April 1774, Rockingham Papers, R1–1487 (Sheffield).

16. Lord Camden's Speech before the House of Lords, 11 May 1774, Hardwicke Papers, Add. Ms. 35912 (BM); for the Duke of Richmond's remark: *Morning Chronicle*, 30 May 1774.

17. *Parliamentary History*, XVII, 1320–25.

18. *Parliamentary History*, XVII, 1351–3; Richmond to Rockingham, 18 May 1774, Rockingham Papers, R1–1490 (Sheffield); *Gazetteer*, 18, 25 May 1774.

19. North: *Parliamentary History*, XVII, 1163–4; Wedderburn: 1206; Burke: 1266–7.

20. Welbore Ellis: *Parliamentary History*, XVII, 1278.

21. *Morning Chronicle*, 10 March 1774; quote from *Morning Chronicle*, 8 March 1774.

22. PALINURUS, *Gazetteer*, 12 March 1774; CINCINATUS, *Public Advertiser*, 18 March 1774; HAMPDEN, *Gazetteer*, 15 March 1774; also MERCATOR AMERICANUS, *Gazetteer*, 10 March 1774; LYCURGUS, *Morning Chronicle*, 16 March 1774; "King, Lords and Commons," T.N., *Gazetteer*, 18 March 1774; *Morning Chronicle*, 22, 26 March 1774; HAMPDEN, *Gazetteer*, 22 April 1774.

23. Benjamin Franklin to Lord Kames, 11 April 1767, Smyth, *Writings of Benjamin Franklin*, V, 17.

24. Rigby: *Parliamentary History*, XVII, 1287; see also, *Morning Chronicle*, 10 March 1774, and POOR OLD ENGLAND, *Public Advertiser*, 13 May 1774; COLUMBUS, *Public Advertiser*, 26 March 1774; Dowdeswell: *Parliamentary History*, XVII, 1198.

25. AN OLD MANUFACTURER, *London Chronicle*, 7 June 1774; PALINURUS, *Gazetteer* 19 March 1774; LYCURGUS, *Morning Chronicle*, 18 March 1774; similar claims are in Z., *General Evening Post*, 10 March 1774; *Morning Chronicle*, 12 March, 9 May 1774, NIMROD, 16 May 1774; *Middlesex Journal*, 8 March 1774.

26. CINCINATUS, *Public Advertiser*, 18 March 1774; see also, C., *Morning Chronicle*, 14 April 1774; SAGITTARIUS, *London Chronicle*, 22 March 1774; *Public Advertiser*, 29 April 1774.

27. *Public Ledger*, 14 April 1774.

28. SAGITTARIUS, *Public Ledger*, 18 March 1774; see also his letters in *London Chronicle*, 22 March 1774; and *Public Ledger*, 31 March and 6 April 1774.

29. E.B., *Morning Chronicle*, 15 March 1774; LYCURGUS, *Morning Chronicle*, 18 March 1774.

30. AN OLD ENGLISH MERCHANT, *Gazetteer*, 12, 14 March 1774; *General Evening Post*, 22 March 1774; *St. James Chronicle*, 31 March 1774; B.T., A PLAIN CITIZEN, *Gazetteer*, 15 April 1774; FABRICIUS, *Gazetteer*, 19 March 1774; CONSTITUTIO, *Public Advertiser*, 22 April 1774; Robin Hood: *Morning Chronicle*, 12 March 1774.

31. *Morning Chronicle*, 14 March 1774; AN OLD ENGLISH MERCHANT, *Gazetteer*, 14 March 1774; *St. James Chronicle*, 15 March 1774; ADAMS, *Public Ledger*, 31 March 1774; *Public Advertiser*, 17 March 1774.

32. John Cartwright, *American Independence the Interest and Glory of Great Britain* (London, 1774); see also his writings under the pseudonym CONSTITUTIO, *Public Advertiser*, 22, 25 April 1774; A.B., *Public Advertiser*, 22 March 1774.

33. *Parliamentary History*, XVII, 1210.

34. *Parliamentary History*, XVII, 1280, 1315–16.

35. Barré: *Parliamentary History*, XVII, 1206; Johnstone and Pownall: *Parliamentary History*, XVII, 1281, 1282–6.

36. Henry Ellison (London) to ———, 18 April 1774; Ellison Family Papers (Columbia).

37. Among the many letters condemning repeal of the Stamp Act are: *Pub-*

lic Ledger, 7 March 1774; *Morning Chronicle,* 10, 11, 22 March, 14 May, NIMROD, 16 May 1774; A PATRIOT, *Gazetteer,* 11 March 1774; *Gazetteer,* 14 March 1774; COLUMBUS, *Public Advertiser,* 16 March 1774; PERIANDER, *Public Ledger,* 10 March 1774.

38. MERCATOR AMERICANUS, *Gazetteer,* 10 March 1774; *Middlesex Journal,* 12 March 1774; *Public Ledger,* 7 April 1774; also CRITO, *Middlesex Journal,* 12 April 1774; COLUMBUS, *Public Advertiser,* 16 March 1774.

39. MERCATOR AMERICANUS, *Gazetteer,* 10 March 1774; CRITO, *Middlesex Journal,* 12 April 1774; *Morning Chronicle,* 24 March 1774; *Gazetteer,* 11 March 1774.

40. Quote from *Gazetteer,* 12 March 1774; see also *Gazetteer,* 15 March 1774.

41. BRECKNOCK, *Morning Chronicle,* 22 March 1774; A LOVER OF MY KING AND CONSTITUTIONAL LIBERTY, *Morning Chronicle,* 23 May 1774.

42. Quote from *Middlesex Journal,* 14 May 1774. Other letters advocating leniency: CATO, *Middlesex Journal,* 12 March 1774; 17 March 1774; JUNIUS AMERICANUS (Arthur Lee), *London Chronicle,* 17 March 1774; *London Chronicle,* 31 May 1774; *Morning Chronicle,* 18 March 1774, MODERATOR, 19 March 1774; MAGNA CHARTA, *Morning Chronicle,* 5 April 1774; VARRO, *Morning Chronicle,* 23 May 1774; *Morning Chronicle* 10 June 1774; *Gazetteer,* 23 March 1774, BRUTUS, 29 April 1774; *Gazetteer,* PHILANTHROPOS, 19 and 23 May 1774; *St. James Chronicle,* 31 March 1774; PHILANTHROPOS, *Public Advertiser,* 15 April 1774; CONSTITUTIO (John Cartwright), *Public Advertiser,* 23 May 1774; *Lloyd's Evening Post,* 6, 9, 11 May 1774.

43. *Parliamentary History,* XVII, 1210–11.

44. Rice: *Parliamentary History,* XVII, 1211–12; Cornwall, 1213–15.

45. Sutherland, *Burke Correspondence,* II, xi–xviii.

46. *Parliamentary History,* XVII, 1218, 1231–3.

47. *Parliamentary History,* XVII, 1234–41.

48. *Parliamentary History,* XVII, 1260–69.

49. *Parliamentary History,* XVII, 1269–73; Brickdale Diary, XI, 9–17.

50. AMICUS, *Public Advertiser,* 4 March 1774; RATIONALIS (Benjamin Franklin), *Public Ledger,* 10 March 1774; CAVEAT, *Gazetteer,* 28 March 1774; MONITOR, *Gazetteer,* 19 April 1774; B.T. A PLAIN CITIZEN, *Gazetteer,* 31 March 1774, and SYDNEY, *Gazetteer,* 7 April 1774; AN AMERICAN, *Middlesex Journal,* 28 April 1774.

51. *Morning Chronicle,* 14 March 1774; AN OLD CORRESPONDENT, *London Chronicle,* 31 May 1774; BRECKNOCK, *Morning Chronicle,* 17 May 1774; TIMOTHY HINT, *Gazetteer,* 14 March 1774; DECAIOPHILUS, *Gazetteer,* 18 March 1774; *Morning Post,* 12 March 1774; HAMPDEN, *Gazetteer,* 21 March 1774; MENTOR, *Gazetteer,* 30 March 1774; A READER, *Lloyd's Evening Post,* 1 April 1774; AN ENGLISHMAN, *Gazetteer,* 6 April 1774.

52. Burke: *Parliamentary History*, XVII, 1269; Fuller: 1320; Rose Fuller chided: VOX POPULI, VOX DEI, *Public Ledger*, 27 May 1774.
53. *Parliamentary History*, XVII, 1320.
54. FABIUS, *General Evening Post*, 10 March 1774; *Morning Chronicle*, 16 March, 14 May 1774; *Public Ledger*, 19 April 1774.
55. "Extract of a letter from Norwich, dated 23 April," *General Evening Post*, 30 April 1774; MYRIAD, *St. James Chronicle*, 14 May 1774; A FRIEND TO HIS COUNTRY, *Gazetteer*, 14 June 1774; *Middlesex Journal*, 16 April, 14 June; *London Packet*, 17 June 1774, as quoted in Fred J. Hinkhouse, *Preliminaries of the American Revolution as Seen in the English Press, 1763–1775* (New York, 1926), p. 176.
56. *Morning Chronicle*, 18, 22 March, 9 April 1774; *Middlesex Journal*, 12 April 1774; "Extract of a letter from Newport, R. I., dated 12 March," *Morning Chronicle*, 23 April 1774; "Extract of a letter from Boston, dated 30 March," *Morning Chronicle*, 30 April 1774.
57. *Morning Chronicle*, 21 March, 4 June 1774; "Extract of a letter from Boston, 6 April," *Morning Chronicle*, 14 May 1774.
58. MAGNA CHARTA, *Morning Chronicle*, 6 April 1774; *Public Ledger*, 21 March 1774; A FREEHOLDER OF OLD SARUM (Benjamin Franklin), *Public Advertiser*, 21 May 1774.
59. "Extract of a letter from Boston, 30 March," *Morning Chronicle*, 30 April 1774; *Morning Chronicle*, 17, 18 March 1774; *St. James Chronicle*, 19 March 1774; B.T.—A PLAIN CITIZEN, *Gazetteer*, 18 June 1774.
60. *Middlesex Journal*, 2 April 1774; *General Evening Post*, 5 April 1774; *Public Ledger*, 6 April 1774; BRITTANICUS, *Middlesex Journal*, 1 March 1774; Henry Ellis to William Knox, 23 March, 27 June, 15 July 1774, Hist. Mss. Comm., *Report on Various Collections*, VI, 111–12.

CHAPTER XI

1. Samuel Adams to Comm. of Corresp. of Marblehead, *et al.*, 24 March 1774, Cushing, *Writings of Samuel Adams*, III, 80–82, and to James Warren (Plymouth), 31 March 1774, in *Warren-Adams Letters*, I, 25; Paul Revere to John Lamb (New York), 28 March 1774, John Lamb Papers (NYHS); Joseph Reed (Phila.) to Dartmouth, 4 April 1774, Dartmouth Papers, I, ii, 965a (WSL), printed in Reed, *Life of Reed*, I, 56–8.
2. John Hancock, *An Oration; Delivered . . . to Commemorate the Bloody Tragedy* (Boston, 1774); Thomas Young (Boston) to John Lamb (New York), 18 March 1774, John Lamb Papers (NYHS); Joseph Reed (Phila.) to Dartmouth, 4 April 1774, Dartmouth Papers, I, ii, 965a (WSL), printed in Reed, *Life of Reed*, I, 56–8.
3. *Morning Chronicle*, 21, 29 March 1774; *Lloyd's Evening Post*, 28 March 1774; *Middlesex Journal*, 29 March 1774.

4. *Boston Gazette*, 4 April 1774.
5. "Extract of a letter from Baltimore, dated 18 March 1774," *Boston Gazette*, 4 April 1774; "Extract of a letter from Norfolk, dated 23 March 1774," *Penna. Journal*, 6 April, and *Boston Gazette*, 18 April 1774; "Extract of a letter from London, dated 18 February 1774," *Penna. Journal*, 20 April 1774.
6. "Extract of a Letter from London, 24 January 1774," [Gaine's] *New York Gazette*, 4 April 1774; *Boston Gazette*, 11 April 1774; *Conn. Journal*, 15 April 1774.
7. *Mass. Spy*, 14 April 1774; *Boston Gazette*, 25 April 1774; John and Abigail Adams (Boston) to James Warren (Plymouth), 9 April 1774, Warren-Adams Papers, I, 22 (MHS).
8. Arthur Lee (London) to Samuel Adams, 8 February 1774, Samuel Adams Papers (NYPL); "Extract of a Letter from London, dated 2 February 1774," *Penna. Packet*, 25 April 1774; reprinted also in *New York Journal*, 28 April 1774; also, "Extract of a letter from London, dated 17 February 1774," *Penna. Journal*, 27 April 1774.
9. Benjamin Franklin (London) to J. Kinsey and T. P. Hewlings (Burlington, N.J.), 18 February 1774, Franklin Papers, XLV, 77 (APS); "Extract of a Letter from a Merchant in London, dated 18 February 1774," [actually Benjamin Franklin to Joseph Galloway], *Penna. Gazette*, 20 April 1774; James Scott (London) to John Hancock, 21 February 1774, Foreign Letters, box 27, John Hancock Papers (HBS).
10. "Extract of a Letter from London, dated 19 February 1774," *Boston Gazette*, 25 April 1774.
11. *Boston Gazette*, 2 May 1774; John Scollay (Boston) to Arthur Lee (London), 31 May 1774, in Lee, *Life of Lee*, II, 213–15; *Boston Newsletter*, 12 May 1774; *Boston Gazette*, 23 May 1774; Thomas Wharton (Phila.) to Samuel Wharton (London), 17 May 1774, Wharton Letterbook, 1773–84 (HSP).
12. Samuel Salisbury (Boston) to Stephen Salisbury (Worcester), 11 May 1774, Salisbury Papers (AAS).
13. Jonathan Jackson (Newburyport) to [Oliver Wendell (Boston)], 13 May 1774, MHS *Miscellany*, No. 2 (15 July 1955); see my *Patriots and Partisans*, pp. 30–32.
14. Wells, *Life of Samuel Adams*, II, 156–8; Cushing, *Writings*, III, 109–11; Cary, *Joseph Warren*, p. 137; Samuel Adams (Boston) to William Checkley, 1 June 1774, Cushing, *Writings*, III, 127–9.
15. Samuel Adams to Elbridge Gerry, 12 May 1774, and to Comm. of Corresp. at Portsmouth, 12 May 1774, Cushing, *Writings*, III, 105–7.
16. *Boston Gazette*, 16 May 1774; *Boston Town Records*, pp. 172–4; Cushing, *Writings*, III, 107–9; Samuel Salisbury (Boston) to Stephen Salisbury (Worcester), 13 May 1774, Salisbury Papers (AAS); Thomas Young (Boston) to John Lamb (New York), 13 May 1774, John Lamb Papers (NYHS).

17. [Wensley Hobby (Middletown) to Samuel P. Savage (Weston)], 17 May 1774, Savage Papers (MHS).
18. "Letter from Farmington, Conn., dated 23 May 1774," *Boston Evening Post,* 30 May 1774.
19. Benjamin Franklin (London) to James Bowdoin, *et al.,* 2 February, 1774, Smyth, *Writings,* VI, 178-80; Adams's remark was allegedly written on the cover of Franklin's letter. Thomas Young to John Lamb (New York), 13 May 1774, John Lamb Papers (NYHS); Stephen Salisbury (Worcester) to Samuel Salisbury (Boston), 14 May 1774, Salisbury Papers (AAS); "Diary of John Rowe," *Proc.* MHS, XXX (March 1895), 85-7.
20. John Andrews (Boston) to William Barrell (Phila.), 18 May 1774, *Proc.* MHS, VIII (1864-65), 327-30.
21. "Extract of a Letter from Boston, 21 May 1774," *New York Journal,* 2 June 1774.
22. "Extract of a Letter from Boston, 2 June 1774." *Penna. Journal,* 15 June 1774.
23. "Extract of a Letter from a Gentleman in Philadelphia, dated 17 May 1774," *Boston Newsletter,* 26 May 1774. This letter was suspected by another correspondent as a fake, for it referred to news of Gage's arrival at Boston as having reached Philadelphia on the 17th, only four days after the event: *Boston Evening Post,* 30 May 1774.
24. *Boston Gazette,* 16 May 1774.
25. G., *Boston Gazette,* 23 May 1774.
26. "Extract of a letter from London, dated 28 March," *Boston Gazette,* 16 May 1774; "Extract of a letter from one of the first character in London, dated 2 April," *Mass. Spy,* 12 May 1774.
27. "America's Friend" (London) to Samuel Adams, 29 March 1774, Samuel Adams Papers (NYPL).
28. "Extract of a Letter from a Gentleman of the first character in London, dated 2 April 1774," *Boston Gazette,* 16 May 1774.
29. John Scollay (Boston) to Arthur Lee (London), 31 May 1774, in Lee, *Life of Arthur Lee,* II, 213-15.
30. *Boston Evening Post,* 23 May 1774; *Boston Gazette,* 23 May 1774.
31. *Boston Evening Post,* 23 May 1774; *Boston Gazette,* 6 June 1774; Edward Winslow to Ward Chipman, 26 September 1783, *Proc.* MHS, XLVI (June 1913), 471-2; Richard Lechmere (Boston) to Lane, Son, & Fraser (London), 30 May 1774, *Proc.* MHS, XXXVI (October 1902), 286-7; "A List of Addressers and Protesters," *Proc.* MHS, XI (October 1870), 392-5.
32. "Extract of a Letter from Boston, dated 2 June 1774," *Penna. Journal,* 15 June 1774.
33. William Pollard (Boston) to Benjamin Bower (Manchester, Eng.), 4 June 1774, Pollard Letterbook, 1772-74 (HSP); Dartmouth to Gage, 9 April 1774, Dartmouth Papers, I, ii, 966 (WSL).
34. AN AMERICAN, *Massachusetts Spy,* 13 June 1774.

35. MERCATOR, *Boston Evening Post*, 13 June 1774; K.D., *Boston Newsletter*, 16 June 1774.

36. *Boston Town Records*, pp. 176–7; *Boston Gazette*, 20 June 1774; *Boston*, 20 June 1774.

37. Albert Matthews, "The Solemn League and Covenant, 1774," *Pubs*. Col. Soc. Mass., XVIII (December 1915), 107–9; Cary, *Joseph Warren*, pp. 140–42.

38. *Boston Gazette*, 13 June 1774; P.R., *Boston Post-boy*, 13 June 1774; "Extract of a letter from Boston, dated 19 June," [Purdie's] *Virginia Gazette*, 28 July 1774.

39. Samuel Salisbury (Boston) to Stephen Salisbury (Worcester), 13 June 1774, Salisbury Papers (AAS); Joseph Warren (Boston) to Samuel Adams (Salem), 15 June 1774, Samuel Adams Papers (NYPL); "Diary of John Rowe," *Proc*. MHS, XXX (March 1895), 86.

40. *Boston Town Records*, p. 176; Worcester's covenant and protest: Matthews, "Solemn League," *Pubs*. Col. Soc. Mass., XVIII (December 1915), 107–9, 113–15; and *Boston Newsletter*, 30 June 1774; see also: *Boston Gazette*, 20 June 1774; X., *Boston Newsletter*, 16 June 1774; *Mass. Spy*, 23 June 1774; *Boston Newsletter*, 23 June 1774; CANDIDUS (Samuel Adams), and A COUNTRYMAN, *Boston Gazette*, 27 June 1774; *Boston Post-boy*, 27 June 1774.

41. *Boston Gazette*, 7 July 1774; *Boston Evening Post*, 4 July 1774; "Diary of John Rowe," *Proc*. MHS, XXX (March 1895), 86; Jonathan Williams (Boston) to John Adams (York?), 28 June 1774, Adams Papers (MHS); "A List of Addressers and Protesters, 1774," *Proc*. MHS, XI (October 1870), 393–5.

42. Force, *American Archives*, 4th ser., I, 491–2; James Warren (Plymouth) to Samuel Adams (Boston), 1, 10 July 1774, Samuel Adams Papers (NYPL); "Extract of a Letter from a Gentleman in Boston, dated 4 July," [Rind's] *Virginia Gazette*, 28 July 1774; "Extract of a Letter from Boston [n.d.]," [Rivington's] *N.Y. Gazetteer*, 28 July 1774; Portsmouth, N.H., Covenant, June 1774, *Proc*. MHS, XXII (May 1886), 481–6.

43. Isaac Sears and Alexander McDougall to Samuel Adams, 15 May 1774, Samuel Adams Papers (Bancroft transcripts, NYPL); *Boston Gazette*, 23 May 1774.

44. *Political Memoranda Relative to the Conduct of the Citizens on the Boston Port Bill . . .*, McDougall Papers (NYHS); Gouverneur Morris (N.Y.) to John Penn (Phila.), 20 May 1774; Force, *American Archives*, 4th ser., I, 342–3; [Rivington's] *New York Gazetteer*, 23 May 1774; [Gaine's] *New York Gazette*, 23 May 1774; Pigou & Booth (N.Y.) to James & Drinker (Phila.), 20 May 1774, Drinker Papers, 1739–79 (HSP).

45. *Political Memoranda*, McDougall Papers (NYPL); *New York Journal*, 26 May 1774.

46. *Political Memoranda*, McDougall Papers (NYHS); *New York Journal*, 26

May 1774; [Rivington's] *New York Gazetteer*, 30 June 1774; Benjamin Booth (N.Y.) to James & Drinker (Phila.), 20 May 1774, Drinker Papers, 1739–79 (HSP).

47. *Political Memoranda*, McDougall Papers (NYHS).

48. *Political Memoranda*, McDougall Papers (NYHS).

49. A PHILADELPHIAN, *Penna. Gazette*, 18 May 1774; Thomas Wharton (Phila.) to Samuel Wharton (London), 17 May 1774, Wharton Letterbook, 1773–84 (HSP).

50. "Joseph Reed's Narrative," Charles Thomson to William H. Drayton, [n.d. post-Revolution], Thomson Papers, *Colls.* NYHS (1878), 269–70, 275–6; Reed, *Life of Joseph Reed*, I, 65.

51. "Joseph Reed's Narrative," and Charles Thomson to William H. Drayton, [n.d., post-Revolution], Thomson Papers, *Colls.* NYHS (1878), 271-2, 277; *Penna. Gazette*, 25 May 1774; *Penna. Packet*, 6 June 1774; Reynell & Coates (Phila.) to Little & Greenleaf (Newburyport), 21 May 1774, Reynell & Coates Letterbook, 1769–84 (HSP); Thomas Wharton (Phila.) to Thomas Walpole (London), 31 May 1774, Wharton Letterbook, 1773–84 (HSP); Reed, *Life of Reed*, I, 66–7; John F. Roche, *Joseph Reed: A Moderate in the American Revolution* (New York, 1957), 41–2.

52. James & Drinker (Phila.) to Pigou & Booth (N.Y.), 24, 31 May 1774, Drinker Letterbook, 1772–84 (HSP).

53. Thomas Mifflin to Samuel Adams, 26 May 1774, and Charles Thomson to Samuel Adams, 3 June 1774, Samuel Adams Papers (NYPL).

54. William Duane, *Passages from the Diary of Christopher Marshall . . .* (2 vols., Philadelphia, 1839), I, 6–7; James & Drinker (Phila.) to Pigou & Booth, 31 May 1774, Drinker Letterbook, 1772–84 (HSP); Robert Morris (Phila.) to James Parker (Norfolk, Eng.), 1 June 1774, Parker Family Papers, PA 18.7 (Liverpool). Jensen, *Maritime Commerce of Philadelphia*, pp. 208–9, rejects the idea that the patriots had made a bargain with Dickinson.

55. *Maryland Gazette*, 26 May 1774; Daniel Dulany, Jr. (Annapolis) to Arthur Lee (London), 1774, Lee, *Life of Arthur Lee*, II, 318–19.

56. *Maryland Gazette*, 2 June 1774; Daniel Dulany, Jr. (Annapolis) to Arthur Lee (London), 1774, Lee, *Life of Arthur Lee*, II, 318–19.

57. *Maryland Gazette*, 2 June 1774.

58. Force, *American Archives*, 4th ser., I. 366–7.

59. [Purdie's] *Virginia Gazette*, 26 May, 2 June 1774; [Rind's] *Virginia Gazette*, 26 May 1774.

60. George Washington (Williamsburg) to George W. Fairfax, 10 June 1774, John C. Fitzpatrick, ed., *The Writings of George Washington, 1745-1799* (39 vols., Washington, 1931–44), III, 224.

CHAPTER XII

1. Samuel Adams to Charles Thomson, 30 May 1774, Cushing, *Writings*, III, 122–4.
2. R. T. Paine's Account, R. T. Paine Papers (MHS).
3. Journal of the House of Representatives, Force, *American Archives*, 4th ser., I, 421; Wells, *Life of Samuel Adams*, II, 176–8; *Boston Gazette*, 20 June 1774.
4. John Scollay (Boston) to Arthur Lee (London), 31 May 1774, Lee, *Life of Arthur Lee*, II, 213–15; "Correspondence in 1774 and 1775 between a Committee of the Town of Boston and Contributors of Donations...," *Colls.* MHS, 4th ser., IV (1858), 1–24; "Extract of a Letter from a Gentleman in Boston, dated 4 July," [Rind's] *Virginia Gazette*, 28 July 1774; Samuel Adams to R. H. Lee, 15 July 1774, Cushing, *Writings*, III, 136–9; Charles Chauncy (Boston) to Richard Price (London), 18 July 1774, *Proc.* MHS, XXXVII (May 1903), 268–9.
5. *Boston Gazette*, 18 July, 1 August 1774; *Boston Evening Post*, 1 August 1774; Dr. William Cooper to Governor Pownall, 12 August 1774, Kings Mss., 203 (BM); *Extract of a Letter from Col. Robertson* (New York), 5 July 1774, Dartmouth Papers, II–948 (WSL); "Extract of a letter from Boston, dated 28 July," [Rivington's] *New York Gazetteer*, 4 August 1774; John Andrews (Boston) to William Barrell (Phila.), 12 June 1774, *Proc.* MHS, VIII (July 1865), 330.
6. For the role of colonial newspapers in promoting the idea of a congress, see Arthur M. Schlesinger, *Prelude to Independence: the Newspaper War on Britain, 1764–1776* (New York, 1958), 204–7.
7. Force, *American Archives*, 4th ser., I, 416–17.
8. *Connecticut Journal*, 15 July, 8 August 1774; Force, *American Archives*, 4th ser., I, 554–5.
9. Force, *American Archives*, 4th ser., I, 893–4.
10. Force, *American Archives*, 4th ser., I, 303–4.
11. Force, *American Archives*, 4th ser., I, 307–9.
12. [Rivington's] *New York Gazetteer*, 14 July 1774; Isaac Sears and Alexander McDougall to Samuel Adams, 25 July 1774, Samuel Adams Papers (NYPL); Force, *American Archives*, 4th ser., I, 312–13.
13. [Rivington's] *New York Gazetteer*, 14 July 1774; Isaac Sears and Alexander McDougall to Samuel Adams, 25 July 1774, Samuel Adams Papers (NYPL); Force, *American Archives*, 4th ser., I, 310–14.
14. [Rivington's] *New York Gazetteer*, 21 July 1774; [Gaine's] *New York Gazette*, 25 July 1774; Isaac Sears and Alexander McDougall to Samuel Adams, 25 July 1774, Samuel Adams Papers (NYPL).
15. [Gaine's] *New York Gazette*, 25 July 1774; [Rivington's] *New York*

Gazetteer, 28 July, 8 August 1774; *New York Journal,* 28 July 1774; Force, *American Archives,* 4th ser., I, 317–20.

16. "Extract of a letter from Philadelphia, dated 4 June," [Rivington's] *New York Gazetteer,* 9 June 1774; "A Few Political Reflections...," *Penna. Packet,* 20, 27 June, 18 July 1774; James Pemberton to John Fothergill (London), 1 July 1774, Pemberton Papers, II, Etting Collection (HSP); *Penna. Packet,* 7 July 1774 (postscript); Joseph Galloway, *et al., Penna. Gazette,* 13 June 1774.

17. *Penna. Journal,* 15 June 1774; *Penna. Packet,* 13 June 1774.

18. *Penna. Journal,* 22 June 1774; *Penna. Packet,* 27 June 1774; Force, *American Archives,* 4th ser., I, 426–7.

19. *Penna. Gazette,* 29 June 1774; Force, *American Archives,* 4th ser., I, 415–16; Edward Shippen (Lancaster) to Edward Burd (Tinian), 28 June 1774, Shippen Papers, VII (HSP); Joseph Reed (Phila.) to Dartmouth, 18 July 1774, Dartmouth Papers, I, ii, 998 (WSL).

20. James & Drinker to Pigou & Booth (London), 29 June 1774, Drinker Foreign Letterbook, 1772–85 (HSP).

21. MARCUS BRUTUS, *Penna. Packet,* 27 June 1774 (postscript); *Penna. Journal,* 29 June 1774.

22. A PLAIN DEALER, *Penna. Packet,* 18 July 1774; *Penna. Gazette,* 20 July 1774.

23. Force, *American Archives,* 4th ser., I, 555–7.

24. Force, *American Archives,* 4th ser., I, 557–60, 564–93.

25. Force, *American Archives,* 4th ser., I, 560–64.

26. Force, *American Archives,* 4th ser., I, 560–64.

27. Force, *American Archives,* 4th ser., I, 601–8.

28. Force, *American Archives,* 4th ser., I, 607–8 n.

29. *Maryland Gazette,* 9, 16, 30 June 1774; *Penna. Gazette,* 29 June 1774 (supp.); Clement Sewell (Maryland) to William Molleson (London), 19 June 1774, Emmett Papers 283 (NYPL).

30. *Maryland Gazette,* 30 June 1774; Force, *American Archives,* 4th ser., I, 438–41.

31. INGENUUS, [Timothy's] *South Carolina Gazette,* 4 July 1774.

32. A CAROLINIAN, [Timothy's] *South Carolina Gazette,* 20, 27 June 1774; NON QUIS SED QUID, [Timothy's] *South Carolina Gazette,* 4 July 1774.

33. [Timothy's] *South Carolina Gazette,* 27 June, 4, 25 July 1774.

34. [Timothy's] *South Carolina Gazette,* 11 July 1774; Force, *American Archives,* 4th ser., I, 525–7, 531–4.

35. Force, *American Archives,* 4th ser., I, 671–2.

36. *Penna. Gazette,* 27 June 1774; Force, *American Archives,* 4th ser., I, 624–5.

37. Caesar Rodney to Charles Ridgely, 21 July 1774, G. H. Ryden, ed., *Letters to and from Caesar Rodney, 1756–1784* (Philadelphia, 1933), pp. 42–3; Force, *American Archives,* 4th ser., I, 663–8.

38. [Rind's] *Virginia Gazette*, 9, 30 June, 14, 21, 28 July 1774; [Purdie's] *Virginia Gazette*, 7, 21 July 1774; *Boston Gazette*, 4 July 1774.

39. [Purdie's] *Virginia Gazette*, 21 July 1774.

40. Julian P. Boyd, ed., *The Papers of Thomas Jefferson* (in progress, Princeton, 1950), I, 117–18; *Boston Gazette*, 8 August 1774.

41. [Purdie's] *Virginia Gazette*, 11 August 1774; Force, *American Archives*, 4th ser., I, 686–90.

42. Thomas Jefferson, *A Summary View of the Rights of British America . . .*, 1774.

43. Worthington C. Ford, ed., *The Journals of the Continental Congress, 1774–1789* (Washington, 1904), I, 25–7, 31–40.

44. Ford, ed., *Journals of the Continental Congress*, I, 43–51.

45. Ford, ed., *Journals of the Continental Congress*, I, 51n–52n.

46. Ford, ed., *Journals of the Continental Congress*, I, 75–81.

47. Ford, ed., *Journals of the Continental Congress*, I, 63–73.

48. Ford, ed., *Journals of the Continental Congress*, I, 81–101, 103, 105–13, 115–21.

BIBLIOGRAPHY

I. PRIMARY SOURCES

A. MANUSCRIPTS

Adams, John, Papers (MHS).

Adams, Samuel, Papers (NYPL).

Additional Ms. 8133B (BM) Manuscripts relative to Britain's tea trade.

Admiralty Papers (PRO).

    Adm 1/3866 — customhouse (London) correspondence concerning smuggling.

    Adm 57/158 — log of H.M.S. *Captain*.

Allen, Thomas, Papers (AAS). Merchant of New London, Conn.

Avery, Samuel, Papers (NYPL). New York Loyalist.

Bernard Papers, Sparks Manuscripts (Harvard). Papers of Governor Francis Bernard.

Bleecker, Anthony L., Letterbook (NYHS). New York merchant.

Boston Committee of Correspondence Papers (NYPL).

    General Correspondence 1772–75.

    Minutes.

    Other colonies.

Boston Private and Business Papers, 1770–83 (BPL). Miscellaneous correspondence.

Bourne, Meletiah, Papers (HBS). The papers of a merchant of Plymouth, Mass.

Brickdale, Matthew, Parliamentary Diary, Bristol. Manuscript diary of the proceedings of Parliament, Vols. VIII–XI, cover the sessions of 1773 and 1774.

Bromfield, Henry, Letterbook, 1773 (NEHGS). A Boston Merchant's correspondence.

Cavendish Debates, Egerton Mss., 246 (BM). Henry Cavendish's manuscript diary of Parliamentary debates from 1768 to 1774, the first two volumes of which were published in 1841–43.

Chatham Papers (PRO).

Clark, Daniel, Letter and Invoice book, 1759–62 (HSP). Philadelphia merchant.

Clarke, Richard, & Sons. One of the Boston consignees.
> Invoice Book, 1767–75 (NEHGS).
> Letterbook, 1767–69 (NEHGS).

Coates, Samuel, Letterbook, 1763–81 (HSP). Philadelphia merchant, John Reynell's partner.

Colonial Office, series 5 (PRO).
> 7   Narrative of the Boston Tea Party.
> 38–9   Copley-Pelham Correspondence.
> 115   Memorial concerning the tea shipped to New York and Philadelphia.
> 133   Lord Dartmouth's correspondence concerning the Boston Tea Party with copies of many important letters.
> 137   Protests of Boston custom house officers.
> 159   Correspondence between Lord Dartmouth and the Attorney General.
> 160   The Case of the Boston Tea Party summarized.
> 226, 243, 247   Colonial Secretary In-letters.
> 756–63 Correspondence from Governor of Massachusetts to the Colonial Secretary.
> 938   Correspondence from Governor of New Hampshire to the Colonial Secretary.
> 1101, 1105 Correspondence from Governor of New York to the Colonial Secretary.
> 1283, 1285 Correspondence from Governor of Pennsylvania to the Colonial Secretary.

Custom House Papers [Philadelphia] (HSP). Correspondence of the Philadelphia collector.

Customs Letterbook, Outwards, 1772–75 [Boston]. Office of the Collector, U.S. Customs, Boston, Mass.

Customs Papers (PRO).
> Series 3/50 through /74 contain statistics of English imports and exports for the period 1750–74.
> Series 16/1 is a volume of statistics covering imports and exports at American customs districts for the period 1768–72.

Dartmouth Papers (WSL). An extensive collection of invaluable reports and correspondence of the Earl of Dartmouth. I have used the cataloguing system adopted by the William Salt Library in citing manuscripts from this collection.

Davis, Caleb, Papers (MHS). A Boston merchant active in the sale of tea.

Drinker, Henry, Papers (HSP). With his partner, Abel James, one of the Philadelphia consignees.
> Foreign Letters, 1772-85.
> Letterbook, 1772-84.
> Papers, 1739-79.

East India Company Papers (Commonwealth Relations Office).
> Committee of Correspondence Reports: vols. 10 and 11.
> Court Minutes: vols. 4, 81, 82, and 83.
> General Ledger, 1773-79.
> Miscellaneous Letters Received: vols. 57 and 58.
> Miscellanies — Home letters sent out: vols. 20, 21, and 22.

Edes Papers (MHS). Contains agreement between Abraham Dupuis & Co. and Richard Clarke & Sons concerning the East India Company's tea; also the draft of the consignees' petition to the Massachusetts Council.

Ellison Family Papers (Columbia). Correspondence between English and American relatives.

Emmet Papers (NYPL). Tea crisis in New Hampshire.

Francis, Tench, Invoice Book, 1759-63 (HSP).

Franklin, Benjamin, Papers (APS).

Greg & Cunningham Letterbook, 1756-58 (NYHS). A New York mercantile firm.

Grenville, George, Papers, Add. Ms. 42086 (BM).

Hall, David, Papers (APS). Philadelphia printer.

Hancock, John, Papers (HBS).
> Letterbook, 1762-83. Mostly business letters.
> Papers. Large collection of commercial correspondence.

Hancock, Thomas, Papers (HBS). John's uncle, a wealthy Boston merchant and smuggler.
> Letterbook, 1750-62.
> Papers.

Hardwicke Papers, Add. Mss. 35375, 35609, 35631, 35912 (BM), Correspondence between a leader of the Old Whigs and his lieutenants.

Hutchinson, Thomas, Papers.
> Letterbooks, Mass. Archives. I have used the transcripts on file at the MHS.
> Papers, Egerton Ms. 2659 (BM). Contains family letters.

Hutchinson-Oliver Papers (MHS). Letters of Boston Loyalists.

James, Abel, & Henry Drinker, Letterbook, 1769-72 (HSP). Business correspondence of one of Philadelphia's tea consignees.

Jones, Owen, Papers (HSP). Contains a paper entitled "Some Observations on the Tea Trade."

Kidd, John, Letterbook, 1749–63 (HSP). A Philadelphia merchant.

King's Mss. (BM). Includes correspondence between Samuel Cooper and Thomas Pownall.

Lamb, John, Papers (NYHS). A New York patriot.

Letters of Boston Merchants Coastwise to Newport, 1732–66 (HBS).

List of Papers Relating to the Disturbances at Boston (HL). Over 100 items submitted by Lord Dartmouth to the House of Lords concerning the Boston Tea Party.

Liverpool Papers, Add. Ms. 38340 (BM). Several important items concerning colonial trade.

Lloyd, Henry, Letterbook, 1766–67 (HBS). A Boston merchant, active in the tea trade.

Ludlow, John, Letterbook, 1752–63 (Columbia). New York merchant.

McAllister Manuscripts (LibCo).

McDougall, Alexander, Papers (NYHS). One of the New York patriot leaders.

"Manuscripts, Large" (MHS). Included is an account of dutied tea imported at Boston.

Manuscripts Relating to Non-Importation Agreements, 1766–75 (APS).

Minutes of a meeting of Boston tea dealers, 1773 (BPL).

Miscellaneous Bound Manuscripts (MHS).

Miscellaneous papers concerning the tea trade, Add. Mss. 8133B, 38334 (BM).

Miscellaneous Unbound Manuscripts (MHS).

Paine, Robert Treat, Papers (MHS). Includes an account of the election of Mass. delegates to the Continental Congress.

Papers of the Committee of the House of Lords inquiring into the Boston Riots (HL).

Papers relating to the shipment of tea . . . (HSP). Contains the only copy I have found of the Company Directors' instructions to the consignees concerning the sale of tea.

Parker Family Papers (Liverpool).

Pemberton Papers. Etting Collection (HSP). Philadelphia merchant family.

Pollard, William, Letterbook, 1772–74 (HSP). A Philadelphia merchant.

Present State of the British Colonies in America, Berkshire Records Office, Reading. Complete copy of the reports sent by American governors to Great Britain in 1773–74 concerning the state of commerce.

Price Papers (MHS).

Reed, Joseph, Papers (NYHS). Papers of the Philadelphia patriot.

Reynell, John, Letterbooks, 1767–69, 1769–70 (HSP). Philadelphia merchant, partner of Samuel Coates.

Reynell & Coates.
    Correspondence, 1769–71 (HSP).
    Letterbook, 1769–84 (HSP).
    Papers (HBS).
Roberdeau, Daniel, Letterbook, 1764–71 (HSP). A Philadelphia merchant.
Rockingham Papers (Sheffield). The papers of this important Opposition leader have been most useful.
Salem Custom House Records (EI).
Salisbury Papers (AAS). Interesting correspondence between merchant brothers in Boston and Worcester, Mass.
Savage, Samuel P., Papers (MHS). Patriot of Weston, Mass.
Shaw, Samuel, Papers (Yale). Merchant of New London, Conn.
Shippen, Edward, Papers (HSP). Patriot of Lancaster, Penna.
Smith, Richard, Mss. (LibCo). Philadelphia merchant.
Smith, William, Letterbook, 1771–75 (HSP). Philadelphia merchant.
Sparks Manuscripts (Harvard). A miscellany of manuscripts pertaining to the Townshend Act crisis are here transcribed.
Stone, Eben F., Papers (EI).
Treasury Papers (PRO).
    Series 1
    433 Tea smuggling into England.
    445 Scheme for a tea tax in America, 1766.
    452 Correspondence of the Lords of the Treasury.
    465 Trade at Boston.
    501 Correspondence of the Lords of the Treasury.
    505 Large collection of papers relating to the Boston Tea Party.
    509 Papers concerning tea at Boston and Portsmouth, N.H.
    522 and 545 The case of Captain Chambers.
    Series 64
    312 Papers relating to the smuggling of tea.
Tudor, William, Papers (MHS). A Boston patriot.
Waln, Richard, Papers (HSP). A Philadelphia merchant.
    Foreign Correspondence, 1763–90.
    Letterbook, 1766–69.
Warren-Adams Papers (MHS).
Wendell, Oliver, Papers (MHS). A patriot merchant of Boston.
Wetmore Collection (MHS).
Wharton, Charles, Cash book, 1765–71 (HSP).
Wharton, Thomas, Letterbook, 1752–59 (HSP).
Wharton Correspondence, 1771–1830 (HSP). Important collection of letters of one of Philadelphia's tea consignees.

Wharton Letterbook, 1773–84 (HSP).
Williams, Israel, Papers (MHS).

B. PRINTED SOURCES

Adams, Charles F., ed., *The Works of John Adams* (10 vols., Boston, 1850–56).
Albemarle, Earl, *Memoirs of the Marquis of Rockingham* (London, 1852).
Andrews-Barrell Correspondence, *Proceedings* of the Massachusetts Historical Society, VIII (1864–65). John Andrews was in Boston during the tea crisis.
Anson, William R., ed., *Autobiography and Political Correspondence of Augustus Henry, Third Duke of Grafton, K.G.* (London, 1898).
Baldwin, Samuel, *A Survey of the British Customs* . . . (London, 1770).
Ballagh, James C., ed., *The Letters of Richard Henry Lee* (2 vols., New York, 1911–14).
Barnwell, Joseph W. and Theodore D. Jervey, eds., "The Garth Correspondence," *South Carolina Historical Magazine*, XXIX-XXXIII (1928–32).
[Boston] *Selectmen's Minutes, 1769–1775. [A Report of the Record Commissioners of the City of Boston* . . . vol. 23, Boston, 1893.]
[Boston] *Town Records, 1770–1777 [A Report of the Record Commissioners of the City of Boston* . . . vol. 18, Boston, 1887].
"The Bowdoin and Temple Papers," *Collections* of the Massachusetts Historical Society, 6th series, IX (1897).
Boyd, Julian P., ed., *The Papers of Thomas Jefferson* [in progress] (Princeton, N.J., 1950–).
Boyle, John, "Journal of Occurrences, 1759–1778," *New England Historic and Genealogical Register*, LXXXIV (April-October 1930).
[Bradford, Alden E., ed.], *Speeches of the Governors of Massachusetts from 1764 to 1775* (Boston, 1818).
Burgh, James, *Political Disquisitions, or An Inquiry into Public Errors, Defects, and Abuses* (2 vols., London, 1774).
Butterfield, Lyman H., ed., *Diary and Autobiography of John Adams* (4 vols., Boston, 1961).
———, ed., *Letters of Benjamin Rush* (2 vols., Philadelphia, 1951).
Carter, Clarence E., ed., *The Correspondence of General Thomas Gage* (London, 1931).
Cartwright, John, *American Independence the Interest and Glory of Great Britain* (London, 1774).
Cavendish, Henry, *Debates of the House of Commons, 1768–1771* (2 vols., London, 1841–43).

Channing, Edward, and Archibald S. Coolidge, eds., *The Barrington-Bernard Correspondence, 1760–1770* (Cambridge, Mass., 1912).

Cobbett, William, *The Parliamentary History of England* . . . (36 vols., London, 1806–20), Vols. XVI and XVII.

Commerce of Rhode Island, 1726–1800 (2 vols., Boston, 1914). A collection of the business correspondence of Rhode Island merchants.

"Correspondence in 1774 and 1775 between a Committee of the Town of Boston and Contributors of Donations . . . ," *Collections* of the Massachusetts Historical Society, 4th series, IV (1858).

"Correspondence of Governor Eden," *Maryland Historical Magazine*, II (September 1907).

Crane, Verner W., ed., *Benjamin Franklin's Letters to the Press* (Chapel Hill, N.C., 1950).

Cunningham, Ann R., ed., *Letters and Diary of John Rowe* (Boston, 1903).

Cushing, Harvey A., ed., *The Writings of Samuel Adams* (4 vols., New York, 1904).

Cushing, Thomas, Letters of, *Collections* of the Massachusetts Historical Society, 4th series, IV (1858).

[Dalrymple, Alexander], *Observations on the Present State of the East India Company* . . . (London, 1771).

DeBerdt, Dennys, Letters, *Publications* of the Colonial Society of Massachusetts, XIII (March 1911).

"Destruction of the Tea in the Harbor of Boston, December 16, 1773," *Collections* of the Massachusetts Historical Society, 4th series, IV (1858). Letters of John Scollay and others.

Documents Relative to the Colonial History of the State of New York . . . (15 vols., Albany, 1856–87).

Drake, Francis S., *Tea Leaves* . . . (Boston, 1884). A collection of documents pertaining to the Boston Tea Party. Several envelopes of notes used by Drake in preparing this volume are on deposit at the New England Historic and Genealogical Society's library in Boston.

Duane, William, *Passages from the Diary of Christopher Marshall* . . . (2 vols., Philadelphia, 1839).

Ellis, John, *An Historical Account of Coffee* . . . (London, 1774).

Fergusson, James, ed., *Letters of George Dempster to Sir Adam Fergusson, 1756–1813* (London, 1934).

Fitzmaurice, Lord Edmond, ed., *Life of William, Earl of Shelburne* . . . (3 vols., London, 1876).

Fitzpatrick, John C., ed., *The Writings of George Washington, 1745–1799* (39 vols., Washington, 1931–44).

Force, Peter, ed., *American Archives*, 4th series (Washington, 1837–46), Vol. I.

Ford, Worthington C., ed., *The Journals of the Continental Congress, 1774–1789* (34 vols., Washington, 1904–37), Vol. I.

Ford, Worthington C., ed., *Letters of William Lee, 1766–83* (2 vols., Brooklyn, 1891).

Fortesque, Sir John, ed., *The Correspondence of King George III* (6 vols., London, 1927).

Gordon, William, *History of the Rise, Progress, and Establishment of Independence in the United States of America* (4 vols., London, 1788).

Goss, Elbridge H., *The Life of Colonel Paul Revere* (2 vols., Boston, 1891). Contains the "Proceedings of the North End Caucus."

Great Britain, House of Commons, *Secret Committee on the East India Company . . . Report . . .* (London, 1773).

——, *Select Committee on the East India Company . . .* (London, 1772).

Grenville, George, *The Regulations Lately Made . . .* (London, 1765).

Guttridge, George H., ed., *The American Correspondence of a Bristol Merchant* (Berkeley, 1934). The business correspondence of Richard Champion.

Hamilton, Stanislaus M., ed., *Letters to Washington . . .* (5 vols., Boston, 1902).

Hancock, John, *An Oration; Delivered . . . to Commemorate the Bloody Tragedy . . .* (Boston, 1774).

Historical Manuscripts Commission, *The Manuscripts of the Earl of Dartmouth* [11th Report, Appendix 5 (London, 1887); 14th Report, Appendix 10 (London, 1895)].

——, *Report on the Manuscripts of the Marquess of Lothian* (London, 1905).

——, *Report on Manuscripts in Various Collections*, vol. VI (London, 1909).

Hutchinson, Peter O., ed., *Diary and Letters of Thomas Hutchinson* (2 vols., London, 1883).

Jefferson, Thomas, *A Summary View of the Rights of British America . . .* (1774).

Johnson, Samuel, *The Works of Samuel Johnson* (12 vols., London, 1806).

Journals of the House of Commons, XXXI.

[Knox, William?], *The Interest of the Merchants and Manufacturers of Great Britain in the Present Contest with the Colonies Stated and Considered* (London, 1774).

Le Marchant, Denis, ed., *Memoirs of the Reign of King George III by Horace Walpole* (4 vols., London, 1845).

Lechemere, Richard, Letters, *Proceedings* of the Massachusetts Historical Society, XXXVI (1902)

Lee, Richard H., ed., *Life of Arthur Lee* (2 vols., Boston, 1829).

"A List of Addressers and Protesters," *Proceedings* of the Massachusetts Historical Society, XI (October 1870).

List of . . . *Proprietors of East India Company Stock* . . . (London, 1773).

Martin, R. Montgomery, *The Past and Present State of the Tea Trade of England and of the Continents of Europe and America* . . . (London, 1832).

Mason, Francis N., ed., *John Norton & Sons, Merchants of London and Virginia* (Richmond, Va., 1937).

Massachusetts Historical Society *Miscellany*, No. 2 (July 1955).

Matthews, Albert, ed., "Documents Relating to the Last Meetings of the Massachusetts Royal Council, 1774–1776," *Publications* of the Colonial Society of Massachusetts, XXXII (1937).

——, ed., *Letters of Dennys DeBerdt, 1757–1770* (Cambridge, Mass., 1911).

——, "The Solemn League and Covenant, 1774," *Publications* of the Colonial Society of Massachusetts, XVIII (December 1915).

Mayo, Lawrence S., ed., *The History of the Colony of Massachusetts Bay by Thomas Hutchinson* (3 vols., Cambridge, Mass., 1936).

"Minutes of the Tea Meetings, 1773," *Proceedings* of the Massachusetts Historical Society, XX (1882–83).

Niles, Hezekiah, ed., *Principles and Acts of the Revolution in America* (Baltimore, 1882).

Parkes, Joseph, *Memoirs of Sir Philip Francis* . . . (2 vols., London, 1867).

Pitkin, Timothy, *A Statistical View* . . . (New Haven, 1835).

Posthumus, Nicholas W., *Inquiry into the History of Prices in Holland* (Leiden, 1946).

Pownall, Thomas, *The Administration of the Colonies* (5th edition, London, 1774).

The Present State of the English East-India Company's Affairs . . . (London, 1772).

Price, Richard, *Letters, Proceedings* of the Massachusetts Historical Society, XXXVII (May 1903).

Proceedings of the Town of Boston on the 5th and 6th November 1773 . . . [1773].

Reed, William B., *Life and Correspondence of Joseph Reed* (2 vols., Philadelphia, 1847).

Report from the Committee of Proprietors, Appointed the 1st of December, 1772 . . . , to Enquire into the Present State and Condition of the Company's Affairs (London, 1773).

[Richardson, ——?], *Advice to the Unwary: Or, an Abstract, of Certain Penal Laws . . . against Smuggling in General and the Adulteration of Tea* (London, 1780).

[Robinson, Matthew?], *Considerations on the Measures Carrying on with Respect to the British Colonies in North America* (London, 1774).

Rowland, Kate M., *The Life of George Mason, 1725-1792* (New York, 1892).

Russell, Lord John, ed., *Correspondence of John, Fourth Duke of Bedford* (London, 1842).

Ryden, G.H., ed., *Letters to and from Caesar Rodney, 1756-1784* (Philadelphia, 1933).

Sharp, Granville, *A Declaration of the People's Natural Right to a Share in the Legislature which is the Fundamental Principle of the British Constitution of State* (London, 1774).

[Shipley, Jonathan], *A Speech Intended to have been Spoken on the Bill for Altering the Charters of Massachusetts Bay* (London, 1774).

Smith, William J., *The Grenville Papers* (4 vols., London, 1852-53).

Smyth, Albert H., *The Writings of Benjamin Franklin* (10 vols., New York, 1907).

Sparks, Jared, ed., *The Works of Benjamin Franklin* (10 vols., Chicago, 1891).

Steuart, A. Francis, ed., *The Last Journals of Horace Walpole* (2 vols., London, 1910).

Stevens, Benjamin F., *Facsimiles of Manuscripts in European Archives Relating to America, 1773-83* (25 vols., London, 1889-98).

Stillé, Charles J., ed., *The Writings of John Dickinson* (2 vols., Philadelphia, 1895).

Strahan, William, Correspondence with David Hall, *Pennsylvania Magazine of History and Biography*, X (October 1886).

Sutherland, Lucy S., ed., *The Correspondence of Edmund Burke, 1768-1774* (Cambridge, England, 1960).

Taylor, William S. and John H. Pringle, *Correspondence of William Pitt, Earl of Chatham* (4 vols., London, 1838-40).

"Tea Party Anniversary," *Proceedings* of the Massachusetts Historical Society, XIII (1873-75).

[Thatcher, Benjamin B.] *Traits of the Tea Party: Being a Memoir of George R.T. Hewes* . . . (New York, 1835). Contains an "Extract of the Journal of the Ship *Dartmouth* from London to Boston 1773."

Thomson, Charles, Papers, *Collections* of the New York Historical Society (1878).

Tradesmen's Protest against the Proceedings of the Merchants . . . (1773).

"Trumbull Papers," *Collections* of the Massachusetts Historical Society, 5th series, IX (1885).

Walker, Lewis B., *The Burd Papers* . . . (2 vols., [Pottsville, Penna.?], 1897-99).

Warren, Mercy, *History of the Rise, Progress, and Termination of the American Revolution* . . . (Boston, 1805).

Warren-Adams Letters (2 vols., Boston 1917, 1925).

[Whatley, Thomas], *Considerations on the Trade and Finances of this Kingdom* . . . (London, 1769).

White, Philip L., ed., *The Beekman Mercantile Papers, 1746-1799* (3 vols., New York, 1956).

Wroth, Kinvin, and Hiller B. Zobel, eds., *The Legal Papers of John Adams* (2 vols., Cambridge, Mass., 1964).

C. NEWSPAPERS

1. *London*

Gazetteer: April-May 1773; January-June 1774.

General Evening Post: January-June 1774.

Lloyd's Evening Post: January-June 1774.

London Chronicle: April-May 1773; January-June 1774.

London Evening Post: January-June, 1774, scattering.

London Gazette: April-May 1773; January-June 1774.

Middlesex Journal: April-May 1773; January-June 1774.

Morning Chronicle: April-May 1773; January-June 1774.

Morning Post: January-June 1774, scattering.

Public Advertiser: January-June 1774.

Public Ledger: January-June 1774.

St. James Chronicle: January-June 1774.

Whitehall Evening Post: January-June 1774, scattering.

2. *American*

New Hampshire Gazette [Portsmouth]: 1773-74.

Boston Post-boy: 1773-74.

Boston Chronicle: 1767-70.

Boston Evening Post: 1773-74.

Boston Gazette: 1767-70; 1773-74.

Boston Newsletter: 1773-74.

Massachusetts Spy [Boston]: 1773-74.

Essex Gazette [Salem]: 1773-74.

Newport [Rhode Island] *Mercury*: 1773-74.

Connecticut Journal [New Haven]: 1773-74.

New York Gazette [Gaine]: 1773-74.

New York Gazetteer [Rivington]: 1773-74.

New York Journal: 1767-70; 1773-74.

Pennsylvania Chronicle [Philadelphia]: 1767-70; 1773-74.

Pennsylvania Gazette [Philadelphia]: 1773-74.

Pennsylvania Journal [Philadelphia]: 1767-70; 1773-74.

Pennsylvania Packet [Philadelphia]: 1773–74.
Maryland Gazette [Annapolis]: 1774.
Virginia Gazette [Purdie] [Williamsburg]: 1773–74.
Virginia Gazette [Rind] [Williamsburg]: 1773–74.
South Carolina and American General Gazette [Charleston]: 1773–74.
South Carolina Gazette [Charleston]: 1773–74.
South Carolina Gazette and Country Journal [Charleston]: 1773–74.

II. SECONDARY WORKS

The following is a selection of secondary works most helpful to the present
study.

Andrews, Charles M., "The Boston Merchants and the Non-Importation Move-
ment," *Publications* of the Colonial Society of Massachusetts, XIX
(1916–17).
Basye, Arthur H., "Secretary of State for the Colonies, 1768–1772," *American
Historical Review*, XXVIII (October 1922).
Becker, Carl, *History of Political Parties in the Province of New York, 1760–
1776.* (Madison, Wisc., 1909).
Brant, Irving, *James Madison: The Virginia Revolutionist* (Indianapolis, 1941).
Brooke, John, *The Chatham Administration, 1766–1768* (London, 1956).
Brown, Weldon A., *Empire or Independence: Failure of Reconciliation* (Baton
Rouge, La., 1941).
Brunhouse, R.L., "The Effect of the Townshend Acts in Pennsylvania," *Penn-
sylvania Magazine of History and Biography*, LIV (October 1930).
Burnett, Edmund C., *The Continental Congress* (New York, 1941).
Butterfield, Herbert, *George III and the Historians* (London, 1957).
Cary, John, *Joseph Warren: Physician, Politician, Patriot* (Urbana, Ill., 1961).
Champagne, Roger, "New York and the Intolerable Acts, 1774," *New-York
Historical Society Quarterly*, XLV (April 1961).
Clark, Dora M., *British Opinion and the American Revolution* (New Haven,
1930).
Davidson, Philip, *Propaganda and the American Revolution, 1763–1783* (Chapel
Hill, 1941).
Dickerson, Oliver M., *The Navigation Acts and the American Revolution*
(Philadelphia, 1951).
———, "Use Made of the Revenue from the Tax on Tea," *New England
Quarterly*, XXXI (April 1958).
Farrand, Max, "The Taxation of Tea, 1767–1773," *American Historical Review*,
III (January 1898).

Glamman, Kristof, *Dutch-Asiatic Trade, 1620–1740* (Copenhagen and The Hague, 1958).

Guttridge, George H., *English Whiggism and the American Revolution* (Berkeley, 1942).

Harrington, Virginia D., *The New York Merchant on the Eve of the Revolution* (New York, 1935).

Hinkhouse, Fred J., *The Preliminaries of the American Revolution as Seen in the English Press, 1763–1775* (New York, 1926).

Hobson, Eric, *The American Revolution in its Political and Military Aspects, 1763–1783* (New York, 1955).

Huxley, Gervas, *Talking of Tea* (London, 1956).

Jensen, Arthur L., *The Maritime Commerce of Colonial Philadelphia* (Madison, Wisc., 1963).

Jervey, Theodore, "Barlow Trecothick," *South Carolina Historical Magazine,* XXXII (July 1931).

Knollenberg, Bernard, "Did Samuel Adams Provoke the Boston Tea Party . . . ?" *Proceedings* of the American Antiquarian Society, LXX (1960).

Labaree, Leonard W., *Conservatism in Early American History* (New York, 1948).

Longley, Robert S., "Mob Activities in Revolutionary Massachusetts," *New England Quarterly,* VI (June 1933).

Meigs, Cornelia L., *The Violent Men: A Study of Human Relations in the First Continental Congress* (New York, 1949).

Milburn, William, *Oriental Commerce . . .* (2 vols., London, 1806).

Miller, John C., *Sam Adams: Pioneer in Propaganda* (Stanford, 1936).

Morgan, Edmund S. and Helen M., *The Stamp Act Crisis* (Chapel Hill, 1953).

Morse, Hosea B., *Chronicles of the East India Company Trading to China, 1635–1834* (5 vols., London, 1926–29).

Mumby, Frank A., *George III and the American Revolution* (New York, 1923).

Namier, Sir Lewis, *England in the Age of the American Revolution* (London, 1930).

——, *The Structure of Politics at the Accession of George III* (London, 1929).

Pares, Richard, *King George III and the Politicians* (Oxford, 1953).

Pownall, Charles A.W., *Thomas Pownall . . .* (London, 1908).

Pritchard, Earl H., *The Crucial Years of Early Anglo-Chinese Relations, 1750–1800* (Pullman, Washington, 1936).

Repplier, Agnes, *To Think of Tea!* (Boston, 1932).

Ritcheson, Charles R., *British Politics and the American Revolution* (Norman, Okla., 1954).

Robinson, F.P., *The Trade of the East India Company: from 1709 to 1813* (Cambridge, England, 1912).

Roche, John F., *Joseph Reed: A Moderate in the American Revolution* (New York, 1957).

Roth, Rodris, *Tea Drinking in Eighteenth-Century America* (Washington, 1961).

Schlesinger, Arthur M., *The Colonial Merchants and the American Revolution, 1763-1776* (New York, 1918).

——, *Prelude to Independence: The Newspaper War on Britain, 1764-1776* (New York, 1958).

——, "The Uprising Against the East India Company," *Political Science Quarterly*, XXXII (March 1917).

Silver, Rollo G., "Benjamin Edes: Trumpeter of Sedition," *Papers* of the Bibliographical Society of America (3rd quarter, 1953).

Smith, Glenn C., "An Era of Non-Importation Associations," *William and Mary Quarterly*, 2nd ser. XX (April 1940).

Sosin, Jack M., "The Massachusetts Acts of 1774: Coercive or Preventive?" *Huntington Library Quarterly*, XXVI (May 1963).

Sutherland, Lucy S., *The East India Company in Eighteenth-Century Politics* (Oxford, 1952).

——, "Lord Shelburne and East India Company Politics," *English Historical Review*, XLIX (July 1934).

Thomas, Peter D. G., *Sources for Debates of the House of Commons, 1768-1774* [Bulletin of the Institute of Historical Research, Special Supplement No. 4, November 1959].

Ubbelohde, Carl, *The Vice-Admiralty Courts and the American Revolution* (Chapel Hill, 1960).

Ukers, W.H., *All About Tea* (New York, 1935).

Walett, Francis G., "The Massachusetts Council, 1766-1774," *William and Mary Quarterly*, 3rd series, VI (October 1949).

Walsh, Richard, *Charleston's Sons of Liberty: A Study of the Artisans, 1763-1789* (Columbia, S.C., 1959).

Warren, Winslow, "The Colonial Customs Service in Massachusetts," *Proceedings* of the Massachusetts Historical Society, XLVI (1912-13).

Watson, Henry C., *The Yankee Tea Party . . .* (Boston, 1851).

Watson, J. Steven, *The Reign of George III, 1760-1815* (Oxford, 1960).

Wells, William V., *The life and Public Services of Samuel Adams* (3 vols., Boston, 1865).

Wolkins, George G., "The Boston Customs District, 1768," *Proceedings* of the Massachusetts Historical Society, LVIII (June 1925).

Zimmerman, John J., "Charles Thomson: the Sam Adams of Philadelphia," *Mississippi Valley Historical Review*, XLV (December 1958).

APPENDIX

TABLE I

English Exports of Tea to America
1750-1774 — in pounds

Year	New Eng.	New York	Penna.	Va. & Md.	Carolina	Georgia	Totals
1750	28,086	64,301	37,590	14,266	14,130		158,373
1751	32,649	67,850	46,248	13,872	15,346		175,965
1752	29,514	34,734	56,099	13,117	15,075		148,529
1753	46,528	25,629	37,800	12,515	21,784	2,273	147,029
1754	63,546	3,911	34,306	14,434	9,754		125,951
1755	53,867	61	16,342	15,485	19,218		104,973
1756	20,099	2,756	7,521	18,130	11,398		89,904
1757	6,011	43,291	25,179	27,044	23,174	334	125,033
1758	16,557	62,733	35,484	26,055	10,875	1,667	153,371
1759	34,790	132,830	41,369	37,014	16,576	992	263,571
1760	58,944	18,732	48,673	14,165	19,622		150,136
1761	6,992	3,837	144	23,290	22,893		57,156
1762	51,618	70,460	7,884	12,773	17,850	1,003	161,588
1763	37,525	83,870	18,281	23,481	22,860		186,017
1764	143,234	265,385	41,949	18,249	18,374	1,989	489,180
1765	175,030	226,232	54,538	20,692	36,067	2,918	515,477
1766	118,982	124,464	60,796	27,240	20,112	6,798	358,392
1768	291,900	320,214	174,883	41,944	34,639	5,212	868,792
1767	252,435	177,112	87,741	36,088	23,865	2,325	579,566
1769	86,004	4,282	81,729	36,733	12,982	4,426	226,156
1770	85,935	269	0	18,270	1,175	2,980	108,629
1771	282,857	1,035	495	32,961	36,385	5,420	359,153
1772	151,184	530	128	78,117	12,916	10,265	263,140
1773	206,312*	208,385*	208,191*	26,166	83,959*	5,070	738,083
1774	30,161	1,304	0	30,372	4,332	3,661	69,830

* Figures for 1773 include tea sent by East India Company but never landed.
Source: Customs 3/50 – /74 (PRO).

TABLE II
Comparative Tea Prices

Year	E.I. Co. Sales	Engl. Wholesale Price	Dutch Wholesale Price	Boston Wholesale Price			New York Wholesale Price			Philadelphia Wholesale Price		
				High	Low	Ave.	High	Low	Ave.	High	Low	Ave.
1750		[3/9]	1/10			[2/3]				3/10	3/9	3/9
1751		[3/1]	1/8							3/11	3/7	3/9
1752		[3/1]	1/6			[3/3]	3/2	3/0	3/1	3/6	3/2	3/3
1753		[3/2]	1/8			[4/4]	3/2	2/10	3/1	3/3	3/2	3/2
1754		[2/10]	1/3			[2/10]	3/3	2/9	3/0	3/4	3/0	3/0
1755			1/8	4/0	3/3	3/7	3/2	2/7	2/10	3/11	2/8	3/2
1756			1/5	4/0	3/1	3/3	3/5	2/10	3/0	3/11	2/8	3/3
1757	2/3	[3/2]	1/10			[3/9]	4/4	3/5	3/7	4/6	3/4	4/0
1758			1/10			[4/1]	4/4	3/9	4/0	4/4	3/7	4/1
1759	4/1			5/10	4/8	5/3	5/0	4/0	4/5	4/6	3/11	4/2
1760	2/3		1/11	4/3	3/9	3/10	4/0	3/5	3/7	4/2	3/2	3/6
1761		[3/6]	2/2	4/6	3/2	3/8	3/11	3/4	3/7	3/4	3/3	3/4
1762		[3/4]	2/4	6/0	3/11	5/3	5/4	4/0	4/8	6/3	3/4	4/9
1763	3/4		2/5	4/8	3/11	4/3	5/2	4/0	4/4	4/2	3/9	4/1
1764	3/6		2/2	4/6	4/3	4/5	4/7	4/4	4/5	4/11	4/0	4/4
1765	3/3		2/2	4/6	3/3	3/10	4/5	3/5	4/0	4/8	3/8	4/2
1766	3/0		1/11	4/3	3/4	3/6	3/9	3/1	3/6	3/11	3/6	3/8

Year												
1767	2/0¾	2/8	1/10	3/6	2/7	2/11	3/9	2/9	3/1	3/8	2/7	3/2
1768	1/9¾	2/6	1/11	3/5	1/9	2/8	2/9	2/5	2/6	2/8	2/4	2/6
1769	1/7½	[2/8]	1/11	3/5	2/2	2/6	2/5	2/4	2/5	2/4	1/11	2/2
1770	1/9¾		1/8	3/8	2/9	3/0	6/0	2/5	3/11	4/6	2/10	3/9
1771	2/3¾	3/1	2/0	3/9	2/9	3/0	3/4	2/7	2/10	3/4	2/6	2/11
1772	2/3¾		2/0	2/10	2/8	2/9	2/7	2/4	2/5	2/7	2/5	2/6
1773	1/9	2/3	1/10	3/10	1/11	2/10	2/7	2/0	2/6	3/7	2/5	2/9
1774	1/8											

NOTES TO TABLE II

1. All prices in pound sterling equivalents.

2. Bracketed averages derived from two or less figures.

3. East India Company prices for the years 1768–73 are adjusted to show effect of drawbacks for which tea exported to America were eligible. Townshend duty is not included.

4. English wholesale price was that charged American importers by English merchants.

5. Dutch wholesale price was that prevailing at Amsterdam.

6. Sources:

   a. East India Co. Sales: "An Account of Tea Delivered from East India Company Warehouses . . . " Add. Ms. 8133B, ff. 326–7 (BM).

   b. English Wholesale Prices: numerous merchants' papers, some of which cited in bibliography.

   c. Dutch Wholesale Prices: Nicholas D. Posthumus, *Inquiry into the History of Prices in Holland* (Leiden, 1946), I, 189–90.

   d. American Wholesale Prices: merchants' papers, correspondence, and ledgers, and Price Currents as published in newspapers.

TABLE III

The East India Company's Tea Trade — 1763-74 — in pounds

Year	Imported	Sold for home market	Sold for export	Total Sold	Annual Surplus	Accrued Surplus
1763	4,190,509	4,259,579	417,192	4,676,771	−426,262	
1764	6,784,276	4,460,721	510,076	4,970,797	1,813,479	1,387,217
1765	6,914,756	4,365,600	785,927	5,151,527	1,763,229	3,150,446
1766	10,176,744	4,285,200	646,102	4,931,302	5,245,442	8,395,888
1767	9,323,051	3,731,903	430,020	4,161,923	5,162,128	13,558,016
1768	4,432,383	6,586,829	1,273,880	7,860,709	−3,428,326	10,129,690
1769	7,032,008	6,687,386	1,640,630	8,328,016	−1,296,008	8,833,682
1770	10,927,999	6,870,691	1,145,368	8,016,059	2,911,940	11,745,622
1771	8,961,687	5,683,570	1,118,128	6,801,698	2,880,989	13,626,611
1772	12,787,113	7,511,907	1,146,255	8,658,162	4,128,959	17,755,570
1773	˜8,799,060	4,134,125	1,187,611	5,321,736	3,477,324	21,232,894
1774	8,848,136	5,925,089	1,273,324	7,198,413	−3,350,277	17,882,617

The effect of the Indemnity Act of 1767 on sales of tea for export is clearly seen in the figures for the years after 1767.

It is also clear that the problem of the Company's surplus of tea in 1773 was caused primarily by repeatedly large importations of tea from China rather than from the boycott of English tea in the American colonies.

Source: "An Account of Tea Delivered from the East India Company Warehouses . . . " Add. Ms. 8133B, ff. 326–7 (BM).

TABLE IV

East India Company's Shipment of Tea to America — 1773

Port Port & Vessel	Number of chests and suggested sale price of each variety					Total lbs.	Invoice value £	Freight one-way £	Total value £
	Bohea @2/0	Congou @2/3	Singlo @2/8	Souchong @3/0	Hyson @5/0				
BOSTON									
Dartmouth	80	5	20	4	5	30,801			
Beaver	80	5	20	2	5	31,212			
Eleanor	80	5	20	4	5	30,573			
William	28	5	20	—	5	12,204			
Total:	268	20	80	10	20	104,790	10,994	243	11,237
NEW YORK									
Nancy	568	20	80	10	20	211,778	21,690	625	22,315
PHILADELPHIA									
Polly	568	20	80	10	20	211,778	21,676	437	22,113
CHARLESTON									
London	182	10	50	5	10	70,304	7,315	157	7,472
TOTALS	1586	70	290	35	70	598,659	61,674	1462	63,136
DESTROYED									
AT BOSTON	240	15	60	10	15	92,586	9,659		

INDEX

CPSIA information can be obtained at www.ICGtesting.com
Printed in the USA
BVOW04s1359130115

382598BV00002B/7/P